# THE YEAR'S WORK IN THE ODDBALL ARCHIVE

## THE YEAR'S WORK: STUDIES IN FAN CULTURE AND CULTURAL THEORY

EDWARD P. COMENTALE AND AARON JAFFE, EDITORS

*The Year's Work in Lebowski Studies*
Edited by Edward P. Comentale and Aaron Jaffe, Endnote by William Preston Robertson

*The Year's Work at the Zombie Research Center*
Edited by Edward P. Comentale and Aaron Jaffe

EDITED BY
JONATHAN P. EBURNE
AND JUDITH ROOF

# THE YEAR'S WORK IN THE ODDBALL ARCHIVE

INDIANA UNIVERSITY PRESS
BLOOMINGTON AND INDIANAPOLIS

*This book is a publication of*

INDIANA UNIVERSITY PRESS
Office of Scholarly Publishing
Herman B Wells Library 350
1320 East 10th Street
Bloomington, Indiana 47405 USA

iupress.indiana.edu



The paper used in this publication meets the minimum requirements of the American National Standard for Information Sciences – Permanence of Paper for Printed Library Materials, ANSI Z39.48–1992.

*Manufactured in the United States of America*

Cataloging information is available from the Library of Congress.

ISBN 978-0-253-01835-9 (cloth)
ISBN 978-0-253-01847-2 (paperback)
ISBN 978-0-253-01851-9 (ebook)

1 2 3 4 5 21 20 19 18 17 16

# THE ODDBALL ARCHIVE

# COLLECTION SUMMARY

TITLE The Year's Work in the Oddball Archive

SPAN DATES ca. 1737–2013

CALL NO. 978-0-253-01847-2

CREATORS Eburne, Jonathan P. (Editor) and Roof, Judith (Editor)

EXTENT 14 items; 4 boxes; 448 p.; 6.125 x 7 in.

LANGUAGE Collection material in English

LOCATION Indiana University Press

SUMMARY A collection of documents addressing topics from the sidebars of mainstream thought and culture; includes essays and brief interventions on topics ranging from fossils to Dixie cups. Contains illustrations.

FINDING AID PERMALINK Cite or bookmark this finding aid as: iupress.indiana.edu

PERMALINK ONLINE Catalog record for this collection: iupress.indiana.edu/product_info.php?products_id=807762

# SCOPE AND CONTENTS

# HISTORY OF THE COLLECTION

## THE ODDBALL ARCHIVE

The Oddball Archive is a collection whose full range we are only beginning to explore. Culled from the sidebars of mainstream culture and thought, its holdings document the eccentricities of culture, thought, and archivization alike. There exists a nearly infinite expanse of such material: anomaly, after all, is the perpetual yield of any system. The history of cultural production is replete with abandoned prototypes, rejected models, crackpot theories, and antiquated media; the permutations are endless. We all too often discount the value of this material, however. Though it may be limitless in scope, its idiosyncrasy makes it difficult to take seriously. Subtending what we think of as the legitimate archive of cultural achievement, such oddball material appears as the trivial, the illogical, the irreverent, the irrelevant, the misled. It is the nutty by-product, we might say, of the procedures that distinguish the true from the false, the major from the minor, or the model from the shards.

The modern age is no stranger to such material. The history of ideas is replete with connoisseurs of the cabinet of curiosities and the loose collection of odds and ends. Medieval church reliquaries and Renaissance collections of natural curiosities gave rise to the taxonomic imperatives of the *Encyclopédistes* and other scientific catalogers of the known world. During the Enlightenment, the *Wunderkammer* gave way to the museum.

Even so, in various guises the cabinet of curiosities has persisted as a lingering testament to the amateurish, the perverse, the experimental, or the unprofessional.[1] Today there are even museums dedicated to conserving and displaying such oddities, from the Museum of Jurassic Technology in Los Angeles to the Museum of Broken Relationships in Zagreb, Croatia, and the Morbid Anatomy Museum in Brooklyn, not to mention the growing ranks of online "museums" dedicated to the odd.[2] P. T. Barnum made a career of institutionalizing the freak show as a cabinet of curiosities for the paying public. What enabled Barnum and his ilk to capitalize on our shared capacity for wonder – our curiosity, our longing for an experience of knowledge that has little to do with reason – was the very recognition that such a capacity exists as an active social demand.[3] Whether the disjecta membra of intellectual history or the very objects of fascination that fuel advances in science, exploration, and industry, these various assemblages of the odd and interesting offer telling lessons about the boundaries of modern reason. Of equal importance is their capacity to record, store, and bear witness to endeavors that might help us better understand the nature of oddity itself. What kinds of ideas and fantasies do such collections hold? Why should we care about the odd?

One of the great contemporary archivists of cultural oddity is the American sleight-of-hand artist and polymath Ricky Jay, whose career traces the conjoined appeal of cultural anomaly and archival collection. His recent book, *Celebrations of Curious Characters* (with David Mamet, 2011), conjures the broad reach of entertainment history as a saga of inventive foolery and expert sleight-of-hand and, most importantly, as an archive of tricks handed down from one con artist to another. Like Harry Houdini, himself the author of at least seven books on magic and deception, cons and escapes, Jay is a fan of conjuring who curates the curious as both exposé and entertainment in itself. Jay's archive of the extraordinary testifies to the collective knowledge of the oddball – to the preservation, presentation, and unmasking of three centuries of diversions whose value lies precisely in the ways they divert spectators' funds, attention, and credulity.

Jay's oddball archive exists in two forms. Not only does he maintain his own extensive collection of original broadsheets, advertisements, descriptions, images, and promotional materials from three centuries of shows, but he has also published materials from his collection in a series of books: in addition to *Celebrations of Curious Characters,* these books include *Extraordinary Exhibitions: Broadsides from the Collection of Ricky Jay* (2005), *Jay's Journal of Anomalies* (2003), *Dice: Deception, Fate, and Rotten Luck* (2002), and *Learned Pigs and Fireproof Women* (1986). Whatever forms of attention or fascination might be said to sustain Jay's devotion to collecting oddities, the urge to publish and circulate a set of essays, lectures, and books dedicated to this collection seems no less strong.

What is it about the "oddball" that invites archivization? The "odd" invites preservation on account of its very idiosyncrasy. Its evident deviation from the typical encourages preservation, admiration, and even fandom. Just as institutions construct archives for their records and proceedings, and just as the state creates archives for documenting the births, marriages, deaths, and laws of its citizens, so too do fans and collectors forge archives for the atypical. Such oddball archives document the idiosyncratic particulars of a collector's experience, or the desire to demonstrate the power of an exception. Not all archives record this kind of data, however. As the German media theorist Wolfgang Ernst reminds us, archives are no longer always dusty and forgotten; the gaps and discontinuities that necessarily open up in the historical record are no longer always secret, owing at once to radical shifts in the technology of data storage and to the resulting availability and global circulation of electronic data.[4] Oddity is more than a by-product of, or exception to, mainstream recordkeeping; bearing an unreason proper to its eccentricity to the broader "order of things," oddity requires an archive of its own.

*The Year's Work in the Oddball Archive* aims to dislodge the "oddball" of alternative knowledge from prevailing assumptions about the intrinsic value of historical progress and the reciprocal worthlessness of the corollary; such assumptions designate only certain species of rationality, visibility, and usefulness as inherently valid. Aberrant data may be embraced when they clear the way toward new truths; forgotten documents testify to repressed historical events. The exception becomes valuable when it can be proven as exceptional. Even when scholars attend to the abnormalities and discontinuities of thought, they tend to do so under the aegis of major figures such as Michel Foucault and Gilles Deleuze. Must oddity always be recuperated into something more valuable, more recognizable? The present volume is governed instead by a provocation: it hypothesizes that archives of idiosyncratic thinking reveal as much about the shape of intellectual history – and the question of what constitutes knowledge itself – as any taxonomy of the work of great minds. Albert Einstein's secretary, Helen Dukas, kept a *komishe Mappe,* a "curiosity file," containing all the crackpot letters and oddball requests sent to the famous physicist during his years at the Institute for Advanced Study. What can such a file tell us about the ideas contained within, or about Einstein's place in intellectual history, or about the intellectual contribution of Helen Dukas?[5] Rather than merely bolstering the iconography of a great scientific genius, Einstein's archive discloses a trove of articulated desires and ideas – from the visionary to the reactionary – that made their way by mail across the great distances of twentieth-century thought. In whose *komishe Mappe* might Einstein's letters be found in turn?

Even as it bears witness to the efforts of marginal thinkers, the Oddball Archive also makes visible the ways in which even the strictest positivist approaches to scientific method have always depended on unreason as a valuable mode of knowing. The archives discussed and examined in this volume collect various modes of offbeat thinking not only as the artifacts of a tradition of unreason but also as integral parts of the rationales for comprehending everyday life, politics, the media, the storage and retrieval of information, the work of theory, and even the very course of history itself. The essays collected here examine the possibilities, as well as the demands and pitfalls, of thinking oddly.

The concatenation of eccentricity you will find in the Oddball Archive organizes many of the forms and varieties of thought proper to oddity and archives alike. The discussions collected in *The Year's Work in the Oddball Archive* select and examine the histories and consequences of wayward, errant, or otherwise offbeat thinking, ranging from Enlightenment theories of extinction and revolutionary "common sense" to outright scams, from pressing questions in contemporary science to the predilections of reality television. While gesturing to the long history of intellectual inquiries deemed heretical or dangerously unorthodox, the volume concentrates on the modern age, featuring key moments in the proliferation of unreason since the so-called age of reason. The essays examine the systems of relations between unreason and reason that unfold among the eccentricities of modern intellectual life, as well as across the fields of literature, philosophy, science, and political theory. Rather than approaching such moments as part of a regressive or self-destructive tendency within Enlightenment reason – as is famously the case in Max Horkheimer and Theodor Adorno's *Dialectic of Enlightenment* – this collection proposes that we approach oddity and even unreason as irremediable elements of all thought.

Unreason, in this context, designates the set of alternative protocols that underwrite extrapositivist modes of knowing. It thus undergirds such cultural phenomena as New Age mysticism, the occult, 'pataphysics, intuition, comedy, avant-garde art movements, alternate cosmologies, games of illusion, and various modes of the absurd. Unreason may not occupy a privileged place in any right-thinking intellectual universe, but it suffuses it all the same. Far from merely a symptom of the twentieth or twenty-first century's lapse into barbarism and degeneracy – characterized by an epistemic shift from rational knowing to irrational leaps of faith – unreason testifies to the discomfiting multiplicity of intellectual and crypto-intellectual practices that comprise the field of knowledge production. Such pursuits, and the forms of reason and unreason they set in motion, demonstrate the extent to which that great trove of unreason that nourishes reason's archive permeates the contemporary world. It counts innumerable adherents and skeptics alike among its constituency, along with a more diffuse body of hobbyists and fanatics. For such audiences, unreason constitutes an urgent appeal to live both ethically and creatively rather than a repressive negation of reason in the name of intolerance or hate. Such oddball unreasonings offer consistent testimony to the pitfalls of certainty, as well as the pleasure – even the jouissance – of the perverse.

## ARCHIVING THE ODDBALL

The very notion of the archive itself harbors traces of the odd. Indeed, the Greek root of the term, ἀρχή, *archē,* meaning "government," suggests a curious paradox at work in the way we think about the storage and retrieval of knowledge. The archive, we might say, designates the place where documents and artifacts that might otherwise bear the full force of law, history, or collective memory instead become the province of functionaries. There is hardly anything more at odds with itself, after all, than the notion of a governmental function whose malfunction is continuous with its proper functioning. This grounding perversity finds its echo in Jacques Derrida's oft-cited thinking: an archive, he writes, "shelters itself from [the] memory which it shelters: which comes down to saying also that it forgets it."[6] Archives forget, institutionally. An archive that governs itself according to a concept of governance (what Derrida calls a "commandment") comes to "forget" the governing concept it safeguards in turn. As a result, we may think that archives are just repositories of inconsequential stuff monitored by a skeleton crew of functionaries, but among all this paperwork lie the foundations of the law. Even so, the governing force of any such law, as the governing concept of the archive, remains suspended, as if forgotten, somewhere among the files. One thinks of the final scene in Steven Spielberg's *Raiders of the Lost Ark,* in which the Ark of the Covenant – the material form of the Law, the Ten Commandments themselves – lies crated up and buried away in the recesses of a government warehouse.

There is much that is bizarre, secondary, corollary, and offbeat about an archive's technology of conservation. Whether institutional repository or virtual data cloud, the archive's preservational and documentary functions collect in order to neglect and conserve in order to remind us that we need not be reminded. Archives are, in this sense, cybernetic: they seek to regulate idiosyncrasy, to forge a manageable equilibrium among odd assortments of data. The odd is what we end up losing sight of when the archive remembers the governing concept it has forgotten. Like data, oddity is all around us, at once everywhere and nowhere at all. And yet such oddity is always there to be culled; its presence attests to the ways oddness is the necessary shepherd to even our most regulated practices, the ovine sanity to which we cling, as to a cherished idol, as we search for truth. Oddity forms the necessary condition, the environment for the archive's perpetual reinterpretation of itself as a legible record of significant events.

At once the terrain upon and against which reason distinguishes itself, as well as the host to reason's exceptional figures, the oddball also constitutes its own series of archives. Such archives are themselves necessarily governed by their own constitutive set of governing logics. They are subject, in other words, to some principle of storage, retrieval, and loss. Yet what distinguishes an oddball archive is that it conserves as archive what the governing imperatives of other archives otherwise seem to forget. The point is hardly to restore to prominence all the nutty things that reason has cast aside in its amnesiac haste to conserve its own proper history. The dustbin of history is replete with unreasonable practices we need hardly extend ourselves too far to bring to mind: Nazi science, human zoos, torture gardens, and the traffic in plundered colonial artifacts. Such practices are, after all, hardly forgotten. On the contrary, they constitute a body of cultural and political tactics that remains all too ready at hand. It is not our intention, therefore, simply to dust off the curiously familiar relics of obsolescence and atrocity in order to stage yet another freak show or Salon des Refusés.

Instead, the governing logic of the Oddball Archive makes it possible to consider the side effects of oversight as more than merely a telling lapse of careful preservation. Oddness rarely crops up in the places where we expect it to be; in this sense it curiously resembles that other slippery fish, the ever-restless event of truth itself. Any "archive" of oddity must instead come to terms with the bizarre and paradoxically oblique functioning of its governance, its principles and technologies of order and neglect alike. The Oddball Archive unforgets, we might say, that the odd is always forgotten in the name of "reason." The Oddball Archive also reminds us – unforgets – that reason can never exist as such without the unreason it pretends to leave behind.

## ODDBALLING

In the United States, "oddball" derives from "screwball," a baseball player's term for a pitch thrown with an outlandish spin (which breaks in the inverse direction to a curveball). The term bears a similar etymology to "queer" and can in fact be considered a Cold War–era substitute for this earlier term, presumably free from the homosexual overtones queerness came to designate after the Second World War. The deployment of "oddball" quickly gained a countercultural flair. Whereas "screwball" came to define a style of Hollywood comedy, the "oddball" became something of a wayward hero, as epitomized by Donald Sutherland's iconic Sergeant Oddball in the 1969 war-heist caper *Kelly's Heroes*. In the film, Sutherland plays a perennially spaced-out tank commander, his stoner ethos gleefully out of step with the 1940s doughboys who surround him. The oddball is, thus, also an anachronism, at once countercultural and counterfactual.

By contrast, in contemporary public life the oddball has become distinctly mainstream in an era when unreason rules. The playing field of twenty-first-century politics has itself become increasingly countercultural and counterfactual. Whether we snicker at the convictions of the Tea Party or the Flat Earth Society or shudder in the face of climate-change denial or the worldwide rise of neofascist groups, our reactions reveal that oddball thinking is everywhere. These unreasonable political and social tendencies are not simply the products of false consciousness or the logic of hate. Often what appears to be "unreasonable" is instead a case of reason taken to unreasonable extremes, involving either a reduction or an exaggeration of centrist logic. In its imperious, totalizing, and even destructive excesses, hyperbolic reason demonstrates what happens when reasonable operations are wielded unreasonably, giving free rein to the excesses Michel Foucault once described as "the torture of the truth."[7] Such excesses illustrate, moreover, the extent to which forms of unreason are inherent in the functioning of what we deem to be reason itself: the risk of error and even madness that shadows every act of thought.

Unreasonable excesses of reason are not, however, the only form of oddball unreason available. As every countercultural movement seems implicitly to recognize, whether Brook Farm collectivists, French Fourierists, punks, Goths, slackers, or hackers, the challenge of experimental or "alternative" ways of living and thinking lies in pursuing alternative forms of knowledge rather than simply resisting mainstream modes. Coextensive with positivist logic and the "scientific" method, in other words, there exist other persistent modes of reasoning, apperceiving, and knowing. Such "discontinuous knowledges" rely on different assumptions about the sources and etiologies of knowledge.[8] They likewise entail alternative means for processing information, institutions for disclosing meaning, and genres and media for representation. To study the history and resonance of such bodies of knowledge is to recognize their pervasive role throughout intellectual history. Such a project thus also begins to account for some of the contemporary habits by which alternate modes of knowing are mitigated or suppressed (such as the pervasive disavowal of the arts, an aesthetophobia that considers aesthetic pleasure as a form of complicity or waywardness), or, reciprocally, the widespread privileging of vocation or ethical good citizenship as the sole raison d'être of intellectual activity. No less prevalent are the vulgarizations of scientific inquiry that posit science as a means for bringing about a technological destiny that always, automatically, knows the future, or the similarly reductive tendency to sanctify historicism and positivism as direct routes to authenticity and truth. To the extent that such tendencies seek explicitly to purge oddity and unreason from contemporary thought, it becomes the task of any oddball archive to take stock of their effects on our reason and unreason alike.

What the "oddball" tells us is that we cannot live without the oddball. The Oddball Archive assembled here is only the most recent in a series of such archives, which range from traveling freak shows to Ripley's Believe It or Not! Odditorium to *Jay's Journal of Anomalies,* as well as to other collections such as the jarring, enjarred anatomical aberrations of the Mütter Museum and the Museum of Jurassic Technology; the Creation Museum and the Museum of Sex; and even the Rock and Roll Hall of Fame and Museum. Although such collections often seek to proffer the necessary evidence for sustaining "alternative" belief systems – whose ideological consequences, like their geographical sites, lie all over the map – other collections seek instead to feed an appetite for fandom or the intellectually salacious. Such exhibitions need not merely reinforce or titillate, however: most broadly, they afford a range of difference that puts culture into perspective not as competing mainstreams but as an inassimilable variety that bespeaks rich interest and possibility.

Such oddity-themed collections thus perform, in their explicit attention to aberration and curiosity, the cultural (as well as the epistemological) patterns of selecting and discarding, of the sorting and storing of anomalies, that the Oddball Archive seeks to unforget. *Wunderkammer* or filing cabinet, the archive's relation to its own intrinsic oddity as an archive – as well as to the vestiges of curiosity and idiosyncrasy that remain sheltered within it – at once obscures and resuscitates the odd as the surprise gem it can, finally, spit out in the end. Such surprise gems may consist of little more than compressed filth, transformed by countless ages of pressure. Yet precisely for this reason they also testify to the tireless processes at work in their creation and discovery alike. We have grown accustomed to such gems but not to the pressure that creates them: this pressure, the force of history, is a property of the ever-accumulating mass of oddity, idiosyncrasy, and error that conditions our production of truth. The oddball is not only what surrounds and suffuses our thinking; it is also what we crave.

## NOTES

1. See Patrick Mauriès's lavishly illustrated *Cabinets of Curiosities.*

2. On the Museum of Jurassic Technology, see the museum's web site (www.jt.org), as well as, for instance, Weschler, *Mr. Wilson's Cabinet of Wonder.* See also www.brokenships.com, as well as www.odditycentral.com.

3. For a sustained consideration of this social demand, see especially Stewart, *On Longing;* and Altick, *The Shows of London.*

4. See Ernst, *Digital Memory and the Archive.*

5. On certain contents of Einstein's *komishe Mappe,* see Turner, "Feet of Genius." See also Rosenkranz, *The Einstein Scrapbook,* esp. chap. 9, "The Curiosity File."

6. Derrida, *Archive Fever,* 2.

7. Foucault, *Discipline and Punish,* 40.

8. See Foucault, *Power/Knowledge,* esp. 81.

## SELECTED BIBLIOGRAPHY


Altick, Richard D. *The Shows of London.* Cambridge, Mass.: Belknap, 1978.

Derrida, Jacques. *Archive Fever: A Freudian Impression.* Translated by Eric Prenowitz. Chicago: University of Chicago Press, 1994.

Ernst, Wolfgang. *Digital Memory and the Archive.* Edited by Jussi Parikka. Minneapolis: University of Minnesota Press, 2013.

Foucault, Michel. *Discipline and Punish: The Birth of the Prison.* Translated by Alan Sheridan. New York: Vintage, 1977.

Foucault, Michel. *Power/Knowledge: Selected Interviews and Other Writings, 1972–1977.* Edited by Colin Gordon. New York: Pantheon, 1980.

Horkheimer, Max, and Theodor Adorno. *Dialectic of Enlightenment: Philosophical Fragments.* Translated by Edmund Jephcott. Stanford, Calif.: Stanford University Press, 2002.

Mauriès, Patrick. *Cabinets of Curiosities.* London: Thames and Hudson, 2002.

Rosenkranz, Ze'ev. *The Einstein Scrapbook.* Baltimore, Md.: Johns Hopkins University Press, 2002.

Stewart, Susan. *On Longing: Narratives of the Miniature, the Gigantic, the Souvenir, the Collection.* Durham, N.C.: Duke University Press, 1993.

Turner, Christopher. "Feet of Genius." *Cabinet* 23 (Fall 2006), http://cabinetmagazine.org/issues/23/turner.php.

Weschler, Lawrence. *Mr. Wilson's Cabinet of Wonder: Pronged Ants, Horned Humans, Mice on Toast, and Other Marvels of Jurassic Technology.* New York: Vintage, 1996.

# ORGANIZATIONAL NOTE

## USING THE ODDBALL ARCHIVE

This sample archive invites you to delve into its four separate collections, each loosely organized around analogous objects or processes. Each archive bears its own governing logic and its own preface. Readers may delve into the holdings in any order they like; there is no progression among the collections, nor is there a logical argument to their ordering. Their distribution into categories reflects merely some thematic or procedural commonality.

Dig in. Enjoy the perverse; revel in the minor; consider the utter importance and irrelevance of it all.

# ACCESS

Readers may use copies of the material rather than the originals. Permission for the use of original material is required from the curator of manuscripts.

# ACKNOWLEDGMENTS

The editors wish to thank Aaron Jaffe – in his role as series coeditor, as well as author – and Ed Comentale for their enthusiasm and support for the project, as well as the two anonymous readers who reviewed it for publication. We also wish to thank Raina Polivka at Indiana University Press for her tenacity in helping to bring this volume to fruition. We also send our warmest thanks to Hanna Biggs for her help throughout the project. Jonathan wishes to thank Carol J. Adams, Richard Barney, David Lynch, and particularly Lynch's assistant Anna Skarbek.

REFUSE

DROWNING

PATHOLOGY

STORAGE

# THE ODDBALL ARCHIVE

## BOX I

## SAVING AMERICA: ARCHIVAL PROLIFERATIONS

AMERICA

REALITY TELEVISION

GERMS

SLAVERY

LIPS

HISTORY

NEW ORLEANS

LAS VEGAS

RAILROADS

KEY WORDS

refuse, storage, drowning, America, germs, pathology, slavery, lips, reality television, New Orleans, Las Vegas, railroads, history

COLLECTION CONTENTS

# COLLECTION SUMMARY

In the United States, even the most confidential archives become the dominion of popular culture; the more secret, the more classified or off-limits, the better. Reciprocally, all popular culture becomes archival material, finding its way into an oddball archive of one sort or another. In its perpetual accumulation of tales, artifacts, and stories about accumulating tales and artifacts, American culture enfolds itself in weirdo predilections.

Littering public consciousness in much the same way that travel stickers adorn the backs of RVs, this pervasive archive situates itself as the perpetual unearthing of material long buried in the back alleys of America's tediously normal and industrious mainstream. The oft-rehearsed rediscovery of these vestiges of the quirky, retro, eccentric, and faddish is part of the show: the entertaining display of perversity allows mainstream America to rest easy, secure in the knowledge that the "oddball" consists of those *other* folks whose well-hidden excesses are now fully on display. The habit of sustaining arcane archives has thus lent America an exciting – even refreshing – diversity as it maintains its quotidian keel. Or, perhaps, such archives obscure the perennial fact that America's keel may not be so even after all.

The spectacular medium du jour for America's popular cultural archive is reality television. Extending archival storage and accumulation into the realm of the sideshow attraction, reality television not only documents but also reproduces the strange archival habits of the American citizenry in its fixation on various forms of "primitive accumulation," the sheer accretion of material things. This accretion might refer, as Joseph Campana and Theodore Bale demonstrate, to the interlinked practices of storing, picking, pawning, and hoarding any and all objects from American life. Such habits might likewise extend, as Atia Sattar traces, to the detritus of the common drinking cup, whether in the Hugh Moore Dixie Cup Collection, the amalgam of pathogens the cups were designed to stave off, or in the broad range of nineteenth-century exhortations against categorical inmixing, from which the disposable paper cup could rescue its thirsty consumers. Or, as Beth McCoy observes, such archival habits might bear a more ominous lesson in the repetitions of history, which McCoy discusses in her comparison of FEMA signs and vévé symbols in post-Katrina New Orleans.

The accretion of anything and everything by the denizens of American "reality" might suggest a culture more engaged in salvage for its own sake than in any sense of preserving history or a bygone Zeitgeist. Yet the boundless archive that ensues divulges a resident ambivalence not only about the sprawling piles of American leavings but also about America itself. Americanness emerges as the sum total of these collections in all their debauched glory, in all their fascinating disgrace. On the one hand, this material is often bizarre, exceptionally detached or displaced from its rightful historical context. An archive of Dixie cups? Any of the numerous hairs, autographs, games, guns, toys, documents, gadgets, and one-of-a-kinds offered for sale to the *Pawn Stars'* discriminating evaluators of cultural value? Spray paint on abandoned buildings? On the other hand, the governing principles for many of these collections point to deep, underlying pathologies that undergird and motivate the choice of objects retained and thus also the narratives they represent and the repressed histories they revive. If, as Campana and Bale suggest, storing is a profitable industry in a culture with too many objects, then hoarding is the often sad and indiscriminate inability to let anything go. If picking rediscovers stylishly valuable remainders – or remainders that become valuable only because they are stylish according to an aesthetic that treasures the patina of age for its own sake – then pawning exposes the all-too-acute need and poverty that accompany, and are perhaps even provoked by, all of the useless accretion of America's junkyards. Likewise, as Sattar illustrates, the preservation of the corporate history of the all-too-disposable Dixie cup elicits an era when protection from the spread of germs also provided an alibi for the continued segregation of classes and types. And as McCoy demonstrates, the likeness of FEMA signs and vévé symbols exposes an archaeology of deluges and drownings that continue to submerge America's history of slavery.

The archive exists in order for us to fail at remembering. What does it mean, then, to exhibit, fetishize, and publicly celebrate the unforgotten collections of an Americana whose predominant forgetability makes such collections all the more nostalgically attractive? In remembering the forgettable, do we forget it all over again? Discussing whether hoarding waste is the equivalent of throwing it away – and gauging the importance of the materials we actually discard – the essays assembled in this box consider the activities and processes that reject, recycle, or salvage cultural value. Indeed, perhaps all this collection and display may well have less to do with the opposition between remembering and forgetting, or between keeping and discarding, than with a far more general opposition to the entire system of production and ideology according to which these bits appear in the first place.

In the midst of this encompassing heap of archives, where, finally, is the proper archive, the archive of America? The essays collected in this portion of *The Year's Work in the Oddball Archive* help us understand the relation between collections of often mass-produced, callous, witnessing detritus and the traditional collections of "official" materials – such as presidential libraries, academic repositories, and the Library of Congress – that would seem to rule the core of any notion of archive. If some version of public significance governs the collections of documents from official bodies, recognized artistic figures, and scientific achievement, what governs the even more pervasive conservation of things without much significance at all?

## HISTORIES OF THE CONTRIBUTORS

**Joseph Campana** is a poet, critic, and scholar of Renaissance literature, with essays on Spenser, Shakespeare, Nashe, Defoe, Middleton, poetry and poetics, and the history of sexuality. He is the author of *The Pain of Reformation: Spenser, Vulnerability, and the Ethics of Masculinity* (Fordham University Press, 2012) and two collections of poetry, *The Book of Faces* (Graywolf, 2005) and *Natural Selections* (University of Iowa Press, 2012), which received the Iowa Poetry Prize. His poems have appeared in *Slate,* the *Kenyon Review, Poetry, Conjunctions,* the *Colorado Review,* and many other venues. He has received the Isabel MacCaffrey Essay Prize, the MLA's Crompton-Noll Award for LGB studies, and grants from the NEA and the HAA. He teaches Renaissance literature and creative writing at Rice University and writes about art, literature, performance, and television for a range of publications, including the *Houston Chronicle, Dance International,* the *Kenyon Review,* and *CultureMap.*

**Theodore Bale** obtained a bachelor's degree from the Hartt School of Music, Theatre and Dance, where he majored in piano, and a master's degree from Northeastern University, where his studies focused on classical rhetoric. From 2000 to 2008 he was dance critic and columnist at the *Boston Herald*. His reviews and features have appeared in many newspapers in Massachusetts and Texas, and he has written extensively on dance for the World Wide Web, including the *Houston Chronicle, Dance International, Dance Magazine,* and *CultureMap,* and regularly as a featured blog called *Texas, a Concept* on *ArtsJournal*. At present he is writing a book titled *Kisses to the Earth: The New Rite of Spring,* a critical study of recent choreographic interpretations of *Le sacre du printemps*. A chapter, "Dancing Out of the Whole Earth: Modalities of Globalization in *The Rite of Spring*," has been published in *Dance Chronicle*.

**Atia Sattar** is Provost's Postdoctoral Scholar in the Department of Comparative Literature at the University of Southern California. She is also cochair of the Committee on the Status of Graduate Students in the Profession for the Modern Language Association. Her research examines the relationship between aesthetics and scientific inquiry from the nineteenth century to the present. Her current book project, *Visceral Aesthetics,* argues for a consideration of aesthetics and embodiment in the epistemology of nineteenth-century medicine. She has published articles in the journals *Configurations* and *Isis*.

**Beth A. McCoy** is SUNY Distinguished Teaching Professor of English at SUNY Geneseo. She edits *Fair Matter,* W. W. Norton & Company's literature blog. Her research interests include (anti)blackness and the paratext.

As much as and more than a thing of the past, before such a thing, the archive should *call into question* the coming of the future.

JACQUES DERRIDA, *ARCHIVE FEVER*

# 1

# PAWNING, PICKING, STORING, HOARDING

## ARCHIVING AMERICA ON REALITY TELEVISION

*Joseph Campana and Theodore Bale*

What kind of archive is America? Let's ask the unforgettable Palm Apodaca (Helena Kallianiotes) in Bob Rafelson and Carole Eastman's 1970 classic film *Five Easy Pieces,* in the midst of which two mismatched lovers (played by Jack Nicholson and Karen Black) on a road trip pick up a stranded lesbian couple (played by Kallianiotes and Toni Basil). As the lesbian couple unloads a heap of luggage and a conspicuous sewing machine, they complain about their unreliable car, a recent purchase. They are headed to Alaska, they reluctantly admit, which they imagine as a clean place free of garbage. Their conversation in the car provokes Apodaca's diatribe on the state of the Union: "I had to leave this place because I got depressed seeing all the crap. The thing is, they're making more crap. . . . I'm seeing more filth. A lot of filth."

The forty years that have passed since *Five Easy Pieces* have witnessed not only an ever-increasing avalanche of mass-produced crap, stuff, junk, and concomitant filth in America but also the advent of a unique medium for the sorting of American things: so-called reality television. We are attracted to certain forms of "trash" viewing, from Andy Warhol's groundbreaking cinema of surveillance (a significant predecessor of reality television), to the nearly grand-opera aesthetic of John Waters's early "trash" oeuvre, to Jim Jarmusch's cinematic surveys of American decay in such films as *Stranger than Paradise, Mystery Train,* and the more recent *Broken Flowers.* Why the attraction? Recent forms of trash television in particular help us unburden our weary minds after a long day of work, and we suspect we aren't the only ones who indulge in such guilty pleasures. Lately, however, we've noticed a hoard developing on television that appears to be growing at a steady rate.

Critical attention to reality television has grown rapidly to keep pace with the multiplying instances of such programming, producing nuanced readings of the cultures of surveillance, the production of authenticities and audiences, and the global reach endemic to the form.[1] And yet our sense is that this accumulating archive of thoughtful scholarship has lavished its attention upon features of reality television that may occlude the very objects that capture our gaze. Understandably, this criticism has primarily concerned itself with novelty, be it in the production of a new self, as in the "makeover" genre admirably detailed by Brenda R. Weber and Katherine Sender, or in the production of new forms of celebrity.[2] Real novelty is elusive, not to mention fleeting, and an unslakable thirst for newness leaves little room for considering how reality television not only has a history, as scholars have traced, but more importantly manufactures history, often through objects, before our very eyes.[3] Moreover, it is understandably hard to resist the allure of personhood and the fascination of narrating the self, which seem to define reality television. Certainly, we wouldn't suggest that people are irrelevant to the medium. The intensity of selves on display, be they tragic or pathetic, overwhelms us, as does the unbearable longing for transformation that fuels so much reality programming.

We would, however, diverge from the primary focus of scholarship in suggesting the thing's the thing wherein to catch the conscience of a nation. Our interest here is not merely to inventory objects or to elaborate an anatomy of postmillennial American kitsch. Rather, we argue that attention to the activity of sorting through the products of American overabundance in an age of decline could reveal a common silhouette of the state of the Union. We're not latter-day Palm Apodacas, anathematizing American excess, but we do argue that America seems to be turning into little more than the warehouse of its Americana. The conventions of reality television, it appears, are dominated by a need to organize this brave new American archive.

Four basic premises guide this essay: (1) America is not only an archive of thoughts, feelings, ideals, attachments, or disappointments but also a collection of the detritus illuminated by the setting sun of American global preeminence; (2) reality television serves as a nearly real-time system for archiving contemporary America as *Americana*, an assortment of variously valued things symptomatic of a mass-produced nation in a period of economic and aesthetic decline; (3) the *acts and processes* of archiving reveal much about contemporary social life that a fascination with the objects themselves, however captivating, cannot; (4) four signature processes – pawning, picking, storing, and hoarding – anatomize this archiving.

We identify the desires and fantasies animating pawning, picking, storing, and hoarding, as well as the drama that plays out as deeply disturbing transactions provoke both unexpected forms of attachment and loathing for television viewers. Often we take single moments, objects, or figures as representative, because even the most compelling reality programming tends toward the highly formulaic, with predictable patterns of pleasure and disgust central to the way networks generate and sustain audiences. We return to *Five Easy Pieces* as a kind of visionary prognosticator of a crisis, the symptom of which is an overabundance of Americana emptied of all but the weariest of genuine ideals. We explore the battle over what forms of value determine the archive, and we examine forms of possessive individualism transacted through objects and validated equally by sentimentality and squalor.

## PAWNING

> They got so many stores and stuff and junk full of crap.
>
> Palm Apodaca, *Five Easy Pieces*

The practice of pawning stretches through history as one of the earliest forms of short-term financing, its longevity and elasticity deriving from a brutal collision of desperation and hope. From the perspective of one who pawns an item, the necessity of short-term cash takes priority over outrageous interest and the specter of long-term cycles of debt. The profit in pawning derives from the extraction of maximum interest from short-term debt and, at times, the retention of collateral. As Gary Rivlin argues, "The business of making money off the poor dates back to the first time a person of means held a ring, a brooch, or a pocket watch in hock in exchange for a cash loan plus interest."[4] Rivlin's *Broke, USA: From Pawnshops to Poverty, Inc. – How the Working Poor Became Big Business* deploys pawning as a kind of historical inspiration for a series of short-term financing options for the working poor (check cashing, payday loans, rent-to-own franchises, tax refund anticipation loans) that extract exceptional profit from those with few assets. Rivlin, for example, narrates the recent history of pawning in America: "To the prosperous, the pawnshop might have seemed an archaic, throwback business that hit its zenith in around 1955 but those with poor credit or no credit knew better. The number of pawnshops in the United States doubled during the 1990s. Though the pawn business can seem penny ante – in 2009 the average pawn loan stood at just $90 – Cash America now tops more than $1 billion in revenues and churns out in excess of $100 million in profits a year."[5] Desperation lending and paycheck-to-paycheck living are nothing new, but they are, in the wake of the recent financial calamity, all over the billboards and the late-night televisions of postdownturn America. So what, then, is the drama of pawning for American reality television viewers? We detect a double move in the television representation of pawning as economic desperation is cloaked in the aura of authenticity or dramatized as often-violent entertainment. In both cases, what is affirmed is the right to an ideal America with a grand history and what seems like a divine right to a family business.

There is what we would like to think of as the "amiable" version of pawning on History's *Pawn Stars*, a popular show tracking day-to-day life at the World Famous Gold & Silver Pawn Shop in Las Vegas, owned by the Harrison family. The program features grandfather Richard ("The Old Man"), son Rick, grandson Corey, and the son's amusing, often incompetent friend, Chumlee Russell, as central players. On a channel named History it's no doubt redundant to say that the show is often animated by a variety of fantasies of the past. On *Pawn Stars* the "Cash in the Attic" fantasy is the mainstay. In the course of sorting through one's attic or basement or someone else's garage sale, treasure awaits. And why not try a pawn shop that traffics in collectibles to avoid the hassle of a private sale or the commissions of an auction house? Each episode includes a series of customers attempting to transform their trash into cash: dolls and figurines, coins, antique guns, classic cars, old (now also classic) video games, celebrity memorabilia, sports memorabilia, antique or simply outdated medical equipment, and more. The drama of pawning in this scenario is in fact a drama of *admiring, historicizing, educating, authenticating,* and *estimating* the worth of history.

This drama oddly obscures any actual economic value, in spite of all the on-camera haggling, by invoking other forms of value. The focus emphatically is not short-term lending. Customers almost never want to pawn an item when they're asked if they would prefer to sell or pawn. Before each episode begins the characters are reintroduced, and Rick Harrison speaks the tagline, "Everything in here has a story and a price." The price of history, it seems, trumps paycheck-to-paycheck living as the focus of *Pawn Stars*.

The Las Vegas location is critical to the fantasies of value emphasized. Although hit hard recently by the great American real estate collapse, the Las Vegas of the World Famous Gold & Silver Pawn Shop thrives. After all, Vegas was founded with criminal enterprises in mind, and its get-rich-quick, boom-and-bust, anything-goes legacy still has a powerful hold on the American imagination. Thus the glamour and risk of gambling help justify and therefore minimize the desperation of pawning.

The role of the family and family drama similarly serve to conceal the uglier side of pawning. The Harrison clan is often tangled up in minor amusing conflicts that provide an oddly if genuinely compelling texture to each episode. What is more American than apple pie if not the family-owned and -operated business? The show often feels like an informal boys' club, with special attention to antique weapons and firearms and excursions to test Gatling guns, canons, muskets and even to experience the "charm" of yesteryear's dueling rituals. After testing a particularly compelling car or weapon, the Harrisons like to emphasize their "priceless" experience.

The impulse of the show is to render *pawning* the work of *restoring* a valuable America. *Pawn Stars* is, of course, shot through with many moments of literal restoration. Repairing at the microlevel, however, is usually deemed undesirable, as when an item is fixed with new parts, resulting in a functioning device that becomes, oddly, worth less than the broken device with its original flawed parts. At other times, a classic car, instrument, or jukebox is restored to working order and therefore possessed of greater financial value or power to please. But *pawning* as an act of *restoring*, rather than merely stripping the desperate of scarce resources, extends beyond the repair of old things.

Take, for instance, the April 8, 2011, episode "Not on My Watch," which features an array of scintillating objects: a massive, deadly, Confederate-era knife known as an "Arkansas toothpick," a classic 1970 Honda Z600, a Rolex watch purchased from the U.S. Marshals Service's auction of Bernie and Ruth Madoff's personal property, a bell from a boxing ring purportedly signed by Sonny Liston (but which turns out to be forged), and a vintage 1957 bowling arcade game. The customer with the Arkansas toothpick is after cash: "The reason I'd like to sell it is I'd rather have the cash. I'm hoping for $5,000." Rick Harrison's motivations are different: "I love rare Civil War pieces, and I would love for this to be the real deal." Thus in this transaction, economic motive is displaced by a drama of authenticity. The pristine handle on the blade makes the story of the knife's origin doubtful. Besides, the prevalence of fake antiques has every true collector on edge. "They ruined the market," Rick's son Corey says in disgust. After an expert partially authenticates the object, Rick acquires it for $400, not even one-tenth of the seller's dream price. The takeaway lesson for this first exchange concerns historical aura and the anxiety that a side industry like forging has damaged real American value.

Contradictory understandings of value are at the heart of another pawn transaction when a seller presents a Rolex watch auctioned from the estate of Bernie Madoff after his conviction. Madoff, of course, engineered what many consider the largest Ponzi scheme in American history, with an estimated loss of $65 billion. The seller, who purchased the item for $32,000, wants $40,000, given the aura the watch possesses from the alleged infamy of its prior owner. Rick Harrison admits he's queasy about buying Madoff's watch, but when there's an eighty-year-old Rolex being offered, money can still be made. However, an attempt to repair the watch has reduced its value: "The people who buy these watches would rather have a messed-up face than replaced parts," he explains. As a result, the watch's link in a historical chain, its authenticity, has been broken. "This is exactly what you don't want to see," Harrison confides. "It ruins the history of the watch."

The success of *Pawn Stars* encouraged History to roll out a spin-off, the short-lived *Cajun Pawn Stars,* which operated under the same principles but more as a regional branch of the franchise shot through with a different brand of local color.[6] Emphasis on a supposed family-neighbor-friend economy dominates the rhetoric of *Cajun Pawn Stars*. In the opening sequence,

Jimmie "Big Daddy" DeRamus, who runs Silver Dollar Pawn & Jewelry Center in Alexandria, Louisiana, with his family, announces: "We're no Sin City. You can give a man a watch, and he'll trade it for a mule, which might be worth a shoe shine. And that watch will move from one hand to the next to the next." The fantasy? One could be separated from the cruel financial realities of Las Vegas living and rely instead on a small-town trade more akin to barter than economic exchange. Of course, the show features much of the exact same activity as *Pawn Stars,* as the array of objects in the June 20, 2012, episode "Trigger Finger" indicates: a 1970 Schwinn adult tricycle, a land grant signed by Andrew Jackson, a 1929 metabolism tester, a rare coin (which turns out to be a copy), and a 1921 Thompson submachine gun, or "tommy gun," which DeRamus tries out with zeal. A similar assemblage of family drama, objects with aura, and local color obscures the economics of pawning. When one seller realizes that his rare coins, potentially worth over $30,000, are in fact copies, he drawls, "When I found those coins I thought I hit the jackpot. Turns out all I have is jack squat. When it comes to luck, I might as well be pooping with the polecats."

Not all pawning obscures the queasiness of short-term lending in contemporary American television. TruTv's rival show, *Hardcore Pawn,* makes a sordid entertainment of the hard times and desperate lives of postdownturn Detroit, Michigan. The show follows the daily business of American Jewelry and Loan, owned and managed by Les Gold and his children, Seth and Ashley. In a half-hearted attempt to lend a certain film noir cachet to the show, the opening sequence announces, "In the heart of Detroit's 8 Mile lies the city's biggest and baddest pawn shop. This is where customers find fast cash and sometimes lose their minds. You won't believe what's in store."

The opening sequence promises viewers outlandish encounters and heightened reality. This show offers more family drama amongst the owners of the shop, but rather than amusing banter we see a struggle for control of the business, the exaggerated presentation of which is made to feel more like classical tragedy than a series of family economic skirmishes. There are fewer scintillating and odd objects featured in *Hardcore Pawn*. More often, the focus is on the financial frustrations of a predominately low-income African American customer base. On *Hardcore Pawn*, some customers still want to sell, but more are looking to pawn, and so promotional scenes for the show are full of tantalizing disputes.

The values associated with history, curiosity, and a grand American past fade before a desperate American present in the Motor City. In the May 22, 2012, episode titled "Devil in Detroit," a man enters looking to pawn a laptop for $150. He and his wife are expecting a baby, and they will need a stroller. The shop offers him $65, which must be repaid over three months at a high interest rate. The cursing begins immediately, and a security guard escorts them out. The store offers loans of only 10 percent of an item's resale value, which causes much consternation to those seeking quick funds. Another customer wants money for an alleged lock of George Harrison's hair, which seems to be little more than five straggly strands framed on a plaque and with a supposed note of authenticity. "Why do you need the money?" the seller is asked. "Gas prices keep rising," the customer responds.

Shots of transactions on computer screens and long, long waiting lines mark the transitions between sellers. In another sequence, a woman comes to the window trying to extend her loan. She had pawned video games months before. By not paying back, she has accrued extra charges, while the principal of her loan has hardly budged. Ashley explains the pawn to her: "It's $10 a month, and we don't take partial payments." But when the customer seeks help from Les, a quarrel ensues, redirecting attention to how a family business survives in a tough economy. Les reprimands Ashley: "Anytime someone wants to pay you, take the money. The key to everything? Taking money."

We've noticed that economic desperation as a form of entertainment is quite a growing empire at TruTV. It extends from pawning into towing, for example, and even repossession programs, which have been exposed as dramatizations of real events. Whereas most reality television seems intensely self-scripted, some shows are shot only *as if* they were reality television. TruTV's *Lizard Lick Towing, South Beach Tow,* and *Operation Repo* are purportedly based on "real" repossessions, but the outlandish characters, frequently damaged property, and bursts of what seems like easily prosecutable violence indicate a brutal and absurd extension of the heightened reality of the conflict-ridden *Hardcore Pawn*. Indeed, after a series of investigations and reports on the "reality" of such shows, the closing credits of at least one, *South Beach Tow,* added the line "The stories that are portrayed in this program are based on real events." We were amused to find that the Wikipedia entry for *Operation Repo* described these repossession shows as a version of cinema verité, which suggests some pretense of art covering over the crass fictionalization and overdramatization of economic woe.[7]

And when we consider the translation of pawning and repossession into common entertainment, it's hard not to recall Theodor Adorno and Max Horkheimer, who said, "Amusement has always meant putting things out of mind, forgetting suffering."[8]

> Those signs everywhere, they should be erased!
>
> Palm Apodaca in *Five Easy Pieces*

Picking relies on a fantasy of durability. American things not only survive and thrive but also proudly and lucratively show their age. Picking over what has been abandoned by more prosperous persons was, perhaps, once practiced primarily only by the lower classes. The idea was well captured, if not strangely sentimentalized, in Jean-François Millet's 1857 painting *Des glaneuses* (*The Gleaners*), which depicts three peasant women gathering up grains of wheat following the harvest. At the time, the canvas bothered both the middle and upper classes of French society, who found the glowing portrayal of the less fortunate distasteful. The theme successfully made its way into art cinema in 2000 with Agnès Varda's award-winning film *Les glaneurs et la glaneuse* (The gleaners and the female gleaner), which offered an intellectually distanced and often heavily sentimentalized portrait of contemporary gleaners. In early twenty-first-century America, successful gleaners are not only respected and admired but also entrepreneurs in service to bourgeois pretensions. They also provide television entertainment to millions of viewers.

By the end of the twentieth century in America, thanks to the pioneering efforts of "extreme homemakers" like Martha Stewart and similar television-based entrepreneurs, it had already become a mainstay of interior design that items decayed and weathered over time (usually neglected in musty barns, attics, and garages) might prove even more valuable than their brand spanking new counterparts. Neglect has its benefits, creating a singular, "true" patina that makes even a formerly mass-produced object into a singular masterpiece.

A rotted look is "in," and not just on television. The French haute couture design house Maison Martin Margiela, for example, experimented with cultivating rust and mold on wearable clothing. One could look back as well to modern painting and sculpture, which had already developed this aesthetic before it emerged within American home design. Marcel Duchamp's ready-mades, Robert Rauschenberg's Gluts and Combines, and even Kurt Schwitters's vast store of collages depended on a steady stream of discarded items, from taxidermy to torn tram tickets.

Picking, however, in recent years has become adapted for everyday tastes. For those average middle- and upper-class Americans who don't have the time to seek out and negotiate the cost of their own one-of-a-kind junk masterpieces, pickers like Mike Wolfe and his sidekick, Frank Fritz, are willing to sift through the landscape, in the long run serving as sort of glorified personal shoppers. Better known to television viewers from the show *American Pickers,* they've been "looking for rusty gold" in front of television cameras since January 2010, when History premiered their unique reality series. The program was eventually picked up by sister network Lifetime. Appealing in its format, it harks back a bit to the early days of PBS's *Antiques Roadshow,* where the financial bottom line is, of course, the most important and determining factor.

Picking is now a well-established genre within greater reality programming. "No longer is clutter the enemy, but a potential gold mine," the *New York Times* declared in its coverage of the phenomenon.[9] Spike aired *Scrappers,* and in History's latest spin-off, *Picked Off,* contestants compete in a series of "picking" challenges. Picking has even developed different gendered styles and markets, with Lifetime's *Picker Sisters* Tanya McQueen and Tracy Hutson and HGTV's *Junk Gypsies* Jolie and Amie Sikes, who are concerned more with design and craft rather than with hard-core negotiating and hauling.

The process seems to look back to the great heyday of American prosperity, whatever that was, as well as to some assertion of stability in the years to come. "When I rescue a rusted piece from a barn or attic, I'm not just thinking about its history: I'm planning its future," claims Wolfe.[10] The objects, then, are valued by the pickers, their fans, and their customers within an extended continuity of use and neglect. The objects have undergone what might be described as a passive fermentation or aging process, and the significant efforts required to obtain them are equally part of how they attain new life as elevated, singular, finished objets d'art.

Wolfe and Fritz do not seek antiques in the traditional sense; rather, they search for old signage, rusted farm machinery, early mass-produced toys, and other similar items with the hope of creating one-of-a-kind valuable "new" home design items. In addition to their website, the enterprising pair has two retail locations for their flourishing business (the primary is located in LeClaire, Iowa, and the other is in Nashville, Tennessee), which offers viewers an opportunity to become bona-fide participants, or "post-pickers." It's intriguing to speculate on the rural "flavor" the men have given to their business and programs. An urban setting, for example, for their gleaning would produce a different look and likely be less profitable. Wolfe and Fritz prefer to buy remnants of a sentimentalized "good old" industrial America, repurpose them, and then sell them back to consumers who share their interest in preserving the past. Moreover, the items look forward in terms of their "green appeal"; they are seemingly eco-friendly and supportive of recent goals to "reduce, reuse, recycle."

Consider, for example, Wolfe's clever Rustorations collection, which "gives new life to old fixtures and vintage lighting parts by forging them into functional, one-of-a-kind furniture for your home or office."[11] The fixtures even have familial, down-home names to make them seem more convincing as true Americana. "Bubba" features two worn green metal shades hanging off an imposing old rusted hay carrier. "Wray" is nothing more than a vintage fire bucket hanging upside down from a piece of weathered rope. Essentially ready-mades rewired, these are the new antiques for America in an age of economic and aesthetic decline.

Enthusiasm for the heyday that produced the picked items seems necessary for their valorization as deteriorated furnishings. While Wolfe has a penchant for vintage bicycles and Fritz for the toys of yesteryear, a significant part of their business centers on old signage, sometimes even in fragments. Even one disembodied letter from an old sign can be turned into a nifty shelf item, signifying something personal to a future consumer, such as initials or the name of a pet, which echoes the musings of Palm Apodaca, who in *Five Easy Pieces* calls for the erasure of all signs as part of her desired regime of cleanliness for America.

But isn't the repurposing of picking also a form of erasure? In one recent episode, the American pickers search for curiosities to decorate William Shatner's "new" Kentucky home. As we'll see, his recently acquired property has a charming legacy. And Wolfe explains that in their general picking, he and his partner "make a living telling the history of America, one piece at a time," so Shatner's home should be the perfect endeavor. The question, however, remains: Exactly what *is* that story, and what role do the material objects in both the interiors and exteriors play in its enactment?

The early scenes of the episode, titled "They Boldly Go" (a play on Shatner's fame as Captain Kirk in *Star Trek*), make it clear that Wolfe and

Fritz are playing a slightly different game this time around. They rarely pick "on demand," as they say, because doing so might stifle their creativity as "expert" pickers. When assistant Danielle Colby Cushman calls to say that Shatner and his lovely young wife, Elizabeth Martin, need items that will amplify the alleged history of their new home, however, they can't refuse. The Shatners have specific needs, it seems, and as the episode proceeds the pickers consult with Cushman about where they might find an authentic millstone and an old-fashioned pie safe, a bakery furnishing with wire shelves to hold plenty of cooling pies. One can almost see the dollar signs in their eyes with the announcement of this wealthy celebrity client. "William Shatner, he's probably got one of everything, doesn't he?" says Frank, imagining that a couple with that much money and a secondary home in Kentucky, of course, must want to spend it on things. When they finally meet up with Shatner, he describes his new house as a "clean slate," despite its legacy as a former mill. The camera pans the scenic location on a bubbling creek as the men receive their first assignment: Shatner wants them to find a "real" antique millstone to reflect the property's history.

In spite of Shatner's theatrical and economic abundance, it seems his old Kentucky home lacks some whiff of the authentic. "This is our equine room," says Martin proudly as she escorts them through the house. The equine room also happens to be her office, where she "designs pictures and furnishings and so on," as Shatner explains only slightly condescendingly. Her career aside, they want what many well-to-do couples want, a room that serves double duty and will also glorify their hobbies and interests. The intent seems genuine, since they breed horses. The office will have to display their trophies and ribbons.

But later on, once the picking is over and the items installed, it's hard not to notice that the couple seems to be overwriting the history they supposedly cherish. The new-old millstone the pickers have found for them stands straight up, contrary to its usage, right in between the autumn-colored mums in their front garden. Shatner calls the decision "genius" and enthuses about the stone's historical aura. "First of all it was made by artisans, whose work resulted in people eating. And then it's antiquity, it's the way people lived," he exclaims in wonderment. His attitude suggests a true kitsch aesthetic, while his wife exclaims that the old millstone is a "work of art." The couple happily lean against it, saying that they are "endowing it with their essence." Everybody chuckles at this strange form of consecration. But it's equally strange, inside the house, to see that the equine room has been well decorated with trophies, ribbons, and other horse memorabilia that have no authentic relationship to Martin or Shatner. They suggest a long legacy of the great heyday of Kentucky horse breeding, but the items have come from other people's garages and barns. Presto! Martin and Shatner now have an impressive material "history," thanks to the resourceful American pickers.

As the episode winds down, Shatner's glowing description of the weary pie safe in his new office articulates his obsession with weathered common items. "Think of all the hands that opened this to get a pie," he says admiringly. "Somebody years ago has touched it, has loved it, has lived it, and for some reason it's been discarded, and now we have rediscovered it, and then it's there in its original beauty, or *even better than its original beauty,* because it now has the patina of age" (emphasis our own). In an aside, Mike says that he and his partner still had to bring something "rusty and metal in in order to get their signature on the room." That item, strangely enough, turns out to be an old commercial sign embedded with a wall thermometer. It's not clear whether or not the thermometer still accurately reads the temperature, but in picking, original use rarely matters.

In this scenario, the value is not "to boldly go where no one has gone before" but rather to boldly seize for historical capital the possessions and places where others have been before. The setting is nostalgically pastoral, the room successfully filled with Americana that speaks of mills, pies, and horses. A history has been successfully repurposed somewhere in Kentucky, complete with a celebrity spokesman. As Palm Apodaca wished, the signs have been erased, and they now point to those who can afford a diligently "picked" aura.

## STORING

> Pretty soon, there won't be any room for man.
>
> Palm Apodaca, *Five Easy Pieces*

The fantasy of storing is the fantasy of endless expansion. The brutal fiction of Manifest Destiny that licensed America's hostile takeover of territory from sea to shining sea now seems directed inward. Neither below the oceans nor above the heavens, a wave of American colonization has taken place in the reterritorializing of a particular interior.

On the website for Storage Mart, a Columbia, Missouri–based business, blogger Abby Bramski traces a "history" of storage from six thousand years ago in "ancient Xian China" when belongings were housed in clay pots placed in public underground pits. American storage seems to begin with "the 1850s, when moving and storage pioneers devised the first warehouse specifically designed for household goods and treasured personal items."[12] In this blogger's mind, at least, the westward expansion of pioneers provoked the invention of storage commerce. And yet mere history is not the primary motivation for storing. According to Bramski, "This was the beginning of an industry waiting to boom." Indeed, innate urges seem to tell the story of storage. She insists, "It is a common fact that as long as there are possessions in this world, there will be a desire to store them" and concludes that "although modern storage units are not exactly underground clay pots, the concept is the same: I need someplace to put my stuff!" So there is, we might say, a storing desire that accompanies but exceeds the mere urge to acquire or possess.

The energies of expansion, either in the psychic terrain of desire or in the geographical space of North America, require forms of commercial space to warehouse the mountains of mass-produced gains of the last decades. The result is a boom in self-storage. According to a 2011 fact sheet from the Self Storage Association, 46,500 of the roughly 58,000 self-storage facilities across the globe are located in the United States, which makes for over 2 billion square feet of space in America: "That figure represents more than 78 square miles of rentable self storage space, under roof [*sic*] – or an area well more than 3 times the size of Manhattan Island (NY)."[13]

If it is reasonable to say that a storing desire produces a storing mechanism, then that mechanism has a number of features worth lingering over before we move to the tele-reality documentation of the storing drama:

**1. Self-storage.** There is much significance and almost no irony in the fact that this phenomenon is referred to as "self-storage." The self can be unburdened of its possessions because possessions can be outsourced, held indefinitely but not in proximity to the self in an ambiguous elsewhere, and preserved in relatively pristine condition, at least with the advent of climate-control units, as if they are beyond time. Unlike picking, which prefers the patina of age, storing prefers the pristine.

**2. Space.** What kind of space is storage space, and what needs does it serve? Is it private or public, commercial or personal? Some of each, no doubt. There's privacy for hire in the act of storing, but there's also something importantly common and shared, if not precisely public, in the expanse of identical storage units lined up, row upon row. We can imagine a number of important descriptors of this space: impersonal, homogeneous, anonymous, transient. The American self needs this peculiar space to hold objects of value colored by complex gradations of attachment.

**3. Security.** According to Bramski, "The first official self storage facility as we know it was in Odessa, Texas and was called 'A1 U-Store-It, U-Lock-It, U-Carry-the-Key.'" Correct or not, the colloquial name of this facility emphasizes all that might be locked away, its value – economic, affective, and otherwise – secure from others and even from oneself.

**4. Density.** While units might be packed tight and messy, the fantasy of storing is that the outsourcing of the hoard or even the archiving of particular goods in particular ways renders storing as a form of civilized hoarding.

Two fictional meditations on storage space clarify what we call the storing desire and its accompanying fantasies, as well as the drama of storing. Frances Thorne, the narrator of Kathryn Davis's lush novel *The Girl Who Trod on a Loaf*, explains a need for space that arises from the desire to rebel against the straitjacket of a privileged upbringing. Her mother is too proper to allow her daughter to send in the tops of cereal boxes in exchange for "a square inch of Texas." She describes the "appeal of the square inch," which was not only that it was part of "an enormous and slowly emerging mosaic" but also that "it would belong to me." Although Frances admits that "the forms taken by this sort of rebellion are essentially the same and consequently boring," her strategy of resistance results from a fascination with storage lockers in transit hubs.[14]

> Silver, mysterious lockers! Walls filled with them, banks and banks and banks of storage lockers! Generally they came in three different sizes: small ones, which could hold a single suitcase and possibly a shopping bag; the medium-sized lockers, two suitcases, maybe one suitcase and a garment bag, maybe up to six shopping bags; and those big enough to accommodate a bass viol or a dead body or a pony – all three, if you were clever at packing. The difficult part came when I had to make a choice. . . . I never deposited luggage . . . but in the rebellious days of my adolescence all I owned was the accumulating square footage of cool mysterious space inside those storage lockers. Once I'd pocketed the key, I'd leave the terminal. . . . I'd find the right place and drop the key; then I'd walk away. After a while, I thought that I must own a space as big as the state of Texas, only what I owned was exotic and unexplored, separate and distinct, and it would forever remain that way because, unlike a real landscape, its parts would never be forced to come together into a single, boring geographic whole.[15]

Although focused on lockers in bus and train stations, *The Girl Who Trod on a Loaf* sees storage as a form of utopia, in spite of its reference to bodies. The gothic version of storage as crypt appears in Jonathan Demme's 1991 *Silence of the Lambs*, as FBI agent-in-training Clarice Starling figures out Hannibal Lecter's anagram and finds a severed head preserved in the back of a classic car in the midst of a decrepit storage unit somewhere in Baltimore.

Even more recently, Andrew Winer's novel *The Marriage Artist* conceives of storage as the hopeless desire to retain the past, describing one of its characters, Max, a Holocaust survivor, as the originator of American self-storage: "The man owns the biggest conglomeration of self-storage chains in the country – he essentially *invented* the business to begin with. Made a fortune out of doing what he has always done anyway: try to hold a vanished world together by storing its chairs and paintings and photos and papers."[16] Still later, another character describes self-storage as simultaneously looking forward and back: "So here he was, using storage to maintain a piece of his old world, while building facilities to allow Americans to hold onto a piece of their brutal and transitory *new* world. The Old World and the New World, all contained right there in storage. . . . And the land was cheap. . . . So Max bought. He bought parcels so fast it took him years to fill them with storage places."[17] The storing desire, it seems, can even outstrip the heap of American things in need of storage.

It's likely that neither Kathryn Davis nor her appealing protagonist could have predicted the surge of storing-oriented reality television programming. But *The Girl Who Trod on a Loaf* identifies the central impetus for the drama of storing: the recuperation of abandoned and unexplored space. Winer, whose incisive *The Marriage Artist* understands storage as invested in both retaining the past and generating the future, published his novel alongside the emergence of the reality tele-visualization of the storing desire. November and December 2010 witnessed the premieres of Spike's *Auction Hunters* and A&E's *Storage Wars*, which were followed by TruTV's *Storage Hunters* and *Container Wars* and A&E's spin-offs *Storage Wars: Texas* and *Storage Wars: New York*. For the sake of brevity, we focus on A&E's *Storage Wars*, which is not only the most compelling but also the one that most clearly elucidates the prime features of the drama of storing. The apparent focus here is the human drama of competition amongst a regular cast of "characters" with varying profiles, organized by the type of storing aficionado: the collector, the gambler, the mogul, the young gun. Bidding against one another on the contents of abandoned units, they foment rivalries in hopes that each unit will provide a return on their investment. Even the auctioneer and his wife are significant characters.

*Storage Wars* is a carefully orchestrated system. A blues harmonica number, "Money Owns This Town," composed especially for the show, announces each episode. A crowd of eager bidders wanders past a series of closed lockers to the unit up for auction. The lock is cut and the door rolls up, provoking a collective gasp in the crowd. Participants have five minutes to look, and they may not enter or touch the unit. The camera pans the unit as the cast of bidders chatters and strategizes about the contents. The camera then picks out items of potential value as the observers discuss the suitability of visible objects for thrift, consignment, or serious collectors. The bidders speculate about what is not visible based on what else is there. The bidding itself is full of facial tics, hand gestures, shouts, cries, and almost-songs. Bidders often drive up the price to trick an opponent into getting stuck with a bad locker. The winner takes possession with his or her own lock and later sorts and appraises the objects. At the end, the profit is tallied amongst the regulars, and a winner emerges.

In "Skullduggery," which aired on April 17, 2011, eager bidders headed to Alpine Storage in Yucaipa, California, a former gold rush town, hoping to strike it rich. The first unit contains Victorian Eastlake furniture: a desk, a table, and a sled. The next is sparser: a few chairs surround a plastic blue seashell light, while a mountable plaster horse head lurks in the corner. In the next, sorting through the hoarded possessions reveals an antique toilet, three used mattresses, and a series of empty boxes and bags. A final unit seems to be entirely full of discarded clothes, until a shiny case containing most of a human skeleton emerges from the mess. Each lucky winner heads to an expert for appraisal. The horse head turns out to be quite valuable: French in origin, made of gold leaf on tin, and indicative of a restaurant licensed to sell horse meat. The human skeleton is quite a commodity, and each bone can be valued specifically and lucratively on the current market: the skull is most valuable at $700, while a hand will go for $300 and a femur for $90. No one, apparently, wants feet. Even the toilet is valuable and makes up for the price of the locker.

In spite of the dramas of economy played out amongst rival bidders, the true heart of *Storage Wars* lies in the fascination that dereliction provokes. What do people have, and what do people abandon? What life do objects have on their own, sequestered from the world of people? The plumbing of these object limbos reveals a whole class of purveyors of the sometimes-valuable detritus of others. Like the figures in *American Pickers*, like the figures in Millet's *Des glaneuses*, the figures in *Storage Wars* live on remainders. Those who buy regularly at auctions to stock their consignment or thrift stores are like parasites cleaning the rotting flesh of the storing system. And what do viewers get from this? We are excited by their finds because it encourages the hope that we are not hoarders and that our things, even abandoned, are treasure and not garbage slowly decomposing beneath us. Even our toilets have value, even our bones.

## HOARDING

> Filth, that's what starts maggots and riots.
>
> Palm Apodaca in *Five Easy Pieces*

Hoarding is perhaps the ultimate financial and emotional investment in objects. Hoarding endows things with such an inestimable worth that letting go, disposing of, cleaning up, or any other form of separation from those objects cannot be endured. No matter what the object and no matter what its condition, value exists all around and without condition, so much so that it's possible to build a blockade of pure value between oneself and the world. All things can (and will) be precious. Waste is not waste – not even one's own waste.

The multilayered psychic and physical worlds of hoarders are built from a complex web of anxieties and unfulfilled aspirations, attachments and endless decisions never made. Hoarders often possess a drive for perfectionism and seemingly peculiar attitudes toward abstractions in life, for example, "opportunity."

The relationship of hoarding to psychiatric problems has been, in the past few decades, extensively described in the clinical literature. Hoarders do not only hoard. Often they suffer as well from organic mental disorders, psychosis, eating disorders, posttraumatic stress disorders, and/or depression, and their various activities could be considered diagnostic criteria for obsessive compulsive personality disorder as well.[18] In other words, to think about hoarding is immediately to think about patients and not merely collectors or debtors.

Despite ongoing attempts to delineate hoarding in the clinical literature, a comprehensive definition of hoarding remains challenging. Scott Herring notes that hoarding "refers to the extreme – and too often *pathologized* – accumulation of material things."[19] According to the International OCD Foundation's website, hoarding is a complex activity with three main branches: hoarders are avid collectors, they have great difficulty getting rid of anything, and they are extremely disorganized.[20]

The tagline of A&E's pioneering, immensely popular *Hoarders* offers an oversimplified summary of this condition: "Compulsive hoarding is a mental disorder marked by an obsessive need to acquire and keep things, even if the items are worthless, hazardous, or unsanitary. More than 3 million people are compulsive hoarders. These are their stories." But what precisely is the overall story of hoarding, and why might viewers flock to watch as "characters" those persons who could be better described as "patients"? Is it merely the "ongoing tension between Before and After" described by Weber?[21]

There is obviously much money to be made in the surveillance of disorder. Three years ago, when the first episode of *Hoarders* premiered, it was the most-watched series in A&E's history.[22] Other networks have jumped on the coattails of the smash hit. The Learning Channel (TLC) offers its own version with the more sensational title *Hoarding: Buried Alive,* and Animal Planet features the melodramatic *Confessions: Animal Hoarding.* The subject shows signs of becoming popular in Europe, having made its way to German television's RTL network with the strangely hopeful name *Das Messie-Team: Start in ein neues Leben.*[23]

Before hoarding became television entertainment, it was a literary draw. Marcia Davenport's 1954 novel *My Brother's Keeper* might have been a fictional account of the lives of the recluse Collyer brothers of Harlem, but it was nonetheless a best seller. The Collyers' cluttered home at Fifth Avenue and 128th Street could be thought of as the birthplace of American hoarding, since the brothers' name was later used in early clinical diagnoses synonymously with hoarding, namely, Collyer brothers syndrome. Among the baby carriages, rusty bicycles, bedsprings, tapestries, and furniture in the Collyers' home were thousands upon thousands of books, bundled newspapers, and magazines, which suggests a unique attitude toward the preservation of information as well. If you save a thing, you'll always have it as a future reference. Also intriguing were the items they saved, allegedly, to perform music: fourteen pianos, a clavichord, two organs, banjos, violins, accordions, and various brass musical instruments, all unusable instances of a potential *Hausmusik*.

We thought of the Collyer brothers when we saw the musical instruments that pervaded the nearly ceiling-high piles of junk in the home of Judi, a sixty-six-year-old recently retired technical writer in Riverdale, Maryland. Judi is poignantly featured in season 2 of A&E's *Hoarders* in an episode called "Judi and Gail" that aired on December 7, 2009. Like that of the Collyer brothers, Judi's hoard seems filled with the possibility of music, even if it is being suffocated by a staggering amount of everyday household clutter and the nearly two tons of her used adult diapers. By the time producers had caught up with her, feces and urine had eaten through some of the walls and flooring of her home. Her daily existence was characterized by an extraordinary isolation. Before she was rescued by an emergency team, she spent most of her time "roosting," as she describes it, in her garbage-filled kitchen, strapped into a toilet chair when she slept so that she wouldn't fall into the mess.

The musical instruments in particular seem to reveal something of her dreams for a refined life dotted with the luxury of charming but modest soirées and chamber performances, and yet Judi's one-time dream of refinement seems to have become a nightmare of an uneventful life occupied now by a massive hoard. As the camera pans her condemned home in the first few scenes, a dusty black-leather and white-stitched guitar case juts out of one heap. The scrolled head of a violin looks as if it is struggling to break free from another pile. A never-used electronic keyboard is found underneath more garbage. An autoharp, abandoned decades ago, sits quietly along with the rubbish. Judi's precious instruments, in a strange echo of modernity, look at times like a neglected canvas of Picasso. There isn't any fruit bowl or pedestal to serve as companion, however. The fractured look epitomized by Cubism circa 1913, strangely, seems to emerge from the setting as if to demonstrate Judi's discursive mind.

In hoarding, things become so laden with value that it becomes impossible to make any choices, still less music. The whole world seems drained of value next to the hoard. "There are things you save that have no value, except for an emotional one," Judi says, almost without any emotion at all, in one of her placid video diaries. "I started hoarding trash and garbage, and that's not good," she adds, as if she's scolding herself. Her shame, what Sender calls "the fundamental affect in this metagenre," is necessary in making the producers feel they have achieved the expected form, perhaps, but it is unconvincing to our eyes and ears.[24] Judi seems almost scripted here, or at least coached, with some intent of letting viewers know she is aware there is a problem, pathological or not. Judi, however, doesn't appear to notice that she has ruined her house beyond repair by never discarding anything, including her own human waste. She looks at the camera blankly as she explains that she needs to sell the house, even though it is about to be condemned.

Like her musical instruments, Judi's vast collection of Bleuettes, Parisian bisque dolls, suggests her hoarding might have developed out of some desire to transcend her middle-class American life. The Bleuettes lean toward a fantasy of elegance, colored as they are by diffuse Francophilia. Did French publisher Henri Gauthier, before the First World War, have hoarders in mind when his company began circulating a wide assortment of clothing patterns for his Bleuette dolls? Or is this just more evidence of the Francophile pretensions of so many American women who watched in envy as Jacqueline Kennedy spoke French with Charles de Gaulle on television? Judi appears to have been hooked on this strange echo of mid-twentieth-century French elegance in her condemned home to the point that she has even come to resemble one of her blank-faced delicate dolls. She has few facial expressions and stares straight ahead most of the time. "I wanted to put out a good image, but I was living in a garbage dump," she admits, again with flat affect.

Little seems authentically refined in the house, despite Judi's constant talk of potential financial and sentimental value. When organization expert Max Paxton and therapist Dr. Elizabeth Moore show up, Judi says from her wheelchair that she wants to get the house cleaned up and for sale, suggesting a happy ending is buried somewhere beneath the dolls and musical instruments. Oddly enough, the "picking" mentality already described in this essay seems to prevail among the clean-up crew and therapists. Everyone talks about what the hoard, even if it is predominantly human waste, might be worth. "As I've told you, we've got a whole lot of feces in the house," says Paxton to his cleaning crew, but he warns them to watch out for those Bleuette dolls. "Even though it's poop, there might be a hundred-dollar bill at the bottom of it," he says to the workers. And this is perhaps the most surprising takeaway from recent attention to hoarding. When faced with a hoard, it seems, everyone is tempted to pick.

With respect to *Hoarders* more generally, Herring finds something "queer" about hoarders, since they, like certain other peoples and populations, resist norms and have been subject to the pathologizing gaze of medical professionals.[25] Jane Bennett, for example, finds in hoarding a vital and sensuous relationship to materiality.[26] We appreciate a healthy skepticism about mental health professionals and the producers and editors of *Hoarders*, and we share a similar desire not to demonize people who are obviously confused and suffering. But in spite of complaints that Herring and Bennett make about the treatment of the hoarders, it's hard not to see in hoarding the manifestation of an extremely American possessive individualism that will let nothing move beyond its grasp.

We find it hard not to notice the dead animals, swarms of insects, feces, tormented family members, and, at the very least, Judi's fragile health. Her daughter Ceci, for instance, breaks into tears as the crew carries the broken toilet out of the house, as if it were the real culprit. "It just all adds up quickly," Judi says matter-of-factly from her wheelchair. She doesn't seem worried about the large sores on the bottom of her feet, so severe that treatment nearly required amputation. "I'm a college-educated woman who didn't get by just by wearing short skirts and sitting in the front row," Judi says with a chuckle.

Hoarding is not only the index of an individual state of mind, way of life, or relationship to pleasure or sensuality. It has a relationship to the uniquely American overabundance of space and goods, from hoarders with secondary homes or storage units to those in precarious rentals or already-dilapidated housing, from pricey collectibles drowning in dross to the piles of cut-rate goods from cut-rate stores. Maybe we should be more anxious about the judgments we make about value. In this, Judi sounds an alarm bell. As the clean-up team removes items from her dilapidated home, therapist Dr. Moore asks Judi to rate their value on a scale of one to ten. Presented with an unsightly, soiled doormat, Judi rates it at "nine."

How did musical appreciation, Francophilia, and visions of Jackie Kennedy yield, gradually, to an endless and anxious squalor? Neither we nor any viewer is qualified to make diagnoses about the "stars" of *Hoarders,* no matter how often we are invited to do so by the rhetoric of the show. Yet it is hard not to see a certain pattern developing in the chaos of the hoard. The very objects meant to anchor the authentic and exhilarating life Judi wishes to live – and perhaps does live in fantasy – are also the revenge of what would never be. It seems no accident that a hoard both enshrines and despoils its objects. Now covered in filth and waste, they are celebrated as indices of a longed-for life while also punished as markers of the failure of American goods to provide the good life, no matter how high or how wide the pile.

## CODA

> I believe everybody should have a big hole where they throw the stuff in and burn it.
>
> Palm Apodaca in *Five Easy Pieces*

An archive is less about the past than it is about the future, Derrida suggests in *Archive Fever.* Above all, he reminds us, an archive is a thing. What future, then, with all this junk? Valuable junk, yes. At least sometimes, depending on how one reckons value. History worth preserving? Sure, although the infinite preservation of the past implies a present as well as a future sterility. Could we admit we're concerned about the state of American things – or, more accurately, about the state of America, which seems, increasingly, no more than its growing piles of things?

For Palm Apodaca, Alaska provides the vital fantasy of a pristine landscape free of junk, the farthest and most frigid reach of the American West, perhaps the last stop on the gold rush. Of course, she's never been there. Arguably, no one has ever *really* traveled to the mythical, authentic America yearned for by pickers, pawners, hoarders, and storers. Reality television archives those Americas: the America in which rust is hidden gold and trash is ready to be revealed as treasure, the America in which restoration retains a glorious past and redeems an equally glorious future, the America in which every home is an empire of self-confirming possessions too dear to part with, and the America in which all trash is surplus and may be held outside of time in anticipation of ever-greater value.

We certainly aren't the first to notice the authenticity industry at work in the constitution of the archive called America. Umberto Eco's *Travels in Hyperreality* pioneered this particular landscape with particular reference to museums and theme parks, tourist traps and animal farms. Eco argues,

> We can identify two typical slogans that pervade American advertising. The first, widely used by Coca-Cola but also frequent as a hyperbolic formula in everyday speech, is "the real thing"; the second, found in print and heard on TV, is "more" in the sense of "extra." The announcer doesn't say, for example, "The program will continue" but rather that there is "More to come." In America you don't say, "Give me another coffee"; you ask for "More coffee" . . . more than you might want, leaving a surplus to throw away – that's prosperity. This is the reason for this journey into hyperreality, in search of instances where the American imagination demands the real thing and, to attain it, must fabricate the absolute fake.[27]

From Eco's depressing and hilarious examples, we learn ultimately that under the sway of American hyperreality "everything must equal reality even if, as in these cases, reality was fantasy."[28]

This argument holds true for the archives we have explored. Certainly, authenticity is fabricated with abandon on a number of the afore-mentioned television programs.[29] And of course, we're not the first to notice.[30]

But we've also noticed how the intensification of this authenticity industry has also led to an ever-greater concern with the aesthetics of authenticity. This manifests itself in various ways. In picking, we noticed the resituating and recontextualizing of American objects for the sake of landscape design. In picking, pawning, and storing, the arts of recognition, authentication, estimation, and restoration come to the fore. Hoarding perhaps offers the most disturbing instance of the aesthetics of authenticity. Here it is not America the authentic but the American individual sitting on his or her heap of trash as a portrait of the artist-oddball refusing to bow to societal or hygienic norms. At least, this is the portrait some have painted lately.

Maybe we do share a little the fiery zeal of Palm Apodaca, that latter-day Nietzsche eager for creative forgetting and destructive renewal. Perhaps we imagine cleansed all the pawn shops with their desperate goods, all the barns packed with pickables, all the storage units full of mysterious treasure, and all the hoarded households stuffed with filth and maggots. How puritanical of us! We're not advocating a twenty-first-century bonfire of the vanities. Instead, we simply wonder about the form of entertainment the sorting of American things provides. What is it to be entertained by the spectacle of the American archive sorting its Americana?

In *Five Easy Pieces*, when Jack Nicholson and his renegade buddy Elton (played by Billy "Green" Bush) are stuck in highway traffic, a bored and discontented Nicholson leaves his own vehicle and climbs aboard a truck trapped in front of them, going straight for the piano nestled in between a gas-powered lawn mower and a used mattress. The piano serves well to suggest refined living, something in one sense completely unnecessary, perhaps only for those who can "afford" such luxuries. The instrument is also redolent with contradiction and regret inasmuch as Nicholson's character has abandoned the refined, artistic life, preferring the dangerous work of a real man in the oil fields of the American West. Yet here it is, and here we are, in the center of horrific congestion: so-called civilization amidst trash. So many cars blaring their horns, and far too many things piled up. As Nicholson delights himself with an impromptu, Liszt-inspired solo amidst the heap, are we appreciating the music, or are we scouring the truck for valuables? Are we listening to an artist transform chaos into beautiful structure, or is it all, in the end, just honking?

## NOTES

1. On reality television and cultures of surveillance, see Andrejevic, *Reality TV.* On the global dissemination of reality television tactics and franchises, see Kraidy and Sender, *Politics of Reality Television.*

2. Laurie Ouliette and James Hay previously addressed the subject of the makeover in a chapter entitled "Makeover TV: Labors of Reinvention" in *Better Living through Reality TV.*

3. A number of scholars address the historical origins of reality television, including Annette Hill's chapter "The Rise of Reality TV," in *Reality TV*; and Bradley Clissold's essay "*Candid Camera* and the Origins of Reality TV."

4. Rivlin, *Broke, USA,* 24.

5. Ibid., 24–25.

6. *Cajun Pawn Stars* ran for two seasons but at the time of this writing appears to remain unrenewed.

7. "Operation Repo," *Wikipedia,* http://en.wikipedia.org/wiki/Operation_Repo.

8. Horkheimer and Adorno, *Dialectic of Enlightenment,* 116.

9. Caramanica, "Reality TV's New Wave."

10. "Rustorations," Antique Archaeology, http://www.antiquearchaeology.com/lighting_gallery/lighting.html.

11. Ibid.

12. Abby Bramski, *StorageMart,* http://pdfsr.com/pdf/history-of-self-storage.

13. Self Storage Association, http://www.selfstorage.org/ssa/Content/

NavigationMenu/AboutSSA/FactSheet/default.htm.

14. Davis, *The Girl*, 122.

15. Ibid., 123–24.

16. Winer, *The Marriage Artist*, 195.

17. Ibid., 289.

18. Frost and Hart, "A Cognitive-Behavioral Model," 342.

19. Herring, "Collyer Curiosa," 159, emphasis added. Herring's essays on hoarding subsequently appeared in *The Hoarders: Material Deviance in Modern American Culture* (Chicago: University of Chicago Press, 2014). That this monograph was reviewed by Joan Acocella in the *New Yorker* ("Let It Go," December 14, 2014) also suggests the widespread interest in compulsive hoarding disorder.

20. "Overview of Hoarding," International Obsessive Compulsive Disorder Foundation, http://www.ocfoundation.org/hoarding/overview.aspx.

21. Weber, *Makeover TV*, 83.

22. "Hoarders," *Wikipedia*, http://en.wikipedia.org/wiki/Hoarders.

23. RTL network, http://www.rtl2.de/72029.html.

24. Sender, *The Makeover*, 84.

25. Herring, "Material Deviance."

26. Bennett, "Powers of the Hoard."

27. Eco, *Travels in Hyperreality*, 8.

28. Ibid., 15.

29. Take, for instance, two recent legal battles involving *Storage Wars*. One of the "stars" of the original series, Dave Hester, sued A&E for wrongful termination after being fired, he alleges, for complaining that the producers of the show planted valuable items in storage lockers to intensify the drama of the show. Although the story was reported in multiple venues, our favorite coverage came from the news section of the ISS: Inside Self-Storage website. Hester is at the heart of another dispute, a legal battle with rapper Trey Songz. Both have used the vocalized "YUUUP!" as a slogan, and each claims ownership. And so it seems even the basic slang of affirmation is now claimed as the authentic property of minor stars practiced in the art of trademark. Hester has, since these legal troubles were reported to the press, rejoined the cast of *Storage Wars*.

30. As Hill perhaps all too obviously distills a staple of reality television criticism, "The debate about what is real and what is not is the million-dollar question for popular factual television" (*Reality TV*, 57), perhaps suggesting that the debate is no longer worth having.

Andrejevic, Mark. *Reality TV: The Work of Being Watched*. Lanham, Md.: Rowman and Littlefield, 2004.

Bennett, Jane. "Powers of the Hoard: Further Notes on Material Agency." In *Animal, Vegetable, Mineral: Ethics and Objects*, edited by Jeffrey Jerome Cohen, 237–269. Brooklyn, N.Y.: Punctum Books, 2012.

*Cajun Pawn Stars*. TV. History. Leftfield Pictures.

Caramanica, Jon. "Reality TV's New Wave: Trash Picking, with a Smile," *New York Times*, January 8, 2011, http://www.nytimes.com/2011/01/09/weekinreview/09caramanica.html.

Clissold, Bradley. "*Candid Camera* and the Origins of Reality TV: Contextualizing a Historical Precedent." In *Understanding Reality Television*, edited by Su Holmes and Deborah Jermyn, 33–53. New York: Routledge, 2004.

Davis, Kathryn. *The Girl Who Trod on a Loaf*. New York: Knopf, 1993.

Derrida, Jacques. *Archive Fever*. Translated by Mark Prenowitz. Chicago: University of Chicago Press, 1995.

Eastman, Carole. *Five Easy Pieces*. DVD. Directed by Burt Rafelson. Culver City, Calif.: Burt Schneider, 1970.

Eco, Umberto. *Travels in Hyperreality*. Translated by William Weaver. New York: Harcourt, Brace, Jovanovich, 1986.

Frost, Randy O., and Tamara L. Hart. "A Cognitive-Behavioral Model of Compulsive Hoarding." *Behaviour Research and Therapy* 34.4 (1996): 341–350.

*Hardcore Pawn*. TV. TruTV. RDF USA.

Herring, Scott. "Collyer Curiosa: A Brief History of Hoarding." *Criticism* 53.2 (Spring 2011): 159–188.

——. "Material Deviance." *Postmodern Culture* 21.2 (January 2011). Project MUSE. Web.

Hill, Annette. *Reality TV: Audiences and Popular Factual Television*. New York: Routledge, 2005.

*Hoarders*. DVD. A&E. Screaming Flea Productions.

Horkheimer, Max, and Theodor Adorno. *Dialectic of Enlightenment*. Stanford, Calif.: Stanford University Press, 2002.

Kraidy, Marwan, and Katherine Sender, eds. *The Politics of Reality Television: Global Perspectives*. New York: Routledge, 2011.

Ouliette, Laurie, and James Hay. *Better Living through Reality TV*. Malden, Mass.: Blackwell, 2008.

*Pawn Stars*. TV. History. Leftfield Pictures.

Rivlin, Gary. *Broke, USA: From Pawnshops to Poverty, Inc. – How the Working Poor Became Big Business*. New York: Harper Collins, 2010.

Sender, Katherine. *The Makeover: Reality Television and Reflexive Audiences*. New York: New York University Press, 2012.

*Storage Wars*. TV. A&E. Original Productions.

Weber, Brenda R. *Makeover TV: Selfhood, Citizenship and Celebrity*. Durham, N.C.: Duke University Press, 2009.

Winer, Andrew. *The Marriage Artist*. New York: Henry Holt, 2010.

2

# GERM WARS

## DIRTY HANDS, DRINKING LIPS, AND DIXIE CUPS

*Atia Sattar*

The conflict between germs and cups first came to my attention in a laboratory at the Indiana Medical History Museum, where I stumbled across an illustration by Hoosier cartoonist Gaar Williams (1880–1935) entitled *Meet Me at the Town Pump. Signed, a Typhoid Germ* (figure 2.1). In this drawing, a typhoid germ appears as an amphibious creature with webbed hands and feet, sitting at the edge of a wooden tub filled with water. In his right hand is the common dipper or public drinking cup of the day, a single metal can for everyone in the town, attached by chain to the water pump. Bearing this instrument of public service near his mouth, drops of water falling from his typhoid lips, the impish germ invites townsfolk to meet him at the pump. His invitation to drink is clear. Williams's striking cartoon, I soon discovered, was not the sole critique of the common dipper, a public service turned danger to public health. In fact, the public war against germs in early twentieth-century America was waged on the rims of drinking cups.

**2.1.** Gaar Williams. *Meet Me at the Town Pump. Signed, a Typhoid Germ.* Indiana Medical History Museum, Indianapolis.

The rise of germ theory and increased awareness of germs as a means of transmitting disease raised great concerns about the public drinking cup at the turn of the twentieth century.[1] The threat of such diseases as diphtheria, typhus, and tuberculosis (a leading cause of death in the United States at the time) was made increasingly visible by scientists publishing research that included photographs of bacteriological slides. In newspapers, magazines, and pamphlets, a concerned public called for the legal banishment of death-bearing communal cups, especially in schools, trains, and other public locales, urging individuals to carry their own cups or to make disposable cups out of paper. In response to this frenzy of germ-infested rhetoric, the disposable Dixie cup emerged on the scene as a veritable twentieth-century cup of life. Indeed, with a slogan informing the public, "your hand and lips the first to touch it," the modest Dixie cup sought to cut off the public path of pathogens.

The archive of this "rim" conflict resides in Easton, Pennsylvania, at the Hugh Moore Dixie Cup Collection at Lafayette College. This collection houses the corporate records of the Dixie cup business under Hugh Moore, pioneer in the paper cup industry and leader of Dixie's individual drinking cup movement until 1986. The earliest records contain material about the development of the paper cup and Hugh Moore's participation in the successful campaign against the common drinking cup. "The bulk of the material," researchers are informed on the collection's website, "pertains to Moore's business activities, and several of the departments which operated under his direction at Dixie's headquarters in Easton, Pennsylvania. Of particular interest are the rich sources for studying the numerous competitors in the cup business, and the role of advertisement and promotion in Dixie's success."[2] The archive is thus intended to function as a bearer and organizer of records pertaining to a specific corporation and its pioneering technological endeavor. Indeed, six of the eight series in the collection are entitled "Competitive Companies," "Legal File," "Department File," "Minutes and Reports," "Home File," and "Product Samples," attesting to the broad focus on corporate history and the cup's technological progress. In the series titled "General Business Files," however, one finds a litany of newspaper articles, marketing brochures, and advertisements for the Dixie cup.[3] These latter documents in the Dixie archive unveil a complex and at times eccentric sociopolitical history undergirding the technological and corporate successes of Hugh Moore. Couched in the language of public health, bacteriological science, and newfound technology, the history of the Dixie cup reveals itself here as a chronicle of conflict between scientifically conceived germs and socially configured lips and hands.

## WAGING A GERM WAR

Initially marketed as the "Health Cup," the Dixie cup was designed by Lawrence Luellen to be "so organized and of such inexpensive material, that it may be automatically delivered by a vending machine from a stock or supply with the liquid contents . . . to be thrown away or otherwise disposed of by the purchaser."[4] The cup-dispensing machine was advertised as the Luellen Cup and Water Vendor. To manufacture, supply, and install this machine, Luellen founded the earliest manifestation of the Dixie Cup Company, the American Water Supply Company of New England, in 1908 with his brother-in-law Hugh Moore. Moore became president of the subsequent Individual Drinking Cup Company in 1910. At the initial price of a penny a cup and with each cup vendor selling two hundred drinks per day, Luellen and Moore soon realized that a thousand machines would mean "taking in two thousand dollars a day, or almost three quarters of a million dollars a year."[5] Whether driven by public health concerns or profit, Moore's corporate venture launched a successful movement against the public drinking cup.

In one of the earliest brochures for Luellen's American Water Supply Company, simply yet pertinently titled *Do You Drink Water?,* readers are faced with the fact that they may well be in a state of war. While much of the brochure describes the technical aspects of Luellen's invention, such as cups made of waterproof fiber or the vendor's insulated ice cooler, it also introduces the individual drinking cup as an essential component of the "present national crusade against the spread of communicable and contagious diseases."[6] Luellen writes most ardently of this crusade in reference to tuberculosis, a disease so rampant at the time that it was often referred to as the "White Plague."[7]

> Were we in the midst of a devastating war with a battle every day leaving the field strewn with four hundred dead, the type of our daily newspapers would prove inadequate in size to emphasize the horror of the calamity. The country would rise in its might and demand that the carnage should cease. . . . Yet how can we reconcile our consciences with the fact that as people we are allowing a constant, unrelenting and remorseless disease to show us each day a list of four hundred dead knowing as we do, that we, the people of this country are guilty and wholly responsible for this result?[8]

Luellen here paints death by tuberculosis as a scene of military carnage. What makes the battle against contagious disease starker is its being fought in our very midst, in saloons, hotels, theaters, parks, and even public schools. As such, it is the responsibility of the public to rise against germs and, in so doing, against the public drinking cup, "one of the most dangerous of public evils."[9] The extensive presentation of stirring war rhetoric, a mainstay for Luellen and eventually for Moore's public health campaign, accompanied by dramatic tales of infection and death, situates the war against germs as an early war on terror in its own right. Using the rhetoric of science and instigated by public fears of infection, this war on terror also called individuals "to respond and fight this evil that is intent on threatening and destroying our basic freedoms and our way of life."[10]

The most significant publication elucidating the terrorizing nature of this war was Moore's self-published newspaper, the *Cup Campaigner,* described on its cover page as "a militant little paper published at intervals by persons striving to banish the most prolific medium for spreading disease – the public drinking cup; containing authentic reports of the rulings of health officials, the growth of public sentiment through the press and other developments of the crusade."[11] Here one sees the war metaphor demonstrated at its finest. Sentimental vignettes of infection accompany calls to arms, declaring those who used and those who provided access to the public cup to be engaged in criminal negligence. In line with Erin Steuter and Deborah Wills's assertions regarding the use of war as a metaphor, "the imagery around [this] figurative war often participates in a lofty range of speech, calling up, through images of flags, banners, and bands of brothers, the sentiments we feel for nation, community, identity, and other such potent values."[12] Indeed, the very first issue of the *Cup Campaigner* featured an illustration of soldiers with guns "on the march" (figure 2.2). Their shirts emblazoned with the names of representative states, these men, led by Kansas, bear a flag declaring "The Public Cup Must Go!"[13] Readers are accordingly urged to "join the fight!" "If all forces unite today," the accompanying article adds, "such a cup will be as much shunned a year from to-day as a city without sewers. The public cup must go. The iron is hot; strike together!"[14] The war against germs is a fight for public health situated within the context of sewage management in cities. Yet it

# The CUP-CAMPAIGNER

**Edited by HUGH MOORE,**
**115 Broadway, New York, N. Y.**
(Copyrighted 1909)

Released for publication to Newspapers, Magazines and Health Authorities or Societies.
Cuts, information and other data furnished on request.

CONTRIBUTIONS SOLICITED.

**JOIN THE FIGHT!**

is the call for abolishment of the public cup here that reeks of propaganda; striking hot iron and shaping the future ultimately require investment in Moore's individual drinking cup.

The rhetoric of military combat continued even in seemingly less propagandist and more scientific publications. The most influential article in this germ war was published by Dr. Alvin Davidson, professor of biology at Lafayette College who conducted a study of bacteria in public school drinking cups in Easton. Published in *Technical World Magazine* on August 1908, "Death in School Drinking Cups" demonstrates that germs bearing diseases such as diphtheria, bronchitis, grippe, pneumonia, and tonsillitis proliferate on school drinking cups. Davidson notes the combative nature of germs early in his article: "At least 700,000 of the million and a half deaths occurring annually in the United States result from the minute parasitic plants and animals gaining access to the body. These invisible foes wage a continual warfare against both strong and weak, rich and poor. Civic duty as well as self preservation demands that these life-destroyers should as far as possible be shut out of the human system."[15] Using such phrases as "invisible foes," "continual warfare," "civic duty," "self preservation," and "life-destroyers," Davidson certainly paints a striking portrait of potential infection by "minute parasitic plants and animals." Furthermore, his choice to foreground "death" in the title of this piece over the mere presence of infectious germs, which are largely the article's investigative focus (consider the impression given by "germs in school drinking cups" as opposed to "death in school drinking cups"), reveals the sensational

**2.2.** *On the March, Cup Campaigner* 1, no. 1 (December 1909): 14, General Business Files, box 1, series 1.1, Hugh Moore Dixie Cup Collection, 1905–1986, Lafayette College Library.

inclinations of his scientific bacteriological work. Similarly, the *Kansas City Star* of July 16, 1909, reports the very urgent nature of the war against germs: "No less than a warren of valuable guinea pigs have been sacrificed on the altars of medical research to demonstrate the truth of the health board's contention, while a microscopic investigation reveals an army of alien germs that threaten the security of the nation."[16] The researcher's laboratory is an altar of sacrifice; the invisible foes are now an "army of alien germs" threatening not only the human biological system, as per Davidson, but also the social and political systems of the nation.

As in the U.S. government's war on terror and its preceding war on drugs in the 1980s and 1990s, the germ war of the early twentieth century was not without its casualties. Ultimately, one needed protection and fortification not simply against germs but also against their identifiable carriers: socially predetermined raced, classed, and gendered types. The campaign for the individual drinking cup notes this need for segregation from its earliest publications: "The public drinking cup has been a menace to the public health (in all communities) bringing the user into intimate contact with all classes of people who may or may not be infected. There is an instinctive aversion felt by all cleanly people in the compulsory use of the public drinking cup."[17] On the one hand, the public drinking cup and its resident germs threatened the security of the nation's citizens alike, unifying its multifaceted public. Even Davidson does not fail to note that germs are nondiscriminatory, affecting all populations, "both strong and weak, rich and poor." On the other hand, in their indiscriminate attack against humans of all classes, genders, and races, germs undermined preestablished and rigid social categories at the turn of the twentieth century. These "invisible foes" brought "into intimate contact" not only strong and weak or rich and poor but also women with men, whites with blacks, and the British with foreigners. Avital Ronell addresses this dual association in her work on the war on drugs: "Under the impacted signifier of drugs, America is fighting a war against a number of felt intrusions. They have to do mostly with the drift and contagion of a foreign substance, or of what is revealed as foreign (even if it should be homegrown). Like any good parasite, drugs travel both inside and outside of the boundaries of a narcissistically defended politics. They double for the values with which they are at odds, thus haunting and reproducing a lexicon of body control and a private property of self."[18] Similarly, at the turn of the twentieth century, "under the impacted signifier of [germs], America [was] fighting a war against a number of felt intrusions. They [had] to do mostly with the drift and contagion . . . of what [was] revealed as foreign [germs, dirt, poverty, nonwhiteness] (even if it should be homegrown). Like any good parasite, [germs] travel both inside and outside of the boundaries of a narcissistically defended politics." That is to say, germs, embodied in their publicized uncultured carriers, simultaneously composed the enemies and constituents of a proud nation called to arms. "They double for the values with which they are at odds, [both threatening and upholding the need for value-laden social hierarchies], thus haunting and reproducing a lexicon of body control [cleanliness and purity] and a private property of self." At the most basic level, germs were an "alien," "invisible" force introduced into the human system. As such, they represented impurity. At the same time, however, "what is impure," highlights Maria Lugones, "is impure relative to some order and . . . order is itself conventional. What is impure is anomalous." The germ-bearing drinking cup, catering to colored men and white women alike, epitomized "the power of impurity in resisting and threatening this oppressive structuring."[19] The eradication of germs was about more than restoring the nation's health; it aimed to maintain preexisting classed, gendered, and raced ideals of purity.

To eradicate germs was to be clean *and* also to be pure. In her article "Tide Whiteness: A Genealogy of Race, Purity, and Hygiene," Dana Berthold confirms, "When we look at purity ideals as having not only physical but also moral aspects, we can see how easily slippage takes place between the exclusion of 'dirt' and the exclusion of 'dirty people.' The function of purity ideals is rarely just about physical dirt – it is about wielding power over 'impure' others."[20] In its quest to eradicate dirt and impure germs, the war against germs in America likewise sought to separate and remove those from society who were marked as dirty and did not conform to conventions of purity. Such a desire for segregation is brought to light in a 1909 editorial in the *New York Herald* that describes a recent train trip:

> I occupied a seat opposite the water cooler, and I noticed that there was one glass for all. The first passengers to use it were two negro girls and a baby they had with them. Then came a white man, then a white woman and two boys, and many more of the perspiring crowd. Some, I confess, did not appeal to me as just the kind you would care to drink after. At one of the stations a Chinaman boarded the train and drank from the glass. A little later a lady with her child and nurse came in, and the nurse gave it a drink from the much used glass. I revolted against the filthy habit, and wondered how many more would use that one glass before the train reached its destination.[21]

The "filthy habit" of using the public drinking cup unflinchingly mediates encounters between the hands and lips of "two negro girls and a baby," "a white man," "a white woman and two boys," "the perspiring crowd," "a Chinaman," and "a lady with her child and nurse." The writer is especially attuned here to race and comportment; the people he/she observes are

**2.3.** *And Then We Wonder at the Spread of the "Black Plague" and the "White Plague," Ladies' Home Journal,* July 1909, General Business Files, box 1, series 1.1, Hugh Moore Dixie Cup Collection, 1905–1986, Lafayette College Library.

either "negro," "white," and "Chinaman" or a nebulous "perspiring crowd" and a more proper "lady." Most telling is the writer's use of the phrase "the kind you would care to drink after," underscoring his/her ideals of purity that there are in fact some *kinds* more pure than others.

The issue of appropriate *kinds* of people is also depicted quite vividly in the *Ladies Home Journal* of July 1909 (figure 2.3). The pertinent illustration juxtaposes two distinct images at the same water fountain. The first presents a man of indistinct race in untidy clothing, hands hidden in his pockets, turned away from the public water fountain. The second consists of a mother and her child, visibly attired as members of a higher social class, with the former holding the dipper to the latter's lips. The caption narrates simply that the man has drunk from the public drinking fountain and the child will drink from the same cup. What the illustration does not need to say but undoubtedly displays is that these two sets of individuals belong to very different *kinds.* This "Public Fountain Story: In Two Pictures," entitled *And Then We Wonder at the Spread of the "Black Plague" and the "White Plague,"* draws a parallel between the spread of the bubonic plague and tuberculosis. The reference to black and white, however, does not refer to the plagues alone. The man of indistinct race may well be black, and his clothes, in any case, are unkempt and blackened: he is covered in dirt and thus, in cartoon logic, also dirty in the moral sense. The mother and child are white of race: their dress and comportment bear the social markers of acceptability. That we should hardly "wonder at the spread of the . . . 'White Plague'" by looking at this comparison exemplifies what Berthold describes as "the concern for hygienic discipline[, which] makes sense within a tradition that has valued mind (or spirit) over body, and culture (or civilization) over material nature." First and foremost, the slovenly figure of the man registers him as lacking hygienic discipline. Second, and perhaps more significantly, the critique of hygiene so visually presented underscores a more jarring critique of race: "In the particular history of hierarchical relations in the United States, whiteness has represented mind/spirit and civilization, and non-whiteness primitive embodiment, closer to nature."[22] At a time when civilization was affiliated with whiteness, a command of nature, and intellectual refinement, the man of questionable race, whose dirt-covered attire and stooping gait position him visibly, physically closer to natural elements, lacks all the markers of civility. It is significant to note, however, that just as this public fountain story rigidly frames impurity and nonwhiteness, it also places women within oppressive gendered categories. The woman is unflinchingly civilized, white certainly, but she has also maintained discipline of form and tidiness of clothing amid the natural scenery that surrounds her. She is also a young mother and, as such, personifies the expected social role for young women. Neither "impure" racialized man nor "pure" white women escapes from the classifications to which they are bound. Yet while the former needed to be protected against, the latter needed most certainly to be safeguarded. The public drinking fountain facilitated the communicability of disease, and it did so by enabling encounters between the hands and lips of undesirable and sinister men of the lower races and classes with those of chaste and highbred young women.

The germ war thus dramatized by the Hugh Moore Dixie Cup Collection commingles scientifically reasoned and empirically proven ideas about bacteriology, disease prevention, and sanitation with unreasonable beliefs about racial purity and morality. The range of public fountain stories found in this collection, whether set in railways, schools, or public parks, inevitably sensationalize the possibility and presence of female victims who have dainty white hands and rosy lips. In fact, the entire assortment of documents on this war may be read as an archive of hands and lips: erring hands and lips, diseased hands and lips, charitable hands and lips, gendered hands and lips, and plenty of hands and lips the *kind* one would not care to drink after.

## WHAT PROMISCUOUS DRINKING!

The necessary use of hands in holding and drinking a cup of water did not by itself pose a problem to public health; rather, the inappropriate, unbridled oversharing of the vessel by hands both healthy and diseased undid the public cup: "The public drinking fountain, what promiscuous drinking does it witness! Placed there by kindly hands, emulous of the praise bestowed upon him who gives a cup of cold water in the name of a disciple, how many has it tempted to premature death! In each instance the hand that holds out the cup is extended in the kindliest spirit, in obedience to a generous impulse, but thoughtless of consequences."[23] While not devoid of alarmist tendencies and several exclamation points, this piece reminds readers of the original public service purpose of the common dipper. Ideally, the hands at a public drinking cup are helping hands that hold out the cup to another, "extended in the kindliest spirit, in obedience to a generous impulse." And yet, this very generosity turned promiscuity imperils drinkers, tempting them to "premature death." The Dixie cup offered itself as a substitute for this thoughtless kindness. The cup's slogan, "your hand and lips the first to touch it" ensured that no one else's hands or lips would have occasion to thoughtlessly endanger one's life.

The marketing documents for the Dixie Cup Company display a conscientious effort to underscore its elimination of promiscuous drinking. The first of these documents found in the collection at Easton consists of an undated list titled "Suggestions for Captions." Among the various points emphasized by Dixie's marketers, one finds here the following: "Though the glass may be polished, consider the hand that polished it, that puts the soda in it. Dixie cups are not touched by human hands till they reach you." Referring here to a glass in a soda shop, the marketers of Dixie warn customers that even the singular hand of the clerk is not to be taken lightly, for who knows which other tainted cups he may have touched with hands unwashed. Dixie offers, instead, the complete removal of other "human hands": "Dixie Cups eliminate the human element."[24] Eliminating the touch of human hands and lips and with them the possibility of human germs, disease, or death, Dixie cups offered a sanitary distance between individuals of different classes, races, and genders. Dixie sold the evacuation of the human element.

On another sheet listing secondary points of emphasis in Dixie's marketing campaign, one finds the following:

> 1. Clerk does not have to stop, wet-fingered, and separate Dixies.
> 2. Dixie paper is made at a country paper mill where air, water and pure materials make for spotless whiteness.
> 3. Dixie Cups are made on wholly automatic machines, almost human in their movements.
> 4. They are sterilized by heat in process and shot off into paper cartons, which are sealed and sent to the fountain.
> 5. You would think you were in a modern bake-shop, seeing the white-gowned, white-capped, white-gloved attendants.[25]

This list suggests that Dixie is modern and mechanized, with machines that are "almost human" and a production process that sterilizes, seals, and sends pristine cups. Dixie embraces purity, from the salubrity of its paper mills and the unsullied nature of its materials to the elimination of

**2.4.** Untitled printed material, General Business Files, series 1.1, Hugh Moore Dixie Cup Collection, 1905–1986, Lafayette College Library.

clerks' wet fingers disengaging cups. And Dixie embraces whiteness, with employees who are "white-gowned, white-capped, white-gloved," sanitary as a laboratory but comforting as a "bake-shop." The Dixie cup is itself made of white paper. Indeed, even when earlier advertised as the Health Cup, the spokespersons for this crusade noted, "This means more than a drinking cup – it is a sanitary drinking cup service."[26] And as a "service," the cup replaces the public dipper.

More dangerous than the promiscuity of dirty hands, however, was the promiscuity of drinking lips. This danger is made most evident in an advertising proof by the Dixie Cup Company that displays a single glass of soda assaulted by an army of lips (figure 2.4). Lips of all shapes and sizes, slightly curved and smiling, stretch back as far as the eye can see. A single drinking cup would hardly survive such an assault by so many varied lips. Neither would a future drinker. The illustration elicits abhorrence, a sentiment evidenced frequently in responses to individuals viewing a barrage of public lips on a single cup. "To see the same vessel," notes a writer for the *Milwaukee Free Press,* "which has but recently left the tobacco stained and pimpled mouth of a diseased man, pressed to the soft and rosy lips of a little child is to become nauseated in body and soul."[27] Moral judgment follows the passage of a public cup from an undoubtedly male "tobacco stained and pimpled mouth," a hotbed of disease, to the "soft and rosy lips" that mark the innocence of childhood. The cup creates potential affiliations of infection between a man whose tobacco-stained mouth betrays some responsibility for his unhealthy condition and a little child who has yet to experience the ways of the world. This newsworthy nausea of both "body and soul" underscores yet again the various unbecoming interactions facilitated by the public drinking cup.

On a more official note, a June 1909 bulletin circulated by the North Dakota State Board of Health, *The Public Drinking Cup,* warned against the unsorted presence of various physical *kinds* on board public trains:

> Enter any ordinary day coach while in transit and it requires no special training for you to divide the passengers into two general classes physically, the normal and the abnormal. Of the latter class there will in all probability be a definite proportion who are suffering from ailments more or less of a contagious nature. There is always left on the edge of the drinking cup after being used more or less of the moisture of the mouth with whatever

> pathogenic organisms that it may contain. The next user will run the chance of having these transferred to his own lips and if there is any abrasion, a local infection is the inevitable result; if this is escaped, intestinal and systemic infection may follow.[28]

That potential harbingers of disease would be so self-evident as to require "no special training" on the part of an observer suggests that divisions of "normal and abnormal" were based not so much on the microscopic scientific evidence upon which the war against germs depended but on the discernment of socially accepted race and class markers. Since the cup alone cannot present contagious germs to the naked eye, individuals must distinguish microbe carriers by discerning the *kind* after whom one does not care to drink. What follows this sorting of "normal and abnormal" is a more technical account of how pathogenic organisms reside at the edge of drinking cups and the potentially harmful presence of an abrasion on one's lips.

The discussions surrounding lips and public drinking cups overflow with sentimentality when compared to accounts of death-dealing hands. This disparity between lips and hands is hardly surprising when one considers that the cases emphasizing lips usually include women. It is bad enough for "normal" men to be infected by the thoughtless likes of the "abnormal," but for white women, paragons of purity and symbols of chastity, to be so tainted with germs is insupportable. The numerous stories of female infection at public fountains hasten to assert the respectability of the inflicted, underscoring the fact that the lady could not have acquired such an infection elsewhere. One such account tells of a Mrs. Olive Peters, age sixty, who died after visiting relatives in Omaha. She took the train, where she "used the public drinking cup on the coach freely." She returned to her daughter's home "with a full developed case of Syphilis of which she died a few days later." Her doctors discovered an abrasion in her mouth and "satisfied themselves by inquiring of the woman that she could have been exposed to the disease in no other way than through the public drinking cup."[29] Mrs. Peters's contraction of disease is certainly dire, leading as it does to her death. Worse nonetheless is the very nature of the illness that she acquired – syphilis, a venereal disease. It is very significant, then, for the sake of maintaining the late Mrs. Olive Peters's respectability that her doctors note that she could only have been exposed to the illness by way of the public drinking cup.

A similar account of infection in the *Cup Campaigner* of December 1909 declares more plainly the value of female reputation and life: "Less than six months ago, an esteemable young woman in Topeka, whose character is above reproach, made a short trip to the Southwest, neglected to take a private drinking cup, drank from the common cup on the train and returned to Topeka with a loathsome disease. That was right here in Topeka. To have protected this one girl would have been of greater value to society and humanity than all the enforcement of the drinking cup order would ever cost the state."[30] In stark contrast to her character, a young woman who is "esteemable" and "above reproach" finds herself to have contracted a "loathsome" disease, most likely syphilis. Her only fault of character, I dare say, was that of neglecting to carry an individual drinking cup. Still, the fact that protecting "this one girl would have been of greater value to society and humanity" than the monetary cost of enforcing the drinking cup emphasizes the characterization of white women as both pure and needing protection. The role of the state is to "protect" white women from disease; the role of white women is to embody all that

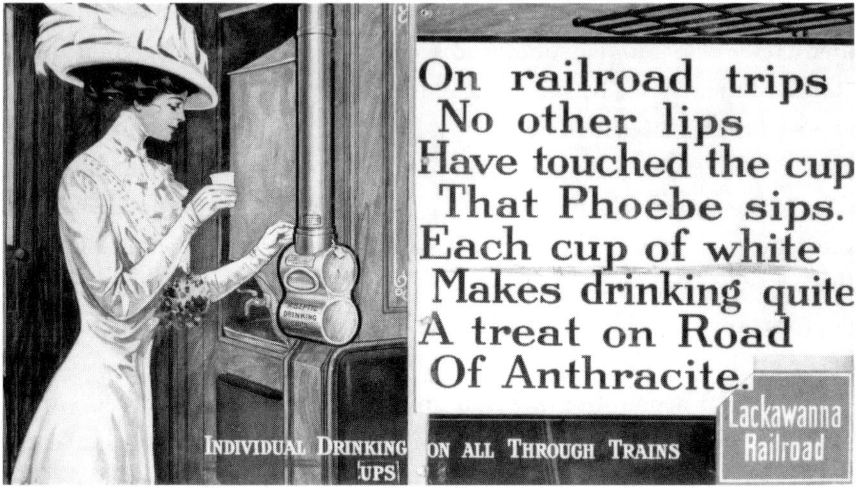


**2.5.** Lackawanna Railroad advertisement, General Business Files, series 1.1, Hugh Moore Dixie Cup Collection, 1905–1986, Lafayette College Library.

is "esteemable" and "above reproach" in society. The author stresses that such an awful thing happened "right here in Topeka." Indeed, if the young women of Topeka aren't safe, who is?

In an effort to assuage the train-traveling female population, the Dixie Cup Company established ties with the Lackawanna Railroad Company. With rail lines connecting New York, Pennsylvania, and New Jersey, the Lackawanna employed locomotives that burned anthracite, a variety of coal that combusts with the fewest impurities. Passengers could thus rest easy about the possibility of having soot-covered "dirty" clothes when travelling on the Lackawanna. Highlighting its cleanliness and hoping to attract a more elite traveler, the Lackawanna developed an advertising character named Phoebe Snow, a young New York socialite, always clad in white, engaged in various activities on the train, juxtaposed with a jingle about the benefits of anthracite and other railroad features. Margaret Young describes Miss Snow's socialite status: "This 'maid in white' with her smooth self-assurance, differed from the grandmotherly image of Lydia Pinkham as well as from the competent home economist image of Betty Crocker. Instead, she hearkened to the more adventuresome New Woman of the new century, who was financially independent and in charge of her own destiny."[31] Phoebe Snow personified the particular kind of woman who rides the rails of her own volition and yet remains above reproach. In her ever-white dress, she advertises for purity of body and mind. The combined advertisement for Dixie and Lackawanna combines Miss Snow's pure whiteness with the individual drinking cup in the image of a finely clad, white-gloved young woman obtaining a drink from a cup and water vendor (figure 2.5). The accompanying rhyme reads as follows:

> On railroad trips
> No other lips
> Have touched the cup
> That Phoebe sips.
> Each cup of white
> Makes drinking quite
> A treat on Road of Anthracite.[32]

In providing "Individual Drinking Cups on All Through Trains," the Lackawanna offers a clean, safe, and moral voyage. The very act of drinking water becomes a "treat," a pleasurable means of restoring the purity ideals that are relentlessly challenged by impure germs. The cup that Phoebe or any other lady daintily "sips" shall be untouched by the lips of another, enabling her to exercise her independence while remaining chaste and safe from infection.

In case general readers were unable to grasp exactly the gravity of female affliction from a public drinking cup, an editorial in the *Ladies' Home Journal* makes it startlingly clear: "The danger here is not fancied but real. The mouth is one of the most sensitive of all our organs for the communication of disease. And any woman with the least common-sense can figure out for herself what it means for us to touch our lips to the same spot where another pair of lips has just been. It is one of the most direct of all human communications."[33] What does it mean to touch one's lips to the same spot where another pair of lips has just been? As a woman with common sense, I would venture that the act is tantamount to a kiss. To drink from a public cup, then, is to render vulnerable "the most sensitive of all our organs"; this is not a fancied fear of germs but the real danger of a kiss, and possibly the undesirable kiss of a mouth carrying loathsome diseases. It comes as no surprise, then, that in his writings on syphilis, the acclaimed "father of modern medicine," William Osler, noted that the disease, and particularly syphilitic chancres, spread "from certain of the contacts of every-day life (contagion from drinking cups, kissing, barbers' utensils, etc.)."[34] Drinking cups and kissing are here juxtaposed as potential causes of syphilitic infection. The very real danger is not simply the sexual connotation of a kiss-facilitating drinking cup but that the act of drinking may well lead to the "loathsome" diseases associated with sexual encounters.

In addition to the unwanted kisses of a public drinking cup, actual kisses were considered carriers of disease and death. A special cable from Paris to the *New York Times* on August 6, 1909, reports: "Mustache Harbors Germs: Kiss Leaves Deposit of Bacilli on French Woman's Lips." Leaving no doubt in readers' minds about the presence of germs on lips, this experiment tested the "most direct of all human communications." The particular conditions of the experiment were as follows: "A Parisienne allowed herself to be kissed by a clean-shaven and then by a bearded man. After each salute her mouth was stroked with a sterilized brush. The microbes thus collected were deposited in a test tube and allowed to incubate four days. It was shown that the clean-shaven man had deposited a small quantity of harmless particles. His rival's kiss had colonized the lady's lips with the bacilli of tuberculosis, diphtheria, pneumonia, and numerous other unpleasant microbes." Engaging voluntarily in two kisses and then the stroking of her lips with a sterilized brush, the "Parisienne" subject finds her lips to be populated by harmful bacilli sheltered in a kisser's mustache. While her clean-shaven kisser merely "deposited" particles, the mustached kisser has "colonized" her lips, depositing a swarm of germs. The report continues its assault metaphors, noting, "The Parisian's affection for his mustache and beard will probably not be affected by it, but savants here have just made an effective demonstration against the malevolent propensity of the hair-adorned lip as a harbor to propagate disease."[35] Harboring germs is like harboring enemies, and any mustached individual is here maligned as the bearer of a "*malevolent* propensity," implicated as an adversary to the woman's state of health.

With its degree of unabashed contact and directness, the previous experiment could perhaps only have been conducted by the French. The American equivalent of such an investigation relies so heavily on norms of womanly respectability that it does away with men entirely. An article titled "Death-Laden Kisses: One Touch of a Healthy Girl's Lips Gave 28 Colonies of Germs" informs readers of the outcome of a study conducted by a Dr. M. F. Schlesinger, who "covered a sterilized culture plate – a transparent glass disc – with perfectly fresh and sterile gelatine, and caused a healthy and vigorous young woman to touch her lips to it." This combination of "fresh and sterile gelatine" meeting "healthy and vigorous" lips nonetheless produces colonies of bacteria, illustrating the unbeknownst dangers lurking in the otherwise sanitary and robust lips of a young woman. The article addresses these perils from its very first words:

> "Where in the world did she get it?" is a question frequently heard after the announcement that Miss So-and-So is ill with pneumonia, or typhoid fever, or some other germ disease; especially if Miss So-and-So is a person who is more than usually fortunate in living in clean and healthful surroundings.
>
> It would shock the one asking the question if she learned that her dear friend's illness sprang from her own friendly kiss; but such might readily be the case.[36]

Further, as the published photograph of the act illustrates (figure 2.6), not only was the woman clean and robust, but she belonged to the upper classes of society, as indicated by her high-necked collar, well-groomed hair, and indications of matrimony (after all, a single young woman could hardly go about offering her lips for a scientific experiment). The unnamed woman in the photograph who is modestly touching her lips to Dr. Schlesinger's culture plate undoubtedly maintains an untarnished reputation.

The caption makes an overt connection between this young woman's lips and the public drinking cup: "Dr. Schlesinger's experiment, which proved that the lips of a healthy young woman swarm with bacteria, and

**2.6.** "Dr. Schlesinger's experiment, which proved that the lips of a healthy young woman swarm with bacteria, and diphtheria and pneumonia germs scraped from a public drinking cup," from "Death-Laden Kisses: One Touch of a Healthy Girl's Lips Gave 28 Colonies of Germs," newspaper clipping, General Business Files, series 1.1, Hugh Moore Dixie Cup Collection, 1905–1986, Lafayette College Library.

diphtheria and pneumonia germs scraped from a public drinking cup." Thus, while the subject of the experiment has kissed a petri dish, she herself, it would appear, has not been kissed. Nonetheless, the fact that a woman accustomed to health and cleanliness and undoubtedly from a socially desirable class could not only be in danger of disease but also bring harm to others as a microbe carrier threatens the very moral underpinnings of society. The public drinking cup, it would appear, leaves a woman unfit to be kissed.

Certainly, by the beginning of the twentieth century, some of the states were already considering enacting antikissing laws. The state of Virginia, for example, proposed a law such that "kissing be permitted only on the certificate of the family physician, and unauthorized kissing by any one with weak lungs or any contagious disease is made a misdemeanor punishable by fine." While the law was proposed with the best of intentions, the difficulties regulating it were noted in the *Journal of the American Medical Association:* "It is difficult to see how such regulations are to be enforced, as kissing and telling are not generally supposed to go together. However unsanitary the practice, it will continue, and a little risk may only add an extra zest to the performance."[37] Indeed, a family physician could really only authorize socially institutionalized kissing in a marriage or engagement, leaving entire congregations of less respectable kissers unchecked.[38]

For some individuals, such as Rev. Dr. John L. Scudder, pastor of the First Congregational Church, Jersey City, the clear solution was to call for an end to the performance altogether. In an article for the *New York World,* he declares that "kissing is a pretty custom, but there is such a thing as kissing a person to death," adding, "If the kisser has tuberculosis or diphtheria, there is great danger that the disease will be communicated to the kissee." The language of infection is here affixed to the "*pretty* custom" of kissing, that is, kissing in its socially acceptable and polite modes, as a "chaste salute." Yet even with this kiss, the danger of imparting infection from one's lips upon another's is entirely too great and all the more sad when one's dear relation risks death itself: "Many a little one has been sent to the grave by the loving kiss of a consumptive mother. Many people have caught tuberculosis by kissing consumptive dogs and cats, canary birds, parrots and other household pets. It is time to start anti-kissing leagues throughout America, and if I could be the agency for this new departure I should consider myself a public benefactor. The whole land should ring with the cry, 'Quit your kissing.'" Certainly, the reverend modestly avoids reference to the kissing that may occur between two loving individuals, mentioning only the kiss of a parent or pet. Scudder offers readers a figure for this "new cult," a Mr. Dowie Jr., who is admirably (and in all seriousness) dubbed "The Great Unkissed." Long Unkissed, Dowie Jr. is undoubtedly free from infection and at no risk of spreading death. Even the chastest of kissing, however, must now be banned, as Scudder goes so far as to call for a ban to the kissing of court Bibles, which are "nests and breeding places of bacilli."[39]

## A HUMANITARIAN ENTERPRISE

Indeed, the role of religion in the war against germs was undoubtedly significant. One could not have congregations infected by the sharing of a single cup, nor could one allow the thought of a chalice as mediator of contact between varying lips. At the sixth annual International Congress on Tuberculosis, held in Washington, D.C., in 1908, a sanitary communion chalice was exhibited for use in churches. Invented by a Rhode Island clergyman, this chalice consisted of a vessel covered at the rim by a number of thin leaves or films assembled together. After each usage, "the uppermost of the leaves or films is removed by the officiating clergyman. When this leaf is detached the next one comes into view and offers a pure, clean surface over which to drink." In contrast to providing a simple individual drinking cup for each communicant, this complicated apparatus, operated by a clergyman, sought to preserve "the symbolism of the sacrament."[40]

At the same time as the church developed a sanitary chalice, the manufacturers of the individual drinking cup sought to sanctify their paper product. The first brochures of Luellen and Moore's American Water Supply Company accordingly urged customers to "Quaff Nature's Nectar from This Chalice." The ornate equivalent of "drink water from this cup," the refrain orchestrates a jump from the language of scientific bacteriology to moral purity; the cup is sanctified as it turns its contents from water into nectar (if not wine). The sacred connotations of the Dixie cup offer purity for body and soul. No longer does the cup merely wage a war against disease, serving as the purveyor of a healthy, germ-free life, but it now offers the triumphant victory of a life that is pure, moral, and sacrosanct.

Thus sanctified, the offering of the Dixie cup to another is nothing short of virtuous. If at first the exclusionary hierarchies of purity were couched in the language of health and sanitation, they are now disguised in expressions of charity, as a benefit for all of humanity. A writer for the *North American* accordingly declared: "Here is an opportunity for co-operation in real humanitarianism, not only for the rich employer of hundreds of workmen, but for the underpaid teacher of the village school."[41] It would appear that the individual drinking cup offers humanitarianism; the Dixie cup and others of its kind bring people of varying classes together, providing them with an opportunity to serve others. In 1909, when Kansas abolished the public drinking cup for all its citizens, effecting the first of the victories in the war against nondiscriminatory germs, many other states followed. The *Larned Chronoscope* fittingly propounded the legal decision: "The removal of this awful menace to public health and happiness from these public places is a step toward a higher civilization, and a better moral and physical condition, and the board of health are entitled to the gratitude of every citizen of the state."[42] That "every citizen of the state" need express gratitude for increased sanitation may well be fitting. Still, this "higher civilization," this "better moral and physical condition" were made possible through the removal of germ transmission from *kinds* one does not care to drink after. The "awful menace" removed is not simply an army of alien germs but the conflicting, commingling lips of various men and women on the rims of drinking cups.

## ARCHIVING GERMS

Even as the Dixie cup was developed as a means for "removing the human element," the Dixie Cup Collection is saturated with it. The rhetoric of the campaign for the individual drinking cup overflows with human sentiment: heart-rending tales of disease and loss, fervent appeals to join the fight, and sympathetic promises of faith and humanitarianism. More than a mere corporate history, this collection of documents concerning a conical piece of waterproof paper can be placed in line with the histories of other U.S. public campaigns metaphorized as wars. And as in the case of other such wars, "persistent metaphors of beast or plague reduce individuals to categories and present these categories as innately dangerous to the human, linking the enemy with things beyond or beneath our own species."[43] In the germ war at the turn of the twentieth century, certain *kinds* of individuals came to stand for nonhuman germs. And germs, represented as imps, corpses, or grim reapers, carved a space for themselves in the cultural imagination as "public evils." Even the scientific methods applied to identify and eventually counter germs exemplify this cultural imaginary, laden with the social, experiential, and emotional inclinations of their human practitioners. Alvin Davidson's article accordingly chose to highlight the threat of death posed by germs at a time when the public crusade against them was gaining momentum. On a similar note, Schlesinger's study of bacteria on the lips of young, healthy women arose out of social anxieties regarding kissing and the unhealthy second-order kisses made possible by public drinking cups. Providing the foundational facts for the war against germs, these scientists affirm how any public health campaign navigates its society's particular preexisting notions regarding an appropriate "public" and appropriate "health." The configurations of knowledge in current popular public health campaigns, such as those against bacteria and obesity, are likewise socially embedded, unable to objectively escape the human element.[44]

As a storehouse of Dixie's lively past, the Dixie Cup Collection preserves the complex networks of human elements that fought the war against germs, offering glimpses into its lines of fire. The war has long been won, and the Dixie cups in our local convenience stores will appear eternally sterile, wrapped in impermeable plastic. But the archive conserves the cup as a hotbed of fear, infection, and calls to valor. Here, the germs of the past adhere to the Dixie cup, hermetically sealed in files and boxes, waiting for us to visit.

## NOTES

1. For a history of germ science in America, see Tomes, *The Gospel of Germs.* On the relationship between germs and early advertising, see McClary, "Germs Are Everywhere"; Sivulka, *Stronger than Dirt;* and Vinikas, *Soft Soap, Hard Sell.*

2. "Scope and Content Note," 1995, Hugh Moore Dixie Cup Company Collection, 1905–1986, http://academicmuseum.lafayette.edu/special/dixie/dixie.html.

3. All brochures, advertisements, and newspaper and magazine articles (including the *Cup Campaigner*) cited in this article are taken from the General Business Files, box 1, Hugh Moore Dixie Cup Collection, 1905–1986, Lafayette College Library, Easton, Pennsylvania. I'd like to thank the staff at the Lafayette College Library Special Collections for being so helpful in this endeavor.

4. Lawrence W. Luellen, Cup, U.S. Patent 1,032,557, filed May 23 1908, and issued July 16, 1912.

5. Henry Petroski, "Design, Design Everywhere," in Petroski, *Small Things Considered,* 34.

6. American Water Supply Company of New England, *Do You Drink Water?* (Boston, 1908), 2.

7. Tuberculosis was often referred to as the "White Plague" because it caused patients to become pale and waste away. For further information on the history of tuberculosis, see, for instance, Dormandy, *The White Death;* Dubos, *The White Plague;* Feldberg, *Disease and Class;* and Rothman, *Living in the Shadow of Death.*

8. American Water Supply Company, *Do You Drink Water?,* 8.

9. Ibid.

10. Central Intelligence Agency, *National Strategy for Combatting Terrorism* (Washington, D.C.: Central Intelligence Agency, 2003), https://www.cia.gov/news-information/cia-the-war-on-terrorism/Counter_Terrorism_Strategy.pdf.

11. *Cup Campaigner* 1.1 (December 1909): 1.

12. Steuter and Wills, *At War with Metaphor,* 8.

13. Kansas was the first state to ban the public drinking cup in 1909.

14. *Cup Campaigner* 1.1 (December 1909): 16.

15. Alvin Davidson, "Death in School Drinking Cups," *Technical World Magazine,* August 1908, 623.

16. "'Twenty-Three' for the Common Drinking Cup," *Kansas City Star,* July 16, 1909.

17. American Water Supply Company, *Do You Drink Water?,* 2.

18. Ronell, *Crack Wars,* 50–51.

19. Lugones, "Purity, Impurity," 468. On the creation of moral panics, see Goode and Ben-Yehuda, *Moral Panics.*

20. Berthold, "Tidy Whiteness," 2–3. For more detailed cultural histories of cleanliness and their relationship to advertising in the American context, see Brown, *Foul Bodies;* and Hoy, *Chasing Dirt.*

21. M. A. Jarnet, letter to the editor, *New York Herald,* August 10, 1909.

22. Berthold, "Tidy Whiteness," 10.

23. "Death in the Cup," *North American,* August 3, 1909.

24. Dixie Cup Company, "Suggestions for Captions," n.d.

25. Dixie Cup Company, "Secondary Points," n.d.

26. Individual Drinking Cup Company, *Health Cup,* brochure (New York, n.d.), 3.

27. Editorial, *Milwaukee Free Press,* July 17, 1909.

28. The North Dakota State Board of Health, *The Public Drinking Cup,* June 1909.

29. *Cup Campaigner* 1.2 (August 1910): 11.

30. *Cup Campaigner* 1.1 (December 1909): 4.

31. Young, "On the Go with Phoebe Snow," n.p.

32. Lackawanna Railroad Company individual drinking cup advertisement, n.d.

33. Editorial, *Ladies' Home Journal* 26.8 (1909).

34. Osler and Churchman, "Syphilis," 156.

35. "Mustache Harbors Germs: Kiss Leaves Deposit of Bacilli on French Woman's Lips," *New York Times,* August 6, 1909.

36. "Death-Laden Kisses: One Touch of a Healthy Girl's Lips Gave 28 Colonies of Germs," source unknown.

37. "The Proposed Virginia Anti-Kissing Law," *Journal of the American Medical Association* 39.25 (1902): 1600.

38. On antikissing campaigns in the Australian context, see Fitzgerald, *Kissing Can Be Dangerous.*

39. "Preacher Would End the Kissing Habit," *New York World,* February 4, 1909.

40. "Sanitary Chalice Now," *Washington Post,* n.d.

41. "Death in the Cup," *North American,* August 3, 1909.

42. “The Common Cup,” *Larned Chronoscope,* September 9, 1909.

43. Steuter and Wills, *At War with Metaphor,* 4.

44. For a comparison between germ discourse at the turn of the twentieth and twenty-first centuries, see Tomes, “The Making of a Germ Panic.”

## SELECTED BIBLIOGRAPHY


Berthold, Dana. “Tidy Whiteness: A Genealogy of Race, Purity, and Hygiene.” *Ethics and the Environment* 15.1 (Spring 2010): 1–26.

Brown, Kathleen M. *Foul Bodies: Cleanliness in Early America.* New Haven, Conn.: Yale University Press, 2009.

Davidson, Alvin. “Death in School Drinking Cups.” *Technical World Magazine,* August 1908.

Dormandy, Thomas. *The White Death: A History of Tuberculosis.* New York: New York University Press, 2000.

Dubos, Jean. *The White Plague: Tuberculosis, Man, and Society.* New Brunswick, N.J.: Rutgers University Press, 1987.

Feldberg, Georgina. *Disease and Class: Tuberculosis and the Shaping of Modern North American Society.* New Brunswick, N.J.: Rutgers University Press, 1995.

Fitzgerald, Criena. *Kissing Can Be Dangerous: The Public Health Campaign to Prevent and Control Tuberculosis in Western Australia, 1900–1960.* Crawley: University of Western Australia Press, 2006.

Goode, Erich, and Nachman Ben-Yehuda. *Moral Panics: The Social Construction of Deviance.* Oxford: Wiley-Blackwell, 2009.

Hoy, Suellen. *Chasing Dirt: The American Pursuit of Cleanliness.* Oxford: Oxford University Press, 1996.

Lugones, Maria. “Purity, Impurity, and Separation.” *Signs* 19.2 (Winter 1994): 458–479.

McClary, Andrew. “Germs Are Everywhere: The Germ Threat as Seen in Magazine Articles, 1890–1920.” *Journal of American Culture* 3 (1980): 33–46.

Petroski, Henry. *Small Things Considered.* New York: Borzoi Books, 2003.

Osler, William, and John Churchman. “Syphilis.” In *Modern Medicine: Its Theory and Practice in Original Contributions by American and Foreign Authors,* edited by William Osler and

Thomas McCrae. Philadelphia: Lea & Febiger, 1914.

Ronell, Avital. *Crack Wars: Literature, Addiction, Mania*. Lincoln: University of Nebraska Press, 2004.

Rothman, Sheila. *Living in the Shadow of Death: Tuberculosis and the Social Experience of Illness in the United States*. New York: Basic Books, 1994.

Sivulka, Juliann. *Stronger than Dirt: A Cultural History of Advertising Personal Hygiene in America, 1875–1940*. New York: Humanity Books, 2001.

Steuter, Erin, and Deborah Wills. *At War with Metaphor: Media, Propaganda, and Racism in the War on Terror*. Lanham, Md.: Lexington Books, 2008.

Tomes, Nancy. *The Gospel of Germs: Men, Women, and the Microbe in American Life*. Cambridge, Mass.: Harvard University Press, 1998.

———. "The Making of a Germ Panic, Then and Now." *American Journal of Public Health* 90.2 (February 2000): 191–198.

Vinikas, Vincent. *Soft Soap, Hard Sell: American Hygiene in an Age of Advertisement*. Ames: Iowa State University Press, 1992.

Young, Margaret. "On the Go with Phoebe Snow: Origins of an Advertising Icon." *Advertising and Society Review* 7.2 (2006). http://muse.jhu.edu/.

As I recall I know you love to show off, but I never thought that you would take it this far. But what do I know?

DWELE IN KANYE WEST'S "FLASHING LIGHTS"

Listen to the cunning exhortations
Wafted to the ears of the big foundations
Blown to the big white boss paymasters
Faint hints of far-reaching grim disasters.
"Be careful what you do
Or your Mumbo-jumbo stuff for Sambo
And all of the other
Bilge for Sambo
Your Mumbo-Jumbo will get away from you."

STERLING BROWN, "THE NEW CONGO"

3

# THE ARCHIVE OF THE ARCHIVE OF THE ARCHIVE

## THE FEMA SIGNS OF POST-KATRINA NEW ORLEANS AND THE VÉVÉS OF VODOUN

*Beth A. McCoy*

### QUADRANT 1: DROWNING

Serving already as archive to the archive of the Atlantic slave trade, the city of New Orleans took on further archival depth when the levees failed after Hurricane Katrina. Throughout the flooded city appeared painted symbols: the cruciform US&R (urban search and rescue) signs devised by FEMA, the Federal Emergency Management Administration enfolded after 9/11 into the Department of Homeland Security. Used by FEMA task forces, the Louisiana Society for the Prevention of Cruelty to Animals, and other private and public entities involved in search and rescue, the US&R signs were to function both as symptom of and vector for achieving through reason and method what the DHS *National Response Plan* calls "the prevention of, preparedness for, response to, and recovery from terrorism, major natural disasters, and other major emergencies."[1] This is what the plan said.

The signs' construction is explained in the DHS FEMA *Field Operations Guide.* They are to be two-by-two-foot-square X's marked near structures' entryways. The first slash indicates that a US&R task force entered a structure, with entry time and task force identifier indicated nearby. Upon exit, a second slash is added, creating a cruciform symbol. The left quadrant identifies the task force, the top quadrant the time and date of exit, the right quadrant the "personal hazards" found (e.g., "RATS"), and the bottom quadrant the numbers (if not zero) of living and dead human beings found inside.[2] Ostensibly, then, X is to mark the spot, to spot the dead, and to begin recovery on the spot.

In "Katrina + 5: An X-Code Exhibition," curator Dorothy Moye observes that the construction of these "enigmatic X-codes" created in New Orleans "a documentary archive with tales to tell." According to the field ops guide, the tales told were to be certain, symmetrical ones full of closure and completion. But to many New Orleanians, the archive's tales were anything but symmetrical or certain. Moye notes, for instance, that the signs bypassed some flooded neighborhoods, descended upon dry ones, and marked some houses as free of human victims while drowned bodies remained inside. For others, however, the signs constituted "a glaring and still present reminder of how our government failed us."[3] Given numerous post-storm performances of governmental incompetence from Condoleezza Rice's *Spamalot* appearance to Michael Brown's concern with sartorial stagecraft, interpreting the signs as evidence of failure is understandable.

What such interpretations do not account for, however, is another possibility, that of success: the signs' hypercompetent execution of a long, fluid performance, one merely symptomatized in Grover Norquist's famous desire to drown government sacrificially "in the bathtub." More specifically, the seemingly banal FEMA signs channel old, old waves propagated by liberalism's irrational antiblack conjure, that which Joan Dayan calls the "sorcery of law . . . hidden at the heart of the modern state."[4] Under cover of the breaking levees, the FEMA signs served up New Orleans's black population, possessions, and property as ritual sacrifice to stave off that which slavery's archive had long predicted: the engulfing of many more into the liquid living death of global capital. Pressing the city into even more extensive archival service, the FEMA signs thus rendered New Orleans as archive to the archive to the archive of antiblackness and the Atlantic slave trade.

The claim that the FEMA archive transacts ritual antiblack sacrifice may seem illogical and impossible to prove, not least because mass sacrifice is still believed to be the province of irrational primitivity, which is antithetical to rational modernity. And the claim itself emerges from what many will count as irrational: an accidental, uncanny hunch. For during a 2008 course on Katrina, I paused Spike Lee's *When the Levees Broke:* amid the film's FEMA-blazoned wrecks, something unnerving jogged my memory. Googling frantically, I displayed onscreen a FEMA sign (figure 3.1) and next to it a vévé – coincidentally, that of Brigitte the lawyer (figure 3.2). Projected in the dark, that which had unsettled me became for one moment clear: the cruciform FEMA signs were stunningly similar to the vévés.[5]

They escaped me then, the words that without recourse to conspiracy theory would articulate the signs' transaction of ritual, antiblack sacrifice. Into the depths of the official, guide-directed archive they vanished, to

**3.1.** Representative FEMA sign from the Lower Ninth Ward. A Wikimedia Commons image released into the public domain by user Berrdatherrd, March 11, 2006, from Wikimedia Commons, March 13, 2009, http://en.wikipedia.org/wiki/File:FEMA_marking.jpg.

quote Carolivia Herron, like "an empty polished enjeweled marble skull washed up and cast down by the waters of the Atlantic Sea."[6] In *Archive Fever,* Derrida explains that "there is nothing accidental or surprising" about this vanishing, for the archive "*shelters* itself from this memory which it shelters: which comes down to saying also that it forgets it."[7] But the logic afforded by vodoun and the vévé counseled patience and urged counting as reasoned methodology that which otherwise would be called mere

**3.2.** The vévé of the vodoun loa Brigitte, May 22, 2007, a Wikimedia Commons image in the public domain, March 13, 2009, http://en.wikipedia.org/wiki/File:VeveBrigitte.svg.

accident. That logic promised that that which had vanished would emerge again from the depths. That which had vanished would become the writing on the wall.

## QUADRANT 2: THE VÉVÉ

Derrida notes that *arkhē,* the Greek word for (and archive for) "archive," carries within it the idea of both *commencement* (beginnings) and *commandment,* or, more specifically, the "*there* where men and gods *command.*"[8] This crossroads of origins and the seemingly irrational intersection of human and divine is performed by the vévé. According to Milo Rigaud's magisterial *Ve-ve: Diagrammes rituels du vodou,* the vévé "bring forth during [vodoun] ceremonies the *loa* or *spirits* for which they serve as geometrical attributes."[9] Each vodoun loa has a vévé (or multiple variations on a vévé) associated with it, and thus the vévé symbolizes the loa. But each vévé does more than that: sketched around the ritual space's central point (or piteaumiton), the vévé summons the loa, effects its crossing of the threshold between the material and the spirit worlds, and thus enables it to possess (or "ride") the attendant priest. In thus connecting the corporeal and spiritual, the vévé is quite active: it demonstrates and enables fluid relationships among seemingly disparate, discrete things.

Indeed, in his structuralist reading of the ground drawings as part of the global "universal tradition" (Hindu to Greek to Hebrew), Rigaud establishes that the vévés both as objects themselves and as part of the worship service are immersed in liquid. The "wands" that make so many vévés cruciform, bilateral, and symmetrical emerge, Rigaud asserts, from primordial water: the "lake," "reservoir," or "basin" that is the source of all, including the crossroads, the doubled road of transit between day and night, life and death.[10] Further, Rigaud's catalog establishes that the drawings' classic cruciform wands are wound frequently with snakes; these resemble waves that suggest actual water, as well as the cross-cultural fluidity of such symbols. The vévés are, thus, immersed both theoretically and literally in water; they are fluid. Or, to choose consciously a word that recalls the language of capital, the geometry of the vévé is bound intimately with liquid.

Serving, then, as nexus for literal and metaphorical liquid, the vévés constitute vivid, rich examples of circum-Atlantic performance, Joseph Roach's term for the violent possession of cultures that accompanied the "transoceanic movement of empire" from Mediterranean to Atlantic. Whether indigenous, European, or African, these cultures were "possessed," Roach observes, of "prolific arts of law and memory," arts that were represented and transacted by performance.[11] Given European genocide of native peoples and the near-simultaneous conflation of blackness with "an ontology of slavery," all such performances – statute to funeral, chant to opera – had to undergo "revisions and amendments" appropriate for "radically transformed circumstances."[12]

The vévés exemplify vividly how some western African strands of circum-Atlantic culture and performance have revised and amended themselves amid catastrophe. According to Robert Farris Thompson, their often-cruciform mappings derive in part from Kongo cosmograms such as the yowa. Though spatially similar to the Christian crucifix, the yowa, Thompson notes, offers a different but "equally compelling" vision, one invested in the crossroads, yes, but one also invested in what might be called the law of liquidity: human souls move continuously through water that constitutes the threshold between the world of the living and that of the dead.[13] As in the vévé, the yowa functions both as symbol of that vision and as vector for enacting it. In other words, the yowa's cruciform, liquidity-enabled shape might be read as doing more than *standing for* the fluidity between life and death: it might be read as also *producing* human beings able to acknowledge the liquid flow between those two states of being.

In the diaspora produced by the Atlantic slave trade, such cruciform performances of law and memory fulfill a related but yet very different function. They establish archivally the fact and memory of the production of black people as what Dayan calls "embodied property": "creatures of law" who are "nonetheless dead to the law."[14] This formulation is not new.[15] European modernity's production of this "embodied property," this communion of property and law, is indeed the "sorcery of law" that Dayan identifies as lying hidden, like Prospero's unseen but oft-cited books, at "the heart of the modern state."[16] At its rational heart, that modern state – and the United States not the least – is irrationally possessed by (embodied) property, the "regulating and preserving" of which is, according to John Locke's rather fluid, magical thinking, the sole purpose for political power, for the "*established,* settled, known *law*" of classical political liberalism.[17]

Liberalism's constitutive dependency on this possession is so crucial and so unflattering to narratives of progress that it is a dependency that liberalism tries mightily to forget, even as its own history pursues it with remembering. Philosopher Charles Mills points out that liberalism has become so "triumphant" to itself that, in the last fifty years, the major debates about political philosophy and ideology are not actually among different frameworks. Rather, Mills says, these debates are merely Lethean variations within the same framework, one that Mills calls "racial," "white," or – in humor so dry as to be nearly incalculable – "just" liberalism. Within this racial liberalism, "white contractors" have agreed to "subordinate and exploit non-white noncontractors for white benefit."[18]

These intramural debates, Mills observes, all take place while trying to ignore another "conflict," one that has "been going on for hundreds of years, if not always in the academy." This conflict, Mills notes, is between white liberalism and what he calls "deracialized" liberalism, that which "confronts" rather than ignores "how the whiteness of the actual American contract and of the actual American community and its conception of the good affects justice and conceptions of the self."[19] It is the conflict, in other words, between white liberalism and that necessitated by the African diaspora, a conflict obscured by Western liberalism's continued, deluded faith that property and possession exist only as concepts that are transitive (i.e., whites own things) and accumulative (i.e., whites will own more and more things) rather than recursive (i.e., whites are possessed by possession[s]).

At the levels of both philosophy and geometry, the yowa's watery threshold between the living and the dead comes to read quite differently in the vévé, where water functions not only as the threshold between two worlds but also as the recognition of the liquid pressure upon whiteness of black living death. As Mills describes this debate, an uncannily familiar geometry emerges: the geometry of the vévé. For deracialized liberalism exists, Mills says, in a relationship "orthogonal" (i.e., perpendicular at point of intersection) to white liberalism. And, he avers, deracialized liberalism's orthogonal – and thus cruciform – relationship is "more pressing" than any of the debates within white liberalism.[20] It is more pressing both because it is urgent and, significantly, because it places actual pressure upon white liberalism.

Under such pressure, the (white) law producing black "embodied property" requires repeated return of that dead-while-living black property and – significantly – *on* it, even if – and perhaps especially when – such return of and on is symbolic. (As Dayan notes, the zombie is vodoun's "answer to being dead in law.")[21] At the same time, the civic death at the heart of whiteness also constitutes that which must inevitably subsume whiteness in one way or another. It is what artist Kara Walker calls the "story of Muck . . . fluidity and the failure of containment."[22] It is what Saidiya Hartman in *Scenes of Subjection* calls white "anxiety about impending *dissolution and engulfment*."[23] And it is what the vévé's geography of liquid pressure witnesses and records.

James Snead would remind us that whether African, European, or indigenous, all circum-Atlantic revisions and amendments represent the "willed grafting onto culture of . . . essentially philosophical insight[s] about the shape of time and history."[24] Mills's description of white liberalism's geometrical and philosophical relationship with black liberalism thus helps to illuminate that the frequently orthogonal vévés are indeed philosophical interventions grafted onto culture. Such illumination might seem unnecessary, but, of course, it's not. Post-Enlightenment Western culture has historically refused to interpret black revision and amendment as rising to the level of philosophy.

Such a liquid lack arises in part, Roach suggests, because of an asymmetry between publication and performance: having little "opportunity to publish" adaptive changes, black people throughout the diaspora often had to turn to performance as the "most readily available medium of cultural recollection and innovation."[25] Rooted in the ostensible permanence of methodology, the state, and possessive individualism, publication confers special value, stable gravitas with which supposedly mere "performance" (kinetic, oral, etc.) has historically had difficulty competing (this, despite the fact that, as Abby Zanger suggests, publication is itself a kind of performance).[26] By contrast, the vévés appear provisional, ephemeral (their chalk washed away by libation, ritual, and time), outside the realms not only of reason and philosophy but also of possessive individualism and – especially – the state.

But it's exactly in these ways that the vévés function as a particularly fluid kind of archive documenting the disaster and catastrophe that the official record desires to forget: the possession of law by the loa or, in what Dayan notes fruitfully as an alternative Kreyol spelling – the lwa of embodied property (*lwa* is also the phonetic pronunciation of the French *loi* [law] governing New Orleans).[27] Whether made and unmade by Haitian vodoun or New Orleans hoodoo, the vévés-as-archive exemplify the kind of rational but "fleeting, disabled, and short-lived practices" that "stand for freedom and its failure" to yield any "absolute distinction" between slave and human.[28] They are symptoms of and vectors for a rigorous practice amid the "cargo cult of Western modernity," a practice that keeps alive the memory of the possession of civic law by the (white) lwa of possession.[29]

But the necessity of memory constitutes only one stroke of the vévé's cruciform lines; a warning against forgetting constitutes the other. For much as other cruciform shapes (e.g., skull and crossbones; National Fire Protection Association symbols) have warning functions, so, too, do the vévés.[30] They warn against the folly of forgetting. Specifically, the vévés' orthogonality warns that forgetting the catastrophic possession of law by the (white) lwa of possession makes further catastrophe inevitable. As Georges Bataille points out in *The Accursed Share,* the pressuring build-up of wealth in a general economy heralds "explosiveness" when that wealth cannot be spent within the system: "If the system can no longer grow, or if the excess cannot be completely absorbed in its growth, it must necessarily be lost without profit; it must be spent, willingly or not, gloriously or catastrophically."[31]

In the United States, that heralded explosion is always already overwritten by a racialized crisscross that represents and adds further pressure. For spending and thus remembering its wealth, whiteness is compelled to remember (anti)blackness, the diaspora without which that wealth could not have been (violently) generated. And because that memory serves as an indictment of white self-generation, it must be forgotten, which makes expenditure more difficult and thus more likely to be made "catastrophically" rather than "gloriously."[32] Again, as Derrida would point out, this archival forgetting is neither accident nor surprise. Regardless, however, it is the "dangerous juncture," to borrow Roach's words, at which "catastrophe may reemerge from memory in the shape of a wish."[33] And the shape of that wish, warn the attendant vévés, will be an X.

## QUADRANT 3: THE FEMA SIGNS

In 2005, situated in the "belly of the basin" and surrounded by water, New Orleans was that liquid, diasporic pressure upon white liberalism.[34] The breaking levees released that pressure and produced the fantasized catastrophe. And the X shape of the wish was to be found in the FEMA signs, orthogonality skewed under diaspora's weight.

To make such claims may seem more than odd: the banal, methodological FEMA signs seem beyond interpretation, not least as the DHS FEMA *Field Operations Guide* purports to have always already explained, directed, and contained their meaning. The vévés' fluid archive acknowledges diaspora (e.g., the visual memory of Kongo culture) and the putatively irrational (e.g., the crossroads of loa/lwa and human). The guide, however, promises a closed, rational system (intra-agency flow charts, checklists, bullet points) proceeding linearly via successive page numbers not only toward completion and future improvement (e.g., "after-action debriefings") but also away from disastrous events safely left behind in early steps and pages. Such a performance of self-containment is in keeping with what Ted Steinberg characterizes as the "freak events" approach that has governed the federal government's handling of disaster in the last century. This approach, Steinberg observes, interprets disasters as utterly separate from such human causes as history, culture, and ideology.[35] To return to Derrida once more, this approach indicates a kind of archival forgetting that is neither accident nor surprise.

But the liquid vodoun logic of the vévé that the FEMA signs so bring to mind counsels attention to history, culture, and ideology, the very things that the guide holds back. Such a logic promises that whatever is submerged in the depths will reappear inevitably. And, indeed, even a tiny dip into FEMA's history reveals that the agency's origins lay in the muck produced at the high-pressure, orthogonal intersection of the African diaspora with white liberalism.

Narrating its history at fema.gov, the agency acknowledges only a very few historical events as leading up to its formal constitution in 1979.[36] One of those events is the Congressional Act of 1803, "generally considered the first piece of disaster legislation." The agency says it "can trace its beginnings" to that act, which "provided assistance to a New Hampshire town following an extensive fire." The return to origins is symptomatically, tantalizingly vague, raising but refusing to answer basic questions. What was the Congressional Act of 1803? What was the town? What was the fire?

Internet resources quickly make clear that the answers to these questions are immersed in the Atlantic slave trade. The Congressional Act of 1803 resolves: "Be it enacted, by the Senate and House of Representatives of the United States of America, in Congress assembled, That the secretary of the treasury be, and he hereby is authorized and directed to cause to be suspended for months, the collection of bonds due to the United States by merchants of Portsmouth, in New Hampshire, who have suffered by the late conflagration of that town."[37] The act's text seems as self-contained as FEMA's signs, but a little more digging reveals otherwise. Historically, Portsmouth functioned as the center of slave trading and holding in New Hampshire, a state whose "white population was notoriously slow to adopt abolition."[38] The city is also the location of the only other African burial ground in the Northeast outside of New York City. The "late conflagration" to which the act refers is the devastating fire of 1802, a fire that destroyed the city's business district and, according to Portsmouth's current municipal website, left "those who lost property and possessions" to the insufficient "mercy of private charity."[39]

And, inviting more scrutiny, the vagueness of that origin story provokes a further dip into the archive, this one bringing the magic informing the signs more clearly into view from the depths. As late as October 2012, a Google search for "Portsmouth fire of 1802" yielded as its second hit the twenty-eighth "ramble" of Charles Brewster, a white nineteenth-century Portsmouth columnist. Brewster begins the column with a strong declaration of purpose: "LET us stir the ashes of the fire of 1802, on Market Square," he writes, "and see what will come up."[40]

At first, what "comes up" is mystifyingly unclear. Establishing first that the fire started in a building that served simultaneously as a bank, an insurance office, and a boardinghouse, Brewster sketches a confusing tangle of stories emanating from the fact that one Hon. Jotham Odiorne had lived in that building almost a century earlier and spawned a rather large family whose members married other people associated with other buildings in Portsmouth.

Appearing to acknowledge that he is being nearly incomprehensible, Brewster declares that to better understand the ramble's "drift," it is necessary to refer to another family: the Whipples. Breathless paragraphs explain in great detail how Mehitable, one of Jotham Odiorne's daughters, *almost* married young William, a Whipple scion who would go on later to fight in the Revolutionary War and sign the Declaration of Independence. Because Mehitable from the building where the fire would later start did *not* marry William the future "founding father," the connection to the building where the 1802 fire took place is rather a stretch. But for Brewster, even this tenuous link is almost too heavy to bear: William Whipple was a slave trader: "Before reaching twenty-one, he had command of a vessel, and afterwards made not only successful voyages to the West Indies and Europe, but also to the coast of Africa; and the blemish of that dark living freight, which his vessel brought away, has not been wholly obliterated by the fame which shines around his name on the immortal scroll of our country's glory." This "dark living freight" that through marriage *almost* became linked to the fire that FEMA holds as ancestor not only serves as a "blemish" on William Whipple's reputation but also pressures Brewster's story to the point of incomprehensibility. Slavery, in other words, constitutes a narrative disaster.

At the same time, however, that same pressure – the living cargo of Dayan's black "embodied property" – becomes a magical vector for relief. For the most intimate point of intersection in Brewster's "ramble" becomes that between William and Prince Whipple, a black man who was the white Whipple's slave. According to Brewster's telling, when William went to join the effort "to stop the progress of the enemy" on the war's northwestern edge, Prince was his only attendant. On the morning they were to depart for battle, Brewster reports, William commanded Prince to prepare the horses; Prince, however, did not "exert his usual diligence" and "appeared sulky and in ill humor." Brewster continues: "His master upbraided him for his misconduct. 'Master,' said Prince, 'you are going to fight for your liberty, but I have none to fight for.' 'Prince,' replied his master, 'behave like a man and do your duty, and from this hour you shall be free.' Prince wanted no other incentive; he performed his duty like a man throughout the campaign, which ended in the surrender of Burgoyne, and from that day he was a freeman." Brewster's retelling does not make it clear what occasions William Whipple's declaration to manumit Prince Whipple. It is evident only that Prince's "sulky" manner places pressure both on William and on Brewster's narrative, the release of which has immediate salutary effects: from here on in, the columnist proceeds with great clarity. Not only is the nascent republic secured, but also the now-free Prince becomes a beloved part of Portsmouth society, the "Caleb Quotem of the old fashioned semi-monthly assemblies," without whom "nothing could go on right." The ashes of the fire of 1802 now having been both stirred and settled satisfactorily, Brewster may return to the purely "antiquarian" matters of the white Whipples, matters of interest to those on "an hour's stroll from Portsmouth to Kittery."

But as Mark J. Sammons and Valerie Cunningham establish in their scholarly history of black Portsmouth, Brewster's ramble carries an important historical untruth: William Whipple did *not* emancipate Prince Whipple before the two rode to war. In fact, the scholars note, Prince was not manumitted until years after the Revolutionary War, and then only after half measures that, "three years before he was actually manumitted," granted him freeman rights while "yet remaining legally enslaved." Sammons and Cunningham suggest that Brewster's tinkering with the historical record emerged from his "desire to improve [William Whipple's] reputation at a time of increasing white abolitionism."[41] In using his print platform to perform such symptomatic archival revising, Brewster deploys a substantial magic: narrative rehabilitation cast as the *real* victim of the slave trade's disaster, the one who merits disaster relief just as Portsmouth's merchants did. Indeed, the flattering-to-William emancipation story persists on whipple.org, especially in "This Was a Man," the telling title and last line of a William Whipple biography presented in 1964 by author Dorothy Mansfield Vaughn.[42]

In the light of Sammons and Cunningham's work, however, the overdetermined Prince fares much differently, emblematizing what Hartman calls the "liminal status of the freed subject, the ambiguity of that status, the impossibility of that status, and the crisis of citizenship" that informs and proceeds from that status.[43] Brewster functionally renders Prince as *fons et origo* of slavery's disaster: the black man becomes both means through which relief for that disaster may be administered to William *and* ungrateful, undeserving resistance to similar relief. For Brewster notes that Prince fights "*like* a man," a simile that recalls white nostalgia for slaves and servants who were "like" (but not quite) part of the family. More importantly, Brewster also acknowledges that whether imaginary or actual, manumission does not relieve Prince's social death. Indeed, to borrow Hartman's words once again, Brewster's ramble suggests that this intransigent "crisis of citizenship" is one that Prince brought down sulkily upon himself, and it is *this* suggestion that lies in 1802's ashes, in the "first piece of disaster legislation," and thus in the cruciform slashes of the FEMA search-and-rescue signs.

After the Congressional Act of 1803, FEMA attended specifically to few other historical moments, but all of these infuse the search-and-rescue signs with abrupt, weird traces of this originary commandment of god and man, of white lwa and law. Glancing, for instance, over a century of "ad hoc" disaster legislation, FEMA paused in the 1930s, a period the history characterizes – somewhat hilariously – as one when "federal approaches to problems became popular." During this time, FEMA says, the Hoover- and Roosevelt-era "Reconstruction Finance Corporation was given authority to make disaster loans for repair and reconstruction of certain public facilities following an earthquake, and later, other types of disasters."[44] The corporation's very name invokes the postbellum period wherein black people were conjured as the origin of disastrous pressure on the (white) union, sacrificed in order to provide whites relief via reunification, and cast as undeserving revenants resistant to that relief. This cascade informs the RFC's eventual immersion in the New Deal's federal disaster relief, waves of which were propagated only after antiblack compromises. And it reemerges in the 1970s when FEMA emerged as a federal agency: from Lee Atwater's "southern strategy" deployment of tax cuts as surrogate for "nigger, nigger, nigger" to Ronald Reagan's deployment of the steak-buying "strapping young buck" as symptom and origin of the "problem" that government had become for America. The archive is nothing if not consistent.

As irrational in its seeming banality as the vévés are rational in their seeming exoticism, the post-Katrina FEMA transacted the business of white law/lwa, manifested in the neoliberal project of "recruit[ing] nature to capital's side in the war against the poor" and/or the black.[45] The X codes magically marked the city's black population and real property for ritual sacrifice, their spray-painted archive signaling (white) corporate repossession of valuable black-owned land, a process that in a 2006 *New York Times* interview former NOLA mayor Marc Morial called "massive red-lining . . . wrapped around a giant land grab." The FEMA signs made visible the crosshairs long trained on the city of New Orleans, yes, but they also promised that those crosshairs were already trained on targets all across the United States, too, as Sarah Palin's infamous 2010 congressional "crosshairs" map later confirmed.

## QUADRANT 4: DROWNING AGAIN

For many gazing with scorn and contempt upon New Orleans's crossroads of diaspora that they had visited only drunkenly, the city's sacrifice perhaps seemed satisfyingly contained, providing fit recompense for 9/11's national humiliation. To this line of thinking, NOLA's sodden agony broadcast worldwide was a terrible but necessary antidote to the attacks on New York and Washington, D.C. Barely alive, New Orleans stood half-dead as proof of the United States' phantasmic ability to select by itself for itself a (black) city to sacrifice with no harm to the nation. Ostensibly.

But there is another way in which the FEMA-marked city may be understood as ritual sacrifice. In 2005 another kind of diasporic pressure also weighed upon liberalism: the global financial markets. These markets were sitting on and in what the eponymously named *This American Life* episode called "The Giant Pool of Money" defined for laypeople as "insurance companies saving for a catastrophe, pension funds saving money for retirement, the central bank of England saving for whatever central banks save for. All the world's savings."[46] By 2000 that already-giant pool, episode narrator Adam Davidson explains, had doubled, because in exporting oil and goods to the United States, "all sorts of poor countries became kind of rich":

> China, India, Abu Dhabi, Saudi Arabia. Made a lot of money and banked it. China, for example, has over a trillion dollars in its central bank, and there are office buildings in Beijing filled with math geniuses – real math geniuses – looking for a place to invest it. And the world was not ready for all

> this money. There's twice as much money looking for investments, but there are not twice as many good investments. So that global army of investment managers was hungrier and twitchier than ever before. They all wanted the same thing: a nice low-risk investment that paid some return.

In other words, the global capitalist diaspora produced by colonialism, imperialism, and the slave trade (but now largely delinked from the nation-state that both produced and was produced by those same projects) turned to the United States for that "nice low-risk investment," identified by "The Giant Pool of Money" as U.S. Treasury bonds.

Federal Reserve chief Alan Greenspan responded to that global pressure, Davidson notes, by stating at the July 2003 Federal Open Market Committee meeting that "the FOMC stands prepared to maintain a highly accommodative stance of policy for as long as needed to promote satisfactory economic performance." One way of parsing Greenspan's statement is, "Go away, diasporic capital, the U.S. is financially autochthonous." Or, as Davidson puts it rather more crudely, "Hey, global pool of money, screw you." In response, Davidson says, the giant global pool of money went elsewhere to get a return on its investment: to new, arcane, barely understood, and largely magical financial products such as mortgage-backed securities and derivatives conjured in the private sector.

Thus, as the citizens of New Orleans drowned, the diasporic giant global pool of money had already expanded catastrophically. Flowing into the stream of U.S. subprime mortgages, the global pool of money helped to birth the housing bubble, pressured from within not only by ever-increasing housing prices but also by ever-increasing "irrational" demand for increasing investment return.[47] In *The Big Short,* his popular 2010 retrospective of the subprime disaster, Michael Lewis describes metaphorically the workings of the collateralized debt obligation, or CDO, the eldritch instrument immersed in the giant diasporic pool. Acknowledging symptomatically the magic employed to submerge subprime risks, Lewis selects the metaphor of a building – a tower – threatened by flood:

> In a CDO you gathered one hundred different *mortgage* bonds – usually, the riskiest, lower floors of the original tower – and used them to erect an entirely new tower of bonds. The innocent observer might reasonably ask, What's the point of using floors from one tower of debt simply to create another tower of debt? The short answer is, They are too near to the ground. More prone to flooding – the first to take losses – they bear a lower credit rating: triple-B. Triple-B-rated bonds were harder to sell than the triple-A-rated ones, on the safe, upper floors of the building.[48]

As it turned out, no floor was safe from the flood. Some – but too few – wise prognosticators warned that the sorcery would get out of control: the bubble would burst, and no sorcerer would come home soon enough to clean up the apprentice's flood.

This fluid – but not quite liquid – pressure weighed down upon Americans who had been living increasingly off of credit, including that drained from housing equity. And as many of these Americans were conditioned to see themselves as rugged individuals understandably unwilling to sacrifice themselves, it is easy to see how, as Katrina approached the Gulf Coast, they began to "take an interest in relieving the consequent pressure" in the ingloriously catastrophic ways described by Bataille.[49] And that interest found a familiar release, disdained and scorned: the drowning human beings constructed on television and computer screens as at once excessive and insufficient amid a majority-black city long interpreted as excessive and insufficient. "*So* black," in Wolf Blitzer's infamous words.

Prompted by such media constructions and possessed by the spirit of dispossession, spectators beyond New Orleans engaged in "empowering the living through the performance of memory" at the expense of the socially dead.[50] I will cite just a few of those performances here: white college students romping and daubing themselves with mud to play "Katrina victim." Images posted on collegehumor.com featuring whites in blackface mimicking Katrina survivors whose images they had seen in the media, replete with beer or wearing a T-shirt reading "Gulf Coast looter." Such performances not only travestied Mardi Gras but also served as anxious containment strategies insisting that the larger body politic could afford the sacrifice. After all, as Newt Gingrich asserted, what happened in the Lower Nine was both a failure of government and a "failure of citizenship." Both failures, the former House Speaker seemed to suggest, were New Orleans born and raised. And as New Orleans had long seemed geographically and morally distant, those who watched the spectacle from afar could believe themselves both inoculated *against* the flood *and* able to thrive *because* of it.

But the law/lwa to which New Orleans was sacrificed was also the same one that the global financial crisis had burst free of the nation-state's levees. It was – and is – a greedy lwa, ill content with engulfing the lower floors and frequencies only. Thus it is striking to consider that as New Orleans residents tried frantically to save and shelter families and neighbors, to cut themselves out from under the very roofs over their heads that pressed them into the fetid water below, the housing bubble burst. Holders of prime mortgages slipped underwater when the houses' value plunged below the amount the owners owed, while holders of subprime mortgages found that the life preserver they thought they held never really existed at all. Credit markets froze, no small thing, as Lewis points out, when Chicago has "only eight days of chlorine on hand for its water supply."[51] Citizens and enterprises private and public were caught in liquidity traps.

Foreclosure waves swept through entire neighborhoods, towns, cities, and regions, while entire families and legacies – helpless despite generations of struggling – drowned in debt, their retirement funds, credit ratings, and savings washed away along with the very documentation that might offer them, if not protection, then, to borrow Toni Morrison's words in *A Mercy*, at least some difference.[52]

And as the waters receded just enough to expose the wreckage, the revenant was pulled from the muck once again, pressed into service in an antiblack carnival asserting that the origin of the flood *this* time could also be found in blackness. The housing activist organization ACORN was posited as the "origin" of the global financial crisis, stripped of its funding, and effectively killed after James O'Keefe and Hannah Giles masqueraded as "pimp and worker" and released a video edited heavily and misleadingly to make it look as if black ACORN workers were helping the pair to hide money earned from prostitution. Since that time, ACORN has not been allowed to rest in peace, having been dredged back up as the origin of everything threatening the law/lwa of white possession from (mythical) voting fraud to the Occupy movement.

I could go on, so assaultively many are the (re)iterations and examples. But it is time to end, even as ending is difficult, not least amid the essay's difficulties. For one thing, my understanding of vodoun is as superficial, provisional, and tentative as my understanding of transnational capital. In fact, vodoun and transnational capital *exceed* my understanding; their complexities seep from, under, and over the essay's attempts at containment, efforts that include its grim attention to liquid metaphor. Such excess, perhaps, is an occupational hazard of the essay's reliance on what Wai Chee Dimock might see as the "cross-stitching of time" she recommends as an approach to a "nonsovereign" historiography taking as its first principle

631
PRAY!

**3.4.** Erzulie's heart over a New Orleans FEMA sign. X on Maurepas Street, Faubourg St. John, New Orleans, Louisiana. Photograph by © Cynthia Scott, 2005.

**3.3.** Erzulie's vévé adjacent to a New Orleans FEMA sign. Photograph by © Paul Conlan, March 23, 2006.

the oceans' fluid connectivity, a connectivity that will only intensify as climate change raises sea levels and returns land to water. Dimock hopes that such nonsovereign "cross-stitching" will bring "attention to the tangled fate of the planet and [urge] us toward an enlarged sense of democracy, an enlarged sense of justice."[53] I consider that hope in the context of these images from Moye's exhibition.

In each image, the vévé is Erzulie's, the lwa associated most often with love. Rigaud notes that she is "*Maîtresse de l'eau* (Mistress of Water) and her traditional posture is to be seated near the water combing her tresses. She walk [*sic*] on water and on fire."[54] The fact that in these images Erzulie's vévé attends the FEMA signs tells me that that vodoun has long anticipated and performed the kind of nonsovereign history Dimock recommends. And it tells me that a globally "enlarged sense" of democracy and justice is impossible without attending to the Atlantic slave trade. I know that to even attempt to get to the urging part, the first step – what Hartman might call the "hint of possibility" suggested by "the presence of that thing that can't be announced within the framework that's already there and legible" – can happen only by wading into the muck, attending to the irrational couched as the rational, and stepping into the archive of the archive of the archive of the Atlantic slave trade, into the antiblack law and lwa of possession.[55] It can only happen, as Jasmine Montgomery points out, by remembering Christina Sharpe's counsel "to stand looking at the door and to build a language that, despite the rewards and enticements to do otherwise, refuses to refuse blackness."[56] By attending, as one stands at the door, to the writing on the wall.[57]

## ACKNOWLEDGMENTS

This essay could not have been shaped and reshaped without insight and encouragement from Judith Roof, Seth Morton, Joseph Campana, Nicole Waligora-Davis, Bill Harrison, Jennifer Katz, Jesse Goldberg, Gretchen Barkhuff, and, especially, Jasmine Montgomery. Audiences at Rice University and SUNY Geneseo graciously provided opportunities to think aloud. Thanks also to W. W. Norton & Company for the opportunity to post an early snapshot of this on FairMatter.com.

## NOTES

1. U.S. Department of Homeland Security, *National Response Plan,* 1.
2. Federal Emergency Management Agency, *Field Operations Guide,* IV-12.
3. Moye, "The X-Codes."
4. Dayan, "Legal Slaves and Civil Bodies," 53.
5. "Katrina + 5" notes a 2009 email correspondence with radio host Nick Spitzer, who observes that the FEMA signs "conjur[e] a cross between the *Vévé* signs of voudun and a kind of military coroner's occupation."
6. Herron, *Thereafter Johnnie,* 163.
7. Derrida, *Archive Fever,* 8.
8. Ibid., 1.
9. Rigaud, *Ve-ve,* 67.
10. Ibid., 67, 68–69.
11. Roach, *Cities of the Dead,* 44, 58.
12. "An ontology of slavery" is from Wilderson, *Red White and Black,* 18; other quotes from Roach, *Cities of the Dead,* 58.
13. Thompson, *The Flash of the Spirit,* 108.
14. Dayan, "Querying the Spirit," 31.
15. The concept of being "dead in law" has been expressed variously by Orlando Patterson (*Slavery and Social Death*) and Saidiya Hartman (*Scenes of Subjection* and *Lose Your Mother*). Frank Wilderson explains it as the "ontological and epistemological time of modernity itself, in which Blackness and Slaveness are imbricated *ab initio*" (*Red White and Black,* 340). And Jared Sexton articulates it as the "living death," in which "black life is not social life in the universe formed

by the codes of state and civil society, of citizen and subject, of nation and culture, of people and place, of history and heritage, of all the things that colonial society has in common with the colonized, of all that capital has in common with labor – the modern world system" ("Ante-Anti-Blackness").

16. Dayan, "Legal Slaves and Civil Bodies," 53.

17. Locke, *Second Treatise of Government,* 75.

18. Mills, "Racial Liberalism," 1382, 1381.

19. Ibid., 1382, 1383.

20. Ibid., 1382.

21. Dayan, "Querying the Spirit," 41.

22. Walker, *After the Deluge,* 9.

23. Hartman, *Scenes of Subjection,* 206.

24. Snead, "On Repetition," 146.

25. Roach, *Cities of the Dead,* 58.

26. Zanger observes that theater is seen as a specific, "ephemeral" art, while the putative standardization of print means it is "often characterized as invariable, identically reproducible over time and across space for individuals reading in private or in small groups." Noting rightly that "such characterizations are clichés" that don't stand up to scrutiny from bibliographers, historians of the book, and poststructuralists, Zanger observes that in the early modern world of theater, print "can be said to intercede in the world of theater and even to perform as an actor in it" ("On the Threshold," 25). Even as Zanger's attentions are devoted to mid-seventeenth-century French frontispieces to published plays, her work is tantalizingly applicable to this essay's concerns.

27. Dayan, "Querying the Spirit," 42.

28. Hartman, *Scenes of Subjection,* 13.

29. Hartman, "Will Answer," 113.

30. My thanks to Claire McLauchlin for this observation.

31. Bataille, *The Accursed Share,* 77, 21.

32. Ibid.

33. Roach, *Cities of the Dead,* 43.

34. I take the phrase from *Belly of the Basin,* a post-Katrina documentary by filmmakers Roxana Walker-Canton and Tina Morton (A Sisters' Eye on Media Production), who screened a draft version of the film at SUNY Geneseo in 2006.

35. Steinberg, *Acts of God,* xxi.

36. Interestingly, as this essay took shape, http://www.fema.gov/about/history disappeared from the agency's website in 2012, apparently as part of a site overhaul. At that time, the history was functionally crossed out / submergedinacache (fema.gov/about/history.shtm) accessible only to those who knew that the history existed in the first place.

By October 2013, the overhaul was apparently complete, and FEMA's history again became visible at http://www.fema.gov/about-agency. I bring this up as an example of the archival churn noted by both Herron and Derrida.

37. Library of Congress, "A Bill for the relief of the sufferers by fire, in the town of Portsmouth" (January 14, 1803), http://memory.loc.gov/cgi-bin/ampage?collId=llhb&fileName=021/llhb021.db&recNum=41.

38. Sammons and Cunningham, *Black Portsmouth,* 123.

39. "Portsmouth's Great Fires," http://www.cityofportsmouth.com/community/markers/PortsmouthsGreatFires-locatedinAldrichParkatCourtatAtkinsonStreets.pdf.

40. Brewster, "Brewster's Rambles about Portsmouth #28." All text quotes are from this website.

41. Sammons and Cunningham, *Black Portsmouth,* 68–69.

42. Vaughn, "This Was a Man."

43. Hartman, "Fugitive Dreams."

44. http://www.fema.gov/about-agency.

45. Steinberg, *Acts of God,* 210.

46. "The Giant Pool of Money," *This American Life,* episode 355, first broadcast May 9, 2008. All text quotes are from this episode.

47. Lewis, *The Big Short,* 47.

48. Ibid., 73.

49. Roach, *Cities of the Dead,* 40.

50. Ibid., 34.

51. Lewis, *The Big Short,* 222.

52. Morrison, *A Mercy,* 166. It is notable that much of Morrison's novel is concerned with water as a warning sign of evil and danger. Indeed, when whites strip Florens of the letter authorizing her to travel, the event is signaled by a kettle relieving its pressure via a release of steam.

53. Dimock, "World History," 144, 157.

54. Rigaud, *Ve-ve,* 87.

55. Hartman, "Fugitive Dreams."

56. Jasmine Montgomery, e-mail message to the author, October 2, 2012; Sharpe, "Response."

57. In the exhibition, figure 3's image carries this caption: "More homey decorations accompany the X-codes on this Marigny home located near Holy Trinity Catholic Church (closed). The door of this residence displays a vévé, a vodou symbol. (A vévé is a linear symbol used to summon spirits in vodou's religious ceremonies.) Other observers of the X-code phenomenon have commented on the resemblance of the graphic to a vévé and viewers can judge by seeing these two side by side."

Bataille, Georges. *The Accursed Share: An Essay on General Economy. Volume 1.* Translated by Robert Hurley. New York: Zone Books, 1991.

Brewster, Charles. "Brewster's Rambles about Portsmouth #28." http://www.seacoastnh.com/brewster/28.html.

Dayan, Colin (Joan). "Legal Slaves and Civil Bodies." In *Materializing Democracy: Toward a Revitalized Cultural Politics,* edited by Russ Castronovo and Dana Nelson, 53–94. Durham, N.C.: Duke University Press, 2002.

——. "Querying the Spirit: The Rules of the Haitian Lwa." In *Colonial Saints: Discovering the Holy in the Americas, 1500–1800,* edited by Alan Grier and Jodi Bilinkoff, 31–50. New York: Routledge, 2003.

Derrida, Jacques. *Archive Fever: A Freudian Impression.* Translated by Eric Prenowitz. Chicago: University of Chicago Press, 1995.

Dimock, Wai Chee. "World History According to Katrina." In *States of Emergency: The Object of American Studies,* edited by Russ Castronovo and Susan Gillman, 143–160. Chapel Hill: University of North Carolina Press, 2009.

Federal Emergency Management Agency. *National Urban Search and Rescue (US&R) Response System Field Operations Guide.* Washington, D.C.: U.S. Department of Homeland Security, 2003.

Hartman, Saidiya. "Fugitive Dreams of Diaspora: Conversations with Saidiya Hartman." Interview with Patricia J. Saunders. *Anthurium* 6.1 (Spring 2008). http://anthurium.miami.edu/volume_6/issue_1/saunders-fugitive.html.

——. *Lose Your Mother: A Journey along the Atlantic Slave Route.* New York: Macmillan, 2008.

——. *Scenes of Subjection: Terror, Slavery, and Self-Making in Nineteenth-Century America.* New York: Oxford University Press, 1997.

——. "Will Answer to the Name Glenn." In *Glenn Ligon: America,* edited by Scott Rothkopf. New York: Whitney Museum of American Art, 2011.

Herron, Carolivia. *Thereafter Johnnie.* New York: 1stbooks, 2001.

Lewis, Michael. *The Big Short: Inside the Doomsday Machine.* New York: W. W. Norton, 2011.

Locke, John. *Second Treatise of Government: An Essay Concerning the True, Original, Extent, and End of Civil*

*Government*. Edited by Richard H. Cox. Wheeling: Harlan Davidson, 1982.
Mills, Charles. "Racial Liberalism." *PMLA* 123.5 (October 2008): 1380–1397.
Morrison, Toni. *A Mercy*. New York: Vintage, 2009.
Moye, Dorothy. "Katrina + 5: An X-Code Exhibition." *Southern Spaces,* August 26, 2010. http://southernspaces.org/2010/katrina-5-x-code-exhibition.
——. "The X-Codes: A Post-Katrina Postscript." *Southern Spaces,* August 26, 2009. http://www.southernspaces.org/2009/x-codes-post-katrina-postscript.
Patterson, Orlando. *Slavery and Social Death*. Cambridge, Mass.: Harvard University Press, 1985.
Rigaud, Milo. *Ve-ve: Diagrammes rituels du vodou*. Trilingual ed. New York: French and European Publications, 1974.
Roach, Joseph. *Cities of the Dead: Circum-Atlantic Performance*. New York: Columbia University Press, 1996.
Sammons, Mark J., and Valerie Cunningham. *Black Portsmouth: Three Centuries of African American Heritage*. Lebanon: University of New Hampshire Press, 2004.
Sexton, Jared. "Ante-Anti-Blackness: Afterthoughts." *Lateral* 1.1 (2012). http://lateral.culturalstudiesassociation.org/issue1/content/sexton.html.
Sharpe, Christina. "Response to Jared Sexton's 'Ante-Anti-Blackness: Afterthoughts.'" *Lateral* 1.1 (2012). http://lateral.culturalstudiesassociation.org/issue1/content/sharpe.html.
Snead, James. "On Repetition in Black Culture." *Black American Literature Forum* 15.4 (1981): 146–154.
Steinberg, Ted. *Acts of God: The Unnatural History of Natural Disaster in America*. New York: Oxford University Press, 2006.
Thompson, Robert Farris. *The Flash of the Spirit: African & Afro-American Art & Philosophy*. New York: Vintage, 1984.
U.S. Department of Homeland Security. *National Response Plan*. Washington, D.C., 2004.
Vaughn, Dorothy Mansfield. "This Was a Man: A Biography of General William Whipple." 1964. http://www.whipple.org/william/thiswasaman.html.
Walker, Kara. *After the Deluge*. New York: Rizzoli, 2007.
Wilderson, Frank. *Red White and Black: Cinema and the Structure of U.S. Antagonisms*. Durham, N.C.: Duke University Press, 2010.

Zanger, Abby. "On the Threshold of Print and Performance: How Prints Mattered to Bodies of/at Work in Molière's Published Corpus." *Word and Image* 17.2 (2001): 25–41.

BIOLOGY

POLITICS

FISH

BODY

# THE ODDBALL ARCHIVE

## BOX II

## COLLECTIVE FIGURES

CONTINGENCY

BED

KITS

CELEBRITY

PHILOSOPHY

CAPITALISM

## KEY WORDS

politics, fish, philosophy, body, contingency, biology, bed, celebrity, capitalism, kits

## COLLECTION CONTENTS

*Robin Blyn*
"Marcuse's Unreason: The Biology of Revolution"

*Dennis Allen*
"The Madness of Slavoj Žižek"

*Jonathan P. Eburne*
"Fish Kit"

Tinkerers or pundits, visionaries or eccentrics, oddballs sometimes make their own archives. Surprisingly, the archives of some of history's most anomalous figures are rarely themselves anomalous but instead come to appear exemplary because their organizing figures have emerged in some way from the pack. Oddball personae collect followings; their followers, in turn, are often the ones left in charge of collecting the oddballs' life's work, their leavings. The Kinsey archives, no less than the papers of the Marquis de Sade or the drawings of Adolf Wölfli, may now be managed by professional librarians, but they were once gathered and conserved by devoted followers: secretaries, experts, epigones, or next of kin.

Even so, such collections nonetheless bear out the oddities and particularities of their governing figures as well. As collections of leavings – correspondence, sketches, draft ideas, manuscripts – such archives also produce themselves virtually from the start and rapidly become an attribute of the oddball personage. Archives sometimes make their own oddballs, in other words. There is rarely an oddball figure who does not have an archival entourage, a set of leavings that matches and sustains his or her body of work and swells the figure's reputation for idiosyncrasy.

As Robin Blyn suggests in her essay on Herbert Marcuse, such archives are often inherited as well. For Marcuse, the human capacity for revolutionary social chance was stored away both in the Left's memory of Marx and Freud and in the Lamarckian notion of biological inheritance that carried through as one of Freud's most anomalous claims. With the mutability of human drives in mind as the basis for his thinking about utopian social change, Marcuse's phylogenetic rationale for the possibility of a new kind of human subject involves a process of "non-repressive desublimation," by which humans could come to embody this mutation in their basic drives and desires. Although Marcuse deploys this concept as a way of describing the liberation of thought in capitalist society, it may just as well characterize how the work of a philosopher whose ideas ran counter to dominant beliefs constitutes an instant archive in itself. Not only does this latter archive crystallize dissent in the very process of its formation, but it also records the larger discussions from which dominant modes of thought emerged. The archives of such figures thus testify to the conditions from which dominant ideologies sprung, as well as preserve the continued objections to such ideologies. Figures of dissenting thought compile archives that represent conditions, ideas, or political intensities that might otherwise have been sublimated: forgotten yet still obeyed.

Archives that accrue around a central oddball figure raise the question of what a revolutionary archive might look like – that is, if the idea of an archive can even sustain such a possibility. Can an archive ever be revolutionary? We might wonder instead about whether the process of archiving oddball figures risks domesticating them as caricatures or curiosities. For such a process also risks pinning down the force of their contestation to a specific – and thus restricted – locus within an archive's governing rule. Archiving oddballs as "oddball" simultaneously includes and excepts them from the political and cultural mainstream. To what extent do the effects of this involvement stem from the process of archivization itself, rather than from the heroic agency of the central figure whose leavings it collects? To what extent, in other words, does the archive's operation already produce the oddball as such? To become a figure, to stand out as an oddball, is already to bear an archival function.

There is a biological, bodily aspect to the oddball figure's archival survival. Any collection organized around such a figure incorporates him or her as part of the collection. The body, as Dennis Allen's mediation on the image of Slavoj Žižek in bed suggests, is an integral part of an oddball figure's archive. Museums dedicated to past presidents, sports heroes, Hollywood celebrities, and even scientific achievement include not only portraiture but also the items used by the subjects of interest and occasionally bodily remnants such as hair and clothing. Žižek is, however, his own museum: for the Slovenian philosopher, the overwhelming physicality of his own body becomes the framework for, rather than the artifact or fetish of, his life's work. Biology becomes epistemological. Marcuse, for his part, renders the unreason of physical persistence in terms of a biological inheritance: Marcuse's Lamarckian biology, Blyn shows, "operates in excess of rational thought." The filmmaker-artist David Lynch, on the other hand, manipulates biological matter as an artistic medium for exercising a particularly unreasoning kind of transcendental thought. Assembling organic matter in tiny archival "kits," Lynch builds imaginative apparatuses for his viewers, his "followers," to use. The kits don't work, however – or rather, they work only insofar as they dismantle their ties to human industry and the generation of discrete logical and bodily wholes. Instead of envisioning humanity as a grand orchestra of seamless biological participation, Lynch's archival kits set biology apart from the bios, enabling humanity to collect, disassemble, appropriate, and rework biology as art in the form of kits and Lynch's broader artistic oeuvre.

The archives of such oddball figures as Marcuse, Žižek, and Lynch operate as synecdoches of both oddball figures and oddball oeuvres. Marcuse's archive becomes visible as a counter to its environment of political philosophy, while Žižek's perpetual recourse to speech self-archives as an unending enunciative project already aimed at its archive. Lynch produces a side-archive of animal kits that extend his cinematic oeuvre not by providing clarity or insight but by pushing the projects even farther along a disassembly line.

## HISTORIES OF THE CONTRIBUTORS

**Robin Blyn** is associate professor of English at the University of West Florida, where she teaches a range of courses in twentieth-century literature and culture. Her published work includes studies of works by Djuna Barnes, Nathanael West, Tod Browning, Toni Morrison, and Gloria Naylor. She is the author of *The Freak-garde: Extraordinary Bodies and Revolutionary Art in America* (University of Minnesota Press, 2013), a study of capitalism, desire, and the American avant-garde.

**Dennis Allen** is a professor in the English Department at West Virginia University, where he specializes in literary and cultural theory, gay and lesbian studies, and the history of sexuality. He is the author of *Sexuality in Victorian Fiction* and has published articles on narrative theory, sexuality studies, and LGBT pedagogy in a variety of edited collections and such journals as *SEL*, *Genders*, and *Narrative*. He is currently working on a book with Judith Roof that examines the impossible status of the contemporary gay and lesbian subject.

**Jonathan P. Eburne** is associate professor of comparative literature and English at the Pennsylvania State University. He is the author of *Sur-*

*realism and the Art of Crime* (Cornell University Press, 2008) and coeditor, with Jeremy Braddock, of *Paris, Capital of the Black Atlantic* (Johns Hopkins University Press, 2013). He is past president of the Association for the Study of the Arts of the Present (ASAP) and founding coeditor of ASAP/*Journal*. He is currently completing a book entitled *Outsider Theory*.

4

# MARCUSE'S UNREASON

## THE BIOLOGY OF REVOLUTION

*Robin Blyn*

"We can use the word revolution again for the first time in many years," Douglass Kellner declared in October 2011.[1] The scene was not Tahrir Square or the streets of Tunis. Nor was it Zuccotti Park. Rather, Kellner was speaking at the University of Pennsylvania, at the Fourth Biennial Conference of the International Herbert Marcuse Society. It was clearly a moment for Kellner and his audience to savor; together, the Arab Spring and Occupy protests of 2011 seemed to vindicate the very idea of revolution and with it the work of a philosopher variously dismissed as impractical, irrational, irrelevant, and dangerously seductive. Thus, when Kellner added that "for those of us who have been doing Marcuse scholarship, this is utopia," he was remarking not only on the large turnout at the conference but also on an historical context that seemed to legitimate the revolutionary aspirations that animate Marcuse's work throughout the 1960s, the decade in which he emerged as the putative father of the "New Left." We can use the word revolution again, Kellner suggests, because the kind of radical break from repressive conditions that Marcuse envisioned is once again within the realm of the possible.

The prospect is understandably giddy for the stalwart who have continued to value Marcuse's work in the face of bemused indifference, if not outright scorn. In the last thirty years, Marcuse's once-popular books have lapsed into near obscurity, their tenor and their goal seemingly out of step with recent history. That goal is nothing less than a society liberated from the domination and repression of corporate capitalism. Only within such a society, Marcuse contends, will humans have the capacity to escape the "Welfare-Through-Warfare State" and thus "function as unmutilated beings."[2] While Marcuse's belief in this radically free society inspired protest movements in the 1960s, the arc of his work owes a great deal to the vitality of the counterculture itself. That is, Marcuse was strongly influenced by the movements that claimed him as one of their own. The result is the hopefulness that distinguishes *An Essay on Liberation* (1969), for example, from the desperate and scathing social critique of *One-Dimensional Man* (1964). Yet, as time marched on, Marcuse's positive prognosis began to diverge from the growing skepticism of his activist base. By the time Ronald Reagan took office in 1981, even the potential for challenging the domination of corporate capitalism seemed inconceivable. Whatever validity Marcuse's theory of liberation once had, it had become the hopelessly naive fantasy of an oddball optimist.

Not coincidentally, in the very same years in which skepticism plagued the Left, Marcuse's most enthusiastic supporters, students and progressive academics, fell under the spell of new trends in critical theory. As French poststructuralism emerged in the academy as the avant-garde du jour, Marcuse's efforts to merge Marxist and Freudian discourses in the name of liberation became passé. Especially from the perspective of the enormously influential work of Michel Foucault, Marcuse's claims that "non-repressive desublimation" could serve as a means of liberation appeared embarrassingly retrograde, a prime example of the "repressive hypothesis" that Foucault so influentially identified and dismissed.[3] As Foucault's star rose, Marcuse's necessarily fell, and the books that had inspired a generation came to be seen as the expression of an atavistic and regressive humanism. In short order, Marcuse's work was domesticated into an intellectual curiosity, an oddball archive as anathema to posthumanists today as it was to mainstream liberals in the 1960s. And yet lurking at the heart of Marcuse's utopianism is a profoundly posthumanist vision, one that has been overlooked precisely because it depends upon the oddest development in Marcuse's work: his turn to biology as the engine of revolutionary subjectivity.

In order to appreciate Marcuse's strange turn to the biological, it is worth recalling that in addition to signifying a major rupture in the established order, "revolution" refers to a circular movement, to the tracing of a path that returns repeatedly to its site of origination. It refers, that is, to repetition, to the return of the same. History is rife with examples of political and social revolutions that follow this conservative path, and it is this trajectory that Marcuse's work attempts to evade by refusing to limit change to that which is already within the realm of the possible. This is because revolution for Marcuse is beyond the power of the liberal subject. On the contrary, it depends upon the generation of a "new historical Subject," a subject who does not yet exist; revolutionary subjectivity for Marcuse is a virtual potential. Precisely because it is virtual, revolution can emerge in Marcuse's discourse as a potential loosed from the confines of what we can currently conceive, as the emergence of that which is genuinely new.[4] So, too, the relevance of this philosopher's work for the twenty-first century lies in the elements of the Marcuse archive that exceed the intellectual imagination of his historical moment, the oddball version of biological evolution that found little traction in the sixties and remains an embarrassment even to those most committed to rehabilitating Marcuse's reputation for the here and now.

The dual requirements of Marcuse's revolutionary subjectivity are that it must be an immanent potential of the existing capitalist regime and, at the same time, resistant to the rationality that secures capitalism's power. The process by which Marcuse's new historical subject emerges is hence necessarily *ir*rational. Yet, Marcuse never celebrates irrationality as a generative psychic state; despite the caricature of him as deranged guru paraded in the press, Marcuse's work never identifies states of psychic unreason as forms of, or avenues to, liberation. On the contrary, the Marcuse archive is an archive of reasoned unreason: it strives to rationally theorize the existence of an irrational and inhuman process through which a revolutionary subject might emerge. The path from *Eros and Civilization* (1955) to *An Essay on Liberation* (1969) is a trajectory that charts the gradual emergence of biology as the irrational engine of the virtual, enabling the generation of a new historical subject and thus a revolution that might genuinely introduce something new into the world.

Marcuse's privileged site of irrationality is the biological process of human evolution, an inhuman process that nonetheless is vulnerable to human intervention. In the Marcuse archive, biological mutation can potentiate social change, but social change can also create the historical conditions for salutary alterations in the evolution of the species. Based on this conception of evolution, Marcuse will go so far as to assert a "biological basis of socialism," and he arrives at this most oddball conclusion through his critical return to the preeminent modern science of the archive, psychoanalysis.[5] As Jacques Derrida has shown us, Freudian psychoanalysis proposes a "new theory of the archive." It posits a psychic archive distinct from spontaneous memory; it conceives of repression as itself a mode of archivization.[6] When Marcuse returns to the Freudian archive, he revives the most embarrassing facet of Freudian theory: its appropriation of evolutionary science. The transgenerational inheritance of repressed memory lies at the heart of Freud's notorious theorization of Jewish national identity, even as it grounds his claims for a universal human condition. Freud thus relies upon Jean-Baptiste Lamarck's theory of phylogenesis, the theory that humans evolve through the inheritance of acquired characteristics. However controversial when Freud turned to it in *Totem and Taboo* (1913) and *Moses and Monotheism* (1937), the theory of phylogenesis was so roundly discredited by the 1950s that the very credibility of psychoanalysis depended upon burying it in the depths of the Freudian archive. In Marcuse's account of the emergence of revolutionary subjectivity, then, we witness the return of the repressed, and like all such returns, the repressed content arrives in an altered state. Where phylogenesis allows Freud to account for the constancy of Jewish identity and to ground an ahistorical human condition, in Marcuse's work it justifies the human potential for genuine change. Phylogenetic inheritance hence becomes Marcuse's biology of revolution.

## THE ACCIDENTAL GURU

However varied their political orientation or approach, Marcuse's critics in the 1960s insisted on the irrationality of his philosophy. Yet a survey of their often vicious and ad hominem attacks reveals a pervasive critical displacement. Effectively, the legion charges of irrationality serve as a screen for the profound discomfort Marcuse provoked in his reasoned critique of the liberal subject that American democracy presupposes. In point of fact, Marcuse's philosophy of liberation depends upon the recovery of rational thought deformed by the camera obscura of liberalism. For this heresy, he managed to earn the wrath of both the conservative Right and the liberal Left, neither of whom ever approach the emergence of that which is truly irrational in his work: the process by which a new historical subject comes into existence.

At the height of his popularity with the counterculture, writers across the political spectrum characterize Marcuse not only as a "guru" but also as a preeminently bad thinker, given to unwarranted generalizations, contradictions, totalizing claims, an absence of evidence, and profoundly irrational arguments dressed up in an "abstruse Teutonic style."[7] As early as 1965, for example, Marcuse was Enemy Number One for the leftist scholars who published in Irving Howe's *Beyond the New Left*. Here, Richard Lowenthal chides Marcuse for dispensing with the "rationality of history" and regressing "to a more primitive kind of secular religion," while Howe charges "the current New Left Guru" with offering disaffected youth "a simultaneous rationalization for withdrawal and wildness, copping-out and turning-on."[8] Both of these assessments find their way into the popular press. Hence, in his article in *Fortune,* Irving Kristol calls Marcuse's work "sheer sophistry," a form of mysticism analogous to "the fantasies of various heretical sects of the early Christian era." Instead of a Christian millennium, Kristol remarks, Marcuse's new order "will be a kind of perpetual 'trip' without the benefits of LSD."[9] According to Herbert Gold, however, the hallucinogenic experience does not abide in Marcuse's fatuous conception of a utopian future; it lies in the experience of reading his books. In the pages of the *Saturday Evening Post,* Gold scornfully concludes, "Like rock 'n roll and some of the mind-expanding drugs . . . Marcuse is a stimulant to fantasy and action."[10] Whether we turn to the pages of mass-market publications or to scholarly collections, then, the upshot is the same: Marcuse's work is a dangerous drug manufactured by an irrational mystic.

By dismissing him as a "guru," Marcuse's critics willfully ignore the determining role of material historical conditions in his philosophy. Indeed, they ignore the specific content of his books. Comparing his work to LSD may link it effectively to sixties drug culture, but Marcuse never urged anyone to "turn on, tune in, and drop out."[11] On the contrary, in *One-Dimensional Man,* the so-called Bible of the New Left, Marcuse concludes, "Self-determination will be real to the extent to which the masses have been dissolved into individuals liberated from all propaganda, indoctrination, and manipulation, capable of knowing and comprehending the facts and of evaluating alternatives" – hardly an injunction to "cop out" or "turn off."[12] As stated here, Marcuse's goals seem entirely consonant with an Enlightenment project. Moreover, there is nothing hallucinogenic about Marcuse's writing. *Eros and Civilization, One-Dimensional Man, An Essay on Liberation,* and even the notorious essay "Repressive Tolerance" (1965) all make for comparatively dry reading. These are politically committed texts, but they are dense and rigorous, ensconced in the philosophical discourses upon which they draw. And all of those influences are insistently Western. Unlike Allen Ginsberg's work, for example, neither Marcuse's critique of the Vietnam War nor his vision of utopia as the "pacification of existence" legitimizes itself by recourse to Eastern religious traditions.[13] There is no Buddhism in Marcuse's work – utopia, perhaps, but not Nirvana.[14]

The distinction here makes all the difference in the world, for Marcuse identifies the human potential for liberation with specific historical conditions; however idiosyncratic, he remains committed to a Marxist tradition grounded in historical materialism. Utopia is not a spiritual state for Marcuse; nor is it a fantasy. It is a way of life potentiated by "the affluent society" and the advanced means of production available to it.[15] The utopian society to which Marcuse refers is a society liberated from the "massive exploitation of corporate capitalism," a form of exploitation accomplished by reducing human existence to "an instrument of labor."[16] Marcuse decries "the performance principle," a repressive ideology that produces a "form of pure servitude" wherein the individual human subject exists only "as an instrument and a thing." His goal is, quite simply, the end of this "technological rationality" and all of the repression and alienation that go with it.[17] Moreover, his critique of "technological rationality" eschews technophobia. On the contrary, it is precisely because of technological advancements that the potential for liberation from instrumentality exists, and if this utopia takes the face of fantasy, it is only because we have so fully absorbed the ideology of the established order. As Marcuse writes, "What is denounced as utopian is . . . that which is blocked from coming about by the power of the established societies."[18] Utopia, in other words, is neither a spiritual state nor an imaginary place; it is a material condition at odds with the state of domination and dehumanization maintained for the profit of corporate capitalism and legitimated through the discourse of liberalism.

Yet for Marcuse this utopia fulfills the double requirement of the term: it is both a "good place" and, as yet, "no place." In other words, we cannot know exactly what a liberated society will look like, for it will be a genuinely new invention produced by revolutionary subjects who do not yet exist. Marcuse is insistent on this point. The struggle for the solution to exploitation, he writes, has "outgrown the traditional forms." Hence, Marcuse is not working toward the communist society envisioned by Marx and Engels; nor does he see the worker as the agent of revolution. On the contrary, Marcuse observes the extent to which the working class has been pacified by unprecedented comforts, the pursuit of commodities, and the extraordinary force of technological rationality. For this reason, the worker "is no longer a living contradiction to the established society."[19] Even more surprising, perhaps, is that Marcuse also refuses to identify the rebels and militants who surround him as revolutionaries capable of the kind of liberation he deems necessary. Rather, their protests inspire him because they lay the groundwork for a new historical subject. They perform "a liberation which must precede the construction of a free society, one which necessitates an historical break with the past and the present."[20] Utopia for Marcuse, then, is a virtual potential immanent in the material conditions of the established order.[21] "Marcuse Leaves It Open," as Gold puts it in the *Saturday Evening Post,* not because he is wanting for ideas or because it would ruin the hallucinogenic experience of "the trip" but because any conception generated from the established order is delimited by the domination and repression that sustain that order. All we could arrive at is the possible, which is to say, more of the same.

The most immediate goal, then, is to create a context in which a genuinely revolutionary subjectivity can emerge. For Marcuse, this entails the rehabilitation of reason and "negative thinking," both of which serve as tools for the penetration of false consciousness.[22] That is, Marcuse locates the means of achieving his goal in a Hegelian-Marxist tradition that identifies revolutionary subjectivity with both a transformation in consciousness and rational enlightenment. "All liberation," Marcuse writes, "depends on the consciousness of servitude," but achieving that consciousness requires the power of negative thinking. Marcuse found the protest movements and countercultures of the sixties so heartening precisely because they represented to him an explosion of negative thinking that he simply did not see coming.[23] He celebrates these movements for performing a conscious and conscientious negation of the establishment, what he calls, after Alfred North Whitehead, "The Great Refusal." Yet though Marcuse also singles out Surrealism as an earlier expression of this act of negation, "The Great Refusal" does not entail the valorization of the irrational. On the contrary, such acts of negation recognize "the degree to which the established society is irrational."[24] Like his colleagues in the Frankfurt School, Marcuse submits "instrumental reason" to a scathing critique, but reason as such is not the problem. The problem, rather, is that we live in a society in which the "web of domination has become the web of Reason itself."[25] The marriage of liberalism and capitalism has rendered reason an ideological tool of disciplinization. Despite the language of his critics, then, Marcuse's work does not exactly dispense with reason or rationality. Rather, its project is more accurately one of salvage.

That much said, there is plenty of ammunition in Marcuse's writing for critics who define the rational in terms of its opposition to the irrational or reason as the antithesis of fantasy and art. Throughout the sixties, Marcuse responded to the unreason of the established order by arguing for the rehabilitation of "higher forms of reason" and by asserting the necessity of "a new idea of Reason, theoretical and practical."[26] It is thus remarkable that, in their attacks on his "irrationality," writers seldom invoke his redefinition of reason or "the new rationality of gratification" Marcuse strives to construct.[27] Nor do they dwell on the biological foundation to socialism he arrives at in his rereading of Freud, a theory, as we shall see, that most pointedly introduces an element of the irrational into his works. Rather, the press baptized Marcuse a "guru" and insisted on his irrationality largely because of an essay entitled "Repressive Tolerance," his contribution to a slender volume named *A Critique of Pure Tolerance* (1965). The content of this essay is so threatening, so intolerable, apparently, that it required even the most sanguine critics to label Marcuse's work irrational without taking into account any of his extended thought on the power and limits of reason.

The most infamous argument of "Repressive Tolerance" is its contention that both the abstract principles of nonviolence and tolerance have become reactionary, a means of sustaining the power of a violent and repressive state. In his view of nonviolence, Marcuse essentially follows Frantz Fanon. He argues that the violence of the regime may well necessitate a violent response and that the insistence on nonviolence in principle is a belated requirement imposed on the weak, on the victims of state-sanctioned violence.[28] The only reason that the question of violence is relevant to Marcuse's essay, however, is that it exemplifies the stultifying effects of "repressive tolerance." Marcuse observes that the entire discussion of the efficacy of violent resistance has been repressed by liberal democracies that define themselves in terms of tolerance. Thus the essay horrified thinkers on the left and the right not only by suggesting the legitimacy of violent revolt but by attacking the sanctity of liberalism's most cherished principle: freedom of expression for dissenting ideas. At its origins at the beginning of the modern period, Marcuse writes, tolerance was "a subversive liberating notion and practice." However, "what is proclaimed and practiced as tolerance today is, in many of its most effective manifestations, serving the cause of oppression." Marcuse thus identifies a gap between the abstract principle of tolerance and its contemporary practice. He contends that the "political locus of tolerance has changed: while it is more or less quietly and constitutionally withdrawn from the opposition, it is made compulsory behavior with respect to established policies."[29] The effect is the perversion of the liberal public sphere, which is no longer a free marketplace of ideas but, on the contrary, a site of indoctrination.

In other words, "Repressive Tolerance" maintains that the illusion of free speech and unlimited tolerance ideologically veils the social engineering of what Marcuse calls, in his most famous book, the "one-dimensional man," a subject who has lost "the mental space for denial and reflection."[30] At stake for Marcuse, then, is not merely the possibility of articulating and disseminating dissenting points of view but also the potential for the new historical subject whose emergence is a prerequisite for revolution:

> When tolerance mainly serves the protection and preservation of a repressive society, when it serves to neutralize opposition and to render men immune against other and better forms of life, then tolerance has been perverted. And when this perversion starts in the mind of the individual, in his consciousness, his needs, when heteronomous interests occupy him before he can experience his servitude, then the efforts to counteract his dehumanization must begin at the place of entrance, there where the false consciousness takes form (or rather: is systematically formed) – it must begin with stopping the words and images which feed his consciousness.[31]

According to Marcuse, the perversion of tolerance in practice, veiled by the sanctified principle of tolerance in the abstract, precludes the demystification of false consciousness and thus prevents the emergence of a new historical subject.

In addition to critiquing the perversion of tolerance, "Repressive Tolerance" offers its own solutions, and it is here that Marcuse earns the wrath of his critics. He argues that "true pacification requires the withdrawal of tolerance before the deed, at the stage of communication in word, print, and picture." Some ideas, he asserts, should not be tolerated, and his evidence is the role of propaganda in Nazi Germany, which he characterizes as the "prologue to massacre." "If democratic tolerance had been withdrawn when the future leaders started their campaign," Marcuse contends, "mankind would have had a chance of avoiding Auschwitz and a World War." This preemptive intolerance, of course, flies in the face of liberalism. Marcuse never invokes the liberal solution; he never suggests that longer and more persuasive dissent could have staved off Hitler's rise to power. This is because Marcuse rejects the a priori autonomy that liberalism imputes to its subject. On the contrary, he maintains that "people exposed to . . . impartiality are no *tabulae rasae;* they are indoctrinated by the conditions under which they live and think." Marcuse hence advocates intolerance of organized repression and indoctrination in order to enable these subjects "to become autonomous, to find by themselves what is true and what is false."[32]

Marcuse's critique and his proposed solution to repressive tolerance are inherently provocative, but they are not irrational, a fact that one is likely to miss in the criticism that the essay inspired. Certainly, the publication of "Repressive Tolerance" was the most immediate impetus for the essays in Howe's *Beyond the New Left,* which, as we have seen, identify Marcuse variously with mysticism, hallucinogens, and the abandonment of reason. Clearly, the issue of violence haunts the writers who contributed to Howe's volume. Hence Howe's fear that Marcuse rationalizes "wildness" and Lowenthal's contention that he feeds "the urge for violent action."[33] Doubtlessly, Marcuse's essay warrants serious critical review, but the excess of the critiques it received is extremely telling; the need to identify Marcuse with the mystical and the hallucinogenic suggests the irrationality of the critics rather than their object of critique.

The ideology of liberalism is so powerful, "Repressive Tolerance" suggests, that it preempts the emergence of revolutionary subjectivity. Thus while Marcuse's theories of liberation depend on the power of reason, he ultimately concludes that the rational demystification of false consciousness will not by itself generate a new historical subject. In addition to a transformation in consciousness, this subjectivity depends on a transformation in needs, and that, in turn, requires exploiting a dimension of human experience resistant to the instrumental rationality Marcuse identified as capitalism's primary disciplinary mechanism. For Marcuse, these dimensions are not only refuges from domination, as Theodor Adorno would argue. They are also grounds for a new kind of subject, one that is ready and willing to undertake the task of social, political, and economic transformation. At different points in his career, Marcuse grounded his new historical subject in fantasy, in the aesthetic, and, finally, in the biology of human evolution. The biological basis of liberation is such an oddball idea that even those who have recently argued for the continuing relevance of Marcuse's work conveniently forget this part of his work. Like Freud's own embarrassing flirtation with Lamarckism, Marcuse's engagement with phylogenesis is a threat to the integrity of the archive. And yet Marcuse's theory for the generation of revolutionary subjectivity emerged specifically by way of the return of the repressed Lamarckism he inherited from Freud.

## EVOLUTION AND THE ARCHIVE

In both *Eros and Civilization* and *An Essay on Liberation,* Marcuse arrives at the ground for the emergence of a new historical subject through a critical return to the psychoanalytic science of the archive. In the Freudian archive, Marcuse rediscovered a rationale for the historicity of the drives and for mutations to human needs provoked by environmental and historical change. Ultimately, Marcuse's revolutionary subjectivity depends on the idea that environmentally induced mutations can be passed on to future generations. Marcuse thus recovers Freud's most disreputable idea: his selective affirmation of a Lamarckian concept of human evolution. Yet though Marcuse inherited the concept of phylogenesis from Freud, in the process of the transfer the concept itself underwent a remarkable mutation. The inheritance of acquired characteristics ceased to be the basis of stable and universal human nature and became, instead, the basis for change. As appropriated by Marcuse, phylogenesis is the irrational biological process that potentiates the emergence of that which is genuinely revolutionary. It is the engine of the virtual.

This mutation in the theory of phylogenesis is itself a product of historical and environmental pressures. Taken in context, Freud's turn to phylogenesis in *Moses and Monotheism* is neither atavistic nor regressive. On the contrary, as Eliza Slavet writes, Lamarckism "was a major subject of scientific and political debates well into the 1930s, if not later."[34] While Freud famously bemoans the "present attitude of biological science" because it "won't hear of the idea of acquired qualities being transmitted to descendents," the fact is that he was hardly alone in entertaining the idea.[35] Certainly, the Nazis would not "hear of it." They favored a neo-Darwinian account of evolution that negated the influence of the environment and regarded Lamarckism as a "liberal-Jewish-Bolshevist science."[36] In the 1930s, Jewish scientists and Bolshevists were, in fact, attracted to Lamarckism, but not because there was some natural affinity between the two. Rather, as Mitchell Hart clarifies, just as Lamarckian environmentalism lent itself to the historical materialism of Bolshevism, it allowed Jewish scientists "to explain the particular physical or mental traits often-times identified as racially Jewish as historically or socially determined."[37] While Freud's own use of Lamarck ultimately diverged from the kind of materialist perspective Hart describes, *Moses and Monotheism* clearly participated in the efforts to turn the discourse of evolution against the biological determinism promulgated by the Nazis.

Although Lamarckism is at work in *Totem and Taboo,* it is in *Moses and Monotheism* that the politics of Freud's use of it come fully into view. In this ambitious latter work, Freud seeks to account for the emergence of monotheism and Jewish identity by recourse to phylogenesis. Specifically, Freud depends on the transgenerational inheritance of repressed memory. Jews are, quite simply, the carriers of the repressed memory of the murder of Moses. No matter what you believe, no matter what rituals you do or do not practice, if you carry the memory-trace of the murder of Moses, you are a Jew. This memory-trace makes Jews what they are. Yet, as it turns out, *Moses and Monotheism* also reveals that this repressed memory, the definitive mark of Jewishness, is a repetition of the prehistoric murder of the primeval father, the memory of which all people carry, in however repressed form. As Freud writes, "The mental residue of those primeval times [is] a heritage which, with each new generation, needs only to be reawakened, not to be reacquired."[38] The "archaic heritage," phylogenetically transported in the archive of the unconscious, is the basis of a universal human nature. Hence, through his appropriation of Lamarckian theories of evolution, Freud was able to develop a Jewish identity that remains constant over time and to identify that particular identity with a universal human condition. The result: Jews are both accorded their particularity and, at the same time, rendered the same as everyone else. *Moses and Monotheism* thus represents a potent intervention into the discourse of Nazism and the brand of anti-Semitism it grounded in a variety of biological discourses, including the discourse of evolution.

While Lamarckism allowed Freud to identify what stays the same over time, it provided Marcuse a means of imagining a basis for revolutionary change. Despite this profound divergence in conclusions, Marcuse viewed his work less as a revision of Freud's than as a critical return to it. In the Freudian archive, he found a phylogenetic rationale for the emergence of his new historical subject: environmentally induced mutations to the drives and to human needs, both of which Marcuse identified, following Freud, with "biology." Biology hence becomes the seat of the drives, the instincts, and organic needs. As Marcuse warns his readers, "I use the terms 'biological' and 'biology' not in the sense of the scientific discipline, but in order to designate the process and dimension in which inclinations, behavior patterns, aspirations become vital needs which, if not satisfied, would cause dysfunction of the organism."[39] On the one hand, Marcuse's biology sounds like a synonym for the naturalization of ideology. When needs become biological, we can say, ideology has become instinctual. Yet by evoking the "organic structure" of man and the "physiological expression and transmission" of needs and by denoting them as "biological," Marcuse reveals his unwillingness to reduce "vital needs" to ideology. It is crucial for Marcuse that they remain ensconced in the realm of the biological, where they can be "transmitted" phylogenetically and remain irrational, resistant, that is, to the rationalization of corporate capitalism.[40]

It is in *Eros and Civilization* that Marcuse first offers his theory of the mutability of the drives. As its title suggests, the book challenges Freud's tragic conclusions in *Civilization and Its Discontents*. In particular, Marcuse takes exception to Freud's working assumption that "the notion of a non-repressive civilization is impossible."[41] For Freud, civilization emerges in the sublimation of Eros. Moreover, the survival of civilization depends upon repression. As *Civilization and Its Discontents* famously argues, Eros, the life drive, is inextricably bound up with Thanatos, the death drive. Unless we repress the one, we cannot repress the other. While the "discontent" of civilization is hence the necessity of repression, Freud paradoxically concludes that the future of civilization depends upon more and better repression. It is a dark vision, one that comes out of Freud's prognosis of the prospects for humankind in 1929. By contrast, Marcuse's more hopeful vision emerges out of the post–World War II boom of the 1950s. As he challenges Freud's arguments for the necessity of repression, Marcuse shares company with the Surrealists he so admired and with a host of radical thinkers of the 1960s, including Wilhelm Reich, Norman O. Brown, and Erich Fromm. The originality of Marcuse's work, however, is that in contrast to the "neo-Freudians" he disparaged, he substantiates his argument against *Civilization and Its Discontents* by turning back to Freud's own writings. Here he finds evidence that the drives and the instincts that Freud locates in biology are subject to change.

Drawing from Freud's *Moses and Monotheism, Beyond the Pleasure Principle,* and *The Future of an Illusion,* Marcuse argues that the biological foundation of the human psyche is given to mutation. Both the drives and the instincts emerge from and respond to specific historical conditions. In the story of human development that Freud tells, instincts first undergo "repressive modification" in response to a "struggle for existence." The pleasure principle gives way to the reality principle as a matter of survival. "If this is true," Marcuse reasons, "the repressive organization of the instincts in the struggle for existence would be due to *exogenous* factors – exogenous in the sense that they are not inherent in the 'nature' of the instincts but emerge from the specific historical conditions under which the instincts develop." In other words, Marcuse contends that "the nature of the instincts is historically acquired."[42] Change the "exogenous factors," change the "reality" of human existence, and the instincts themselves will be subject to change. Repression is thus not a precondition for civilization as such, Marcuse concludes, because the death drive is only operative under the pressure of specific exogenous conditions of scarcity. From Marcuse's point of view, repression is utterly redundant in the affluent society of the United States in the 1950s.

Marcuse complicates this view of repression in the very section of *Eros and Civilization* in which he explicitly introduces the idea of phylogenesis. The third chapter of the book is entitled "The Origin of the Repressed Civilization (Phylogenesis)." In this chapter, Marcuse essentially recounts Freud's argument in *Moses and Monotheism*. Surprisingly, the tone is largely affirmative. That is, even though he suggests that we can never prove the story of prehistoric man that Freud tells, Marcuse appears to accept Freud's view of the origin of repression in the murder of the primeval father. "We use Freud's anthropological speculations," Marcuse writes, only for their "*symbolic* value," and yet he never objects to Freud's account of the origin of repression or to Freud's claims for the inheritance of memory-traces of external events. Doubtless, Marcuse approves the "disturbing implications of Freud's theory" for liberalism. According to Marcuse, Freud's theory "reveals the power of the universal in and over the individuals," thus undermining "one of the strongest ideological fortifications of modern culture – namely, the notion of the autonomous individual." Yet the idea that "the individual lives the universal fate of mankind" hardly bodes well for the generation of revolutionary subjectivity or the potential for genuine change. The enabling assumption that Marcuse reads out of Freud's account, rather, is that even though the "universal fate is in the instinctual drives," those drives "are themselves subject to historical modification."[43] What matters to Marcuse, then, is not the phylogenesis of repressed memories but the transmission across generations of modifications to the drives.

Thus, according to Marcuse, Freud's mistake is neither his Lamarckism nor his account of the origin of repression; it is his "assumption that scarcity is as permanent as domination," an assumption belied by the current condition of affluence in the United States.[44] At this point, Marcuse observes, an abundance of resources and technological innovations precludes the need for constant, laborious work. Under these conditions, Eros is freed from its bondage to Thanatos, and repression is no longer the necessary condition of civilization. On the contrary, the nonrepressive desublimation of Eros potentiates new kinds of civilization. Yet in spite of these potentials, repression persists *as if* humankind continued to live in the conditions of scarcity that Freud describes as the determining historical fact of our biological nature. Marcuse explains this fact as the effect of the ideological imperatives of corporate capitalism. Instrumental reason legitimates the "performance principle." As a result, "body and mind are made into instruments of alienated labor," sexuality is put in the service of reproduction, and our very instincts and needs are deftly organized to support the powers that be.[45] Repression is thus no longer a biological condition but a social condition we can change.

Although the explicit language of phylogenesis disappears from Marcuse's discourse in the intervening decades between *Eros and Civilization* and *An Essay on Liberation,* the concept itself remains vital to his construction of revolutionary subjectivity. The Lamarckian memory-trace functions most powerfully in the chapter in *An Essay on Liberation* entitled "A Biological Basis for Socialism?" Here Marcuse argues that "the radical change which is to transform the existing society into a free society must reach into a dimension of the human existence hardly considered in Marxian theory – the biological dimension in which the vital, imperative needs and satisfactions of man assert themselves." We will never achieve a free society, he contends, until rebellion has "taken root in the very nature, the 'biology' of the individual." What we need, in short, is a "biological need for freedom." As he theorizes how the need for freedom can become biological, Marcuse seems to reduce biology to social and historical determination. He claims that "patterns of behavior" and "certain cultural needs" "can 'sink down' into the biology of man," creating a "second nature." Socially or culturally constructed needs, in other words, can become "organic."[46] Thus biology can serve as the basis for socialism but only as long as the right social instincts become biological. In order to change our biology, it seems, we have to change our society. Just as exogenous factors have modified our drives, they can modify our needs.

For Marcuse, however, there is no direct cause-effect relation between social modifications and biological mutation. On this point, he differentiates his view from the neo-Freudians who, he argues, mistakenly shift the emphasis from "biological to cultural factors: they have no conceptual basis outside the established system; their ideas and values are provided by the repressive system."[47] In other words, reducing biology to history brings us back to the trap of one-dimensional man, to a state of affairs that precludes the potential for the emergence of a new historical subject. In order to potentiate revolutionary subjectivity, Marcuse insists that biology is historically informed but ultimately irreducible to that history. Hence Marcuse's discourse introduces a gap between a "cultural need" and the "biology" into which it "sinks," and it is in this way that he renders human evolution the seat of the virtual. In the end, what biology does with this socially informed need remains unknown. Biology thus exceeds the rationality of the social. It refuses the instrumental reason of the established order, even when that ideology includes the social instinct for freedom. Hence, Marcuse's theory never actually arrives at a new historical subject as such. Revolutionary subjectivity remains on the horizon, a virtual potential of the phylogenetic transmission of our biologically altered needs. In this way, Marcuse's Lamarckism licenses his imagination of an escape from the realm of the possible. It allows Marcuse to account for the emergence of that which cannot be engineered: the unpredictable, the genuinely new, the truly revolutionary.

## POSTHUMAN FUTURES

As Marcuse turns to the evolution of the human species to theorize revolutionary potential, his work approaches – even embraces – what we now call the "posthuman." Thus Marcuse's ideas ultimately have more in common with the posthuman philosophy of contemporary feminist Elizabeth Grosz than with his neo-Freudian contemporaries in the 1960s. Like Marcuse, Grosz grounds her "politics of surprise, a politics that cannot be mapped out in advance," in the biological dynamism of the human species. Grosz, too, relies on an evolutionary theory that insists on the interaction of nature and culture, biology and human history. Where Marcuse turns back to Freud and thereby to a revised Lamarckism, Grosz returns to Darwin. In Darwin's writing, she discovers a construction of human evolution that accounts for radical ontological indeterminacy and thereby validates the incessant becoming of human being. As she writes, "Darwin has bequeathed to the humanities and social sciences, as well as the natural sciences, a new conception of life, defined not in terms of any given characteristics, any essence or being, but in terms of an openness to history, contingency, and events."[48] For this reason, Grosz identifies "nature" and "biology" as difference machines, irrational engines of the virtual. Posing Marcuse's "biology of revolution" beside Grosz's work reveals the extent to which he breaks with the retrograde humanism that detractors so often attribute to him. Ironically, the most oddball ideas in the Marcuse archive turn out to be the most contemporary.

Yet as the polarized reception that Grosz's work has received reveals, the similarities between Marcuse's theorization of revolution and contemporary posthumanism are unlikely to inspire a Marcuse revival among political activists today. In an historical context in which the social constructivism of gender and sexuality still reigns supreme, Grosz's call for "a feminism without end, without definitive goal, without pregiven aims or objects" remains deeply controversial.[49] Doubtless, Marcuse's assertion of a "biological basis of socialism" invites the same kinds of anxieties as Grosz's feminism. On the surface, it smacks of the kind of biological determinism that still haunts the memories of feminists and socialists alike. Likewise, both Grosz and Marcuse open the future to an indeterminacy that plays havoc with assumptions about the ideal society that have long informed progressive politics. What exactly, feminists and socialists might ask, are we fighting for? As long as we demand an answer to that question that addresses finite material conditions, Marcuse's philosophy is destined to disappoint.

"As much as and more than a thing of the past," Derrida writes, "... the archive should *call into question* the coming of the future." More literally than Derrida perhaps intended, Marcuse's theory of the emergence of revolutionary subjectivity creates an archive endowed with this power. It is the archive of the evolving human being. In Marcuse's hands, this human being becomes a storehouse of acquired needs and drives. Its power as an archive lies in its capacity to bring into being a future that is not only unknown but also unknowable as such. In Derrida's terms, the Marcusan archive points to an indeterminate future that "no longer come[s] under the order of knowledge or . . . a horizon of preknowledge." The future, in other words, is a virtual potential. As archive, however, Marcuse's evolving human being diverges finally from Derrida's conclusions. Specifically, it resists the "messianic" character that Derrida attributes to the Freudian archive. Certainly, the generation of revolutionary subjectivity from the Marcusan archive is loosed from that which is "*actually* present." Otherwise, the future would be shackled to the impoverished realm of the possible as defined by the established order. However, Marcuse's human archive is, in fact, related to what "will have been *actually* present."[50] In fact, the hope for a revolution that is not a return of the same depends, for Marcuse, on the events that the virtual *will have made* "actually present." It is for this reason that hope for the future, according to Marcuse, is less a matter of faith than of potentialities immanent to the world in which we live.

## NOTES

1. Quoted in Romano, "Occupy This."

2. Marcuse, *Eros and Civilization,* xiv, xxv.

3. Marcuse advances "non-repressive desublimation" in ibid., 208. For Foucault's most detailed exposition of the "repressive hypothesis," see his *History of Sexuality.*

4. Throughout, I use the terms "virtual" and "actual" as Gilles Deleuze defines them in *Difference and Repetition.* Specifically, Deleuze contrasts the virtual to the possible. In contrast to the process of realizing the possible, Deleuze writes, "The actualisation of the virtual . . . always takes place by difference, divergence or differenciation. Actualisation breaks with resemblance as a

process no less than it does with identity as a principle. Actual terms never resemble the singularities they incarnate. In this sense, actualization or differenciation is always a genuine creation. It does not result from any limitation of a pre-existing possibility" (ibid., 212).

5. Marcuse, *Essay,* 7–22.

6. Derrida, *Archive Fever,* 29, 19, 64.

7. "Professors," 38.

8. Lowenthal, "Unreason and Revolution," 71; and Howe, "Confrontation Politics," 44–45.

9. Kristol, "The Improbable Guru," 191, 194.

10. Gold, "California Left," 59.

11. That, of course, was Timothy Leary's refrain. Marcuse does write that "the awareness of need for such a revolution in perception, for a new sensorium, is perhaps the kernel of truth in the psychedelic search" (*Essay,* 37).

12. Marcuse, *One-Dimensional Man,* 252.

13. Ibid., 235.

14. Marcuse does often refer to Eros as the "Nirvana principle," and he identifies the desire to return to the womb as the desire for "Nirvana," but Nirvana, in both of these cases, marks an impossible goal, a desire beyond satisfaction.

15. In the debate that followed the 1958 publication of John Kenneth Galbraith's *The Affluent Society,* the book's title became part of a public discourse.

16. Marcuse, *Essay,* vii; and Marcuse, *Eros and Civilization,* 155.

17. Marcuse, *One-Dimensional Man,* 41, 2.

18. Marcuse, *Essay,* 3–4.

19. Marcuse, *One-Dimensional Man,* 256, 31.

20. Marcuse, *Essay,* viii.

21. While I am using the terms "virtual" and "actual" as Gilles Deleuze defines them in *Difference and Repetition,* I do not mean to suggest that Marcuse was proto-Deleuzian. Nor do I contend that Marcuse's account of the potential for emergence of the new converges on all points with Deleuze. However, Marcuse's bid for escaping the confines of the possible depends upon the generation of the virtual as a potentiality whose effects are both inconceivable and indeterminate. See Deleuze, *Difference and Repetition,* 208–212.

22. Marcuse, *One-Dimensional Man,* 7.

23. *One-Dimensional Man* testifies to a sense of entrapment. On the one hand, Marcuse maintains that "forces and tendencies exist which may . . . explode society," but he also insists that "advanced industrial society is capable of containing qualitative change for the foreseeable

future" (ibid., xv). Thus rather than ending the book with a call to action, he ends the book with the melancholic yearning of Walter Benjamin: "It is only for the sake of those without hope that hope is given to us" (ibid., 257).

24. Ibid., 225. Marcuse identifies the Great Refusal as the extant power of the aesthetic.

25. Ibid., 169.

26. Marcuse, *Eros and Civilization,* 130; and Marcuse, *One-Dimensional Man,* 228.

27. Marcuse, *Eros and Civilization,* 224.

28. Marcuse, "Repressive Tolerance," 102–103. I am referring here to Frantz Fanon's exposition in "On Violence," which appears as the first chapter of *The Wretched of the Earth,* 1–51.

29. Marcuse, "Repressive Tolerance," 81, 82.

30. Ibid., 112.

31. Ibid., 111.

32. Ibid., 109, 98–99.

33. Howe, "Confrontation Politics," 45; and Lowenthal, "Unreason and Revolution," 57.

34. Slavet, "Freud's 'Lamarckism,'" 39.

35. Freud, *Moses and Monotheism,* 127–128.

36. Slavet, "Freud's 'Lamarckism,'" 39.

37. Hart, *Social Science,* 12.

38. Freud, *Moses and Monotheism,* 170.

39. Marcuse, *Essay,* 10.

40. These terms circulate in *An Essay on Liberation* and in *Eros and Civilization.*

41. Marcuse, *Eros and Civilization,* 17.

42. Ibid., 134, 138.

43. Ibid., 60, 57, 58.

44. Ibid., 134.

45. Ibid., 46.

46. Marcuse, *Essay,* 16–17, 4–5, 10–11.

47. Marcuse, *Eros and Civilization,* 5–6.

48. Grosz, *Time Travels,* 8.

49. Ibid., 183.

50. Derrida, *Archive Fever,* 33–34, 72.

## SELECTED BIBLIOGRAPHY

Deleuze, Gilles. *Difference and Repetition.* Translated by Paul Patton. New York: Columbia University Press, 1994.

Derrida, Jacques. *Archive Fever: A Freudian Impression.* Translated by Eric Prenowitz. Chicago: University of Chicago Press, 1998.

Fanon, Frantz. *The Wretched of the Earth.* Translated by Richard Philcox. New York: Grove Press, 2004.

Foucault, Michel. *History of Sexuality: An Introduction.* New York: Random House, 1978.

Freud, Sigmund. *Moses and Monotheism.* New York: Random House, 1939.

——. *Totem and Taboo.* Edited by James Strachey. New York: Norton & Co., 1950.

Galbraith, John Kenneth. *The Affluent Society.* New York: Houghton Mifflin, 1998.

Gold, Herbert. "California Left: Mao, Marx, et Marcuse!" *Saturday Evening Post,* October 19, 1969.

Grosz, Elizabeth. *Time Travels: Feminism, Nature, Power.* Durham, N.C.: Duke University Press, 2005.

Hart, Mitchell Bryan. *Social Science and the Politics of Modern Jewish Identity.* Stanford, Calif.: Stanford University Press, 2000.

Howe, Irving, ed. *Beyond the New Left.* New York: McCall Publishing Co., 1965.

——. "Confrontation Politics Is a Dangerous Game." In *Beyond the New Left,* edited by Irving Howe, 40–54. New York: McCall Publishing Co., 1965.

Kristol, Irving. "The Improbable Guru of Surrealist Politics." *Fortune,* July 1969, 191–194.

Lowenthal, Richard. "Unreason and Revolution." In *Beyond the New Left,* edited by Irving Howe, 55–84. New York: McCall Publishing Co., 1965.

Marcuse, Herbert. *Eros and Civilization: A Philosophical Inquiry into Freud.* Boston: Beacon Press, 1955.

——. *An Essay on Liberation.* Boston: Beacon Press, 1974.

——. *One-Dimensional Man.* Boston: Beacon Press, 1964.

——. "Repressive Tolerance." In *A Critique of Pure Tolerance,* edited by Robert Paul Wolff, Barrington Moore, Jr., and Herbert Marcuse, 81–117. Boston: Beacon Press, 1965.

"Professors: One-Dimensional Philosopher." *Time,* March 1968, 38–40.

Romano, Carlin. "Occupy This: Is It Comeback Time for Herbert Marcuse?" *Chronicle of Higher Education,* December 11, 2011. Web.

Slavet, Eliza. "Freud's 'Lamarckism' and the Politics of Racial Science." *Journal of the History of Biology* 41 (2008): 37–80.

Wolff, Robert Paul, Barrington Moore, Jr., and Herbert Marcuse. *A Critique of Pure Tolerance.* Boston: Beacon Press, 1965.

5

# THE MADNESS OF SLAVOJ ŽIŽEK

*Dennis Allen*

There are literally thousands of clips of Slavoj Žižek available on the Internet, but perhaps the most entertaining one is a YouTube excerpt from Astra Taylor's succinctly entitled 2005 documentary, *Žižek!* Posted as "Philosophy from a Bed View (by Žižek)," the clip seems singularly apt for our purposes if only because, in the process of defining the project of philosophy, Žižek touches on one of the key questions that this collection of essays is intended to address: What is the relation between reason and unreason? Sliding across a series of binaries, Žižek articulates the difference between "true" philosophers and "madmen" as the difference between metaphysics and hermeneutics. His meditations are worth quoting at some length:

> What is philosophy? Philosophy is not what some people think, some crazy exercise in absolute truth, and then you can adopt, you know, this skeptical attitude: "We, through scientists, are dealing with actual, measurable, solvable problems. Philosophers just ask stupid metaphysical questions and so on, play with absolute truth, which we all know is inaccessible." No, I think philosophy's a very modest discipline. Philosophy asks a different question, the true philosophy. How does a philosopher approach the problem of freedom? It's not, "Are we free or not? Is there God or not?" It asks a simple question which would be called a hermeneutic question: "What does it mean to be free?" So this is what philosophy basically does. It just asks: "When we

> use certain notions, when we do certain acts and so on and so on, what is the implicit horizon of understanding?" It doesn't ask these stupid ideal questions: "Is there truth?" No. The question is: "What do you mean when you say this is true?" So you can see it's a very modest thing, philosophy. Philosophers are not the madmen who search for some eternal truth and so on and so on.

So madmen ask unanswerable questions with inaccessible answers, like "What is truth?," while philosophers interrogate the "horizon of understanding" of any utterance: "What do you mean when you say this is true?" The difference between insanity and philosophy thus becomes the difference between the absolute and the contingent, the eternal and the historically situated, between Truth and "what do you mean?" Moreover, the "crazy" metaphysical questions, the questions that true philosophers wouldn't ask, are made to seem even more crazy through an implicit contrast with that touchstone of post-Enlightenment ideas of rationality: the scientific method. In contrast to science, which deals with measurable problems that have solutions, there's no point in seeking an absolute truth that is, in its very nature, unknowable. That does sound kind of crazy.

What Žižek is doing here, of course, is responding to a popular conception of philosophy as abstract speculation. Perhaps the best example of this notion can be provided by the Philosophy Department at my own university, which, faced with shrinking enrollments and dwindling resources in an era in which higher education is increasingly understood as job training, launched a highly successful series of monthly public forums called The Question, designed primarily to demonstrate the link between "deep philosophical questions" and contemporary "controversies and decisions." Each month a huge banner on the bridge over a major traffic artery through campus asks the deep question that will be addressed in that month's forum, such as "What is race?" or "Do we have a soul?" Now, these are clearly the wrong sorts of questions, and not simply because they bear very little relation to the actual questions asked by most college students, which nowadays tend to run more along the lines of "How will I ever pay off my student loans?" For Žižek, the Philosophy Department's questions are the wrong questions because they raise the discussion to an unanswerable transcendental level, and what I take to be the main point of the videoclip is Žižek's articulation of the project of "true" philosophy as a different sort of enterprise from metaphysical speculation: as, instead, the critical/interpretive interrogation of our knowledge itself. In other words, the question should be not "What is race?" but "What do we mean when we say race exists?"

I think this clip provides a good starting point for an analysis of Žižek's conception not only of how philosophy should work but also of how rational thought functions, always one of Žižek's major concerns. Before we go any further, however, there's one detail about the video that I need to add, especially because it is itself fairly oddball. The scene from which the clip is taken features Žižek sitting up in bed, shirtless, with the covers pulled up to his waist while he's delivering his reflections.

Now, it seems fairly obvious that this may not be the best way of presenting a philosopher who is insisting that philosophers are not insane. Yet, I think that there may be a method to what seems like madness here, which we can understand by focusing on what this clip does, as well as on what Žižek actually says. In the pursuit of such an analysis, I'll begin with a review of Žižek's interrogation of the nature of reason, or, more aptly, his assertion that unreason, in the form of ideology, always returns within the process of rational thought, haunting it at its core. What I hope to show is that this dynamic is also true, inevitably, of Žižek's thought itself, which must be based on certain blind spots or omissions in order to articulate itself. Both the content and the form of Žižek's philosophical work force us to reexamine the project of academic discourse itself and to interrogate the extent to which it is based on reason. Perhaps most crucially, however, this essay will also address the central question raised by the video: Why is Žižek in bed?

## THE UNREASON OF REASON

We can begin, then, by looking at the basic premises of Žižek's own hermeneutics, and one of Žižek's recent and relatively "easy" texts, 2009's *First as Tragedy, Then as Farce,* provides a good example of his philosophical project. Clearly designed as a crossover book aimed at a mass market (or as much of a mass market as a book labeled "philosophy/politics" is likely to have in America), the book addresses the reasons for the current economic crisis. Since this is Marxist/political Žižek rather than Lacanian/psychoanalytic Žižek or even cultural studies Žižek, the answer is, of course, capitalism, or, more properly, the ideology of capitalism, and the proposed solution is a reconceptualized notion of communism. What is most relevant for our purposes, however, is less the exact content of the book than its function as an example of Žižek's analytic assumptions and method, which, at their most basic level, are essentially unchanged since *The Sublime Object of Ideology.* While the text directly asks one of the wrong questions ("What is ideology?"), the discussion itself threads through a series of the right questions, which are situated in a particular historico-ideological context, such as "Why do the members of the Tea Party act against their own best interests?" Ultimately, the text is designed less to convey the specific answers to these questions, although they are important, and more to illustrate, precisely, a critique of the "horizon of understanding" in which what we take to be reason functions.

Thus, one way to read *First as Tragedy* is as yet another example of Žižek's ongoing project of demystification, his continual unmasking of the unreason of reason. The first half of the book deals specifically with the continued dominance of the ideology of laissez-faire capitalism after the economic meltdown despite the fact that it is precisely this set of beliefs – that capital will behave rationally, that government regulation stifles economic growth – that caused the financial crisis in the first place. Moving through a series of examples ranging from pronouncements by George Soros to the Tea Party, Žižek articulates his standard argument: even when an idea can be shown to be false, and even if we are overtly cynical about it, we will still act as if the idea were true, because it is based on a deeper belief, an ideological fantasy, that is designed precisely to conceal something that we cannot admit to ourselves. His classic formulation for this is: "They know very well, but still they are doing it." In the case of contemporary capitalist ideology, of course, that bit of the Real that we can't acknowledge is class antagonism, which, as Žižek notes, currently takes the form of the growing economic disparity between the extremely wealthy and everyone else. Because conscious awareness of class antagonism would call the entire system into question, there are thus a variety of unconscious or unexamined beliefs that, depending on your conscious assumptions, allow you to suture over that antagonism.

As one might expect, contemporary politics provides a good example of this. Public Policy Polling is a North Carolina–based company that specializes in opinion surveys focused on political races. In addition to its usual research, the company will occasionally do a more lighthearted poll, like the one it did in March 2011 in which pollsters asked respondents to choose between Charlie Sheen and a number of political figures as a candidate for president. Now, Charlie Sheen is apparently one of the least popular celebrities, with only a 10 percent approval rating and a 67 percent disapproval rating that crosses party lines, and the news story that emerged out of this poll was that independent voters would choose Sheen for president over Sarah Palin (41 percent to 36 percent).[1] In and of itself, this is a fairly interesting result, but the comments posted in response to the story on the company's website are even more amusing. Most of these decried the poll as "stupid," but one anonymous commentator then went on to make a larger point about democracy and the American political process: "They ridiculed Obama when he started his 2008 presidential campaign, and he is now our president. Don't write off anyone in America – a country of unparallel [*sic*] possibilities."[2]

In a sense, this quote provides the perfect summary of the first half of *First as Tragedy,* and the only problem with it is that an ideological analysis of it is almost too obvious to require explication. "Anonymous" is, of course, appealing here to one of the founding premises of American culture, the ideology of the land of opportunity, the notion that hard work and talent will be rewarded with success, and, to be fair, Palin's meteoric rise from relative obscurity as the governor of a sparsely populated state to the national spotlight as a vice presidential candidate in 2004 can indeed be taken as a reflection of this principle at work. Yet, as Žižek would note, this perspective leaves something out or, rather, is designed precisely to conceal that omitted element, although Žižek always insists that we live in a cynical age and that such assertions reverse almost immediately into an awareness of their opposite. In this case, because the symptom appears on the surface of the text, in the typographical error by which "unparalleled" is transposed into "unparallel," the conventional platitudes of bootstrap capitalism and of democratic equality are openly inverted into a gesture toward a "truer," more cynical perspective. This is the liberal political notion that the playing field is not really level, that the children of the 1 percent and the children of the 99 percent do not start out in life with the same set of possibilities, or, to return to Sarah Palin, this is the view that her rise to national prominence had little to do with any innate talents or abilities she may have had and much more to do with a calculated set of decisions, themselves very cynical, made by a small number of people in the Republican Party's inner circle about the selection of a vice presidential candidate for strategic reasons (to appeal to the ultraconservative portion of the base, for example, or to counter Hillary Clinton's popularity as a woman candidate).

At the risk of overreading, I'll just add that the fact that the symptom here is precisely an omission (the missing letters "ed") gestures nicely toward the continual Žižekian reminder that both of these perspectives are incomplete and can only constitute themselves through an unconscious omission. In the case of the ideology of the land of opportunity, what is elided is the obvious reality of social inequality, but Žižek's point is always that the cynical reading – here, the liberal reading – also omits something: in this case (and this is the point of the second half of *First as Tragedy*), the cynical view is also wrong, and not simply because a foreign-born Muslim raised by Al Qaeda did, after all, become president. Finally, the cynical view is wrong because it fails to fully engage with the Real of class antagonism. If what most liberals want is a redistribution of the wealth or of "possibility," this perspective, however critical, still takes place within the horizon of capitalist ideology, not simply because it implicitly appeals to a bourgeois value system predicated on ideas of equity or equality but, far more importantly, because it continues to assume the necessity of capitalism and does not truly confront the blind spots inherent in that assumption, including a recognition that class antagonism may be inextricable from capitalism itself.

If we take this example as an accurate illustration of Žižek's premises and method, then we can summarize these by saying that, regardless of the topic at hand, Žižek's project is always to demonstrate the unreason of any assertion that presents itself as reason, to articulate the blindnesses and occlusions that make the statement possible, and to uncover the absence at its core that, if only because it is an absence, is always something other than reason. Seen in this light, Žižek's conception of "true" philosophy is thus not just hermeneutics but a particular version of it. Based on Žižek's analytic practice, the right sort of philosophical question is not simply "What do we mean when we say *x* is true?" but, more accurately, "What are the assumptions that lead us to think *x* is true?" As such, the emphasis in his discussion of the "horizon of understanding" has to be placed not on "understanding," on what we (think we) know, but on "horizon," on the conceptual preconditions for the way we think in the first place. Žižek's hermeneutics is finally less about knowledge or interpretation than about what we will find plausible. To put it as simply as possible: this is a hermeneutics that is not about understanding but about belief. The true Žižekian question is finally not "What is race?" or even "What do we mean when we say race exists?" but, finally, "Why do we believe in the existence of race?"

## THE REASON OF UNREASON

If such a hermeneutics provides a clear interrogation of rational thought and, by extension, of the enterprises of philosophy in particular and academic discourse in general, it also serves to undermine our conception of the philosopher himself. The problem is not simply the familiar post-structuralist conundrum, one that most contemporary undergraduates recognize immediately and that is usually phrased this way: While the concept of the horizon of understanding clearly suggests that there is no transcendental truth, isn't the assertion that there is no transcendental truth itself presented as a transcendental truth? Here that recursive moment also involves the rational subject so that we can rephrase the previous question a bit more specifically: If all beliefs are ideologically inflected, isn't this also true of Žižek's beliefs? In what sense can we take what he says to be itself beyond ideology in a space that we can designate as the site of both truth and disinterested reason? Or, to put the matter in the formulation that Žižek himself would use, if Žižek knows very well that every truth is ideological, is partial and contingent, why does he speak as if he doesn't know this, making apparently universal pronouncements about, say, what philosophy is or is not?

The immediate answer to the question is that Žižek does know this. In both *First as Tragedy* and the film *Žižek!,* he points out that many leftists expect him to identify a political agenda, to delineate a path that can take us beyond capitalism, although, he continues in *Žižek!,* "What do I know?" Typically, his response to this situation is to identify the position into which he's placed as that of the *sujet supposé savoir,* the one presumed to know, to remind us that this position is always the result of a projection, and then to turn the question around: What does this say about the ideological fantasies of his audience? As Adrian Johnston points out, this denial of the position of the *sujet* has an added benefit, since, once one subtracts the ideological critique from Žižek's political writings, there is not much left that could stand as a political agenda. As Johnston says, it may not even be clear to Žižek what Žižek desires politically.[3] It's apt, for more reasons than one, then, that Žižek makes his own rhetorical position a matter more of belief than of truth.

Yet there is, I think, another twist here. However much Žižek may disclaim the position of the *sujet,* if only because that position is impossible to occupy, I would suggest that, in certain situations, the position of the *sujet* is also impossible not to occupy. One of these situations is academic discourse, which, whether in the form of the lecture or the written text, is presented, by convention, from a position of mastery, from the position of the one presumed to know. However much I erase myself from the text and however much I qualify my assertions, the rhetorical stance is that I know the truth and that I am telling it to you. When in the clip Žižek says, "Philosophers are not the madmen who search for some eternal truth," he's making an apparently universal pronouncement, even if his discursive position as the sujet is contradicted by the content of the statement itself. To put this in slightly different terms, then: even if the aim of Žižek's discourse is always to uncover the unreason – the ideology – that shapes what we take to be reason, the form of that discourse, the rhetorical stance from which it must issue, continues to insist on the possibility of a transcendental truth that is beyond ideology.

## THE PHILOSOPHER'S NEW CLOTHES

I'm not catching Žižek out on anything here. He knows this too, just as all academics know it on some level. To put it in the terms with which I began, the persistence of the position of the *sujet* is the inevitable intrusion of the illusions of metaphysics into Žižek's project of a hermeneutics, and it is part of the reason why, even when we know that reason is always inextricably based on unreason or that "truth" is always ideological, we are able to pretend that this is not the case, at least in those instances where we too believe. Yet, Žižek's own awareness of this becomes a matter for further consideration. The point is not simply that, despite his disclaimers, Žižek is still forced to occupy the position of the *sujet*. Even more importantly, here again Žižek himself becomes a textbook example of his own critique of the subject of ideology: although he knows very well that the rhetorical stance of mastery is a false one, still he is doing it. By the same token, his audience, seeing Žižek as an avatar of truth or reason or looking to him to articulate a political agenda, should know very well that he can't really be the one presumed to know and yet act as if they don't know that. The question that follows, as is always the case in a Žižekian analysis, is: "What, then, is the blind spot that allows Žižek to act as the *sujet* even though he knows very well that nobody is the *sujet*?" Perhaps not too surprisingly, I will argue that Žižek's blind spot, what he must forget, is the existence of the Real, but, to understand that, we first need to answer another question, the one with which this essay began: "Why, in this video, is Žižek in bed?"

The obvious answer to that last question is that the "bed view" of Žižek depends in part on certain very basic conventions, both of film in general and of the documentary in particular. Shot in the cinema verité style, *Žižek!* simply follows the philosopher around with a handheld camera, recording his reflections or observations, and, in accord with the premises of the documentary genre, the aim of *Žižek!* seems to be, precisely, documentation, to provide a more complete portrait of its subject than can be obtained by attending one of his lectures or reading his work. Thus, in classic direct cinema fashion, the film records Žižek's thoughts wherever he happens to be: on the street or having lunch in a café or even in bed. Moreover, the Žižek who is the subject of the film is Media Žižek, the Žižek who has an international cult following, which explains all those YouTube videos.[4] This is the Žižek of the exclamation point in *Žižek!,* the Žižek whose speech to Occupy Wall Street in Zuccotti Park on October 11, 2011, received extensive coverage by the press.[5] Taylor's film explicitly presents this Žižek as "the wildman of theory," and it would certainly be in keeping with that image that Žižek would allow himself to be filmed in a way that, if it's not exactly shocking, is at least somewhat unexpected. Moreover, since this is Intellectual Celebrity Žižek, and since celebrity status is now almost entirely dependent on a self-referential loop in which you are primarily a celebrity because the camera is always on you and the camera is always on you because you are a celebrity, then this is the intellectual version of that: what Žižek has to tell us is sufficiently important that we have to keep the camera rolling at all times. Speaking in terms of celebrity culture, this is a philosopher's version of a sex tape.

Yet, what's striking about Taylor's film is where it deviates from most biographical documentaries, which, in their desire for completeness, usually attempt to capture their subject's psychological interiority or subjective depth.[6] Instead, the Žižek that Taylor presents is almost entirely the public Žižek, Žižek as celebrity philosopher. In effect, this is precisely Žižek as the one presumed to know, endlessly relating his thoughts, and what is striking about the film is how it continually veers away from any extended presentation of the private Žižek or "Žižek the man." For example, although we briefly see him in his apartment with his son, the scene almost immediately shifts to Žižek providing an ideological critique of his son's toys so that the philosopher steps in in place of the father. In fact, the scene does not even make his domestic situation clear. (Where is his wife?) In a sense, it's surprising how little we actually learn about Žižek in *Žižek!,* which seems designed to respect his insistence, quoted in the film, that "I like philosophy as an anonymous job." All of this makes seeing Žižek

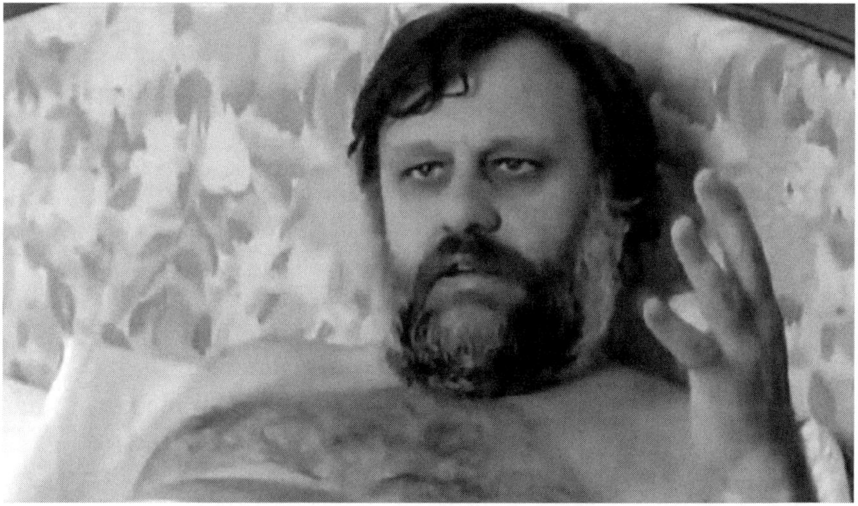

in bed even less expected, but I would argue that the scene is actually a lure or a distraction. Initially, it seems to take us even closer to the film's subject, to give us an even more intimate portrait of him, both figuratively and literally, an effect enhanced by the use of a zoom shot to bring his face into close-up during the scene.

Yet, despite the visual presentation of what we might call Žižek's bedroom eyes, the focus still is on the aural, on what he is saying. In direct contrast to the illusion of personal intimacy the scene seems designed to create, this is once again the transcendental philosophical *sujet* speaking to us, talking about the nature of philosophy no less. In a certain sense, Žižek himself is not here at all.

Except that, in another sense, he is. It's the tiny moment of shock or surprise when the viewer encounters Žižek in bed that tells us where he actually might be. That moment, or the lingering sense of oddity that may come after it, suggests that Žižek himself acts here as what Roland Barthes has called a punctum, that irrelevant detail that stands outside of the intended meaning and the representational codes of a visual image and speaks directly to us, often affectively, in a way that eludes interpretation.[7] If the intended point of the scene is, as we've seen, to have Žižek speak as the *sujet* about philosophy, and if a secondary intention seems to be to bolster Žižek's image as an edgy and groundbreaking figure, the scene nonetheless does not seem to be able to contain or control all the energies it unleashes. As Barthes says, "No analysis would be of any use" in perceiving the punctum, since it is "the passage of a void" that resists "the possibility of a rhetorical expansion."[8] In other words, for Barthes, the punctum is equivalent to what, in the work of Jacques Lacan, would be the site of the eruption of an awareness of the unsymbolizable Real into the culturally coded meanings of the image. As such, Žižek's body, his sheer corporeal materiality, opens onto this void here, points toward a place that is not simply beyond reason but where, by definition, reason cannot go.

To understand how Žižek's body acts as a punctum that gestures toward a space beyond symbolization, we'll need to take a closer look at it, although, fortunately, only in the figurative sense. The point is not that material reality simply stands as the Real in contrast to the abstract meditations of philosophical thought. Material reality is itself already part of the Symbolic Order, always heavily symbolized. Thus, the "set," if you will, of this shot can easily be understood as a group of signifiers that designate "bedroom," and we could go on from there to read it in terms of cultural codes of national and class differences in taste, modes of decorating hotel rooms as opposed to bedrooms in private homes, and so on. Nor is it the materiality of the unclothed body that resists symbolization. We can think of any number of celebrities (Ryan Gosling and Kristen Stewart come immediately to mind) whose corporeality is part of what Barthes calls the studium, the intended meaning of many of the images we see of them. In fact, both of these points suggest ways in which Žižek's body does, indeed, "make sense." One fairly obvious, perhaps even automatic, response to the scene, especially given that Žižek is in bed and at least partially naked, is for the viewer to do a quick assessment, if only on a visceral level, of his attractiveness. This would certainly be an affective response that doesn't seem to be the intended meaning of the scene, yet even this reaction doesn't really invoke the ineffable, if only because any consideration of the question "Slavoj Žižek: Hot or not?" simply pulls his body back within a set of (personal and cultural) erotic codes, making it once again symbolizable. By the same token, we might see this scene as a literal representation of that old philosophical staple, the mind/body problem, noting the contradiction between the transcendental truths uttered by the sujet and the contingent, particular body from which they issue. Once again, however, such a reading serves to fit the body into a familiar conceptual paradigm, as one pole of a binary in which it stands as matter as opposed to thought.

Still, there's a way in which Žižek's body here seems to stubbornly exceed any interpretation we can give to it, and I would locate the evidence of that precisely in the response it provokes in the viewer, in the initial shock or surprise at the image, and in our lingering sense of the comedy or oddity of it as the scene continues. Perhaps the best way to understand how Žižek's body resists "the possibility of a rhetorical expansion," how it functions here to point toward the Real, is to realize that it acts primarily as a distraction. Even if we try to attribute meaning to Žižek's body by analyzing it, it finally works in the scene to subtly and continually draw our attention away from the scene's meaning, whether we take that to be the content of the philosophical discourse itself or the filmmaker's apparent intent ("Here is Žižek philosophizing"). It's that very process of distraction, which does not itself mean anything at all but which gestures toward a place beyond meaning, that serves to remind us of the existence of the Real, of what lies beyond the possibility of cultural coding and rational thought. Nor is this an isolated example. Such distractions, uninterpretable intrusions of the corporeality of Žižek into the scene of philosophical discourse, happen more often than you might think. In the hour-long video of his presentation for Authors@Google, a series of lunchtime talks for employees at Google headquarters by such nonbusiness people as John Searle and Bernard-Henri Lévy, Žižek repeats the characteristic gesture of pulling on his nose so frequently that the clip becomes almost unwatchable.[9]

## PHILOSOPHY IN THE BEDROOM

Just as Žižek's philosophical enterprise is always to uncover the irrationality, the ideology, that underlies reason, it's precisely in moments where Žižek's corporeal materiality creates a sense of distraction or discomfort that Žižek himself inadvertently reminds us of what he must forget in order to be "Žižek the Philosopher." Žižek's gestures while giving a talk are unconscious, of course, just as it's clear in Taylor's film that, expounding on the mission of philosophy, he's literally forgotten that he's in bed, and I would argue that this obliviousness about his corporeality stands as the perfect synecdoche for a certain larger amnesia on Žižek's part that makes the rhetorical stance of the *sujet* possible in the first place: a repression of any awareness of the Real, which, in this context, we might best understand, following Sarah Kay, as "the resistance offered to thought by material reality," although it can simply be seen as the very limitations of reason itself.[10] We can even read those instances where Žižek is Žižek "in person" (in the partial nudity of the "bed view" or in the compulsive gestures) as a sort of return of the repressed, as the literal, material intrusion into the scene of philosophy of a distracting "something more" that the philosophy does not and cannot address.[11]

Yet, if *what* Žižek must ignore or forget in order to take the position of the one presumed to know is the existence of the Real, of the unsymbolizable remainder that makes that position impossible, we might now ask *how* he forgets it. In both Lacan and Žižek, of course, the Real cannot be confronted directly, and in a classic Lacanian analysis, the subject focuses instead on the *objet petit a,* an object of desire that sutures over the sense of constitutive lack produced by the Real, a concept that Žižek's work glosses extensively. As we've seen, in Žižek's political analyses, the place of the *objet petit a* is taken by the ideological fantasy, the unconscious belief that persists beneath the cynical calculations of reason, but, in Žižek's more psychoanalytic register, he presents the *objet petit a* as the site of *jouissance,* of a surplus enjoyment that functions as a substitute for the lack of satisfaction, the incompleteness, of the Symbolic order. As such, the obvious question thus becomes: What is Žižek's *objet petit a*? I'd like to suggest that this too is evident in the excerpt from Taylor's film and lies in the very fact that Žižek is talking, although, to be clear, I don't think it can be found in the content of what is said or even in the phenomenality of the voice, in the sound or the material aspects of his speech. Rather, Žižek's *objet petit a* is the very act of speaking or writing itself, the production of discourse.

By all accounts, Žižek is a compulsive talker, a point that features crucially in Robert Boynton's oft-cited and gossipy character study of him published in 1998 in *Lingua Franca.* Meeting Žižek for tea in London, Boynton reports that Žižek launched into a monologue almost before he sat down, talking nonstop and speeding up even as he asked Boynton to cut him off. The effect is overwhelming, Boynton says, even for Žižek himself, noting Žižek's tendency toward "head problems" and panic attacks. In a nice touch, Boynton suggests that even a scholar as verbose as Judith Butler may also find the stream of Žižekian discourse to be a bit much. Boynton quotes her as saying that "discussing Hegel and Lacan is like breathing for Slavoj. I've seen him talk about theory for four hours straight without flagging." Boynton then adds, "As his eyes dart around the room and his manic monologue becomes even more frantic, I fear that I may be his last interviewer. Žižek is like a performance artist who is terrified of abandoning the stage; once he starts talking, he seems unable to stop."[12] As such, it's not really surprising that more than 80 percent of Astra Taylor's film consists simply of Žižek talking.

I will come back to Boynton's implicit diagnosis of obsessive-compulsive disorder, but, for the moment, I'll note that, although Boynton says that Žižek talks the way he writes, it might be more accurate to say that he writes the way he talks. Certainly, there's a nonstop quality to Žižek's written work too. An amazingly prolific writer, Žižek has published more than sixty books since *Sublime Object* appeared in 1989. To take only the recent past as an example and to focus only on book publication, ignoring occasional essays and articles, *Living in the End Times,* 432 pages long, appeared in May 2010, followed by *Less than Nothing: Hegel and the Shadow of Dialectical Materialism,* 1,056 pages, in May 2012. In between, the afterword to the paperback edition of *End Times,* published in April 2011, adds an additional 79 pages to that text. Finally, *The Year of Dreaming Dangerously,* a mere 128 pages, came out in October 2012, bringing his total number of pages in print to nearly 1,700 during a two-and-a-half-year period. As John Gray notes in a review of *Living in the End Times* and *Less than Nothing,* one of the problems with determining Žižek's stance on any issue is "his inordinate prolixity, the stream of texts that no one could read in their entirety, if only because the torrent never ceases flowing."[13]

This sense of an ongoing textual flow is enhanced by the fact that the structure of Žižek's writing seems to owe as much to the rambling informality of everyday speech as it does to the conventions of academic writing. Certainly, Boynton's characterization of Žižek's conversation as a "nonstop pastiche of Hegelian philosophy, Marxist dialectics, and Lacanian jargon leavened with references to film noir, dirty jokes, and pop culture ephemera" anticipates a number of the critical complaints that have been leveled at his prose style.[14] For example, Sarah Kay, noting that Žižek often approaches an argument obliquely and that his examples have a tendency to take on a life of their own and move beyond their typical function as simple illustrations of a point, says that his writing can seem "utterly chaotic."[15] Similarly, Geoffrey Galt Harpham, heavily critical of Žižek's failure to follow the conventions of academic writing, may go too far when he argues that Žižek's work is "a stream of nonconsecutive units arranged in arbitrary sequences that solicit a sporadic and discontinuous attention," but there is nonetheless some truth to this charge.[16] Certainly, Žižek's style is heavily metonymic, moving endlessly from topic to topic, and he refuses the standard academic technique of periodic summaries designed to demarcate the stages of an overarching argument. Ultimately, this creates the impression of a certain logorrhea, a continuous stream of written discourse whose segmentation, not just into separate chapters but into separate books, begins to seem artificial. Much of Žižek's recent work, in which he struggles in book after book with the problem of redefining communism so that it provides a viable alternative to an increasingly destructive (and self-destructive) capitalism, thus reads like parts of one endless, ongoing monologue. Simply put, Žižek does run on.

I won't attempt a full-scale psychoanalytic reading of Žižek here, if only because he has already undergone analysis, and with no less an analyst than Jacques-Alain Miller, but if we take the Real in this context as, precisely, the very existence of an unsymbolizable "something more" that reveals the very limits of reason or knowledge or truth, and Žižek's *objet petit a* is the production of discourse, then it's striking that Žižek's logorrhea provides an almost textbook case of his concept of jouissance as surplus enjoyment, his adaptation of Lacan's notion of the *plus-de-jouir.* As the source of Žižek's surplus enjoyment, this discourse would be obsessively compelled (Žižek always stresses the role of the superego here), which would certainly explain why an interviewer like Boynton might depict you as manic, and, because the *objet* is only a substitute and because satisfaction can thus never be obtained, it makes sense that Žižek's production of discourse must be endless. Moreover, Žižek himself seems to illustrate his insistence that surplus enjoyment is the site not only of pleasure but of pain.[17] This is the sort of thing that would lead to an obvious delight in endlessly professing but that might also cause what Boynton calls "head problems." Most interesting, however, especially given our concern to find the "real Žižek," is Žižek's continual assertion that the dissolution of the *objet* and the confrontation with the Real lead to a "nauseating" encounter with the void.[18] As such, if the production of discourse is Žižek's objet, then Boynton's portrayal of him as a performance artist terrified to leave the stage is singularly apt. As Žižek himself notes in Taylor's film, "My eternal fear is that if, for one brief moment, I stop talking, the whole spectacular appearance will disintegrate. People would think there is nothing and nobody there. This is my fear, as if I was nothing who pretended to be somebody." Žižek then adds that his goal is thus "to fascinate people enough so that they don't notice there is nothing." Deprived of the *objet,* "the real Žižek" turns out to be the Real Žižek.

At this point, it does become tempting to attempt to plumb the Žižekian unconscious. For example, since Žižek posits that his discourse can be the *objet petit a* for others as well as for himself, we might analyze Žižek's "desire to be desired," one classic Lacanian response to the sense that you are nothing. Yet, for our purposes, it seems more useful to approach the identification of discourse as Žižek's *objet petit a* from a slightly different direction. If we remember that the *objet petit a* is always an object of desire, then we can see Žižek's unconscious selection of discourse as itself a symptom, and we might then ask: What does Žižek want? What does Žižek's choice of discourse as an *objet* tell us about Žižek's desire? The answer, I think, is suggested both by what his *objet* is and by his "eternal fear" that there is nothing and nobody behind that discourse. What Žižek wants is simply the possibility of philosophy or reason or academic discourse itself. Ultimately, this desire is, in fact, the desire for two related things: for the possibility of a "full discourse," a discourse without an unsymbolizable remainder, and for the possibility of a subject without lack, of a *sujet.* Simply put, what Žižek wants is the possibility of the sort of metaphysics that he disavows as impossible in the quote with which we began. And this desire thus answers the questions raised by that quotation: if Žižek knows very well that there is an uninterpretable Real and that nobody can be the *sujet,* the blind spot or screen that allows him to forget this (and that crystallizes his desire that this not be the case) is to obsessionally enact, to take as an *objet,* the process that defines the desired identity of the one presumed to know, the process of talking and writing. In effect, Žižek thus embraces the form of knowledge to occlude the fact that the content of such discourse, complete knowledge or absolute truth, is impossible. To put it another way, the real function of Žižek's logorrheic discourse may finally be to fascinate *himself* enough that *he* doesn't notice there is nothing.

## AND SO ON . . .

This brings us back to the larger issues at stake here and allows us to draw some conclusions about reason in general and about the nature of philosophy and academic discourse in particular. If, as Žižek argues, reason is always haunted by the unreason, the ideology, at its core, then we can now see that the critical or analytic enterprise is itself fraught with a similar paradox: the necessity of being the one presumed to know and the impossibility of that position because of the limitations of the Symbolic Order and of reason itself. Žižek's source of jouissance, the continual production of discourse, is thus the perfect response to the paradoxical position of the *sujet supposé savoir,* the absolute necessity of speaking "the truth," and the impossibility and endlessness of that task. And this too is evident in the video with which we began, in Žižek's definition of the philosophical enterprise, appearing right on the surface, if only as a symptom. The phrase "and so on" occurs early on in his discussion ("stupid metaphysical questions and so on") and then, doubled, appears twice more ("when we do certain acts and so on and so on), including serving as the conclusion to his meditations ("Philosophers are not the madmen who search for some eternal truth and so on and so on"). In a sense, it's the perfect academic phrase about the impossibility of the academic enterprise, since it suggests that rational analysis could continue, that the "and so on" could be spelled out more precisely if he wanted to, while simultaneously functioning as an ellipsis, as an implicit admission that not everything can be articulated, that there is always more that could be said, which means there is always something more than *can* be said. And, if we have any doubts about the limitations of philosophy or reason or academic discourse, their continual collision with the unsymbolizable Real, even the "and so on" needs an "and so on." Even beyond everything else we could say there will always be another "everything else we could say" . . . and so on.

Clearly, this is not simply a problem for Žižek alone but an issue that lies at the heart of all academic work. Frustrated with Žižek's failure to follow the conventions of academic writing, with his blending of concepts and objects of study from different disciplines, and with his refusal to follow a conventional line of argument that begins with a hypothesis and leads to a conclusion, Harpham finally argues that we must reject the style of Žižek's work itself, since it functions as an implicit critique of the ideology of academic writing and an interrogation of the basic mechanisms that serve as the deep structure of academic discourse. If we accept this critique, he says, the implications are overwhelming:

> For this option would require us to admit the inadmissible: that the phrase of probing or testing in a standard argument is an engineered illusion, a charade performed for the benefit of the credulous en route to a predetermined conclusion; that what appears to be rational argumentation is actually a subtle doctrinal practice designed not to arrive at truth by "legitimate" means but simply to explicate a truth already possessed as a matter of faith; that disciplines achieve their specificity by making an unsupportable claim to have eliminated all that is not in their domain. If we took Žižek as a guide to the real character of conventional methods and practices, we would be forced to revise – actually, to discard – all our assumptions about academic work and indeed about rational thought as such.[19]

Well, yes. Harpham would like to see Žižek's work as "para-academic," as something like the conversation that takes place in coffeehouses near college campuses, but to marginalize it, literally, in this way ignores some of the valuable if potentially terrifying insights about the underlying ideology of academic work that Harpham recognizes in Žižek. It's not just that, as Michel Foucault pointed out long ago, the academic disciplines are indeed artificial – and often territorial or even imperialistic – divisions of the pursuit of knowledge. It also seems true that, whatever the research process itself may be, the presentation of the results of that research in the finished talk or essay does indeed involve leading the audience to a predetermined conclusion. In fact, one could argue that teaching undergraduates to do precisely that is the point of the composition courses almost universally required by American universities. Perhaps most importantly, however, Žižek may very well be right when he argues that all hermeneutics is a question of belief rather than of truth precisely because, as all of his work continually reminds us, rational argumentation really is on some level always ideological and thus, inevitably, a "subtle doctrinal practice." That may sound like madness, but I actually think that it's philosophy.

## NOTES

1. Public Policy Polling, "Palin Trails Sheen with Independents," March 17, 2011, accessed September 12, 2013, http://publicpolicypolling.blogspot.com/2011/03/palin-trails-sheen-with-independents.html.

2. Anonymous, March 17, 2011 (1:00 PM), comment on ibid.

3. Johnston, "From the Spectacular Act," 2.

4. There are currently about 144,000 YouTube videos featuring or discussing Žižek, compared to 25,000 for Derrida. Moreover, the videos themselves seem relatively popular. Vice's interview with Žižek, "Vice Meets Superstar

Communist Slavoj Žižek," received 100,000 hits within the first two weeks of being put online (October 11, 2013, accessed October 27, 2013, http://www.youtube.com/watch?v=XS_Lzo4S81A). In contrast, Jay Kirby and Amy Ziering Kofman's documentary on Derrida recorded 31,000 views in the first year and a half following its posting on YouTube ("Derrida [2002]," April 25, 2012, accessed November 1, 2013, http://www.youtube.com/watch?v=CtcpwJCC6Co). If Žižek's popularity can be explained on a superficial level as a response to his unique blend of leftist political analysis, humor, and fondness for popular cultural references, on a deeper level, as I suggest below, his appeal might lie in his function as a sort of intellectual fetish in the psychoanalytic sense as someone who simultaneously undermines and affirms the possibility of truth and reason. Since his fans not only "know very well" but also know that "still they are doing it," such an indeterminate suspension between the inevitability of cynicism and the possibility of belief would be precisely the point.

5. See, for example, Gell, "Slavoj Žižek Speaks."

6. In this respect, *Žižek!* is oddly positioned within the spectrum of the (minuscule) film subgenre of the "philosopher documentary." On the one hand, there is Astra Taylor's *Examined Life* (2008; Zeitgeist Films, 2010, DVD), which features ten philosophers articulating their ideas. In this instance, the focus is on the philosophy rather than the philosopher, whose personal life is essentially irrelevant, an emphasis that is signaled by the camera's continual tendency to pan away from the speaker, such as Peter Singer on Fifth Avenue or Avital Ronell walking in a park, to the passersby around them. On the other hand, from its opening scenes, Jay Kirby and Amy Ziering Kofman's *Derrida* (2002; Zeitgeist Films, 2004, DVD) is directly concerned with the question of the relation between the philosopher and his or her ideas. Although Derrida sometimes refuses to answer personal questions, and although the film includes a number of "deconstructive" *mise-en-abime* moments (Derrida watching a clip of himself watching a clip of himself being interviewed, for example) that are designed to interrogate the artificiality of the documentary genre itself, the viewer nonetheless gets a sense of Derrida as a person, if only from the mundane scene of him putting the plastic wrap back on a pan of leftovers, not to mention his discussion of experiencing anti-Semitism as a child. In a sense, then, *Žižek!* is

the inverse of *Derrida*. If the latter film continually claims it cannot provide a personal portrait of Derrida even while it does so, Žižek consistently seduces us with the promise of showing us who Žižek really is while continually frustrating that desire.

7. Barthes, *Camera Lucida,* 42–55.

8. Ibid., 42, 49.

9. "Authors@Google: Slavoj Žižek," October, 3, 2008, accessed August 25, 2013, http://www.youtube.com/watch?v=_xoeyNkNpLo.

10. Kay, *Žižek,* 5.

11. The notion of the return of a certain repressed materiality is not entirely fanciful here, if only because the "bed view" pose may be a favorite of Žižek's. The photo that accompanies John Gray's review of Žižek in the *New York Review of Books* for July 12, 2012, shows Žižek, fully clothed this time, at home in bed with the covers pulled up to his waist.

12. Boynton, "Enjoy Your Žižek!"

13. Gray, "Violent Visions."

14. Boynton, "Enjoy Your Žižek!"

15. Kay, *Žižek,* 6.

16. Harpham, "Doing the Impossible," 455.

17. Žižek, *Living,* 304.

18. Žižek, *Enjoy Your Symptom!,* 148.

19. Harpham, "Doing the Impossible," 467–468.

## SELECTED BIBLIOGRAPHY

Barthes, Roland. *Camera Lucida.* Translated by Richard Howard. New York: Hill and Wang, 1981.

Boynton, Robert S. "Enjoy Your Žižek!" *Lingua Franca* 8 (1998), accessed September 1, 2012, http://linguafranca.mirror.theinfo.org/9810/zizek.html.

Gell, Aaron. "Slavoj Žižek Speaks to Occupy Wall Street." *New York Observer,* October 9, 2011, accessed September 5, 2013, http://observer.com/2011/10/slavoj-zizek-speaks-to-occupy-wall-street/.

Gray, John. "The Violent Visions of Slavoj Žižek." Review of *Less than Nothing* and *Living in the End Times,* by Slavoj Žižek. *New York Review of Books,* July 12, 2012, accessed September 5, 2013, http://www.nybooks.com/articles/archives/2012/jul/12/violent-visions-slavoj-zizek/.

Harpham, Geoffrey Galt. "Doing the Impossible: Slavoj Žižek and the End of Knowledge." *Critical Inquiry* 29 (Spring 2003): 453–485.

Johnston, Adrian. "From the Spectacular Act to the Vanishing Act: Badiou, Žižek, and the Politics of Lacanian Theory." *International Journal of Žižek Studies* 1 (2007). http://zizekstudies.org/index.php/ijzs/article/view/1.

Kay, Sarah. *Žižek: A Critical Introduction.* Malden, Mass.: Blackwell, 2003.

"Philosophy from a Bed View (by Žižek)." February 17. 2010, accessed September 10, 2012, http://www.youtube.com/watch?v=dp8aTYUrPio.

Žižek, Slavoj. *Enjoy Your Symptom!* 2nd ed. New York: Routledge, 2001.

———. *First as Tragedy, Then as Farce.* Brooklyn, N.Y.: Verso, 2009.

———. *Living in the End Times.* Brooklyn, N.Y.: Verso, 2011.

*Žižek!* Directed by Astra Taylor. Zeitgeist Films, 2005.

Ideas are like fish.

If you want to catch little fish, you can stay in the shallow water. But if you want to catch the big fish, you've got to go deeper.

Down deep, the fish are more powerful and more pure. They're huge and abstract. And they're very beautiful.

DAVID LYNCH, *CATCHING THE BIG FISH*

To a fish, the depths and expanses of its waters, the currents and quiet pools, warm and cold layers are the element of its multiple mobility. If the fish is deprived of the fullness of its element, if it is dragged on the dry sand, then it can only wriggle, twitch, and die. Therefore, we always must seek out thinking, and its burden of thought, in the element of its multiple meanings, else everything will remain closed to us.

MARTIN HEIDEGGER, *WHAT IS CALLED THINKING?*

6

# FISH KIT

*Jonathan P. Eburne*

## STICK TO YOUR DAY JOB

In the summer of 2000, an event billed as the New York City CowParade exhibited roughly five hundred fiberglass cow statues around the city. Decorated "by artists and schoolchildren" and displayed on sidewalks throughout the five boroughs, the statues were the trademark of CowParade Holdings, a private, for-profit development company that sponsors such "CowParades" in cities around the world.[1] As the company's website explains, "CowParade is helping to showcase the local arts community and stimulate civic spirit and pride which ultimately raises funds for local charities that in turn benefit the community." Though a private corporation, its interests are manifestly public: "CowParade is designed to make art accessible to the masses by bringing it out of the museum and onto the streets and parks of a city. People are able to touch as well as to see these unique canvases, making the art interactive and unlike anything that has ever been seen."[2] Unlike the urban sheep-protests featured in Roman Polanski's *Chinatown* (1974) or, more recently, in contemporary Madrid (2012), the presence of hundreds of decorated cow statues on urban sidewalks offers an explicit, if unthreatening, appeal to both the comforts of urban space and the approachability of contemporary art. Cities and concept art alike can be breezy and even pastoral, the event proposes; CowParade offers both cities and artists a ready-to-assemble kit for raising public arts awareness and corporate buy-in all at once. Indeed, even before the New York event opened, lawsuits over brand naming and the rights to the cow-display concept suggested precisely how profitable such CowParade kits might be.[3]

At the same time, the New York CowParade yielded at least one other "happening," albeit on a somewhat less consumer-friendly order of interactive public art than the happy synergy to which the company's website beckons. True to the Actionist-Fluxus pretensions of the CowParade's foray into public art, the filmmaker David Lynch contributed a statue that invoked the company's tenuous links to experimental art, though a bit too literally for the organizers' tastes. Rather than approaching the fiberglass cow as merely a surface to be decorated, Lynch altered the very form of the "unique canvas" itself: Lynch's cow had been beheaded, partially butchered, and stabbed with forks.

Entitled *Eat My Fear,* Lynch's sculpture evokes the abattoir rather than the pasture or the Big Apple; its figural violence appears to designate the mortal "cow parade" that leads from farm to table, recalling the role of the slaughterhouse in the path from country to city. As a number of critics have noted, Lynch's statue thus calls to mind "real" animal properties (or fates) that the other decorated urban interlopers refuse: *this* is what happens to cows when they enter the city.[4] On a more formal register, the violence of the sculpture exercises itself reflexively as a demonstration of what it means to use a fiberglass cow as artistic raw material. In a manner consistent with the unsettling physicality of his cinematic work, Lynch's

**6.1.** David Lynch, *Eat My Fear,* ca. 2000, from the New York City CowParade. Mixed media. Private collection. ©2014 David Lynch.

*Eat My Fear* recalls the Viennese shock-art of the 1960s, likewise notable for its recourse to bodily mutilation, animal slaughter, and the commingling of food (and sexual activity) as artistic materials. In its discomfiting, if playful, act of formal mutilation, Lynch's cow might be said to confront at once the historical fate of real cows – or at least steers – and the historical antecedents of his own gesture of disfiguration, insofar as it takes on the Actionist pretensions of CowParade itself.

Like the work of Viennese Actionist artists Günter Brus, Otto Muehl, Herman Nitsch, and Rudolf Schwarzkogler, Lynch's mutilated cow is striking less for its sensationalism or provocation alone than for its alarmingly literal recourse to bodily forms as artistic raw material. *Eat My Fear* suggests an affinity with the Viennese avant-garde, that is, in its approach to the cow's fiberglass body as a form to be manipulated rather than as an unimpeachable living surface. Whether animal or human, living or synthetic, such bodies constituted repositories of artistic materials to be appropriated within the artistic process. As Muehl puts it in his 1964 "Material Action Manifesto," writing of the human actors used in Actionist performances (who were often the artists themselves): "a person is not treated in the material action as a person but as a body. the body, things, are not viewed as objects for our purposes, but have all the purpose radically removed from them. everything is understood as form. the human being is not seen as a human being, a person, but as a body with certain properties. material action extends reality."[5] The repurposing of bodily forms for "material action" demanded both use and abuse: any "radical" removal of their (human, animal) purpose bore the discomfiting echo of the body's presumed former integrity, no longer inviolate.

To suggest that Lynch's *Eat My Fear* bears art-historical continuities with Viennese Actionism is hardly to presume a stable historical frame of reference for explaining his sculpture; rather, it highlights the extent to which its violence and dark humor have to do with the work's formal approach to the cow as a medium.[6] As elements of a figure modeled in fiberglass, the "violence" exercised in *Eat My Fear* is strictly allegorical, prompting an association of the CowParade statues with slaughter and the production of meat. No real cows were harmed in the process of making *Eat My Fear;* Lynch simply assembled the elements of his kit in a different way. Rather than embellishing one of the several stock cow poses offered by the CowParade organizers, in other words, Lynch altered the medium itself, taking advantage of the plastic and formal properties of a fiberglass statue, which has precisely to do with its ability to evoke violence without inflicting bodily harm. Even without a head, it still stands up.

Lynch's contribution to CowParade was, notoriously, banned from the exhibition. Joining it in ignominy was the cow submitted by PETA (People for the Ethical Treatment of Animals), which bore slogans testifying to the kinds of cruelty Lynch's design seemed to figure explicitly: "Cattle are castrated and dehorned without anesthesia" and "A lot of times the man skinning the cow finds out an animal is still conscious – USDA Inspector Timothy Walker."[7] The censorship of Lynch's cow had more to do with anticipated judgments of obscenity and bad taste, however, than with any testament for or against animal cruelty. For the organizers, that is, it mattered little whether *Eat My Fear* was to be viewed as Actionist aesthetic or as animal rights invective. The cow was an indulgent exercise of the filmmaker's inveterate weirdness: Lynch's oddity had crossed the line. In the words of Parks Commissioner Henry J. Stern as cited by the Associated Press, "I don't know whether it's shock art or schlock art. David Lynch should stick to his day job, making movies."[8]

Perhaps for this very reason, the CowParade incident has become virtually as central to the public and scholarly understanding of Lynch's career as the products of his "day job." For not only does the incident testify to the curious and often ambivalent popular reception of Lynch's cinematic work – a body of work more suited, it would seem, to late-night repertory theaters and other cult venues than to crowded daytime streets – but it also yields critical insights into Lynch's artistic process as a film auteur. According to Greg Olson, for instance, the statue is consistent with Lynch's noirish attention to the dark underbelly of commodified US culture: "Once again, Lynch has probed beneath the surface of a seemingly benign all-American institution (beef-eating) and revealed raw, disturbing truths."[9] Like the severed ear that opens *Blue Velvet* (1986), Lynch's mutilated cow exposes a violent underworld of "raw" animal cruelty and fear. Yet as gainfully as *Eat My Fear* may present itself as a critical device for approaching Lynch's cinematic oeuvre, it is no less striking as an example of the kind of work Lynch has continued to produce throughout his career both on the margins of his Hollywood day job and, increasingly, independently from it.

Indeed, before announcing his return to television in 2016, Lynch seemed increasingly to have left his Hollywood day job behind. For even as film buffs have lamented the growing span of years between his feature-length films (*Mulholland Drive* [2001] and *INLAND EMPIRE* [2006] are his two most recent as of 2015), Lynch himself has kept remarkably busy, producing commercials, furniture, an album of original songs, a musically oriented website, an eponymous brand of coffee, a series of art and photography exhibitions, a nightclub in Paris, and, perhaps most distinctively, a nonprofit foundation devoted to transcendental meditation, "consciousness-based education," and the teachings of Maharishi Mahesh Yogi. Even as a major career retrospective in late 2014 sought to consolidate his status as a visual artist, Lynch's body of work remains strikingly diffuse, unfolding as a seemingly limitless proliferation of minor projects and business ventures. Of course, Lynch's films have always featured other forms of artistic labor, from his early art-school "filmed paintings" such as *Six Men Getting Sick* (1967) – which strongly resembles Muehl's live-action films from the same period – to the set constructions of *Eraserhead* (1977) and *INLAND EMPIRE,* as well as the *tableaux-morts* of *Blue Velvet.* Not only was Lynch heavily involved with the set design and sound editing of his films, but he also built furniture and produced a body of still photography and painting related to their production, as critics have long noted.[10] Yet in terms of his continuing artistic and commercial projects, it seems as though these supplemental arts have exceeded the parameters of filmmaking altogether. We have the set designs, tableaux, and quirky auteurist habits without the cinematic apparatus to bind them together in a meaningful synthesis.

For some, Lynch's ever-expanding body of odds and ends might seem to be bound up in his absorption by New Age spirituality, symptomatic of a retreat into the inland empire, we might say, of his "consciousness-based" project. His sole authored book, *Catching the Big Fish* (2007), is devoted far more centrally to Transcendental Meditation than to cinema. Yet it would be a mistake to be cynical about either Lynch's artistic output or his interest in Transcendental Meditation. The continual, even intensified, productivity of his work in media other than film suggests not only that Lynch's career as an artist transcends the singular medium of feature-length Hollywood movies but also that his particularity as an artist, filmmaker, or even "transcendental" thinker has very much to do with this attention to *medium* as constitutive of artistic works and the ideas that animate them. Indeed, the work of thinking – what Lynch refers to as the harmonics of "ideas" – is indispensably bound up with the material action of his art. As Michel Chion has noted, Lynch's creativity functions through the mechanical, corporeal, or otherwise material components of the media forms within which he works, whether animal or human bodies, assemblages, mechanical artifacts, or the cinematic apparatus. Such components become at once the archive and the apparatus for Lynch's creative thinking, that is, at once the documentary trace and the technical means of its effects. As Chion writes, "Creation, for Lynch, thus consists of building kits which do not exist in nature but which derive their parts from it."[11] These "kits," as we will see below, bear an intellectual as well as aesthetic function, yet the precise nature of their functioning is rarely furnished with a concrete explanation.

Unlike the Viennese Actionists or other experimental art groups, for instance, Lynch refuses to supplement his works with anything resembling a manifesto; his interviews and commentaries are often maddeningly vague or matter-of-fact. "Interviewing Lynch," writes Richard Barney, "can be an experience of sinuous indirection."[12] Even so, I propose that we look to Lynch's statements about creativity, intuition, and Transcendental Meditation as a kind of composite, ersatz manifesto that testifies to his painstaking attention to the intricacies of thinking and artistic production alike. In place of any stable hermeneutic platform for understanding or explaining the curiosities of his work, we instead find insights about the way his "kits" function creatively and epistemologically.

This is an essay, therefore, about Lynch's kits. My contention here is twofold. First, I propose not only that there is a unifying or underlying logic to David Lynch's odd bits and pieces of artistic production but also that this body of work proposes a distinctive kind of thinking, if a decidedly oddball one. For Lynch, the curious functioning of his "kits" and contraptions serves as a means for gathering ideas, themselves particular to the medium through which they are grasped. Second, I propose that for Lynch, an "idea" refers to the object-cause of a material action rather than to the product of any purely cognitive function. Ideas are the key operative elements in the assemblages that make up the "kits" of his creative labor. Unlike, however, the "desiring-machines" described by Gilles Deleuze and Félix Guattari (with whose writings Lynch's career is roughly contemporaneous), his "kits" are very much rooted in a notion of consciousness, understood as an unknowable totality that exceeds the human. The point, for Lynch, is less to map out this consciousness – or to dislodge its privilege as a metaphysical construct in favor of apparatuses and mechanisms – than to exercise and perpetuate its effects. Such effects are available, however, only by proxy: the process of grasping or "catching" ideas demands a "transcendental" form of creative thinking that functions intuitively to bear them out, a curious form of pragmatism. Lynch's kits exercise rather than constitute this thinking; they comprise its medium. Like his cow sculpture, that is, Lynch's oddball assortment of paintings, photographs, assemblages, videos, advertisements, songs, furniture, and commercial ventures are productive engines and repositories alike of this thinking, a creative discipline that can be exercised and even taught.

### PARTS ARE TO BE ASSEMBLED

How does one go about catching ideas? According to what procedures, that is, does it become possible to grasp hold of something called "an idea"? This, we might say, is one of the constitutive questions of Lynch's work across its many forms and apparatuses. In interviews throughout the past twenty-five years, as well as in *Catching the Big Fish,* Lynch voices his insistence on "catching" ideas, as if an idea were a concrete object in itself. "Ideas are the strangest things," he notes, "because they suddenly enter into your conscious mind and you don't really know where they came from – where they existed before they were introduced to you. They could mean something, or they could just be there for you to work with. I don't know."[13] Lynch's notion of an "idea" has less to do with knowledge than with the processes that comprise creative thinking. Lynch's ideas function, in other words, as vessels or devices for both gathering and conveying the work of thinking, insofar as thinking designates a procedure that can be exercised but never fully known. "An idea," Lynch puts it in *Catching the Big Fish,* "is a thought. It's a thought that holds more than you think it does when you receive it."[14] An idea is something we receive, like a radio signal, or a gift. But it is something we also use in turn. Neither simply the outward appearance of an ideal thought nor the mystical essence of all thinking, an idea instead inaugurates the possibility of *gathering,* the material action of assembling and dissecting that comprises the work of thinking

Without in any way seeking to collapse Lynch's thinking about ideas (or his ideas about thinking) into that of existential philosophy, it is nonetheless striking to note how strongly his terms resonate with the artisanal figures of Martin Heidegger's philosophy, which is likewise replete with jugs and vessels, fish, cabinetry, and the emphatic distinction between thinking and knowing. For Lynch, however, the distinction between thinking and knowing is a procedural rather than an ontological one, as it is for Heidegger. Lynch is interested in creative practice and in well-being rather than in philosophy. Lynch's devotion to ideas has little to do with *knowledge* as either an intellectual faculty or a body of truth-claims, moreover; his "ideas" may think, but they do not know. Famously, Lynch himself makes no claims to know or fully comprehend his own work; for instance, writing of the blue box and blue key, two major structuring objects in *Mulholland Drive,* he confesses, "I don't have a clue what those are."[15]

Rather than considering such claims as either an antitheoretical rhetorical ploy or as auteurist mumbo-jumbo, Lynch's other writings encourage us to take them literally. On the one hand, to refuse knowability in this way is to propose a hermeneutics of "open" artistic works, indicating art that is to be inhabited rather than merely deciphered by its audience. Here we encounter Lynch in a more traditional, Kantian guise as an engineer of "aesthetic ideas," that is, of a set of sensory presentations, distinct from rational concepts, that enable a spectator to experience the same harmonious state of mind that the artist experienced in creating the idea.[16] As Lynch writes, reflecting on his day job, "A film should stand on its own. It's absurd if a filmmaker needs to say what a film means in words. The world in the film is a created one, and people sometimes love going into that world. For them that world is real. And if people find out certain things about how something was done, or how this means this or that means that, the next time they see the film, these things enter into the experience." Thinking, in this light, extends from spectatorial experience: as a hermeneutic process of interpretation ("find[ing] out certain things") that nevertheless remains rooted in experience, it is subject to emotional and sensory absorption as much as to understanding. "I think it's so precious and important to maintain that world," Lynch concludes, "and not say certain things that could break the experience."[17]

At the same time, Lynch's procedural attention to "ideas" as thinking-kits is consistent with his artisanal prerogatives in its dedication to the properties and possibilities of artistic media. His fetishistic attention to ideas proposes that thinking emerges from processes other than cognition, as a function that owes more to solicitation and invocation, we might say, than to deductive or inductive reason. Lynch has described this process on numerous occasions to the extent that it too has become part of his mythos, his public persona; in a 2006 interview, he notes that his overriding approach to the construction of a film is to focus not on its structure but on "the ideas": "An idea comes. You get an idea and the idea tells you everything. I understand the idea enough to translate it to cinema and stay true to that and try to get everybody in tune into that idea that's driving the boat. Sometimes, if you're true to the idea, these ideas have 'harmonics' and someone may pick up a harmonic like you – some kind of angle – and, if you're being true to the idea, then the harmonics are true."[18] Thinking – the grasping of ideas – is thus intimately bound up with the material action of Lynch's artistic tinkerings, and in turn their "truth," their harmonics, has to do with the formal properties of the materials and media in which he works. Indeed, in a 1990 interview Lynch describes this truth-procedure in almost childlike terms as a kind of happiness: "If you're kind of into it, it's a certain kind of happiness: happy gluing one piece of wood to another. You kind of like the wood, and the sun is just right, and the glue, you've got enough of it. Some little bit of wire. And you know what the wood does and you know what the glue does, and the wire, and your imagination is seeing the whole thing. And a little bit of action and reaction."[19] The harmonics of thinking are continuous, according to Lynch, with his own practical relationship with such materials. In place of a Kantian harmony among the faculties of the mind, in other words, Lynch stresses a harmony among mental faculties and concrete materials alike, a being-among-things.

All the same, Lynch's "harmonics" are often far from harmonious, as his fans and detractors alike are well aware. As in the case of his contribution to the New York CowParade, Lynch's imaginative attention to the material properties (rather than bodily integrity) of his artistic medium can render the "little bit of action and reaction" of his happy tinkerings into a spectacle of violent dismemberment. What is at stake, I propose, is the literalness with which the logic of kits – the apparatus of gluing and ungluing, disassembly and assembly – plays out in the practical construction of some of his most unsettling works.

In *Fish Kit* and *Chicken Kit,* two photographed assemblages from 1979, Lynch offers instructions for reassembling a living fish and a living chicken

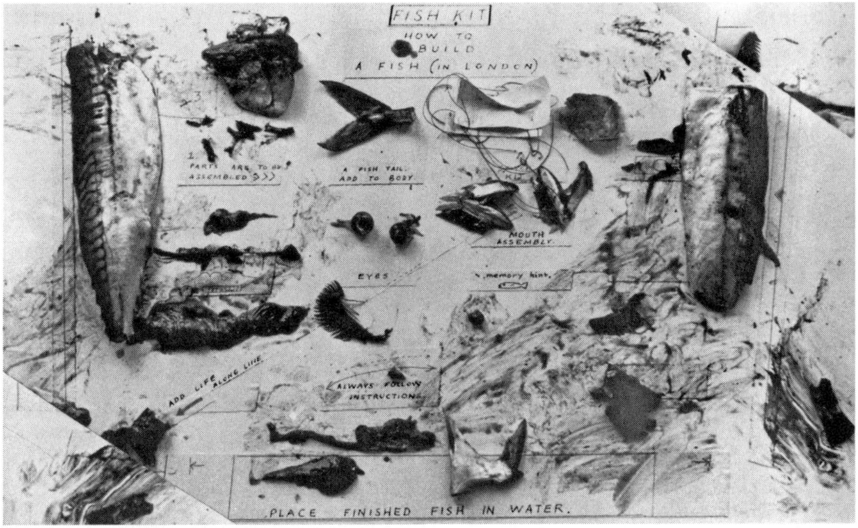


**6.2.** David Lynch, *Fish Kit,* ca. 1980. Photograph. Private collection. ©2014 David Lynch.

from dismembered parts. The assemblages are comprised of the bodies of commercially available animals regularly displayed in supermarket coolers, butcher shops, and fish markets for their food-grade attractiveness.[20] Only here, the aesthetics of consumption have been dramatically inverted: both *Fish Kit* and *Chicken Kit* lay out the disarticulated parts according to a taxonomic scheme familiar to any veteran of hobby model kits. "Parts are to be assembled," read the instructions on each of the two extant versions of *Fish Kit.* In place of a neatly butchered corpse presented hygienically as food, we witness an array of viscera, organs, and severed limbs that – if one were to follow the instructions – could be reassembled into living organisms that swim or cluck. The compositions are, in spite of their rather clumsy attempt at anatomical precision, disconcertingly messy: the white surfaces on which the fish and chicken parts are mounted are smeared with blood and gore. In this sense, the kits recall the gruesome dissection scene in *Eraserhead* in which the protagonist, Henry Spencer, cuts through the bandages of his monstrous infant, only to find – to his and our horror – that he has disemboweled it. Here, as in the film, the inanimate prosthesis (bandage, "kit" apparatus) likewise becomes indistinguishable from the animate, mortal organism that it binds together (its living tissue, its very life).

Indeed, no less than in *Eraserhead,* the *Fish Kit* and *Chicken Kit* images confront us with spectacular dismemberment. The instructions for "assembling" a living body from these parts confront us, in turn, with the no less spectacular irony of their presentation as kits to be assembled. Their mortality is thus doubly accentuated. "The idea came," Lynch reflects, "from model airplane kits, where you get a box and you take out the parts and you have to read the instructions and assemble them. And then, when you're finished, you have what is on the cover of the box."[21] Needless to say, the project is an impossible one. The nonreversibility of dissection constitutes the very premise of the works. This is played, in part, for laughs: regarding the inner organs of the chicken, the instructions insist on proceeding with exceptional care, since even though this part of the kit cannot be seen once the chicken kit is complete, the organs nonetheless remain important. "Will you earn a star?" beckons the simpler of the two *Fish Kit* assemblages.

The gruesome mortal content of the kits provides a vehicle for their conflicting affective registers of humor and revulsion. No less significant to the kits is the experience of confronting the technical-conceptual problems they pose. The hortatory language of the instructions induces us to build rather than merely reflect. Yet we cannot actually attempt to recompose the dissected animals, since *Fish Kit* and *Chicken Kit* are photographs; we are thus redirected, thanks to the particularity of the photographic medium, back to our reflections. The result is a second-order assemblage: a second, conceptual version of the kit. It works like this: the kits propose the assembly and disassembly of one apparatus, an "impossible" one, in favor of another apparatus, conceptual yet no less bound up in the specificity of its materials. As Lynch reflects, "Well, it makes you think about things like, 'What makes this thing work?' If you put it all together, you'd have a 'chicken,' but what makes it walk around, you know? And peck at bits of gravel? Pretty weird."[22] The technology of the kit – its instructions, as well as its taxonomic, pedagogical means of presentation – is instrumental, in other words, in staging the imaginary reassembly, the monstrous projected apparatus, which, of course, falls infinitely short of replicating the "true" apparatus of a living chicken or a living fish.[23] The irony of this confrontation, animated by humor and disgust, is neither cynical nor simply cruel; rather, it is constitutive of the kits' conceptual function and, in turn, constituted by their scrupulous attention to the potentials and limits of their media.

*Fish Kit* and *Chicken Kit* demand reflection on their recourse to artistic materials, to artistic media. Unlike, say, the edible art of the Romanian-Swiss artist Daniel Spoerri, whose 1960s "snare pictures" are comprised of the actual remnants of meals, Lynch's kits exist as photographic images: we see a photographic double rather than the actually decomposing assemblages of body parts themselves.[24] The difference, I propose, is constitutive: whether photographic or cinematic, film images can successfully be cut and reassembled; the static objects and images they depict can be animated. With living tissue the limitations of cutting and pasting become far more consequential; but so, too, does any claim to "animation" and life.

In the guise of a gruesome assortment of part-objects – living organisms reduced to bloody odds and ends – Lynch's kits thus exercise their "material action" among the media they bring into contact. *Fish Kit* and *Chicken Kit* propose an experience of being-among-media as much as an experience of being-among-things. Two orders of medium-oriented irony open up here: the first adheres to the impossible reversibility of the butchered animal parts and the living assemblage; the second occupies the irreconcilable gap between the photographic image and the tableau-mort assemblage. The kits "work" as conceptual art insofar as they rehearse their failure to work as objects or living beings. The result is no longer a work of figural art that allegorizes the politics of dismemberment (as in the case of *Eat My Fear,* we might say) but a photographic record of once-living bodies appropriated as artistic material and exploited for their formal properties, that is, for their parts and organs but also for their eliminated "purpose" of organic functioning, their claim to life, which has been removed in order to render the body parts ripe for art, even as it is recalled in the future-perfect of the kit to be assembled. What becomes allegorical here is thus less the mortality and suffering of animal bodies than the vanity of creative tinkering as it encounters the limits of its organic and inorganic materials. Yet even as the technical means of Lynch's creative process might seem to reach its material limit – in real, biological death – this limit is what makes the pictures work: the fish and chicken kits maintain their epistemological function in their very insistence on the mortality of artistic raw material. In doing so, *Fish Kit* and *Chicken Kit* introduce the possibility of keeping "ideas" alive and functional in spite – or precisely because – of the spectacular and insistent deadness of their animal parts. The finite plasticity and foreclosed combinatory possibility of its raw materials, organic and inorganic alike, open up to the plasticity of thinking. My point here is less to exhaust the full conceptual harmonics of such kits – whether as shock art, schlock art, or meta-artistic reflection – than to suggest how these kits both allegorize and exercise how "tinkering" itself becomes one of Lynch's privileged mediums, that is, the assembling and disassembling, combining and recombining, of artistic materials, which functions as Lynch's principal method of soliciting the work of thinking, of "catching the big fish."

## SYNCHING WITH DAVID LYNCH

More archive than oeuvre, Lynch's heterogeneous body of work continues to proliferate and expand. From sketches, songs, and photographs to feature-length films, this archive is comprised of countless kits devotionally attuned to the harmonics of pulling apart and synching up their constitutive bits and pieces. Lynch's films, no less than his other artistic tinkerings, abide by the truth-procedures of gathering, dissecting, combining, and, most of all, thinking: the intuitive process of staying "attuned" to an idea. Any discussion of Lynch's creative work would thus be remiss not to consider his cinematic career, given especially the extent to which his films both incorporate and build upon the procedural logic of his other work. Yet whereas scholars have long discussed the formal intricacies of Lynch's cinematic imagination, they have tended to register discomfort with the notion that his "ideas" constitute the procedural means rather than the exegetical payload (or wacky auteurist origin) of his work.[25]

As a filmmaker, Lynch has been canonized in academic scholarship as a poet of the unknown or the unknowable, concepts most often addressed in psychoanalytic terms that draw from the work of Jacques Lacan or, in certain cases, Carl Jung. The result is a curious tendency for critics to reframe Lynch's explicitly "transcendental" devotion to thinking according to the scale of their own reductive rationalism, as Robert Sinnerbrink has put it, wherein his films come to illustrate a priori concepts or theories rather than sustaining their own intellectual demands.

The problem lies in viewing the films as illustrations in the first place. Even critics attentive to the impersonality and "ontological" fixation of Lynch's cinematic work tend to seek comfort in interpretations that confirm such an illustrative or allegorical function: Lynch's films are *about* medium; their "ideas" demand the *a priori* rejection of any and all concepts or narrative expectations; they reflect the perverse afterimage of US history, or of cinematic history itself; they disclose the horror of subjectivity, the Real, and so forth. Such claims are all perfectly compelling and reasonable; indeed, they are all more or less equally convincing as interpretive horizons for viewing Lynch's films. Yet they fail to exhaust the procedural insistence of Lynch's broader artistic project, within which such intense bursts of interpretive energy themselves comprise a key ingredient. I thus propose instead that we heed the oddball logic of Lynch's medium-specific ideas, that is, that we attempt to "stay true" to the project Lynch himself outlines – albeit less in deference to the auteur than in an effort to play out the logic of the kits themselves. As I have been arguing, such a project has less to do simply with illustrating the unknown, or the unknowable, or the unthinkable than with exercising the work of "catching" such slippery conceptual fauna.

In this regard, it is important to take Lynch's films literally, just as in the case of his artistic assemblages, that is, with their material structure, their attention to medium, in mind. Chion sums up the technique of Lynch's early films in precisely such terms. "A literal film-maker," he writes, "Lynch takes old formulae concerning parallel editing and 'thought-shots' and makes them new. He often connects images with the same sense of freedom in editing reminiscent of the silent film era."[26] In his films, thinking can be represented formally through montage as well as enacted by characters; yet in each case the constitutive ideas are dependent on the technical particulars of the medium. As his films grew more narrative in structure during the early years of his cinematic career, Lynch's formal interests began to take on increasingly "subjective" or "psychological" resonances. In addition to the harmonics, we might say, of dead and living animals, Lynch's narrative films take up the representational possibilities of characters as thinking, feeling, human subjects. All the same, such subjective effects are the consequence, the ghostly echo, of the formal demands of the cinematic medium. In a manner consistent with his other work, the narrative construction of fictional characters is a function of the same set of procedures that bring about the radical removal of all human "purpose" from living bodies and things in favor of their formal "properties" as artistic raw material. Lynch's films are haunting precisely for their capacity at once to present us with "a series of images, sounds, gestures, bodies and actions which must be grasped literally before any attempt at interpretation," as Chion puts it, and yet also to present us with the "subjective," psychological echo of narrative consequences.[27] The films enact diegetically the paradoxes that *Fish Kit* and *Chicken Kit* engender through static photographs. In Lynch's films, that is, we not only witness the accumulation of his cinematic ideas but also watch his characters think, struggle, live, and die: a cinematic illusion, certainly, but, as a function of the narrative medium, an illusion no less intrinsic to its formal properties.

*Mulholland Drive* (2001), which may stand as Lynch's most self-reflexive, even "archival" film, is composed of an interlocking series of moving parts. The dynamic of synching up and splitting apart is replicated in the overall narrative structure of the film, as well as in individual scenes and even shot sequences. Like its predecessor, *Lost Highway* (1997), *Mulholland Drive* bears a bifurcated plot structure; its lead actors, Naomi Watts and Laura Harring, play different roles in the first and second sections of the film. The two narrative sequences are brought into painful contact during the course of the film, pivoting on the appearance of a mysterious blue box and a haunting set piece staged at a nightclub called Silencio. Critics and fans have sought to reconcile the film's structural discontinuities by speculating about various combinations of dream, illusion, hallucination, multiple dimensions, reincarnation, and so forth.[28] Curiously, a scholarly consensus has emerged about the status of its two basic sequences. To wit: the first act, in which Naomi Watts plays the impossibly sunny Hollywood ingénue Betty Elms, constitutes a wish-fulfillment or fantasy reconstruction of the more sordid events of the second act, in which Watts plays the more haggard, failed actress Diane Selwyn. The film's tragic second act thus emerges as the uncanny, nightmarish double of the first; the crucial twist here, though, is that the nightmarish second act constitutes the "real" version. The conspiracy-laden story of Betty Elms is thus relegated to an impossible fantasy – akin, we might say, to the reassembled fish or chicken we are instructed to reconstruct from bloody pieces. Theories abound about the details of this understanding of *Mulholland Drive,* as well as its conceptual significance; yet the consensus is largely bound up in the interpretive process of resolving how the narrative structure works.

The problem here is not that such a resolution is unreasonable (certainly, the film's opening gesture to Billy Wilder's 1950 film *Sunset Boulevard,* which Lynch claims to be one of his favorite films, raises the possibility that the film could be narrated from the point of view of a corpse). Rather, the abundant set pieces, red herrings, and other marvelous excesses of *Mulholland Drive* render such schematic explications unsatisfying. Why, for instance, must we accede to the "reality" of the nightmarish second act, which, in its tragic lesbian melodrama, is hardly any less fantastic – or bound up in generic conventions – than the Betty Elms story (or, for that matter, the film-within-the-film, the *Sylvia North Story*)? As Heather Love has noted, Lynch takes up stereotypical lesbian romance plots and clichés in *each* of the film's sequences, paying equal heed to the poignancy of the Betty-Rita and Diane-Camilla plots. "While it is possible to read this film as a depiction of a confrontation between fantasy and real life," Love writes, "fantasy, in fact, has a much more diffuse presence in the film, underwriting 'real life' at every moment."[29] Clichés, generic conventions, and role-playing permeate the film in a manner that complicates the ready identification of stable characters. The point, in other words, is not simply that Betty is too good to be true, or that "Rita" is a pure invention, but that Diane Selwyn, Camilla Rhodes, and, for that matter, Sylvia North are no less provisional than these other personae – even within the logic of the film.

The film's multiply doubled or folded structure thus functions instead as a kind of mechanism for marrying and breaking apart its constitutive parts. No less than in works such as *Fish Kit* and *Chicken Kit,* the moments of combination and separation become the source of great drama. "For Lynch," George Toles reminds us, "the fact of a character's conspicuous fabrication is no safeguard against real hurt."[30] Whether occupied seamlessly, fused disjointedly, or pulled apart tragically, the viability of such combinations determines the way we feel and think about the film's characters and structures alike. To view the film in terms of its "ideas" this way hardly signifies a retreat into pure formalism, ignoring the fates of its characters in favor of pure sounds and images. Rather, it accounts for the extent to which the fates of the characters are largely determined by the formal and material demands of the cinematic medium, in its promiscuous abundance of apparatuses, from the gadgetry of sound editing and set construction to the procedures of auditioning, acting, and making a living in Hollywood.

The pivotal "Silencio" scene quite literally stages the characteristic effects of this structure. In the wee hours of the morning, the protagonists of the film's first sequence, Betty and Rita, arrive by taxi at a late-night theatrical spectacle in which the club's master of ceremonies announces: "No hay banda! There is no band! And yet we hear a band." The ensuing performance plays uncannily on the illusory possibilities of lip-synching, a signature element throughout Lynch's body of cinematic work.[31] Onstage, the singer Rebekah del Rio performs a Spanish-language rendition of Roy Orbison's torch-song "Crying." At the song's dramatic climax she collapses and is carried offstage, but her voice continues independently. Where we may have presumed a unity of singer and song, there unfold instead two separate soundtracks, the "live" and the recorded, which spin out autonomously – analogous, we might say, to the separation between celluloid and soundtrack in early film production. The *Silencio* MC's announcements that their performance is an illusion synchronized to a prerecorded tape reveals the affective overlap between production-level dubbing (*doublage,* doubling) and the intradiegetical synchronizing of bodies and voices. In turn, we watch the powerful effects of this "illusion" upon the film's protagonists – themselves doubled within the film – who watch the spectacle, convulse, and weep. For them, as for us, it remains unclear as to whether the singer's collapse is part of the club's scripted performance, which capitalizes on such separations of singer and voice, or whether it constitutes the actual collapse of the spectacle. Does the singer "die" onstage? We can of course safely presume that the real Rebekah del Rio, who plays herself in the film, survived the production either way. Yet beyond the question of how much of the performance is "real," the Silencio scene challenges us with the spectacle of how exhaustively it has been scripted and rehearsed. To what extent, we might wonder, does the rigorous orchestration of the performance not only coordinate the movements of its onstage actors but determine a broader choreography as well? How far does the spectacle extend? The consequences of the Silencio spectacle upon its immediate spectators are, for instance, quite disturbing: as if scripted herself, Betty shudders uncontrollably in response to the illusion of thunder onstage, and the two women both weep in response to del Rio's performance of "Llorando" as if heeding the implicit command to be crying.

The Silencio club's evidently mortal divorce of singer from soundtrack functions, as critics have pointed out, as the fulcrum or navel of the film. For it is at this point where the intradiegetic peeling away of "Rebekah del Rio" from her song plays out at the level of the film's diegesis, in the fatal separation of "Betty" from "Diane" (as played by Naomi Watts) and a corresponding separation of "Rita" from "Camilla Rhodes" (as played by Laura Harring), as well as in the separation of the Camilla Rhodes played by Harring from the Camilla Rhodes played by Melissa George, and so on. Sinnerbrink inventively reads the startling performance at Silencio as a staged version of the disavowed yet diegetically "real" death(s) that govern each of the film's two principal sequences: the (failed) assassination attempt that opens the film, and the (presumably successful but unseen) assassination of Camilla Rhodes that takes place in the second act. For Sinnerbrink, the Silencio performance reenacts this twice-suppressed death of Rita/Camilla, "recorded and transfigured through beautiful cinematic illusion."[32] At the same time, this logic can also be reversed: the tragic doubling of Betty and Diane, "Rita" and Camilla, constitutes the narrative reenactment of the singer's desynchronizing collapse, likewise recorded and transfigured through beautiful cinematic illusion, however tragic. The Silencio performance thus becomes the "script" or microcosm of the film itself. The reversibility of death and celluloid resurrection is sustained by the paradoxical status of fantasy in the cinematic medium: as a psychological function it never "belongs" to a character, comprising instead a second-order fantasy production of the film medium.

In *Mulholland Drive* and throughout Lynch's films in general, there is no shortage of such paradigmatic set pieces, kits that by turns wrench apart and resynchronize their "living" elements. What takes place in such cinematic kits, I maintain, is thus less a diegetical switch between a realized fantasy and a more sordid narrative "reality" than a moment of encounter between two distinct formal registers typified by, but not limited to, the technical procedures of lip-synching, dubbing, rehearsing, and enacting. These procedures, these registers – soundtrack and "singing," rehearsal or "live" performance – confront one another and become synchronized or pulled apart according to their status as doubles or echoes of one another. The medium for such kits is no longer dismembered animal bodies and their photographic doubles but the imaginative totality of Hollywood cinema. Reducible neither to simulacra or illusion nor to material reality alone, these procedures rehearse the ironies and paradoxes of their construction as cinematic kits, wherein the seamless, living entities of "illusion" and "reality" have been chopped up into their basic elements. In recombining these elements throughout the film, moreover, Lynch's formal procedures take on narrative as well as conceptual significance; their affective resonance – indeed, their tragic consequences – not only induces us, the film's spectators, to think and feel our way through but also reflexively governs the unfolding melodrama of Betty and Diane themselves. This, Lynch's film suggests, is how Hollywood works.

Indeed, it could be said that Hollywood film – the "dream factory" of cinematic production – constitutes both the medium and the setting for *Mulholland Drive*'s cinematic approach to thinking through its characters. As critics have noted, the film can be viewed as a compendium of Lynch's ideas about Hollywood, or, as Justus Nieland aptly puts it, as "a well-timed exploration of the experience of cinema amid millenarian fears of a morbid medium."[33] This exploration is not limited, however, to a simple pastiche of or panegyric to other Hollywood films (such as *Sunset Boulevard, Vertigo,* and *Gilda,* from whose lead actress, Rita Hayworth, Laura Harring's character takes her name). Rather, *Mulholland Drive* presents a phenomenal working-through of an industry whose geographical and symbolic site is the district of Hollywood itself and whose industrial product is precisely the synching up and peeling away of performances with scripts. Put otherwise, *Mulholland Drive* dramatizes Hollywood "fantasy" as the systematic production of dead starlets such as Diane, of aspirations to stardom such as Betty's, of vanishing signifiers such as Rita and Camilla Rhodes, and of resurrected careers such as that of the fictional director Adam Kesher.

One such resurrection, I should add, has to do with the character of Coco, the concierge to the Hollywood apartment complex where Betty first meets "Rita." Reemerging spectrally late in the film as the director's mother, Coco is played by the actress and dancer Ann Miller, a former dance sensation who started in Hollywood at age fourteen (Lynch's film, we might recall, begins with a dance contest) and continued as a long-standing contract actor and dancer for RKO, Columbia, and MGM. Before Lynch cast her as Coco, Miller had not appeared regularly in films for forty-five years – she performed largely on Broadway in the 1960s and 1970s – and she died of lung cancer three years after the film was released.[34] Thus "resurrected" by *Mulholland Drive,* Miller's career as a former starlet contracted by the film industry might be considered a figure for the film's notions of fantasy production. In a manner that notably recalls *Sunset Boulevard,* longevity in Hollywood is measured less in years than in the persistence of a spectacle of being "in synch" with the film industry. Once this spectacle is disrupted – as was the case for Ann Miller when she broke her studio contracts to give birth – one becomes dead to the world of filmmaking. *Mulholland Drive* systematizes this phenomenon as part of the very structure of Hollywood itself. As in *Eat My Fear,* a work roughly contemporaneous with the production of the film, Lynch recasts the city as a virtual slaughterhouse.

For the fictional Diane Selwyn, such deaths are literal as well as symbolic: Diane is both cast out of the Hollywood system *and* left as a decaying corpse (to be discovered twice: first by Betty and second by the spectators as a suicide). Yet as Toles has noted, the same film that makes Diane die twice (and which makes Betty and Rita disappear into thin air) also gave birth to Naomi Watts's rise to stardom.[35] Hollywood is, in this sense, as much a resurrection industry as a death machine. Such a redemptive assessment of the dark, nocturnal setting for *Mulholland Drive* demands not only that we leap out of the narrative confines of the film but also that we subject Hollywood itself to the "Actionist" prerogatives of Lynch's broader body of work. That is, the film recasts the landscape of Lynch's day job as an artistic material rather than as a material condition alone. The film industry loses its veneer of totality and integrity, becoming instead a set of basic functions, from the staging of auditions, scenes, and incomplete films to the processes of dubbing and synchronizing and the manufacture of stars and failures. This is the universe Lynch himself occupies, in spite of his folksy identification with his childhood Montana and Idaho; in his cinematic work, it becomes a milieu and, most importantly, a medium in which Lynch is happy to work. "The golden age of cinema is still alive there," Lynch writes, "in the smell of jasmine at night and the beautiful weather. And the light is inspiring and energizing. Even with smog, there's something about the light that's not harsh, but bright and smooth. It fills me with the feeling that all possibilities are available."[36] By recasting Hollywood as one of the media in which he works, rather than accommodating himself to its industrial and ideological demands – as in the case of the fictional Adam Kesher – Lynch derives his creative ambitions, as well as his very thinking, from the causality he ascribes to ideas. In this way Lynch can be "true" to the harmonics of the Hollywood industry without becoming grist for its mill.

In turn, Lynch has sought to institutionalize his own mode of training for staying true to the idea, seeking not only his own artistic freedom from the ravages of Hollywood but a systematic means to supplant the deadly effects of contemporary existence with a salutary, "transcendental" form of mental discipline. The David Lynch Foundation has become a platform for Lynch's public visibility as an advocate of Transcendental Meditation.[37]

"When you dive within," Lynch explains in reference to the rigors of TM, "the Self is there and true happiness is there. There's a pure, huge, unbounded ocean of it. It's bliss – physical, emotional, mental, and spiritual happiness that starts growing from within. All those things that used to *kill* you diminish. In the film business, there's so much pressure; there's so much room for anxiety and fear. But transcending makes life more like a game – a fantastic game. And creativity can really flow."[38] Such statements may confound the likes of more politically militant thinkers such as Slavoj Žižek, in whose philosophical work Lynch's films figure prominently, in spite of Žižek's dedication to expunging such New Age fantasies, which, for him, amount to little more than egoistic striving toward an impossible goodness. For Žižek, in the words of Kant, such endeavors "expose us to the danger of mysticism, to the illusion of omnipotence which, in the practical domain, is called the delirium of holiness."[39] Even so, in his abundant – one might even say insistent – writings on Lynch, Žižek returns devotionally to the formal composition of Lynch's films as a powerful conceptual apparatus in their own right; the structure of their "noir universe" (and their sound editing in particular) calls forth the "ontological horizon, the frame of reality itself, the very texture that holds reality itself together."[40] Žižek's work has sought to instrumentalize this capacity in Lynch's films toward a distinctive brand of psychoanalytic Marxism engineered against the artificial paradises of New Age transcendentalisms and the restorative bliss of the creative process.

There is, however, no paradox here. The persistence of Lynch's films in Žižek's work is consistent, I maintain, with the very logic of Lynch's own "transcendental" imagination, insofar as the *films* – and the ideas within them – do the thinking. Lynch's own public persona as both a masterful auteur and a full-blown mystic is, in other words, an effect of the films, a product of their structural logic rather than their authorial source. That is, what is fascinating about Lynch's work is that "the idea" is so impersonal as to structure the very existence of the filmmaker himself. David Lynch, by this logic, is one of his own "big fish."

Yet to insist too forcefully on this possibility – that is, to privilege the films over the "naive" figure of Lynch himself – suggests a reification of the notion of Lynch as a know-nothing mystic, a product of the very "New Age" criticism from which Žižek seeks to distinguish his own work. Lynch is no less an intellectual, however, for the "sinuous indirection" or apparent lack of sophistication of his performance as a public figure. And indeed, Lynch's thinking acknowledges the antihumanism implicit even in his so-called mysticism in a way that is similarly consistent with the way the structure of his films derives from "ideas." For Žižek's claim is, for all its antipathy to the New Age resonances of Lynch's devotion to TM, consistent with Lynch's own. "David Lynch," the Hollywood oddity, the postcinematic artisan-transcendentalist, is himself the product of an idea.

## NOTES

1. Associated Press, "Lynch Too Gruesome."

2. See CowParade's "Frequently Asked Questions," http://edinburgh.cowparade.com/contact/faq/1; also http://kansascity.cowparade.com/contact/faq/1.

3. On the legal skirmishes, see Hedges, "Is Nothing Sacred?"

4. See, for instance, Adams, "Post-Meateating," esp. 48–50.

5. Muehl, "Material Action Manifesto," 87. Muehl's capitalization.

6. In interviews, Lynch is often reluctant to plot a definitive art-historical genealogy for his early career as a painter, citing interests in and affinities with the work of Francis Bacon and with American action painters; his largest

"influence" is Bushnell Keeler, the father of his best friend.

7. PETA sued for the release of its cow. See People for Ethical Treatment of Animals v. Giuliani, 105 F.Supp.2d 294 (2000), United States District Court, S.D. New York, July 25, 2000, http://www.leagle.com/xmlResult.aspx?page=5&xmldoc=2000399105FSupp2d294_1366.xml&docbase=CSLWAR2–1986–2006&SizeDisp=7.

8. Associated Press, "Lynch Too Gruesome."

9. Olson, *David Lynch,* 516.

10. In his foreword to the exhibition catalog *David Lynch: Dark Splendour,* Achim Sommer writes that Lynch "had the opportunity, within the framework of film productions, to try out everything, including stage and furniture design. He in no way limited his creativity to one direction, but instead continued to develop it in painting, drawing, collage, and photography" (Spies, *David Lynch,* 12).

11. Chion, *David Lynch,* 182.

12. Richard A. Barney, introduction to Barney, *David Lynch,* vii.

13. Lynch, in Rodley, *Lynch on Lynch,* 48.

14. Lynch, *Catching the Big Fish,* 23.

15. Ibid., 115.

16. On Lynch's Kantian "ideas," see Sinnerbrink, "Cinematic Ideas."

17. Lynch, *Catching the Big Fish,* 19.

18. Interview with John Esther, in Barney, *Interviews,* 247.

19. Interview with David Breskin (1990), in ibid., 99–100.

20. The chicken in *Chicken Kit,* purchased in Mexico City, is marked as "naked" because Lynch presumably bought it plucked and ready to cook. Lynch's commentary on its featherless condition is characteristically amusing: "Then I did *Chicken Kit.* That was my most advanced work in the Kit department! I got into a lotta things with that one, like there was a note that told you the feathers were not included – with a lot of kits you have to buy extra stuff. It's a rip off. And then there were instructions about how to put the feathers in – not the soft, fluffy end, but the more pointed, harder end [laughs]. Really dumb stuff" (Rodley, *Lynch on Lynch,* 110).

21. Ibid.

22. Ibid., 113.

23. Another of Lynch's formal apparatuses from this period, the "Bee Board" or "Ricky Board," made with dead bees, highlights this taxonomic quality. As Lynch explains in a 2006 interview, "A Ricky Board was based on my idea of a Japanese kind of formal art and so you

would arrange your – whatever they were . . . they're all going to be suddenly different but mainly look the same, like rows of bees. I think four rows of five was what it was but then you would name your Ricky, name your Rickies, and so they look the same but they've all got different names." For Lynch, in other words, the naming becomes the formal element of the apparatus that both legitimates the taxonomic logic of its formal presentation of the bees and yet, paradoxically, disrupts it. "When you put a name to them they kind of separate out and it's true, you could look at a bee named 'Riley' and the bee would take on a certain character. A bee named 'Bob' would suddenly be unique" (David Lynch, interview with Kristine McKenna, in Fondation Cartier, *The Air Is on Fire,* 16).

24. On Spoerri's work and other comestible art, see Novero, *Antidiets.*

25. Michel Chion's 1995 study of Lynch's films, which does not discuss TM, is the most attentive to Lynch's procedural logic; it notably features its own "Lynch Kit" of paradigmatic Lynchian motifs and techniques.

26. Chion, *David Lynch,* 42. Chion's example is characteristic of Lynch's auteurist signature: "In *Eraserhead,* Henry is stuck in his room while expecting a message to be delivered to his letter-box in the building's lobby. His thoughts are expressed by a shot of the letter-box, but it is impossible to say whether this is a mental shot or an objective shot of the letter-box edited in parallel. The insert counts as an idea, a thought, but it is objective at the same time" (ibid., 40).

27. Ibid., 21.

28. For a thrilling set of speculative essays and interpretations on *Mulholland Drive,* see http://www.mulholland-drive.net/. For the most thorough scholarly explications, see, for instance, Sinnerbrink, "Cinematic Ideas"; McGowan, *The Impossible David Lynch,* esp. 194–221; Nieland, *David Lynch,* esp. 94–110; and Hayles and Gessler, "The Slipstream of Mixed Reality."

29. See Love, "Spectacular Failure."

30. Toles, "Auditioning Betty," 4.

31. In earlier films, such as the related scene in *Blue Velvet* in which Ben (Dean Stockwell) lip-synch's Roy Orbison's "In Dreams," what becomes disturbing instead is the seamlessness of the synchronization of performance with song, played intradiegetically as a threatening moment of performative illusionism. See Vass, "Cinematic Meaning," 12. On Lynch and synaesthesia, see Barker, "Out of Sync."

32. See Sinnerbrink, "Cinematic Ideas."

33. Nieland, *David Lynch*, 95.

34. Severo, "Ann Miller."

35. Toles, "Auditioning Betty," 9.

36. Lynch, *Catching the Big Fish*, 31–32.

37. http://www.davidlynchfoundation.org/.

38. Lynch, *Catching the Big Fish*, 51–52. For a discussion of the collective possibilities of such bliss, see Barney, *Interviews*, 258–260.

39. Immanuel Kant, quoted in Žižek, *Enjoy Your Symptom*, 164.

40. Žižek, *The Metastasis of Desire*, 115.

## SELECTED BIBLIOGRAPHY


Adams, Carol J. "Post-Meateating." In *Animal Encounters*, edited by Tom Tyler and Manuela Rossini, 47–72. Leiden: Brill, 2009.

Associated Press. "Lynch Too Gruesome for NYC." August 3, 2000, http://www.apnewsarchive.com/2000/Lynch-Too-Gruesome-for-NYC/id-eda18460eabdb58feded536ca40ed9a0.

Barker, Jennifer. "Out of Sync, Out of Sight: Synaesthesia and Film Spectacle." *Paragraph* 31.2 (July 2008): 236–251.

Barney, Richard A., ed. *David Lynch: Interviews*. Oxford: University of Mississippi Press, 2009.

Chion, Michel. *David Lynch*. Translated by Robert Julian. London: BFI, 1995.

Fondation Cartier. *David Lynch: The Air Is on Fire*. London: Thames and Hudson, 2006.

Hayles, N. Katherine, and Nicholas Gessler. "The Slipstream of Mixed Reality: Unstable Ontologies and Semiotic Markers in *The Thirteenth Floor, Dark City*, and *Mulholland Drive*." *PMLA* 119.3 (May 2004): 482–499.

Hedges, Chris. "Is Nothing Sacred? International Discontent Erupts over a Cow Parade." *New York Times*, May 31, 2000, http://www.nytimes.com/2000/05/31/nyregion/is-nothing-sacred-international-discontent-erupts-over-a-cow-parade.html?pagewanted=all&src=pm.

Heidegger, Martin. *What Is Called Thinking?* Translated by J. Glenn Gray. New York: Harper & Row, 1968.

Love, Heather. "Spectacular Failure: The Figure of the Lesbian in *Mulholland Drive*." *New Literary History* 35.1 (Winter 2004): 117–132.

Lynch, David. *Catching the Big Fish: Meditation, Consciousness, and Creativity*. New York: Penguin, 2007.

McGowan, Todd. *The Impossible David Lynch.* New York: Columbia University Press, 2007.

Muehl, Otto. "Material Action Manifesto" (1964). In *Writings of the Vienna Actionists,* edited by Malcolm Green, 87. London: Atlas Press, 1999.

Nieland, Justus. *David Lynch: Contemporary Film Directors.* Champaign-Urbana: University of Illinois Press, 2012.

Novero, Cecilia. *Antidiets of the Avant-Garde: From Futurist Cooking to Eat Art.* Minneapolis: University of Minnesota Press, 2010.

Olson, Greg. *David Lynch: Beautiful Dark.* Lanham, Md.: Scarecrow Press, 2008.

Rodley, Chris, ed. *Lynch on Lynch.* London: Faber and Faber, 1997.

Severo, Richard. "Ann Miller, Tap-Dancer Starring in Musicals, Dies." *New York Times,* January 23, 2004, http://www.nytimes.com/2004/01/23/arts/ann-miller-tap-dancer-starring-in-musicals-dies.html.

Sinnerbrink, Robert. "Cinematic Ideas: David Lynch's *Mulholland Drive.*" *Film-Philosophy* 9.34 (June 2005), http://www.film-philosophy.com/vo19–2005/n34sinnerbrink.

Spies, Werner, ed. *David Lynch: Dark Splendour. Space. Images. Sound.* Osftildern: Hatje Cantz, 2010.

Toles, George. "Auditioning Betty in Mulholland Drive." *Film Quarterly* 58.1 (Fall 2004): 2–13.

Vass, Michael. "Cinematic Meaning in the Work of David Lynch; Revisiting *Twin Peaks: Fire Walk with Me, Lost Highway,* and *Mulholland Drive.*" *Cine-Action* 67 (Summer 2005): 12–25.

Žižek, Slavoj. *Enjoy Your Symptom: Jacques Lacan in Hollywood and Out.* London: Routledge, 1991.

——. *The Metastasis of Desire: Six Essays on Women and Causality.* London: Verso, 1994.

EVOLUTION

BIG BONE LICK

INHUMAN

ELOI

EXTINCTION

GENERATION

# THE ODDBALL ARCHIVE

# BOX III

# UNTIMELY ARCHIVES

CLIMATE

HUMAN

DNA

FOSSIL

MAMMOTH

TIME MACHINE

MORLOCKS

KEY WORDS

Big Bone Lick, climate, DNA, Eloi, evolution, extinction, fossil, generation, human, inhuman, mammoth, Morlocks, time machine

COLLECTION CONTENTS

*Timothy Sweet*
"The Eighteenth-Century *Archives du monde:* The Question of Agency in Extinction Stories"

*Charles M. Tung*
"Modernist Heterochrony, Evolutionary Biology, and the Chimera of Time"

*Aaron Jaffe*
"THERE IS AS YET INSUFFICIENT DATA FOR A MEANINGFUL ANSWER: Inhumanism at the Literary Limit"

## COLLECTION SUMMARY

All archives promise – and ineluctably fail – to offer a bulwark against the passage of time. In their task of making up for lost memory – that is, for the loss of ways of thinking, as well as for the passing of successive eras – archives carry out their functions incompletely. Archives mark what has been lost in their preservation of remnants that remain incomplete in what we imagine to be their testimony to a much fuller moment. Can we think of archives as time machines that bring us into direct contact with the documents and relics of a forgotten age? Or do they instead function as measures of time's inexorable passage and the losses that ensue: not simply time's movement, but also its tendency to wash away its own footprints, to eradicate its traces? As time machines, perhaps archives confront us most profoundly with the inhuman scale of this passage: a time no longer measurable according to the term of a human life.

This box collects three essays that discuss conversations about archives that reflect fascinations with the scale and measurability of time, and the longue durée, in three successive centuries. Beginning with the eighteenth-century musings on the fossil record of North America by European, white American, and Native thinkers, Timothy Sweet's essay reconstructs eighteenth-century thinking about the agency of extinction, whether through supernatural, human, or climatic intervention. The archive of the dinosaurs' disappearance is the archive of a Paleolithic mythos, whereby the wanderings of mammoths become the imaginative terrain for exploring the reasons why extinctions occur. Natural history inquiries and Native myths about the extinction of the woolly mammoth became a "meta-archive" of the geological record through which thinkers weighed the relative powers of human and nonhuman agents within the natural world.

Next, Charles Tung's essay moves to the evolutionary biology of the nineteenth century, which sought to understand how the human body could form the archive for the history of evolution itself. In Tung's estimation, genetic aberration and seemingly atavistic developmental phases in humans comprise an archive of the phylogenetic history of mankind, which became a modernist obsession. From nineteenth-century biology through the fictional works of H. G. Wells, the paintings of Picasso, and the poetry of T. S. Eliot, there is a veritable fascination with the ways in which the long, aching histories of biological and even geological time leave their traces within human genetic matter. Through this imaginary genetic archive, modernist "time machines" explore the possibility for alternative timelines and experiences of duration beyond the scale and scope of human history.

An archive of speculations about impossibly distant futures shifts fully into the real production of science fiction. As Aaron Jaffe shows us, the work of writers such as H. G. Wells, Isaac Asimov, and J. G. Ballard attempts to chronicle impossible or inhuman timescapes; it does so from within a modern age characterized by the ever-increasing measurement and regulation of time by devices such as clocks, alarms, schedules, and the five-day workweek. In such literary works, the "time machines" of Paleolithic wandering, which offered access to evolutionary periods prior to definitive standards of human measurement, give way to imagined versions of a future no less beyond human grasp. With a futurism no less bound up in a melancholic fascination with the sublimity of evolutionary time, such writers call out to the extinction of human memory: the constitutive problem, we might say, of any archive.

## HISTORIES OF THE CONTRIBUTORS

**Timothy Sweet** is professor of English at West Virginia University, where he teaches courses in American literature and ecocriticism. His publications include *Traces of War: Poetry, Photography, and the Crisis of the Union* (Johns Hopkins University Press, 1990), *American Georgics: Economy and Environment in Early American Literature* (University of Pennsylvania Press, 2002), and articles on early American, Native American, and Civil War literature. His contribution to this collection is drawn from work in progress on extinction narratives.

**Charles M. Tung** is associate professor of English at Seattle University, where he teaches twentieth-century literature, literary theory, and race. He has published articles on modernist temporalities and is completing a book called *Modernism, Time Machines, and Alternate Histories,* which examines the relationships among the modernist time obsession, the rise of time-travel narratives, and the desire for alternate histories.

**Aaron Jaffe** is professor of English at the University of Louisville. Since publishing *Modernism and the Culture of Celebrity* (Cambridge University Press, 2005, 2009), his major project has been writing and researching a new book called *Second Modernism: Risk, Modernity and Cultural Value.*

7

# THE EIGHTEENTH-CENTURY *ARCHIVES DU MONDE*

## THE QUESTION OF AGENCY IN EXTINCTION STORIES

*Timothy Sweet*

Reckoning with the fossil remains of unfamiliar creatures, naturalists in the eighteenth century began to historicize nature. The era's preeminent naturalist, Georges-Louis Leclerc, comte de Buffon, articulated the program for this new kind of history by conceptualizing the earth itself as an archive: "As in civil history, one consults titles, one researches medals, one deciphers antique inscriptions to determine the epochs of human revolutions and discover the dates of moral events; similarly, in natural history, one must search the archives of the world, draw old monuments from the bowels of the earth, collect their debris, and assemble in a body of evidence all indices of physical changes that can take us back to the different ages of Nature."[1] Playing etymologically, by way of the analogy with civil history, on the root of *archive* in beginnings and government (*archē*), Buffon defines natural history as an inquiry into the original and ongoing government of the world. The conception of the *archives du monde* thus raises the question of that which governs, that is, the question of agency. Attempts to answer this question in eighteenth-century North America produced an intercultural meta-archive in which Native American and European American interpretations of the earth's ancient *débris* offered conflicting accounts of the interactions of human, animal, and natural/supernatural nonanimate agents. The archives du monde became a site of contest between Enlightenment reason and unreason, as European Americans disavowed Native American supernaturalist ontologies even as they adhered to their own supernaturalist assumptions concerning an extrahuman creating and regulating power. The archives remain a site of contest as attempts to explain the extinction of Pleistocene megafauna according to scientific or traditional indigenous frames take on new urgency within the discourses of climate change and ecological catastrophism.[2]

A potentially rich archive for the new kind of history proposed by Buffon was Big Bone Lick, a salt lick near the Ohio River southwest of present-day Cincinnati. In 1739 a military expedition of French soldiers and Native American warriors, mostly Iroquois, encamped near Big Bone Lick, found fossil bones, teeth, and tusks of creatures that later came to be classified as mastodons and mammoths.[3] One of the expedition's officers, Charles Le Moyne de Longueuil, baron de Longueuil, shipped some of the remains back to Paris, where they were placed under Buffon's direction in Louis XV's cabinet of curiosities. Subsequently collected remains found their way, often by circuitous routes, into other repositories of curiosity, including the private collections of Benjamin Franklin and other members of the Royal Society, the Royal Society's museum, the Tower of London, the American Philosophical Society, the great hall at Monticello, Charles Wilson Peale's Philadelphia Museum, and P. T. Barnum's American Museum.[4] Most recently, the Grand Rapids, Michigan, Public Museum acquired some mastodon remains that were found in a box of miscellaneous items donated to a local charity, which the museum's collections manager characterized as "kind of an oddball way for something to come in," especially because no accompanying story explained the remains' provenance.[5]

The provenance of the Big Bone Lick collection was obvious to Longueuil's Iroquois warriors: they knew from traditional stories that the remains belonged to the "grandfather of the buffalo."[6] To European naturalists, the remains suggested not so much a buffalo as an elephant. This raised numerous questions: How could elephants have survived in a cold climate? Had the climate changed over time? Were the animals in fact elephants, or another species? In any case, were such animals still living, and if so, where had they gone? Or if they had become extinct, how long ago and of what cause? Subsequent collectors followed Longueuil's practice of eliciting stories from local informants. The most widely circulated of these stories appears in *Notes on the State of Virginia* (1785), where Thomas Jefferson claims the existence of the mammoth as a key piece of evidence in his refutation of Buffon's theory of the inferiority of the American environment.[7] Jefferson opens his argument by integrating Native American narrative into the European discourse of natural history: "Our quadrupeds have mostly been described by Linnaeus and Mons. de Buffon. Of these, the Mammoth, or big buffalo, as called by the Indians, must certainly have been the largest. Their tradition is, that he was carnivorous, and still exists in the northern parts of America." Jefferson then transcribes a Delaware story concerning "the animal whose bones were found at the Saltlicks, on the Ohio." Jefferson does not make much of the narrative's historical claims, presumably because the story described the action of a supernatural actor, a "Great Man above" who killed all the mammoths but one by hurling lightning bolts. However, he renders from the archive of mammoth bones a similar claim, arguing that mammoths were likely still living somewhere north of the Great Lakes, where the "aboriginal state" of the environment provided habitat. "To add to this, the traditionary testimony of the Indians," he concludes, "would be adding the light of a taper to that of the meridian sun."[8]

Jefferson's treatment of the Delaware story typifies eighteenth-century naturalists' ambivalence toward Native American interpretations of fossils. For example, in an essay promoting the first museum exhibition of a complete mammoth skeleton in 1803, Rembrandt Peale argued that the indigenous tradition of the "great Buffalo" from Big Bone Lick was "clouded with fable" but "not improbable" at its core.[9] Similarly, American Philosophical Society Vice President Benjamin Smith Barton explained in a treatise on method, "I am far from insinuating, that such traditions should be received as *pure history:* but I am persuaded that, on some occasions, much interesting information might be educed from them. . . . To a discerning and virtuous naturalist, they are like mines, among the rubbish of which we dig, with success, for the most precious metals."[10]

As European Americans developed narratives of environmental history through critical readings of both the fossil remains and indigenous stories of the remains, an internally contradictory meta-archive came to be layered onto the archives du monde. This meta-archive of environmental history registered two kinds of disagreement, one regarding agency and one regarding effect. Most naturalists – with the prominent exception of Jefferson – agreed with Native Americans that mammoths had threatened the security of humankind in ancient times and that the extinction of the mammoth had shaped the environment for the benefit of humankind. How to understand the cause of that effect was another matter, however. Different conceptions of causal agency emerged from different positions of power. During the mid- to late eighteenth century, indigenous cultures in the Ohio River valley saw themselves as threatened, especially after the British defeat of the French in the Seven Years' War and the failure of Pontiac's Rebellion in 1763. Stories from these cultures minimized human agency with respect to the environment or relegated it to the past and emphasized supernatural agency – though the particular conception of divine agency, monotheistic or pantheistic, again varied with local context. European American naturalists suggested that certain truths could be mined from these indigenous stories through the disaggregation of fact from "fable," as Peale put it. This suggestion took shape within the larger Enlightenment context of the disavowal of supernatural intervention into the natural world, as wonders were conceptually reduced to a regular order of nature.[11] Eighteenth-century naturalists thus anticipated modern cognitive-linguistic theories of myth, which purport to refine truth from the "rubbish" of mental distortions.

Despite their assumption that the truth of Native American environmental narratives was occluded by fictions of supernatural actors, eighteenth-century naturalists also assumed a supernaturalist ontology, positing an implicitly Christian or deist conception of the world that included superhuman agents.[12] However, some who were invested in westward colonial expansion proposed an alternative account of the Big Bone Lick extinctions (without explicitly disavowing a supernaturalist ontology), developing a speculative political fiction of collective human agency according to which ancient inhabitants of North America had banded together to remove the threat of the mammoth. Jefferson alone among the commentators wanted to hold on to the belief that the mammoth was still living, though he did imagine that human activity might have diminished its range. As he eventually came to accept the fact of extinction, he posited that a supernatural agent ordered particular extinctions but kept nature from degenerating into chaos.

If Jefferson's narration of extinction as loss marks him as peculiarly modern, anticipating our own elegiac response, his recourse to supernatural agency invites us to interrogate the ontological grounding of modern extinction discourse, which must account for the interaction of human and other-than-human agents. Shifting our interpretive focus from ontology to agency may lead to a more productive form of environmental history, as we see examples of how environmental change manifests as felt consequences in the present experience of locally situated narrators. This shift from questions of ontology to questions of agency follows the recent work of Bruno Latour, who argues that modern science, the legacy of Enlightenment reason, cannot settle the question of ontology because strict naturalism proliferates endless causal chains culminating only in an appeal to an undifferentiated Nature. A focus on agency makes no judgment regarding ontology, although Latour argues that "there is no way to devise a successor to nature, if we do not tackle the tricky question of *animism* anew."[13] Within an agent-oriented frame, the extinction meta-archive remains anthropocentric, concerned ultimately with human desires, regardless of competing ontological claims.

* * *

The Native American meta-archive of Big Bone Lick includes four stories transcribed prior to the late nineteenth-century era of salvage ethnography (although others may persist in oral traditions). In the multicultural, multilingual context of the Ohio Valley in the eighteenth century, such stories must have been widely shared among Shawnees, Iroquois, Delawares, and others. Variably inflected according to context, audience, purpose, and taste, the stories bear two core motifs: giant animals pose a threat to the people, directly or indirectly; and all or most of the giant animals are killed by lightning bolts. Whereas some other eastern North American indigenous stories associate fossil remains of late Pleistocene megafauna with water monsters or humanoid giants, the stories from Big Bone Lick identify the remains as belonging to a large, carnivorous mammal.[14] The tellings of the earlier Big Bone Lick stories bracket Pontiac's Rebellion of 1763. Two were recorded in 1762, each collected independently and transmitted to the Philadelphia Quaker naturalist John Bartram. One of these comes via Bartram's English patron Peter Collinson, who had heard from Indian trader and deputy superintendent for Indian affairs George Croghan about the discovery of the giant skeletons at Big Bone Lick.[15] Croghan, who was based at Fort Pitt after its rebuilding in 1759, visited Big Bone Lick several times while traveling the Ohio River on diplomatic and trading voyages; he heard a story about the giant animals from his escorts, who were probably Delaware, Shawnee, or Sandusky Wyandot. Croghan evidently sent Collinson a story along with a description of bones and teeth, which Collinson then passed on to Bartram: "The Indian tradition [is] that the Monstrous Buffalos so called by the Indians was all struck dead with Lightning at this licking place." Collinson doubted that the story fully explained the creatures' disappearance, asking Bartram, "But is it likely to think all the Race was here Collected & was Extinguished at one Stroke[?]"[16] Evidently Croghan or Collinson had isolated the story's core motif, the lightning strike. While the adjective "Monstrous" characterizes the animals as a threat to humankind, the narrative is attenuated, leaving the agent of the lightning strike implicit.

After hearing from both Collinson and the commander at Fort Pitt, Colonel Henry Bouquet, about the bones at Big Bone Lick, Bartram evidently wrote to James Wright, a fellow Quaker curious in natural history, to request more information. Working with an interpreter, Wright interviewed "two Sincible Shawanese Indians" who gave a detailed description of the site, including the positions of five skeletons of the giant animal in question, and a story about their extinction, which Wright transmitted to Bartram in 1762.[17] The Shawnees reported that although such bones were "Scattered here & there" across the Ohio Valley, nowhere else was there a large group such as this, all apparently killed at one stroke. At the time that these animals lived, according to the Shawnees, there also lived "men of a size proportionable to them, who used to kill them and tye them in their noppusses [sic] and throw them on their Backs As an Indian now does a deer." When this race of giant men disappeared, "God killed these mighty creatures, that they should not hurt the present race of Indians." The Big Bone Lick animals specifically were "supposed . . . to have been Kild by lightning."[18]

Another version was told on site at Big Bone Lick in the summer of 1766, although it was not published until 1795. In the new and tenuous accommodation between the British and various Native American polities following the failure of Pontiac's Rebellion, George Croghan organized an expedition down the Ohio River to distribute presents to cement alliances as the French formerly had done. George Morgan, a Philadelphia merchant, acted as supercargo. At Big Bone Lick, the British party met a raiding party of Iroquois and Wyandots headed south against the Chickasaws. The eighty-four-year-old head of the raiding party, most likely an Iroquois, told Morgan that he had traveled this road against the Catawbas many times in his youth and had often heard his grandfather's story about the bones.[19] This version begins with a familiar account, which emerged in the context of Ohio Valley revitalization movements, of the Great Spirit's separate creations of the white, black, and red races, each on its separate continent. The "Red Man" was happy for a time, but "the foolish young people, at length forgetting his rules, became exceedingly ill-tempered and wicked." Unique to the version of the separate creations story told to Morgan is an episode in which the Great Spirit punishes the red race by creating "the great buffalo," who "made war upon the human species and destroyed all but a few." When these remaining few "repented," the Great Spirit killed the buffalos by means of lightning bolts, all but a male and female pair, whom he "shut up in yonder mountain, ready to let loose again, should occasion require."[20]

Jefferson attributes the story he published in *Notes on the State of Virginia* to the "chief speaker" of a Delaware delegation who had visited him in his capacity as governor of Virginia, probably during 1781 in Charlottesville. After "matters of business" pertaining to the war "had been discussed and settled in council, the governor asked the delegation some questions relative to their country, including what they knew or had heard of the animal whose bones were found at the Saltlicks, on the Ohio." The chief replied that according to "a tradition handed down from their fathers," "in antient times, a herd of these tremendous animals came to the Big-bone licks, and began an universal destruction of the bear, deer, elks, buffalos, and other animals, which had been created for the use of the Indians." The "Great Man above" was "enraged" by this behavior and killed all the giant animals but the largest bull, who was wounded but escaped, "bound[ing] over the Ohio, over the Wabash, the Illinois, and over the great lakes, where he is living at this day."[21] This story includes neither the 1762 Shawnee version's account of a prior hunting culture technologically adapted to killing the giant animals nor the 1766 Iroquois version's moral narrative of separate creations followed by sin, repentance, and salvation. If Jefferson was gratified to hear from an indigenous informant that the mammoth was living in the present day, he was skeptical of the means by which that information was transmitted, via what he would have regarded as an allegory in which one mammoth, retreating from an angry god, stands in for a population that actually migrated for some material reason to the northwest. Yet while Jefferson expanded on the critique of the indigenous meta-archive as suggested by Collinson, he agreed with his Delaware informant that the mammoth "may as well exist there [in the unexplored northwest] now, as he did formerly where we find his bones. If he be a carnivorous animal, as some Anatomists affirm, his early retirement may be accounted for from the general destruction of the wild game by the Indians, which commences in the first instant of their connection with us, for the purpose of purchasing matchcoats, hatchets, and firelocks, with their skins."[22]

* * *

Thus attempting to disaggregate fact from fable by correlating narrative detail with observable material truth (market hunting was generally known to cause a game population to decline), Jefferson anticipated the modern cognitivist theory of myth. Working backward from assumptions about narrative distortions imposed by mental structures, the cognitivist approach attempts to discern the material truth of the geohistorical or astronomical event that the story seems to witness. For example, following this method, a Klamath story recorded in 1865, shorn of its fabulous aspects and correlated with geological evidence, seems to record eyewitness memory of the formation of Crater Lake some 7,700 years ago from the eruption of a volcano.[23] The cognitivist approach assumes the possibility of the unbroken continuity of oral tradition over millennia. Here some ethnohistorians, Native American scholars, and activists agree. Sioux activist Vine Deloria, Jr., claims absolutely that traditional stories bear witness to events such as the creation of Crater Lake.[24] Pawnee historian Roger Echo-Hawk more cautiously writes that "verbal literature arguably preserves glimpses and echoes of the long-vanished Pleistocene world of our ancestors."[25]

A cognitivist approach to the Big Bone Lick meta-archive would begin with the analysis of one core motif, the killing of giant animals by means of lightning bolts, because archeological evidence could be sketchy at best for the other core motif, the claim that the animals posed a threat to humankind. Cognitivists would shear away any consideration of divine agency as a mental distortion (the belief that if something happens, some agent must have willed it to happen) in order to read the lightning-bolt motif as evidence of a natural phenomenon. Thus the story might be interpreted as a garbled explanation of the onset of the Younger Dryas climate phase, a thousand-year period of cold and drought from about 11,000 to 10,000 years ago. The hypothesis is that a comet crashing to earth some 11,000 years ago caused widespread fires, the ash from which induced cooling by partly blocking solar radiation.[26] In North America, the timing of the Younger Dryas climate phase correlates with the extinction of the mammoth, as verified by radiocarbon dating, and with the demise of the Clovis culture, whose technology was specifically adapted to hunting the mammoth and other late Pleistocene megafauna. The 1762 Shawnee story maps most closely onto the Younger Dryas scenario, identifying a premodern culture "proportionable" to the mammoth, which seems to correlate with archaeological evidence of Clovis culture.[27] Yet the story seems to want to refute the controversial hypothesis that this culture hunted the mammoth to extinction, because here the humanoid giants (the Clovis people) disappear *before* the mammoths do, to be replaced by the present-day Shawnees, who hunt smaller animals such as deer, although no reason is given for the disappearance of the giants.[28] In this evaluative context, the Shawnee version would seem to point to climate change as the cause of the late

Pleistocene extinctions, the compression of time between the lightning strike / comet event and the eventual disappearance of the mammoths being a cognitive accommodation of long-scale environmental observation to conventional narrative chronology.

However, none of the other Big Bone Lick stories preserves the Shawnee version's elements of the replacement of one culture by another. Without these elements, the story loses its window onto the late Pleistocene epoch. Reduced to the core motif of an extinction-causing fiery event, the Big Bone Lick story stands only to lose authority as further geological and paleontological findings confirm or disconfirm the impact of a comet and any resulting climate change and ecological consequences. The cognitivist approach thus allows the primitive subject to witness but not to understand. In this way it reproduces the eighteenth-century naturalists' critique of Native American environmental narratives as so much raw ore, valuable only insofar as it might be "mine[d]" for the "precious metals" of original witness.[29]

* * *

The ground of dispute concerns the naming of other-than-human causation – that is, the question of agency, which as we have seen remained implicit in Buffon's archival conception of environmental history. The modern cognitivist interpreters of myth merely defer the question of agency to the physical sciences, where it becomes a matter of specifying geophysical, astrophysical, or biological forces. Since these forces have their causes in turn back to some unknown origin in the beginning of the universe, such a deferral instantiates, as Latour puts it, a "contradictory notion of an *action without agency*."[30] However, the eighteenth-century European American naturalists did not discount the question of agency but rather named it in three forms, sometimes intermixed in a single narrative. Some, such as Jefferson, substituted a European conception of superhuman agency, vaguely equivocating "God" and "Nature," for the more localized conceptions of superhuman agency deployed by the Native American stories. Some naturalists appealed to geophysical forces such as a great deluge, thus deferring causation to an unspecified (though implicitly superhuman) origin. Others, however, developed a fiction of cooperative human agency that was no more verifiable (especially given the absence of any such motif in traditional stories) than the apparently more magical accounts of agency given by their naturalist colleagues or by Native Americans.

In the first European American contribution to the Big Bone Lick meta-archive, a paper published in 1768 in the Royal Society's *Philosophical Transactions,* English physician and anatomist William Hunter argued that the fossil remains, like similar remains found in Siberia, were not those of the elephant but rather represented a distinct species. Hunter's speculation regarding the extinction of this species, which he thought "in former times has been a very general inhabitant of the globe," shares with the Native American stories a project of moral evaluation. Hunter asserts that "if this animal was carnivorous, which I believe cannot be doubted, though we may as philosophers regret it, as men we cannot but thank Heaven that its whole generation is probably extinct."[31] Even as he invokes a supernatural agent by "thank[ing] Heaven," Hunter does not speculate on the mechanism of extinction, a question that Native Americans had answered by reference to lightning strikes. Eighteenth-century naturalists were divided over question of mechanism. Buffon would posit a gradual climate change, regarding the Big Bone Lick and Siberian fossils as remains of a tropical elephant species that had either died out or migrated as the earth cooled. Many others, such as Buffon's successor Georges Cuvier, posited a catastrophic climate event such as a flood rather than a gradual cooling. With the weight of Christian tradition behind it, the story of the flood had remained the default narrative, first invoked in this context by German naturalist Johann Breyne in 1737 to explain the location of elephant-like remains in Siberia.[32] The sublimity of the biblical flood matched the scale of the creature. Thus Rembrandt Peale, for example, found the "sudden and powerful cause" of a great "deluge" the likeliest cause for the extinction of such "tremendous animals . . . which at all times must have filled the human mind with surprise and wonder."[33]

However, some European Americans argued that humankind, rather than a supernatural agent or a nonhuman natural agent, was the beneficent shaper who had removed a threatening excess from the environment. These European Americans developed a speculative political fiction centered on human agency. In a short book published in 1784 to promote the settlement of Kentucky, land speculator John Filson reviewed the territory's "Curiosities" of natural history, including the extant literature on the remains at Big Bone Lick. Dismissing the stories told about Siberian remains by "ignorant and superstitious Tartars" but apparently unaware of Native American accounts, Filson takes a moral stance similar to that of Hunter and the indigenous Big Bone Lick stories but shifts the attribution of agency:

> Can then so great a link have perished from the chain of nature? Happy we that it has. How formidable an enemy to the human species, an animal as large as the elephant, the tyrant of the forests, perhaps the devourer of man! Nations, such as the Indians, must have been in perpetual alarm. The animosities among the various tribes must have been suspended till the common enemy, who threatened the very existence of all, should be extirpated. To this circumstance we are probably indebted for a fact, which is perhaps singular in its kind, the extinction of a whole race of animals from the system of nature.[34]

In this scenario, the normal politics of warfare and diplomacy is suspended in favor of international cooperation to remove a threat to humankind. Imagining human rather than supernatural agency as causal, Filson develops a politics rather than a theology of extinction.

This political fiction was reiterated by George Turner, a federal judge in the Ohio country who had personally traveled to Big Bone Lick.[35] In a scientific paper arguing that the mammoth was carnivorous, Turner concludes, "With the agility and ferocity of a tiger; with a body of unequalled magnitude and strength, it is possible that the Mammoth may have been at once the terror of the forest and of man! – and may not the human race have made the extirpation of this terrific disturber a common cause?"[36] Filson's and Turner's narrative of cooperative human action fit the late eighteenth-century context that is the occasion for Filson's promotional tract, the shaping of American nature for European culture – a project that would require the removal of Native Americans. (Filson's text includes the first biography of the Indian fighter Daniel Boone.) Like the indigenous narratives, this narrative takes an anthropocentric stance toward the shaping of the environment. However, the imperial prospect elicits an emphasis on the potency of collective human agency where the indigenous narratives relegated shaping power to superhuman actors.

* * *

Even as we translate between Native American and European practices for naming other-than-human agency, we can observe that the meta-archive as a whole is fundamentally concerned with one primary distinction, between the human and the nonhuman. That is, the meta-archive becomes a site for the examination of the powers and capacities of human and other-than-human agents with respect to a given world. With this modal approach, we can reread the Big Bone Lick meta-archive more closely as shaped by environmental concerns in the present of the telling.[37] All the Native American stories make three claims: (1) giant animals are associated with past environmental conditions that are less hospitable than present conditions to humankind; (2) human beings do not possess the capacity to manage this kind of environmental threat; and (3) some superhuman power does possess that capacity. The nature of that superhuman power remains in question, however, indicating a conflict between monotheistic and pantheistic cosmologies. Monotheism was a central component of the Pan-Indian revitalization movements that emerged beginning in the mid-eighteenth century in the Susquehanna and Ohio Valleys, so it is not surprising to find it manifest here in the Great Man who hurls lightning bolts.[38] Another motif bears on the question of power, however, as evidenced by Longueuil's Iroquois's 1739 identification of the bones as those of the "grandfather of the buffalo." This motif is a "master of the game," an embodied tutelary spirit who organizes the behavior of a species of game animal and mediates human interaction with it, as, for example, the Great Beaver was said to do in northeastern Algonquin territory.[39] Similarly, from European American hunters and traders working west of the Mississippi in the early 1760s came indigenous accounts of "the Rhinosses or Elephant Master," which became associated with the bones at Big Bone Lick.[40] The master-of-the-game motif, traditional in the pertinent indigenous cosmologies, is absent from the 1762 Shawnee version, which is told at the moment of monotheistic revitalization's greatest promise, just prior to Pontiac's Rebellion. However, in the versions told after the failure of Pontiac's Rebellion the motif returns in altered or attenuated form, indicating the persistence of traditional pantheistic cosmologies. The 1766 Iroquois story imports the motif into the revitalizationist master narrative of sin, repentance, and salvation: the Great Spirit creates the great buffalo as an agent of punishment and preserves that agent should humankind need to be punished for future transgressions.[41] In the 1781 Delaware story, the big bull is evidently more powerful than the others of his kind, able to fend off the lightning bolts with his forehead until he is wounded, and even then he is able to escape to safety. The struggle between the big bull and the Great Spirit suggests a tension between a residual pantheistic cosmology, in which environmental agency is dispersed and accessible to humankind through ritual interaction with natural-supernatural agents such as masters of the game, and an emergent monotheistic cosmology, in which environmental agency is consolidated in a single supernatural force that is comparatively remote from human access. Read as a political allegory in the context of the Delawares' concerns with the colonial militia's occupation of several Ohio River settlements, with the Great Man standing in for colonial power and the big bull for the Delaware people, the 1781 Delaware story projects a geographic limit on European American expansion.[42] Read ecologically, with the people as beneficiary of the Great Man's good will, the story projects a benevolent supernatural agent with strong but limited power to shape the environment. Unforeseen changes, such as the disruptive mammoths, may yet appear at any time. The Delaware version draws out the anthropocentrism of the earlier versions, stating specifically that the game animals "had been created for the use of the Indians."[43] The Great Spirit decides who has a greater right to eat the game animals, the mammoths or the Indians. The decision is not based so much on moral evaluation, as in the 1766 Iroquois version, but rather on the assumption of the centrality of (indigenous) human culture to ecosystem dynamics. Anthropocentrism thus receives both theological and ecological warrants. At the same time, the debilitating effects of European colonization on Native American polities seem to have precluded any narration of a political account of environmental management in the manner of Filson and Turner – even though such an account could conceivably have drawn on the transmitted memory of Clovis culture mammoth hunting as a collective enterprise.

* * *

Much of the Big Bone Lick meta-archive, European American as well as Native American, characterizes the mammoth as an environmental excess, not merely a superfluous presence but an invasive agent that threatens the well-being of humankind (albeit with a jeremiadic twist in the 1766 Iroquois version). By contrast, Jefferson's story (as distinct from the Delaware story he transcribes) anticipates the modern narration of extinction as loss. Arguing against mounting claims by European naturalists that the mammoth was likely extinct, Jefferson asserts that "such is the oeconomy of nature, that no instance can be produced of her having permitted any one race of her animals to become extinct; of her having formed any link in her great work so weak as to be broken."[44] Jefferson shares with the indigenous stories an assumption that a larger-than-human force shapes the environment. Here a powerful agent, "nature," acts on the world, figured as both structure (chain) and system ("oeconomy," i.e., household management). Reprising these figures in a scientific paper on the fossil remains of another giant animal he named the Megalonyx (great claw), Jefferson again argues against extinction: "The movements of nature are in a never-ending circle. The animal species which has once been put into a train of motion, is still probably moving in that train. For if one link in nature's chain might be lost, another and another might be lost, till this whole system of things should evanish by piece-meal; a conclusion not warranted by the local disappearance of one or two species of animals."[45] In the fear that "this whole system of things should evanish," Jefferson confronts the possibility of the extinction of humankind. Thus he pushes the personified, superhuman shaping agent into the background, imagining its work both as an initial act of propulsion whose momentum continues perpetually and as an initial act of creation whose structure endures indefinitely.

After Buffon's successor Cuvier made an overwhelmingly persuasive case, in his *Recherches sur les ossemens fossils* (1812), that the mammoth and Megalonyx were in fact extinct, Jefferson revised his view of this environment-shaping agent, imagining a more active role:

> It is impossible, I say, for the human mind not to believe, that there is . . . design, cause and effect, up to an ultimate cause, a Fabricator of all things from matter and motion, their Preserver and Regulator while permitted to exist in their present forms, and their regenerat[or] into new and other forms. We see, too, evident proofs of the necessity of a superintending power, to maintain the universe in its course and order. Stars, well known, have disappeared, new ones have come into view; comets, in their incalculable courses, may run foul of suns and planets, and require renovation under other laws; certain races of animals are become extinct; and were there no restoring power, all existences might extinguish successively, one by one, until all should be reduced to a shapeless chaos.[46]

While the context, a debate with John Adams over Calvinism, required theological speculation, it is clear that Jefferson had come to believe that the careers of species are initiated, governed, and terminated by a supernatural agent. This agent, external to the material universe, quite actively exercises its power to "restore" order in the face of matter's inherent tendency to disorder. Thus while Jefferson reversed his position on extinction, he retained his notion of a divine, ordering force. The apparent modernity of Jefferson's response – his narration of extinction as loss – thus remains bound up with a premodern appeal to supernatural agency.

* * *

To return to Buffon's figure: if the notion of the archive in general presupposes absence, the notion of the archives du monde did not fully take shape until naturalists accepted the fact of extinction, the absence of certain species of life once present on the earth. The acceptance of extinction, as we have seen in the case of both Native American and European American accounts, required the narration of some agent as the author of the archives du monde. This agent is understood to have caused the deaths of the animals whose remains became legible as traces of the agent's action. Be it superhuman, other than human, or a human collective, this agent works on a scale beyond that of the individual. Thus where an ontological frame would differentiate between human and supernatural beings, an agential frame differentiates on the basis of individual and larger-than-individual powers and capacities.

Current extinction discourse takes yet another turn on the shifting alignments of agency and the master tropes of excess and loss. It has been argued, most familiarly by Bill McKibben, that the human power to shape the environment, both deliberately and collaterally, has been exercised so extensively as to bring about an enormous absence, the disappearance of "nature" itself as a domain outside of human culture.[47] As Filson and Turner imagined ancient peoples joining together to extinguish the mammoth, so McKibben describes a cooperative human effort, that is to say a politics, that has worked to extinguish the category of "nature" itself, whose absence is documented in the archives du monde. Individual extinctions accumulate, whether accomplished in fact (the dodo, the passenger pigeon) or narrated in the future tense (the polar bear), thus warranting an understanding of the Anthropocene epoch as the era of the sixth mass extinction event in geologic time.[48] Although human beings are clearly implicated in these losses, the causes seem beyond humankind's capacity to address because the required powers exceed individual actions. (Even if each American started driving a hybrid car, the polar ice would still melt.) Submitting to a theology of extinction, as the indigenous narrators had done and Jefferson came to do, we have not yet been able to imagine a politics of preservation, as Filson, Turner, and McKibben have been able to imagine a politics of extinction. Is this because any extinction narrative ultimately implies the disappearance of the human species (a Darwinian inevitability) and, nearer to us, our own death?

## NOTES

1. "Comme dans l'Histoire civile, on consulte les titres, on recherche les médailles, on déchiffre les inscriptions antiques, pour déterminer les époques des révolutions humaines, & constater les dates des événemens moraux ; de même, dans l'Histoire Naturelle, il faut fouiller les archives du monde, tirer des entrailles de la terre les vieux monumens, recueillir leurs débris, & rassembler en un corps de preuves tous les indices des changemens physiques qui peuvent nous faire remonter aux différens âges de la Nature" (Buffon, *Les époques,* 1:1, my translation).

2. On the debate concerning the causes of the Pleistocene extinctions, see Krech, *The Ecological Indian*, 29–43; Mithen, *After the Ice*, 246–257. For a provocative critique of ecological catastrophism, see Bruckner, *The Fanaticism*.

3. For an account of the 1739 expedition, see Mayor, *Fossil Legends*, 1–15.

4. On the reception of the fossils, see Semonin, *American Monster*; Rudwick, *Bursting the Limits*, 263–271.

5. *Grand Rapids Press,* October 9, 2013, http://www.mlive.com/news/grand-rapids/index.ssf/2013/10/mastodon_tooth_tusk_found_in_g.html. The story was picked up by media networks including Fox, ABC, NBC, PBS, and the syndicated children's feature "The Mini Page" (KidsPost, *Washington Post,* October 13, 2013). The item's headline in "The Mini Page" – "My, what big teeth he had!" – suggests how deeply

embedded in this archive are questions of power and agency.

6. Quoted in Mayor, *Fossil Legends,* 13.

7. On the debate over the premise that American nature was degenerate, see Gerbi, *The Dispute.*

8. Jefferson, *Notes,* 43–44, 55. Reflecting eighteenth-century practice, I will use "mammoth" to refer to the animal that would later be identified as the mastodon, *Mammut americanum.*

9. Peale, *An Historical Disquisition,* 2:577.

10. Barton, *A Discourse,* 59–60, italics in original.

11. See Daston and Park, *Wonders.*

12. The homonym of *naturalist* as one who studies natural history (a standard eighteenth-century usage) and as one who holds a naturalistic (i.e., materialistic) ontology may cause some terminological confusion. However, this confusion underscores the confusion of the students of natural history who excoriated Native Americans' supernaturalism while adhering to their own supernaturalism.

13. Latour, "An Attempt," 481. A similar shift is suggested by recent work in anthropology, for example, Descola, "Who Owns Nature?"; Cadena, "Indigenous Cosmopolitics."

14. On water monsters, see Mayor, *Fossil Legends,* 9, 12–13. Edward Taylor recorded a local indigenous tradition about a humanoid giant; see Stanford, "The Giant Bones."

15. Bartram, *The Correspondence,* 563.

16. Ibid., 566.

17. It is not clear where the interview took place. Wright resided in Delaware County, outside of Philadelphia. However, it is unlikely that Bartram would have written to him unless he were in a location where he could meet someone who knew about the bones. Mayor thus places Wright at Fort Pitt in 1762; see *Fossil Legends,* 53.

18. Bartram, *Correspondence,* 569. Stories of humanoid giants among New England Algonquin peoples evidently cited isolated mammoth teeth or bones as evidence; see Stanford, "Giant Bones."

19. On Iroquois raids into the Carolina Piedmont in the late seventeenth and early eighteenth centuries, see Merrell, *The Indians' New World,* 5, 41–42, 78.

20. Winterbotham, *An Historical,* 3:139. On the emergence of a story of separate creations in the Ohio Valley in the mid-eighteenth century, see Dowd, *A Spirited Resistance,* 30; Cave, *Prophets,* 13–14.

21. Jefferson, *Notes,* 44. A version of the Delaware story, evidently deriving

from Jefferson's text but stylistically embellished so as to sound more "Indian," was published in the *American Museum* in 1790 and reprinted in Peale, *An Historical Disquisition,* 2:577–578. On the composition of the 1781 delegation to Charlottesville and Jefferson's address, see Jefferson, *Papers,* 6:60.

22. Jefferson, *Notes,* 56.

23. Barber and Barber, *When They Severed,* 6–11.

24. Deloria, *Red Earth.* Dismissing scientific techniques such as radiocarbon dating, Deloria's postflood chronology encompasses three thousand years and places indigenous Americans in an environment that includes dinosaurs.

25. Echo-Hawk, "Ancient History," 273. See also Echo-Hawk, "Oral Traditions," 41–42; Bruchac, "Earthshapers." Peter Nabokov's comprehensive study of Native American historical narration leaves the question open; see *A Forest of Time,* 72–75.

26. On the hypothesis that a comet caused the Younger Dryas phase, see Dalton, "Blast."

27. Archaeological evidence of human coexistence with mammoths and other extinct megafauna was discovered in France by Jacques Boucher de Crèvecoeur de Perthes beginning in the 1830s; see Grayson, "Nineteenth-Century Explanations," 25–27. Clovis culture artifacts were first discovered, in association with mammoth remains, at Blackwater Draw (Texas and New Mexico) in the 1930s.

28. For overviews, see Krech, *The Ecological Indian,* 29–43; Mithen, *After the Ice,* 246–257.

29. Barton, *A Discourse,* 60.

30. Latour, "An Attempt," 482.

31. Hunter, "Observations," 45.

32. On Buffon's theories of extinction and climate change, see Semonin, *American Monster,* 111–135; Cohen, *The Fate of the Mammoth,* 94–100; Rudwick, *Bursting the Limits,* 139–150. Buffon explained the absence of elephants from tropical South America by arguing that they were stopped by a mountain barrier north of the Isthmus of Panama. On Cuvier, see Cohen, *The Fate of the Mammoth,* 105–121; Rudwick, *Bursting the Limits,* 353–388. On Breyne, see Cohen, *The Fate of the Mammoth,* 70–73.

33. Peale, *An Historical Disquisition,* 2:579.

34. Filson, *The Discovery,* 34, 36.

35. On Turner's western career, see Semonin, *American Monster,* 306–307.

36. Turner, "Memoir," 518.

37. Nabokov argues in *A Forest of Time* that Native American historical narration, be it legend, myth, or folktale,

is always oriented toward the present of the telling. The modal approach to the narration of environmental agency that I am suggesting here owes much to White, *Metahistory*.

38. On revitalization in the Ohio Valley, see Dowd, *Spirited Resistance*, 27–35; Richter, *Facing East*, 180–181, 193–199; Cave, *Prophets*, 11–44.

39. On such "masters of the game" in Algonquin territory, see Martin, *Keepers of the Game*. On the Abenaki Great Beaver, see also Brooks, *The Common Pot*, 14-24; Bruchac, "Earthshapers," 70–73.

40. Jordan, "Journal," 180.

41. As the Ottawa leader Pontiac explained the Delaware prophet Neolin's vision, the Master of Life told Neolin that he had sent the game animals away as punishment for the people's dependence on the whites and would bring the animals back when the people returned to the old ways and followed his teachings; see Burton, *Journal*, 22–32. In Neolin's vision, the Master of Life acts as master of the game; in the Iroquois Big Bone Lick story, the creator spirit controls the giant buffalo, a traditional master-of-the-game figure.

42. On the Revolutionary War context, see Wallace, *Jefferson and the Indians*, 62–66.

43. Jefferson, *Notes*, 44.

44. Ibid., 55.

45. Jefferson, *Papers*, 29:297. The remains were discovered in a cave in western Virginia by workers digging nitrous deposits for a saltpeter works. The animal was soon classified by Cuvier as a species of giant ground sloth.

46. Jefferson to John Adams, April 11, 1823, in Jefferson, *The Writings*, 15:427.

47. McKibben, *The End of Nature*.

48. Leakey and Lewin, *The Sixth Extinction*.

## SELECTED BIBLIOGRAPHY

Barber, E. J. W., and Paul Barber. *When They Severed the Earth from the Sky: How the Human Mind Shapes Myth*. Princeton, N.J.: Princeton University Press, 2004.

Barton, Benjamin Smith. *A Discourse on Some of the Principal Desiderata in Natural History*. Philadelphia: Denham and Town, 1807.

Bartram, John. *The Correspondence of John Bartram, 1734–1777*. Edited by

Edmund Berkeley and Dorothy Smith Berkeley. Gainesville: University Press of Florida, 1992.

Brooks, Lisa. *The Common Pot: The Recovery of Native Space in the Northeast.* Minneapolis: University of Minnesota Press, 2008.

Bruchac, Margaret. "Earthshapers and Placemakers: Algonkian Indian Stories and the Landscape." In *Indigenous Archaeologies: Decolonizing Theory and Practice,* edited by Claire Smith and H. Martin Wobst, 56–80. London: Routledge, 2005.

Bruckner, Pascal. *The Fanaticism of the Apocalypse.* Cambridge: Polity Press, 2013.

Buffon, Georges-Louis Leclerc, Comte de. *Les époques de la nature.* 2 vols. Paris, 1780.

Burton, Agnes M., ed. *Journal of Pontiac's Conspiracy.* Translated by R. C. Ford. Detroit: Clarence Munroe Burton, 1912.

Cadena, Marisol de la. "Indigenous Cosmopolitics in the Andes: Conceptual Reflections beyond 'Politics.'" *Cultural Anthropology* 25.2 (2010): 334–370.

Cave, Alfred A. *Prophets of the Great Spirit: Native American Revitalization Movements in Eastern North America.* Lincoln: University of Nebraska Press, 2006.

Cohen, Claudine. *The Fate of the Mammoth: Fossils, Myth, and History.* Chicago: University of Chicago Press, 2002.

Dalton, Rex. "Blast from the Past?" *Nature* 447.7,142 (May 17, 2007): 256–257.

Daston, Lorraine, and Katharine Park. *Wonders and the Order of Nature, 1150–1750.* New York: Zone Books, 2001.

Deloria, Vine, Jr. *Red Earth, White Lies: Native Americans and the Myth of Scientific Fact.* New York: Scribner, 1995.

Descola, Philippe. "Who Owns Nature?" *Books & Ideas,* January 21, 2008, http://www.booksandideas.net/Who-owns-nature.html.

Dowd, Gregory Evans. *A Spirited Resistance: The North American Indian Struggle for Unity, 1745–1815.* Baltimore, Md.: Johns Hopkins University Press, 1992.

Echo-Hawk, Roger. "Ancient History in the New World: Integrating Oral Traditions and the Archaeological Record in Deep Time." *American Antiquity* 65 (2000): 267–290.

———. "Oral Traditions and Indian Origins: A Native American Perspective." In *Exploring Ancient Native America: An Archaeological Guide,* edited by David Hurst Thomas, 41–42. New York: Macmillan, 1994.

Filson, John. *The Discovery, Settlement, and Present State of Kentucke.* 1784. Reprint, Ann Arbor: University Microfilms, 1966.

Gerbi, Antonello. *The Dispute of the New World: The History of a Polemic, 1750–1900.* Translated by Jeremy Moyle. Pittsburgh, Pa.: University of Pittsburgh Press, 1973.

Grayson, Donald K. "Nineteenth-Century Explanations of Pleistocene Extinctions: A Review and Analysis." In *Quaternary Extinctions: A Prehistoric Revolution,* edited by Paul S. Martin and Richard G. Klein, 5–39. Tucson: University of Arizona Press, 1984.

Hunter, William. "Observations on the Bones, Commonly Supposed to be Elephants Bones, Which Have Been Found Near the River Ohio in America." *Philosophical Transactions* 58 (1768): 34–45.

Jefferson, Thomas. *Notes on the State of Virginia.* Edited by Frank Shuffelton. New York: Penguin, 1999.

——. *Papers of Thomas Jefferson.* Edited by Julian P. Boyd et al. 40 vols. to date. Princeton, N.J.: Princeton University Press, 1950–.

——. *The Writings of Thomas Jefferson.* Edited by Andrew A. Lipscomb and Albert Ellery Bergh. 20 vols. Washington, D.C.: Jefferson Memorial Association, 1903.

Jordan, John W., ed. "Journal of James Kenny, 1761–63." *Pennsylvania Magazine of History and Biography* 37 (April 1913): 152–201.

Krech, Shepard, III. *The Ecological Indian: Myth and History.* New York: Norton, 2000.

Latour, Bruno. "An Attempt at a 'Compositionist Manifesto.'" *New Literary History* 41 (2010): 471–490.

Leakey, Richard E., and Roger Lewin. *The Sixth Extinction: Patterns of Life and the Future of Humankind.* New York: Anchor, 1996.

Martin, Calvin. *Keepers of the Game: Indian-Animal Relationships and the Fur Trade.* Berkeley: University of California Press, 1978.

Mayor, Adrienne. *Fossil Legends of the First Americans.* Princeton, N.J.: Princeton University Press, 2005.

McKibben, Bill. *The End of Nature.* New York: Random House, 1989.

Merrell, James. *The Indians' New World: Catawbas and Their Neighbors from European Contact through the Era of Removal.* Chapel Hill: University of North Carolina Press, 1989.

Mithen, Steven J. *After the Ice: A Global Human History, 20,000–5000 BC.*

Cambridge, Mass.: Harvard University Press, 2004.

Nabokov, Peter. *A Forest of Time: American Indian Ways of History.* New York: Cambridge University Press, 2002.

Peale, Rembrandt. *An Historical Disquisition on the Mammoth, or, Great American Incognitum* (London, 1803). In *The Selected Papers of Charles Willson Peale and His Family,* edited by Lillian B. Miller. 5 vols. Vol. 2, 543–581. New Haven, Conn.: National Portrait Gallery, Smithsonian Institution, Yale University Press, 1983.

Richter, Daniel K. *Facing East from Indian Country: A Native History of Early America.* Cambridge, Mass.: Harvard University Press, 2001.

Rudwick, Martin J. S. *Bursting the Limits of Time: The Reconstruction of Geohistory in the Age of Revolution.* Chicago: University of Chicago Press, 2005.

Semonin, Paul. *American Monster: How the Nation's First Prehistoric Creature Became a Symbol of National Identity.* New York: New York University Press, 2000.

Stanford, Donald. "The Giant Bones of Claverack, New York, 1705, Described by the Colonial Poet, Reverend Edward Taylor (ca. 1642–1729) in a Manuscript Owned by Yale University Library." *New York History* 40 (1959): 47–61.

Turner, George. "Memoir on the Extraneous Fossils, Denominated Mammoth Bones." *Transactions of the American Philosophical Society* 4 (1799): 510–518.

Wallace, Anthony F. C. *Jefferson and the Indians: The Tragic Fate of the First Americans.* Cambridge, Mass.: Harvard University Press, 1999.

White, Hayden. *Metahistory: The Historical Imagination in Nineteenth-Century Europe.* Baltimore, Md.: Johns Hopkins University Press, 1973.

Winterbotham, William. *An Historical, Geographical, Commercial, and Philosophical View of the American United States.* 4 vols. London: J. Ridgeway, 1795.

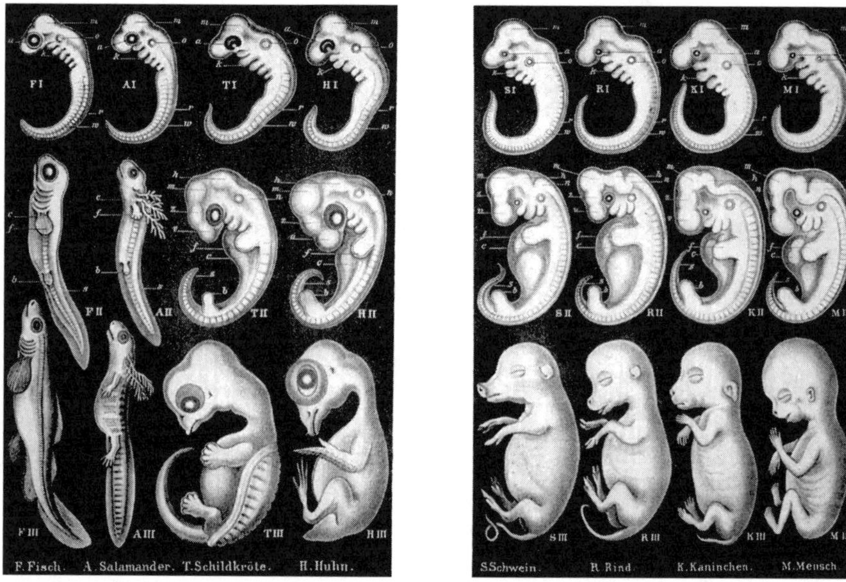


**8.1.** *Haeckel Anthropogenie 1874.* Lithograph by J. G. Bach of Leipzig after drawings by Ernst Haeckel in *Anthropogenie, oder, Entwicklungsgeschichte des Menschen* (Leipzig: Engelmann, 1874). Nick Hopwood, "Pictures of Evolution and Charges of Fraud: Ernst Haeckel's Embryological Illustrations," *Isis* 97 (2006): 260–301, PDF. Licensed under public domain via Wikimedia Commons, https://commons.wikimedia.org/wiki/File:Haeckel_Anthropogenie_1874.jpg#mediaviewer/File:Haeckel_Anthropogenie_1874.jpg.

8

# MODERNIST HETEROCHRONY, EVOLUTIONARY BIOLOGY, AND THE CHIMERA OF TIME

*Charles M. Tung*

Spencer Wells, in his PBS documentary *Journey of Man,* claims that there is "a time machine hidden in our genes."[1] This Wells, unrelated to the literary figure H. G. Wells (at least in the short term), is the genetic anthropologist in charge of the Genographic Project, an international study funded by *National Geographic* and IBM that traces individual Y-chromosomes from all corners of the earth back to a recognizably "modern" human leaving Africa around sixty thousand years ago. The time travel central to Wells's research is guided by two-hundred-dollar self-testing kits, tracking devices sold in large part to ancestry-obsessed Americans, and, more controversially, by the institutionalized DNA collection from indigenous populations around the world, whose clustering of genetic markers helps to sketch a roadmap of major ancestral migrations. For Wells, deep in every modern human's body is not only a vehicle that returns us to a "Y-chromosomal Adam" (and a much earlier "mitochondrial Eve" living 150,000–200,000 years ago) but also, according to his mixing of metaphors, "the greatest history book ever written," an archival record of our Paleolithic wanderings.[2]

In this context, while the biblical analogy might raise eyebrows, the mixed metaphor – *the body as time machine as archive* – usually does not, since both the transporter and the repository share the commonsense view of time as frame independent and unilinear, and both function at their most conventional as devices that reveal the truth about our past.[3] Our DNA can move us backward on our time line to our evolutionary point of origin, because inscribed in it is the record of our steady movement through history. Indeed, this view of time and our access to it accounts for the fact that the trope of the archival time machine and its functions often appear in the discourses of many academic disciplines – history, archaeology, and cognitive psychology, to name just a few. The trope serves as an effective rhetorical and conceptual device for transporting us to a hitherto unfamiliar and hard-to-imagine past (or future) and transforming it into a well-furnished present. In collecting and recording the accumulation of time, the archival time machine makes available the range of perceptual and imaginative conditions for understanding not only what is absent but also the direct relationship between what is absent and what is present. The pedagogical power of sliding back and forth in history derives from a unification of time that allows us to track a current state of affairs to its cause and vice versa, a cause to its consequence.

However salutary such diagnostic (and prognostic) operations often are, this epistemological function is not all there is to the time machine's work, and especially not to time travel in the corporeal archive. It is rarely recognized that the trope of the time machine often functions unconventionally – not merely to move in time and clarify sequences but also in fact to defamiliarize time, the very medium taken for granted in our movements and historiographies. If Wells is right that the body is a time machine and an archive, then it is a time machine and an archive of the oddest kind, one that allows us to see that our corporeal present contains the strangest history book ever written, a book that resembles a modernist text. One of modernism's achievements, long overlooked, is its treatment of the physical and figural body as an archival time machine that produces temporal estrangement and reveals the alternative timespaces cutting across an apparently singular present. In fact, beginning with what I see as the modernist aspiration to the condition of the time machine and spanning many areas of twentieth-century culture, such as evolutionary biology, modernist painting, science fiction, and literary and filmic forms, the refiguration of time as an assemblage of heterogeneous strands running at varying rates often proceeds as an exploration of embodied heterochrony.[4] Heterochrony – the body's hodgepodge of disjunctive timings and times – reveals that our physical present is not the end of a long line nor the ultimate storehouse of a single-file history shared with all living things. Rather, to use Wells's description in *Deep Ancestry,* we – and time itself – "are in fact chimeras."[5]

* * *

The refiguration of time as a plurality of times has appeared with increasing frequency in discussions that reconsider modernity's historical and aesthetic dimensions. In Dilip Parameshwar Gaonkar's collection *Alternative Modernities,* for example, the pluralization of modernity marks a rejection of the way modernization theory's global frame has assumed a single, uniform process modeled on the course of history in the West. The idea that different nations and cultures enter the process of modernization at "different starting points . . . [and with] different outcomes" is not simply to say that diverse contexts are not all equally secular, scientific, bureaucratic, and industrialized. It also implies that the "course of history" itself – the very temporal infrastructure of modernity, with its "twin matrix" of "incessant change and deadening routine" – must be further reconceptualized as site specific and therefore always multiple.[6] Peter Osborne makes this rethinking of time explicit in his most recent book on contemporary art, *Anywhere or Not at All:* "The changing temporal quality of the historical present over the last few decades is best expressed through the distinctive conceptual grammar of con-temporaneity, a coming together not simply 'in' time, but *of* times . . . a coming together of *different but equally 'present'* temporalities or 'times,' a temporal unity in disjunction, or a *disjunctive unity of present times.*"[7]

Osborne briefly uses the term "heterochronic" to describe an unexpected danger of this "contemporaneity": its disruption of modernity's "permanent transitoriness" and constant change by the "conjuncture, or at its most extreme, the stasis of a present moment," that is, by an "annihilation of temporality" characteristic of a "culture of the image."[8] By contrast, I would like to linger on the concept of heterochrony in order to emphasize not the simultaneity or stasis of the disjunctive coming together of times but the multiplicity of ongoing trajectories figured in and as the chimerical body. The archival body of plural times – whether in the form of global history in Gaonkar or in the tissue of presentness in Osborne – is always in danger of becoming a detemporalized convergence in the space of "the present." Even so, what seems "all here now" should instead be seen as cuts or fragments of various historical trajectories assembled in relation to each other *as* a "now."

One of the most famous uses of the idea of heterochrony – by Michel Foucault in his 1967 lecture "Of Other Spaces" – exemplifies this danger, while its nineteenth-century context grounds heterochrony's reconception as a multiplicity of temporal tracks.[9] Foucault used the term to argue that the countersites of heterotopia involve not just the reflection and contestation of spatial orders but an "absolute break with . . . traditional time." His first examples of the way heterotopias are linked to heterochronies are "museums and libraries . . . heterotopias in which time never stops building up . . . a sort of general archive, the will to enclose in one place all times, all epochs, all forms, all tastes."[10] While his concept of heterotopia, like heterochrony, is thought to be incomplete or even incoherent, Foucault's idea of the archive has a fairly secure meaning: in *The Archaeology of Knowledge* (1969), the archive is theorized not merely as "that whole mass of texts" in a repository but as the "law of what can be said, the system that governs the appearance of statements as unique events."[11] However, to emphasize the structure and regulation of the rules of discourse would be to miss the very strange pluralization that Foucault's less polished thinking might have briefly identified in archives conceived heterochronically.

The heterogeneous pluralization of times suggested in Foucault's idea of the rupture with "traditional time" is in fact already present and explicit in the very first context from which the word "heterochrony" comes: nineteenth-century evolutionary developmental biology. In 1875, almost a century before Foucault's formulation and before we had the technology to access the genetic code informing morphology, the German embryologist and ardent Darwinist Ernst Haeckel coined "heterochrony" (along with "heterotopy") to describe deviations in the "traditional time" of the body.[12] In his famous biogenetic law or "recapitulation theory," ontogeny always smoothly recapped phylogeny; that is, an organism's development from embryo to adult always replayed every adult stage of its entire species' evolution. In other words, the part not only stood for the whole but also archived within it the whole's entire phylogenetic history, one that was always getting longer, growing denser, and playing faster. Haeckel imagined, as Stephen Jay Gould points out, "an even and integrated acceleration of the [series] of entire adult ancestor[s] into earlier and earlier ontogenetic stages of descendants."[13] However, variations in the onset or offset or pacing of development fragmented both the coherent form of the descendant and the history that it stood for into a desynchronized set of individual organs, each with its own ontogenetic trajectory. Heterochrony referred to these aberrations in the timing and rate of embryonic development that Haeckel believed prevented the otherwise single-file rehearsal of the past in the morphology of the present. These anomalies notwithstanding, the body was thought to contain regular records of our ancestral past, which Haeckel's well-known and widely disseminated illustration of eight vertebrates at different stages of development made clear (see figure 8.1).[14]

Although recapitulation theory has been discredited, Haeckel's concept of heterochrony – the deviation from smooth recapitulation – has remained an important idea in the life sciences, since it is able to account for variation as such. In fact, as a result of Gould's work, contemporary developmental biology sees heterochrony not as an aberration of evolution but as one of its primary mechanisms for generating difference itself. The complete adult image of any previous ancestor never appears in any of the stages of a creature's development, but "underdeveloped" and "overdeveloped" traits appear in the hodgepodge of the present. As Cambridge paleobiologist Kenneth McNamara claims, heterochrony is the missing link between the external pressures of natural selection and the internal directives of genetics and is precisely the way that evolutionary variation is achieved: "It explains everything, from the shape of the delphinium flower, to a horse's foot, to the song of a bird." It explains how some finches develop slightly bigger bills than others, why dogs resemble juvenilized wolves, and why humans are paedomorphic apes with baby faces but with peramorphic brains that grow for much longer than do the brains of other primates. Heterochrony reveals that our corporeal present is not the culmination of a progressive and uniform linear time; we are, rather, a "mosaic of characters, some speeded up, other slowed down, producing one of the more potent cocktails" concocted by over three and a half billion years of life on the planet."[15]

If for Haeckel the body was a figure for linear developmental time, heterochrony's dismemberment of phylogenetic history – its presentation of a mosaic of different temporal signifiers, many of which evoke pasts completely beyond narrowly constructed lineages – reconfigured the body as a figure for multiple times and different rates of change. The body is indeed an archive, but it is a deeply disorderly one. The pasts contained in it are not neatly arranged like library stacks but scattered about in strange arrangements and at different points in their ongoing trajectories. Thus, learning to be modern, as Ezra Pound said of T. S. Eliot's self-modernization, may have involved "remember[ing] the date (1914) on the calendar," but it also involved – in so many canonical modernist literary texts and paintings – the proliferation of clocks and the clash of time-telling devices in disjunctive assemblages.[16] The very concept of generation as a period term was in fact revised in the first third of the twentieth century by sociologists such as Karl Mannheim in order to get beyond the inadequacies of positivist chronologies and successive "spirits of the age" and to acknowledge "the mutually fructifying co-existence of multiple times . . . co-existent multiple worlds."[17] Modernism's time obsession contributed to this revision by pushing the metaphorics of kinship at the heart of generational periodization to their extreme, calling attention not just to parents and peers but also to coeval ancestors from disparate periods and emphasizing not lineage but the biological assemblage of anachronisms.

The heterochrony of modernist figures and techniques is at the heart of what I see as an alternate history of the modernist time fixation, which extends far into the twentieth century, an alternate history whose "Jonbar hinges" or points of divergence include the growing awareness of the multiplicity of temporal scale and pace.[18] In standard histories of modernism, this multiplication of clocks is swallowed up by depth – of either subjective temporality and its repudiation of the clock's fractioning of time or the long, subsuming distances of paleomodernism's timescales.[19] The nineteenth-century currents that flow into these typical readings of the early twentieth century's well-known obsession with and reaction to time are, first, the technologies of ever-faster production, transport, and communication, which contribute to an acceleration of changes in social life; a radical compression or "annihilation" of space; and a temporal contraction in which, as David Harvey argues, "time horizons shorten to the point where the present is all there is."[20] Second is the "fall into deep time," a fall brought about by evolutionary theory's long processes (Charles Darwin's publication of *The Origin of Species* in 1859), the paleontological discoveries of Neanderthal and Cro-Magnon skulls (in Engis Cave, 1829, Gibraltar, 1848, and the Neander Valley, 1856, and in Les Eyzies, 1868, respectively), and the geological bottoming out of the age of the planet (James Hutton's *Theory of the Earth* in 1795). Together, these two currents produce the common account of modernist time consciousness as the experience of rupture with the anchoring power of eternity and tradition; the awareness of being adrift among "the transient, the fleeting, the contingent," separated by precipitous and ever-lengthening distances from primordial substructures; and the sense of the present nested squarely in the deep past that constitutes it.[21]

In deep time, the connection between the present and the past was expanded so much that either it snapped, producing only a contrast between overwhelmingly large durations and the increasingly small interval once at its head, or it dilated and thickened to the point that the present became nothing other than the radically deepened past. But in its tension with deep time, the impact of shifting rates of change did not just result in the cultural ambivalence between an "aesthetics of transitoriness" and the "timeless world of myth," as critics so often say.[22] It also generated the much weirder vision and aesthetics of heterochrony. To rethink this history of modernism by returning to figurations of temporal scale, especially as it was inscribed on the human body and the body of the text, is to see that the crisis of "deep historicism" yielded not just a dwarfing of the frame of human experience or an enlargement of the segment of historical process that we occupy. The discovery of the presence of the deep past also provoked what we might call a compound vestigialization of the present. As I have pointed out, evolutionary biology's conceptualization of the body became a figure for the temporal hodgepodge of differential rates of change constituting the corporeal present.

This vestigialization of the present differs from both the phenomenological narrative of multiple temporalities and the usual "primitivist" framework. The former derives from past uses of Henri Bergson's philosophy, which have dominated literary criticism's understanding of the modernist "time cult" since Wyndham Lewis's treatment of his contemporaries' "Time-mind" in *Time and Western Man*. Because Bergson's theory of *durée* was, in Adam Barrows's words, "both backward and inward looking in its orientation," the heterogeneous agglomeration of nonpsychological times in modernist cultural production often got melted down into Bergson's conception of time as interior, "a succession of qualitative changes, which melt into and permeate one another, without precise outlines, without any tendency to externalize themselves in relation to one another, without any affiliation with number . . . pure heterogeneity."[23] Bergson's resistance to time as a homogeneous, uniformly divided, and singular line has been recast in recent years as support for external and political conceptions of history – for example, in Elizabeth Grosz's treatment of durée as a repository of "virtualities," a set of "resources for multiple futures, for open pathways, for indeterminable consequences."[24]

The heterochrony housed in the material body must also be distinguished from another dominant discourse in modernist studies that swallows up modernism's multiple clocks: primitivism. While it is tempting to think of all instances of heterochrony as examples of paleomodernism's inscription of myth and the deep past in the present, the primitivist framework treats heterochrony's "temporal otherness" as the difference between present and past. Disjunctions, mosaics, and assemblages are reduced to simple markers of pastness and therefore become expressions of the period's reactionary pathologization of the other, its fears of degeneration, and its evasions of the complexities of the historical present. To read heterochrony in this way places it within discourses that affirm the rectilinear unity of time, with primitive on the one end and civilized on the other, whereas heterochronic bodies suggest a multiplicity of varyingly deep and heterogeneous time lines, in which the present would be construed not only as points on individual lines containing separate pasts but as a cross section of a plurality of those histories. As Dana Seitler's work on atavism shows, the appearance of the archaic past in the present disrupts "the modern construction of time as linear and continuous . . . [which] undergirds a cause-effect understanding of history." It does not do this simply by suggesting a reversible, backward-moving time or a discontinuous eruption of ancestral moments into an "out-of-order" present; rather, "atavism offers up a notion of time as multidirectional and of the body as polytemporal."[25]

To fully account for this polytemporality, the story of modernist heterochrony must return to a key moment in the exploration of time's disjunctive plurality, H. G. Wells's *The Time Machine* (1895), which was roughly contemporary with the high point of Haeckel's career. The text's interest in the progressive or degenerative direction of history – its obvious query about the evolutionary fate of Victorian humanity and its socioeconomic structures – might appear to be the primary focus. But the novel also functions as a heterochrony machine, its alternative function less obvious, as if hidden in the pedestal of the sphinx. Not just a vehicle of adventure and prognostication, Wells's *Time Machine* defamiliarizes the very medium in which we live and move by featuring a device able to manipulate and outstrip the putatively universal pace of one second per second, the commonsense rate of temporal passage itself.[26] The speed of the machine, relative to the rate at which the experience of the dinner guests elapses, varies from "over a year a minute," to a pace so fast that "the thousands [of days] hand [on his dial] was sweeping round as fast as the seconds hand of a watch," to the unimaginably "great strides of a thousand years or more." If the machine's ability to "controvert . . . ideas that are almost universally accepted" exposes the fact that our experience of the steady flow of a single, uniform, natural time is a fiction built on the "infirmity of the flesh" (i.e., the limitations of the human sensorium), then "the" history of that flesh is an even greater mystery than the Traveller suspects.[27] His own trip contrasts with the model of time that underlies all his hypotheses about what has happened over the span of 800,807 (and then 30 million) years.

The Traveller keeps guessing as to how his nineteenth-century present – "this ripe prime of the human race" – could have culminated in the Eloi and the Morlocks, the two species into which humans have evolved over the 800,807-year period. But he remains unable to generate an adequately complex narrative of "change over time," given the dimensions in which and with which he is thinking.[28] His discovery that the paedomorphic Eloi, with their "juvenile" traits, are not the evolved masters of but instead livestock for the Morlocks clarifies the power relations of this future present, but it does not solidify in any way his "developing" explanation that *Homo sapiens* split into two species based on nineteenth-century class divisions.[29] In the largest timescale, those two species seem to become huge crabs and then, finally, a black, flopping, tentacled creature. But it is clear by this point that connecting the Golden Age to the sunset of humanity to the red death of the sun continually falters because the slices of analysis, figured by the discussion of four-dimensioned cuts and the Kodak that the Traveller goes back for, are spaced too far apart. Those slices are, moreover, too uniform. Wells's novel calls its main epistemological trajectory into question by likening the creatures of 802,701 to a number of other animals, such as apes, lemurs, and ants, and by peppering itself with chimerical figures such as the sphinx, griffin, and faun. The other possible pasts of the Eloi and Morlocks, and the human-animal hybrids, together suggest how any slice reveals an interpenetrated cross section of heterogeneous strands running through it at different and variable rates.

The "hysterical exhilaration" that the Traveller feels is generated, according to Paul Cantor and Peter Hufnagel, by his typically Victorian "journey to the imperial frontier," where European explorers, including modernist protagonists like Conrad's Marlow, encounter exotic "cultures at very different stages of historical development."[30] But it is important to point out that this exhilaration of going-forward-to-go-back on the progressive line of history is also balanced by a disorientation that the Traveller calls "excessively unpleasant" and that is not caused by his vertiginous slide through time alone.[31] The dissonance seems to exceed the distaste for the colonized and their often unheard claim to coevalness in imperialist romances. The Traveller's confusion is in fact an index of the disintegration of the imperial universal time underwriting the diagnosis and prognosis of both self and other.[32] The hybrids and chimeras that haunt the text, while normally located in the critical discourses of racial hygiene and pathology, also allow us to think the radically heterogeneous forms of the body and history that make normativity and the identity of pure wholes over time impossible.

These visions of the chimerical body can be linked to a wide range of aesthetic experiments after Wells. For instance, as Susan Squier points out in her work "Embryologies of Modernism," they speak to the modernist interrogation of character, the reconfiguration of "identity not as stabilized in space and in one time period, but rather as diffused and disseminated across different spaces and times."[33] For some writers such as George Bernard Shaw, the primary goal of this deep reconfiguration of identity seems to be to respond to the political problem of the brevity of generations. Just when people gain enough experience to govern complex civilizations, they get old and die. In his 1921 play *Back to Methuselah* (subtitled *A Metabiological Pentateuch*), Shaw imagined that, in the year 31,920 ("As Far as Thought Can Reach"), humans would be able to live indefinitely (until killed by accidents). However, the diffusion and dissemination across spatiotemporal difference for which Squier argues are not just about extension and longevity. Instead, they mean fragmentation and recombination of temporally significant parts. Shaw's characters may say that they want to escape the temporal condition of the body: his "She-Ancient" laments her eight hundred years of life, one in which she has been "all sorts of fantastic monsters. I walked upon a dozen legs: I worked with 20 hands and a hundred fingers: I looked to the four quarters of the compass with eight eyes out of four heads."[34] But it is these figures that show how modernist experiments in multidimensional being go beyond identities "stabilized in space and in one time period" to more radical queries on the relation of the body itself, aesthetic form, and new ways of conceiving the temporalities proper to the uneven and inconsistent topographies of timespaces.

In the visual arts, Picasso provides a nearly perfect example of the connection between these figures, forms, and timespace, since no one depicts strange growths and appendages, surreal human-animal hybrids, and temporal dismemberment better than he. One even gets the sense sometimes that twentieth-century "evo-devo" – from Julian Huxley's work *The Problems of Relative Growth* (1932), to Richard Goldschmidt's "hopeful monsters" experiments in the timing of fruit-fly development (in which arms and legs could be made to grow in the place of wings and antennae), to Maurice Kottelat's studies of fish with larval, newborn bodies but adult gonads – turned to modernists like Picasso for their vision of the body's disjunctive timings and times. To see how the latter is related to aesthetic form and historiography, let us examine a painting that is likely to be the most difficult to dislodge from the framework of social and racial hygiene and imperialism's self-serving views of progressive history. Picasso's *Les demoiselles d'Avignon* is the first painting of his "African" period, one of the most famous works of primitivism, and arguably the incipient moment of cubism.

Contemporary interpretations of this painting emphasize the historical pathologization of the other, fears of racial and sexual degeneration, and the evolutionary justifications for the colonization of Africa, and they warn us off midcentury interpretations that redeployed the framework in which non-Western subjects and artifacts were uprooted from their contexts and relocated to the back of a typological scheme, the front of which was modernity and civilization. Both threatening and celebratory encounters with the primitive have always seemed to involve, as Mark Antliff and Patricia Leighten point out, a movement "into an 'infantile' past, as if travelling through time rather than space."[35]

It is important to contextualize the painting, but we should note that the canvas provides no simple dramatization of backward time travel. While the painting tempts us with the vision of unilineal human development and cultural hierarchy, its shifts across the canvas from left to right resist any reading centered on the trip from the now of the French brothel, to the Spanish prehistory of the Iberian figures, to the deep African root of "time immemorial." As even William Rubin notes, "None of the African pieces Picasso saw in his first few years of fascination with 'art nègre' were more than just decades old."[36] That is, all signifiers of Africanness were drawn from contemporary tribal art, whereas the Iberian elements – the bulging, lozenge-shaped eyes, huge scroll-like ears, and wedge noses – were inspired by stone reliefs dating from the fifth to third centuries BCE.[37] The present of the French bordello is neither the end of the evolutionary line nor the archive that contains all pasts. Likewise, the African past is not the ultimate deep frame containing Spanish and French history, if we can even use these adjectives of continent, race, and nationality without scare quotes.

Instead, the painting jarringly stages different histories and cultures in a way that exposes the bodies to be discontinuous amalgams and the timespace of the canvas itself to be deeply irregular. Each figure is not a pure representative of a particular people and a historical stage but an obvious hybrid resisting typological and individual consistency: mask-like faces rest atop bodies that do not match up, and limbs are in several instances incongruous. Both the bodies and the stylistic discontinuity express the heterochronic event space of the canvas and "history" itself. If it is true that the painting anticipated, if not initiated, cubism's radical defamiliarization of rational, regularized space measured by static, single-point perspective, then it is also true that it broke decisively with unilinear developmental time. Instead of unifying temporal diversity by collapsing the divarication of branches back into the length from trunk to root, *Les demoiselles* figures the collisions, overlappings, and coeval nonintersections of a plurality of histories. Hence, the absence of a discernible single light source for the various hatchings and shadings, as well as the painting's extreme crinkling of timespace itself.

Likewise, in literary productions, the heterochronic body of the modernist text itself ought to be seen as figuring the larger nature of the body of time. If narratives have been seen as "tales of time" because they organize our experiences sequentially and generate our understanding of time itself in the process of the telling, then modernism's nonnarrative experiments can be seen as a kind of alternate-historicity technology designed to defamiliarize everything from plot sequence to what Virginia Woolf derided as "the formal railway line of a sentence."[38] Modernism's stylistic discontinuities and disjunctions have for many decades been construed as the frozen simultaneities of fleeting instants or the static juxtapositions of the deep past and the present in what Joseph Frank called "spatial form." The "timeless unities" that Frank thought were examples of "the transformation of the historical imagination into myth[,] . . . which sees the actions and events of a particular time only as the bodying forth of eternal prototypes," should perhaps be reread heterochronically as transverse sections of different pasts existing side by side, each with a different historical depth and pace.[39] Instead of signifying any "simultaneous order" or the universal stages of deep ethnological time, the techniques of a text such as *The Waste Land,* and critical moves such as T. S. Eliot's insertion of the Paleolithic into the "historical sense" in his essay "Tradition and the Individual Talent" (i.e., his mention of "the rock drawing of the Magdalenian draughtsmen"), can be seen as gestures similar to H. G. Wells's stretching of human history onto multiple scales of deep time (Darwinian, Marxian, astronomical): less a simple mythic inscription of the past in the present, more a reconceptualization of time as a plural.[40]

Modernity, Zygmunt Bauman has pointed out, is "more than anything else, [the] *history of time:* the time when time has history."[41] A major aspect of this temporal history is the exceedingly odd vision of time as a heterochronic archive that I have been describing. This peculiar kind of time machine, one that generates or reveals the compound vestigialization of the present and alternative notions of history, continues to build its machinic network into our end of the long twentieth century, even if we now believe we have moved on to some phase beyond the modern. After the turn of the millennium, the "resurgence of interest in the science fiction subgenre of the alternate history," as Phillip Wegner describes it, is itself an important node in the larger cultural machine that produces the sense of "a variety of epochs liv[ing] side by side in the same areas."[42] For Wegner, as his recent book on the long 1990s argues, the reason for the revival of interest in the "what if" of counterfactual narratives is that the period "between two deaths" – defined on the one end by the fall of the Berlin Wall and the end of the Cold War and on the other by 9/11 and the beginning of the War on Terror – sparked a widespread reimagination of "the present as history" rather than the end of history that neoliberal accounts first heralded. This rethinking of the present is neither the "stereotypically modernist totalitarian closure of rigid historical determinism" nor "the postmodern free play of radical contingency" but a hopeful and political specification of the possibilities that follow from a determinate past. Wegner's view of the value of alternate history can be summed up by his quotation of Michael Löwy on Benjamin: "Against the history written by the victors, the celebration of the *fait accompli,* the historical one-way street and the 'inevitability' of the victory of those who triumphed, we must come back to this essential proposition: each present opens up onto a multiplicity of possible futures. In every historical conjuncture, there were alternatives."[43]

However, as the very first pulp SF alternate history shows us, equal to the utopian investment in not-yet-ness is the ability to read the multiplicity of possible futures back into the many presents to which they belong (rather than solely into the potentiality of a singular present) and to see the larger historical present as the cross section of those strands. Murray Leinster's "Sidewise in Time" (1934) focuses less on a single forking of human history than on the jumbled and patchwork geography composed of many unfamiliar times and historical outcomes. Moving sideways in that short story produces a vision of the North American present as comprising a "Post-Cambrian jungle left in eastern Tennessee," a Russian Alaska and California, an East Coast ruled by a Confederacy that won the Civil War, and preindustrial Chinese settlements around the Potomac.[44] As W. J. T.

Mitchell has pointed out recently, our age requires not just anthropologies and archaeologies of the present but a "'paleontology of the present,' a rethinking of our condition from the perspective of deep time"; insofar as both the rethinking and the condition are "after" modernism, we could add at the very least the complications introduced by evolutionary biology, Marxist approaches to uneven development, time geography, and astronomy.[45]

The combination and collaboration of disciplinary lenses required to understand heterochronic complexity and the interrelations of temporal scales brings me to my last example of anachronistic bodies: Terrence Malick's deployment of a disparate range of scales and cinematic-narrative rhythms to represent the body of all times in his Palme d'Or–winning film *Tree of Life* (2011). None of the approving viewers – those who were not bored or put off by Malick's very obvious desire to create a unified explanatory structure for the appearance of everything in the universe – would be likely to construe the film as a Leinsterian alternate history, but this may be the best way to read *Tree of Life.* Only by reading the film outlandishly can one see its contribution to the century-long thematic and formal exploration of the nonsubjective plurality of strange timespaces and concurrent histories and thereby discern in the film a clear counterpoint to its most obvious features: the religious themes generating the structuring tension between nature and grace, violence and compassion; the "mythopoetic" trope of the tree of life itself suggesting arboreal nesting structures that finally collapse in a single common origin; and the overemphasis on the human scale and the 1950s family drama in Waco, Texas, intensified by some truly awful voice-over.

That list of attributes is at the heart of why half of the film's viewers loved it, while the other half of the audience, as was widely reported, booed, stood up, and walked out of the theater. On first glance, *Tree of Life*'s cosmic vision of the interconnectedness of all things, as Kent Jones points out, seems to express a majestic unity in a "grand consistency of forms ( . . . the same spindly tentacles in a ball of primal energy, in a waving undersea plant, in a dinosaur's tale [*sic*], in the branches of trees blowing in the wind, in human hands and fingers)." Citing the film's "fluid shifts of scale" and "the film's signature action of dilation and contraction," Jones quotes Emerson on "the whole of history . . . in one man . . . a relation between the hours of our life and the centuries of time."[46] Similarly, David Sterritt, riffing on Baudelaire, writes that the mercurial scenes and highly mobile camera blend "the transitory and the enduring, the breathless and the timeless. From the standpoint of eternity, Malick poetically suggests, the feeling of an instant and the meaning of a lifetime are interwoven parts of a seamless whole." For Sterritt as for so many others, the movie ultimately makes sense because the jarring juxtapositions of scale "eventually jell into a fairly linear, if highly unconventional, narrative," one that privileges the human drama of the O'Brien family as the perfect aperture onto the cosmic story of the origins of life, consciousness, and conscience.[47]

However, the reactions of the disapproving audience – the extreme impatience with the film's shifts from cosmic montage to microscopic footage, or, in my first viewing, the attempt to ameliorate the taxing unevenness of pace with the ten-second skip function of VLC Media Player – register what I think is the film's equally important failure to make sense. The counterpoint to the emphasis on seamless wholes, jelling, and the nested scales of narrative (i.e., the resistance to ultimate sense making in the shifts, dilations, and contractions of the camera and story) is generated by the very content of the film itself: the multiplicity of time lines. Our expectations of both cinema and narrative as conventional time machines are frustrated by this content. The film's grating failure to jell and nest makes us recognize that, as physicist Robert Jaffe points out, "the times of our lives . . . are not the natural rhythms of the world," which include such irreconcilable scales as the electron's orbit ("the beat of the electromagnetic force," $10^{-16}$ second), the quark's vibration ("the natural rhythm of the strong force," $10^{-22}$ second), and "the unit of cosmological time" of 10 billion years, measured, of course, from our reference frame.[48] Unhappy viewers were most frustrated by the film's incommensurable scales and images, expressed most efficiently by the title of this blog post, "Daddy didn't love me. Hey look, a dinosaur!"[49] But perhaps the film's greatest contribution is in fact indexed by frustration, since this reaction is produced by the film's demonstration of the impossibility of making the pathos of the narrative mode universal. While the drama of 1950s American life is placed in the blink-of-an-eye flashback of a middle-aged Jack, the whole of history cannot be simply in one man. The theological emphasis on the problem of evil, evoked by the quotation from Job at the beginning of the film and the sermon in the middle and of course by the death of Jack's brother, is indeed a result of the *incompatibility* of the processes of larger natural scales with the human frame.[50] It is this inability of scales to be reducible to one another in some final cosmic totality that is the real subject of *Tree of Life,* perhaps in spite of itself.

To refer to the cosmos – in those gorgeous manipulations of Hubble images, shots of the formation of the universe, slow views of the flame-like coalescence of gas and dust into galaxies – is already to acknowledge the relativity of reference frames and what modernism troped as the proliferation of clocks. The twenty-minute stretch in the film that time-travels from the earliest moments of the universe, to the birth of microbial life on the planet, to the plesiosaur on the prehistoric beach, to the birth of consciousness in the predatory Troödon, to the birth of Jack seems to form a single, thin, long line, resulting in "the dawn of all human life" and the appearance of grace.[51] But in fact we have many disparate lines, some of which make their way into the present, some of which have completely independent trajectories and pace, some of which are long extinct. The visual clash of the various scales, if it is the function of any tree, is the result of the dense entanglements of Darwin's "great Tree of Life," the only illustration in his *On the Origin of Species* (1859), which he described as "fill[ing] with its dead and broken branches the crust of the earth, and cover[ing] the surface with its ever-branching and beautiful ramifications."[52] While the film appears to use its voice-overs as a way of unifying and arborealizing the lineage, I think the weird way in which the soundtrack and monologue carry over impossibly across a series of shots produces not theophanic transcendence but cineophanic immanence in which frame rate is not in any natural relation to the rate of occurrence within any particular reference frame. Moreover, as Martin Woessner has pointed out, Malick has used voice-over before, in *Badlands,* as the vehicle for cliché, and thus the film invites a *suspicion* of the voice-overs, the visual rhymes, and the homological power of the human drama in general.[53]

Like H. G. Wells's *Time Machine, Tree of Life* appears to conclude with a vision of the end of human time – after the death of the sun. But Malick gives his ending a distinctly Christian cast: the beach, where the dead have risen and are walking around, is a literalization of the mother's insight about time dilation ("unless you love, your life will flash by") and the site of her graceful release of her dead son ("I give you my son") in divine sacrifice. However, this closure, like Wells's Traveller's theories, is clearly facile in contrast to the rest of the film's interest in the relations and interference of timescales that produce all temporal effects, including the dilated instant that Jack is in fact experiencing outside his office building and in which modernism was clearly invested not as a point but as a portal to just this temporal difference. As Eliot's J. Alfred Prufrock says before he too ends up on a beach, "In a minute there is time."

In this newly estranged time is the play of relations among locally inflected sequences and disparate lines of occurrence. Our perception of something condensed or capacious, fast or slow, modern or archaic is not a feature of the event alone, measured in some singular abstract medium, but is a function of the pace of these time lines or reference frames in relation to one another. For Wells's Traveller, it might be the difference between "the spoke of a wheel spinning, or a bullet flying through the air" and the perceptual rates of the human sensorium.[54] For Henri Lefebvre, in his description of "rhythmanalysis," it might be the contrast between "an apparently immobile object, the forest" and some smaller scale in which "the movements of the molecules and atoms that compose it" become visible.[55] It might also be the difference among multiple histories running concurrently through the body of the present.

## NOTES

Thanks to Lois Cucullu, Rudolph Glitz, and Aaron Jaffe for organizing a set of productive conversations at their 2012 conference "Generation M: Resetting Modernist Time" (Amsterdam, Netherlands), which contributed to the evolution of this essay.

1. Wells, *Journey of Man*. The documentary is based on Wells, *The Journey of Man: A Genetic Odyssey*.

2. Wells, "Spencer Wells Builds" (TED talk). The combination of the tropes of time machines and archives occurs in numerous places in Wells's broadcast and printed work. In Wells's TED talk, the combination becomes a conflation: "Written in our DNA, in our genetic code, we have a historical document that takes us back in time to the earliest days of our species." Wells's work

focuses on the Y chromosome, "a large piece of DNA that doesn't recombine" (*A Genetic Odyssey,* 38) and that therefore allows us to follow ancestral lines far into the past. The patrilineal Y-chromosomal research was meant to test the earlier genetic work first published in *Nature* in 1987 by Rebecca Cann, Mark Stoneking, and Allen C. Wilson. This group's research had focused on the DNA in mitochondria, which is inherited intact from the mother, that is, without mixing mother's and father's genes in a way that obscures history.

3. The "Adam and Eve" narrative was invoked by the media to understand the research of Cann, Stoneking, and Wilson. See the cover of the January 11, 1988, issue of *Newsweek,* which depicts an African couple in the Garden of Eden. As many scientists have pointed out, the analogy is poor for several reasons. First, mitochondrial Eve and Y-chromosomal Adam did not live at the same time and therefore did not reproduce with each other; second, this Eve and Adam were not the only humans alive during their respective times; third, they represent not an absolute origin but a "coalescence point" – the most recent common ancestor whose existence accounts for a particular DNA sequence.

4. My manuscript "Modernism and Time Machines" examines time travel as a modernist device for defamiliarizing time itself – especially its pace, scale, and number.

5. Wells, *Deep Ancestry,* 58.

6. Gaonkar, *Alternative Modernities,* 17, 3.

7. Osborne, *Anywhere,* 17.

8. Ibid., 24. In his discussion of the problematic nature of contemporaneity, Osborne says that the "co-presentness of a multiplicity of times associates the contemporary . . . with the theological culture of the image," and he cites Michael Fried's famous line "presentness is grace" (24). The presentness in the representational form of the image is an "annihilation of temporality" (24).

9. Gaonkar pushes against the detemporalized space of world history by foregrounding the "critical band of variations consisting of site-specific 'creative adaptations' on the axis of convergence (or societal modernization)" (*Alternative Modernities,* 18). Convergence is the "acultural theory" of the unilinear and "inexorable march of modernity [that] will end up making all cultures look alike," regardless of culturally specific conditions and interactions (17).

10. Foucault, "Of Other Spaces," 26. Foucault's next example is the opposite

and related "to time in its most fleeting, transitory, precarious aspect": fairs that "teem once or twice a year with stands, displays, heteroclite objects, wrestlers, snakewomen, fortune-tellers" (26).

11. Foucault, *Archaeology of Knowledge,* 126, 129. "Heterotopia" appears in the preface of *Les mots et les choses: Une archeÏologie des sciences humaines* (Paris: Gallimard, 1966), a year before the lecture "Of Other Spaces," which was never published in Foucault's lifetime. The 1967 lecture was published in 1984, several months after Foucault's death; the English translation was published in 1986. Edward Soja calls Foucault's account of heterotopia "frustratingly incomplete, inconsistent, incoherent" (*Thirdspace,* 162). For a good summary of similar complaints, as well as a clear articulation of the usefulness of the concept, see Johnson, "Unravelling Foucault's 'Different Spaces.'"

12. The term first appears in Ernst Haeckel, "Die Gastrula und die Eifurchung der Thiere," *Jenaische Zeitschrift für Naturwissenschaft* 9 (1875): 402–508. For its first appearance in English, see Haeckel, *Evolution of Man.*

13. Gould, "The Uses of Heterochrony," 2.

14. Plates IV–V in Haeckel, *Anthropogenie.* J. G. Bach's lithograph of Haeckel's illustrations shows a fish, salamander, turtle, chick, pig, cow, rabbit, and human, as well as "the more or less complete agreement, as regards the most important relations of form, between the embryo of man and the embryo of other vertebrates," which is "more complete, the earlier the periods of development," and "retained for longer, the more closely the corresponding mature animals are related in descent" (quoted in Hopwood, "Pictures of Evolution," 292).

15. McNamara, *Shapes of Time,* 46, 282.

16. Ezra Pound to Harriet Monroe, London, September 30, 1914, in Pound, *Letters,* 80.

17. Kettler and Loader, "Temporizing with Time Wars," 157. Karl Mannheim, in "The Problem of Generations," complicated the biological fact of common chronological location by breaking the interval of generation into other necessary and sociologically relevant elements, such as different participations in different shared fates and perceptions of history ("actual generations") and different responses within a cohort to these shared experiences (which he called "generational units").

18. The term "Jonbar hinge" comes from Jack Williamson's pulp novel *The Legion of Time.* As Edward James puts it, the "classic image [of a divergence point]

is that of John Barr . . . standing in a field; if he picks up a magnet, rather than a stone, the history of the galaxy will be transformed. SF writers have come to call these decisive moments 'Jonbar points'; they range from the non-arrival of the comet which caused the extinction of the dinosaurs . . . to the non-occurrence of the Protestant Reformation" (*Science Fiction,* 113).

19. The term "paleo-modernism," paired with "neo-modernism," comes from Kermode, "The Modern," in Kermode, *Modern Essays,* 39–70.

20. Harvey, *The Condition of Postmodernity,* 240.

21. Baudelaire, "The Painter of Modern Life," 403. The standard sites that express these currents include the pace of urbanization, mass production, railways, automobiles, telegraphs, and the vertiginous elongation of human and planetary history.

22. Calinescu, *Five Faces of Modernity,* 3; Frank, "Spatial Form," 60.

23. Barrows, *The Cosmic Time of Empire,* 11; Bergson, *Time and Free Will,* 104.

24. Grosz, *The Nick of Time,* 253. The Darwinian language in Gaonkar's idea of "variations consisting of site-specific 'creative adaptations'" (*Alternative Modernities,* 18) and the brilliant combination of Darwin and Bergson in Grosz's work resonate in exciting ways with heterochrony. The Deleuzean distinction between the virtual and actual is in some ways less radical than the actual multiplicity of histories running through heterochronic bodies, but the critical potential – of opening up a "nick" in time to refuse the inevitability of the present and to sponsor multiple futures – is similar.

25. Seitler, *Atavistic Tendencies,* 172, 7. In this excellent study, the idea of heterochrony is implicit in Seitler's references to polytemporality, which can be defined, by way of her examples of atavisms, as the existence of different moments from the past in the present, different "times" bubbling up into what is otherwise "continuous forward movement" (7). It would hardly be a giant leap to see some of those coeval moments not as coming from "the" past but as synecdochic vestiges of different pasts as such, pasts that are still ongoing.

26. According to Harry Turtledove, "We're all time travelers, whether we know it or not. We go into the future at a steady rate of one second per second" (introduction to Turtledove and Greenberg, *The Best Time Travel Stories,* ix).

27. Wells, *The Time Machine,* 78, 144, 47, 59, 60.

28. Ibid., 120.

29. For more on neoteny and paedomorphic characteristics, see Farrell, "Wells and Neoteny." As far as I know, Farrell is the only critic ever to have written on some aspect of biological heterochrony in Wells.

30. Cantor and Hufnagel, "The Empire of the Future," 36, 37.

31. Wells, *The Time Machine,* 77.

32. I agree with Cantor and Hufnagel that "the imperialist expansion of Europe in the nineteenth century opened up the imaginative possibility of time travel" and that the machine itself is constructed out of "the raw materials of empire . . . ivory and crystal" ("Empire of the Future," 37, 54). But the ultimate effect of coming into contact with a primitive past is not only and always a strengthening of the historiographic or evolutionary line stretching from exotic other to civilized self. It very often produced a sense of what Johannes Fabian calls "coevalness" and, moreover, a sense of multiple historical tempos whose coevalness is an effect of a specific kind of cross-sectioning.

33. Squier, "Embryologies of Modernism," 147. Squier's examples include Susan Glaspell's 1922 play *The Verge,* whose female botanist sees social potential in embryological fragmentation and recombination: "I want to break it up! . . . There would be strange new comings together" (quoted on 147), and Julian Huxley (the brother of Aldous and grandson of anatomist T. H. Huxley), the zoologist who worked with Wells on a textbook and who wrote a short story, "The Tissue-Culture King," centering on "one of the most celebrated modern embryological techniques" of growing tissue and body parts outside of the body (147).

34. Shaw, *Back to Methuselah,* 296.

35. Antliff and Leighten, *Cubism and Culture,* 28. "African, Oceanic and even Middle Eastern and North African cultures have been said to mirror the 'childhood' of Western civilization. . . . As such the term 'primitive' is part of a larger discourse concerning the role of temporal constructs in power relations between cultures, propped up by racial theories of inferiority" (28).

36. Rubin, "Picasso," 243.

37. Rubin nevertheless maintains that "tribal works were associated by Picasso's generation with the earliest phases of civilization, in accordance with a highly simplistic model of world history" (ibid.).

38. See Ricoeur, *Time and Narrative;* Woolf, *A Writer's Diary,* 136.

39. Frank, "Spatial Form," 50.

40. Eliot, *The Sacred Wood,* 46.

41. Bauman, "Time and Space Reunited," 172, italics in the original.

42. Wegner, "Learning to Live in History," 98; Paz, *The Labyrinth of Solitude,* 11.

43. Wegner, *Life between Two Deaths,* 175, 101; Löwy, *Fire Alarm,* 115, quoted in Wegner, *Life between Two Deaths,* 100.

44. Leinster, "Sidewise in Time," 140.

45. Mitchell, *What Do Pictures Want?,* 491.

46. Jones, "Light Years," 26, 28.

47. Sterritt, "Days of Heaven and Waco," 55, 53.

48. Jaffe, "As Time Goes By," 16, 21.

49. Greg Christie, "'Daddy didn't love me. Hey look, a dinosaur!' Boozie Movies Waxes Philosophical on *Tree of Life,*" *Twitch* (blog), June 19, 2011, http://twitchfilm.com/2011/06/daddy-didnt-love-me-hey-look-a-dinosaur-boozie-movies-waxes-philosophical-on-tree-of-life.html.

50. The film quotes the book of Job 38:4, 7–8: "Where were you when I laid the foundations of the earth? . . . When the morning stars sang together, and all the sons of God shouted for joy?" This is the reply to Job's question about why a just god would allow Job's ten children to die.

51. Jones, "Light Years," 26.

52. Charles Darwin, *On the Origin of Species by Means of Natural Selection* (London: J. Murray, 1859), 105, quoted in Plate, "Visualizing the Cosmos," 533.

53. According to Woessner, Malick's "Heideggerian Cinema" always calls attention to the horizons and limits of worlds. See "What Is Heideggerian Cinema?," 144–145, 40.

54. Wells, *The Time Machine,* 67.

55. Lefebvre, *Rhythmanalysis,* 20.

## SELECTED BIBLIOGRAPHY

Antliff, Mark, and Patricia Dee Leighten. *Cubism and Culture.* New York: Thames & Hudson, 2001.

Barrows, Adam. *The Cosmic Time of Empire: Modern Britain and World Literature.* Berkeley: University of California Press, 2011.

Baudelaire, Charles. "The Painter of Modern Life." Translated by P. E. Charvet. In *Selected Writings on Art and Literature,* 390–435. Harmondsworth: Penguin, 1992.

Bauman, Zygmunt. "Time and Space Reunited." *Time & Society* 9.2–3 (June 2000): 171–185.

Bergson, Henri. *Time and Free Will: An Essay on the Immediate Data of Consciousness.* New York: Harper, 1910.

Calinescu, Matei. *Five Faces of Modernity: Modernism, Avant-Garde, Decadence, Kitsch, Postmodernism.* Durham, N.C.: Duke University Press, 1987.

Cann, Rebecca L., Mark Stoneking, and Allan C. Wilson. "Mitochondrial DNA and Human Evolution." *Nature* 325 (1987): 31–36.

Cantor, Paul A., and Peter Hufnagel. "The Empire of the Future: Imperialism and Modernism in H. G. Wells." *Studies in the Novel* 38.1 (2006): 36–56.

Darwin, Charles. *On the Origin of Species by Means of Natural Selection.* London: J. Murray, 1859.

Eliot, T. S. *The Sacred Wood: Essays on Poetry and Criticism.* London: Methuen & Co., 1920.

Fabian, Johannes. *Time and the Other: How Anthropology Makes Its Object.* New York: Columbia University Press, 1983.

Farrell, Kirby. "Wells and Neoteny." In *H. G. Wells's Perennial Time Machine,* edited by George Edgar Slusser, Patrick Parrinder, and Danièle Chatelain, 65–75. Athens: University of Georgia Press.

Foucault, Michel. *The Archaeology of Knowledge.* Translated by A. M. Sheridan Smith. New York: Pantheon Books, 1969.

——. "Of Other Spaces." *Diacritics* 16.1 (Spring 1986): 22–27.

Frank, Joseph. "Spatial Form in Modern Literature." In *The Widening Gyre: Crisis and Mastery in Modern Literature,* 3–62. New Brunswick, N.J.: Rutgers University Press, 1963.

Gaonkar, Dilip Parameshwar. *Alternative Modernities.* Durham, N.C.: Duke University Press, 2001.

Gould, Stephen Jay. "The Uses of Heterochrony." In *Heterochrony in Evolution: A Multidisciplinary Approach,* edited by Michael L. McKinney, 1–13. New York: Plenum Press, 1988.

Grosz, Elizabeth. *The Nick of Time: Politics, Evolution, and the Untimely.* Durham, N.C.: Duke University Press, 2004.

Haeckel, Ernst. *Anthropogenie, oder, Entwicklungsgeschichte des Menschen.* Leipzig: Engelmann, 1874.

——. *The Evolution of Man: A Popular Exposition of the Principal Points of Human Ontogeny and Phylogeny.* New York: D. Appleton, 1879.

Harvey, David. *The Condition of Postmodernity: An Enquiry into the Origins of Cultural Change.* Cambridge: Blackwell, 1990.

Hopwood, Nick. "Pictures of Evolution and Charges of Fraud: Ernst Haeckel's Embryological Illustrations." *Isis* 97.2 (2006): 260–301.

Jaffe, Robert L. "As Time Goes By." *Natural History* 115.8 (2006): 16–22.

James, Edward. *Science Fiction in the Twentieth Century.* Oxford: Oxford University Press, 1994.

Johnson, Peter. "Unravelling Foucault's 'Different Spaces.'" *History of the Human Sciences* 19.4 (November 2006): 75–90.

Jones, Kent. "Light Years." *Film Comment* 47.4 (2011): 24–29.

Kermode, Frank. *Modern Essays.* London: Collins, 1971.

Kettler, David, and Colin Loader. "Temporizing with Time Wars: Karl Mannheim and Problems of Historical Time." *Time & Society* 13.2–3 (September 2004): 155–172.

Lefebvre, Henri. *Rhythmanalysis: Space, Time, and Everyday Life.* London: Continuum, 2004.

Leinster, Murray. "Sidewise in Time." In *The Time Travelers: A Science Fiction Quartet,* edited by Robert Silverberg and Martin Harry Greenberg. New York: D. I. Fine, 1985.

Lewis, Wyndham. *Time and Western Man.* London: Chatto and Windus, 1927; Santa Rosa: Black Sparrow Press, 1993.

Löwy, Michael. *Fire Alarm: Reading Walter Benjamin's "On the Concept of History."* Translated by Chris Turner. London: Verso, 2005.

Mannheim, Karl. "The Problem of Generations." In *From Karl Mannheim,* edited by Kurt Wolff, 351–398. New Brunswick, N.J.: Transaction Publishers, 1993.

McNamara, Ken. *Shapes of Time: The Evolution of Growth and Development.* Baltimore, Md.: Johns Hopkins University Press, 1997.

Mitchell, W. J. T. *What Do Pictures Want? The Lives and Loves of Images.* Chicago: University of Chicago Press, 2005.

Osborne, Peter. *Anywhere or Not at All: Philosophy of Contemporary Art.* London: Verso, 2013.

Paz, Octavio. *The Labyrinth of Solitude and Other Writings.* 1961; New York: Grove Press, 1985.

Plate, S. Brent. "Visualizing the Cosmos: Terrence Malick's *Tree of Life* and Other Visions of Life in the Universe." *Journal of the American Academy of Religion* 80.2 (2012): 527–536.

Pound, Ezra. *The Letters of Ezra Pound, 1907–1941.* Edited by D. D. Paige. New York: Harcourt Brace, 1950.

Ricoeur, Paul. *Time and Narrative.* 3 vols. Chicago: University of Chicago Press, 1984.

Rubin, William. "Picasso." In *"Primitivism" in 20th-Century Art: Affinity of the Tribal and the Modern,* edited by William Rubin, 241–343. New York: Museum of Modern Art, 1984.

Seitler, Dana. *Atavistic Tendencies: The Culture of Science in American Modernity.* Minneapolis: University of Minnesota Press, 2008.

Shaw, Bernard. *Back to Methuselah: A Metabiological Pentateuch.* London: Penguin, 1921.

Soja, Edward. *Thirdspace: Journeys to Los Angeles and Other Real-and-Imagined Places.* Cambridge: Blackwell, 1996.

Squier, Susan M. "Embryologies of Modernism." *Modernism/Modernity* 3.3 (1996): 145–153.

Sterritt, David. "Days of Heaven and Waco: Terrence Malick's *Tree of Life.*" *Film Quarterly* 65.1 (Fall 2011): 52–57.

Turtledove, Harry, and Martin Harry Greenberg, eds. *The Best Time Travel Stories of the 20th Century.* New York: Del Rey, 2005.

Wegner, Phillip E. "Learning to Live in History: Alternate Historicities and the 1990s in *The Years of Rice and Salt.*" In *Kim Stanley Robinson Maps the Unimaginable: Critical Essays,* edited by William J. Burling, 98–112. Jefferson, N.C.: McFarland, 2009.

———. *Life between Two Deaths, 1989–2001: U.S. Culture in the Long Nineties.* Durham, N.C.: Duke University Press, 2009.

Wells, H. G. *The Time Machine: An Invention.* Edited by Nicholas Ruddick. Peterborough: Broadview Press, 2001. First published in 1895 by Heinemann.

Wells, Spencer. *Deep Ancestry: Inside the Genographic Project.* Washington, D.C.: National Geographic, 2006.

———. *Journey of Man.* Directed by Clive Maltby. Alexandria, Va.: PBS Home Video, 2003.

———. *The Journey of Man: A Genetic Odyssey.* Princeton, N.J.: Princeton University Press, 2002.

———. "Spencer Wells Builds a Family Tree for Humanity." Filmed June 2007. TED video. Posted August 2008. http://www.ted.com/talks/spencer_wells_is_building_a_family_tree_for_all_humanity.html.

Williamson, Jack. *The Legion of Time.* Reading: Fantasy Press, 1952.

Woessner, Martin. "What Is Heideggerian Cinema? Film, Philosophy, and Cultural Mobility." *New German Critique,* no. 113 (Summer 2011): 129–157.

Woolf, Virginia. *A Writer's Diary: Being Extracts from the Diary of Virginia Woolf.* Edited by Leonard Woolf. London: Hogarth Press, 1953.

9

# THERE IS AS YET INSUFFICIENT DATA FOR A MEANINGFUL ANSWER

## INHUMANISM AT THE LITERARY LIMIT

*Aaron Jaffe*

Among its other merits, Vilém Flusser's strange treatise on *Vampyroteuthis infernalis* is a fable about information at the literary limit. Comparing "the vampire squid from hell" and *Homo sapiens sapiens,* Flusser proposes a fantastic convergence that links the odd existence of a tentacled life-form, complexly equipped for probing the deep ocean, to the inhuman consequences of our emerging system of new media. Humans increasingly approximate the strategies of invertebrate life, he writes: "As our interest in objects began to wane, we created media that have enabled us to rape human brains, forcing them to store immaterial information. We have built chromatophores of our own – televisions, videos, and computer monitors that display synthetic images – with whose help broadcasters of information can mendaciously seduce their audiences."[1] Is this assessment hyperbolic? Probably not. Recumbent with chromatophoric gadgets, humans become more and more cephalopodan, probing, probed by, and propelled through an endless ooze of immaterial information. Increasingly, our environment is, in so many words, the seemingly unfathomable abyss of big data plumbed fitfully by inhuman algorithms.

Like the vampyroteuthic dataverse, big data presents a literary problem that defies sensible human scales.[2] Big data signals an endgame for a literary humanism that depends on the kind of specially selected, reasonably portioned, yet easy-to-lose information anyone might come to value in the reference frame of a single lifetime. Formerly, humans worked hard – and mostly failed – to give their information durable form in terms of finite objects – grasping problems, transforming "intractable things into manageable ones," coming up against the "last things" that "could not be transformed or overcome," archiving what they found out as best they could for later. Now things have changed; the sheer pile-up of inexpensive, new-style stuff overwhelms us from all sides with unmanageable nonthings "negligible from an existential point of view."[3] "Humans," returning to the ever-prescient Flusser, "no longer realize their creative potential by struggling against the resistance of stubborn objects. . . . From now on, humans can realize their creative potential by processing new and immaterial information" and then by selling it back at "inflated prices" to a "dominated" humanity.[4] The change from handling in-formed objects to processing an abyss of potential information is decisive. In effect, Flusser observes a state-shift from an age when the inevitability of further processing was not a given – when *raw data* was *not* an oxymoron, to invoke Lisa Gitelman's recent collection – to a time when it is inevitably so. The idea of unprocessed information – and things that are intractable to processing – increasingly seems like a naive archaism to those saturated with so much potential information.[5] Now every nonthing comes preformed with massive quantities of metadata – date and time stamps, above all else – a vapor-trail of data-as-waste, which our insidious gadgets leave us behind willy-nilly, whether it matters or not. Mostly not – we hope.

Hovering in the background here is the "friendly reminder" from new media studies that data are always already "cooked" and never entirely "raw," an allusion to Claude Lévi-Strauss's structuralist classic *The Raw and the Cooked,* invoked to emphasize that data are cultural, not natural, phenomena.[6] One way or another, data always come prepared, it's held. Yet, following Lévi-Strauss, raw and cooked are *linked* empirical categories, and cooking is the middle phase – "a form of mediation," he repeatedly intones.[7] Perhaps it's worth pressing a poststructuralist point: *raw* is a discourse effect of *cooked;* the unmarked/marked pair is mutually constitutive. *Raw* is more than relational, in other words; it's also meditational and semiconductive. In later work, Lévi-Strauss nuances his culinary-cultural matrix, adding gradients extending from *almost raw* to *more than cooked* and including such additional states as *burnt* and *rotten* as well as *bland* and *spicy.*[8] The inevitability of such category shifting – changes in state from *given* to *taken,* for example – indicates that, despite appearances, categorical terms like *data* have little self-sufficiency. If *data* implies something like *available for further processing,* it manifests the same problems as *guest* and *host,* eating off one another. In the beginning, as Michel Serres reminds us, comes the parasite: "Real production is unexpected and improbable, it overflows with information and is always immediately parasited."[9] The break in the flow – the interruption – is formative static.

In other words, data don't need to be raw to be considered oxymoronic. Contradiction is already on board, yoking the sharp and the dull, as the etymology of "oxymoron" suggests. *Raw data* is a kind of pleonastic oxymoron, presupposing multiplicity as accumulation – processing plural to singular into a set, a matrix, a database, and so forth. The ambition is to fit all data – to process everything – *they* becomes *it*. Switching to singular, then, data comes always already sharpened, the argument goes; data is less raw than it is constitutively messy. Raw and/or cooked, the massive amounts of static implicated in inhuman scales make archival issues conspicuous in several ways. For better or worse, hangovers of obsolete form – skeuomorphs – hover about our metaphors about managing data, information, and knowledge. Google isn't an archive per se. It's an inhuman finding aide for making sense of its monstrously expanding archives.

For all their ubiquity, analogies drawn between in-formed objects with finite capacities and the nebulous communication dataverse designated by the cloud are also simultaneously monstrous and clumsy.[10] Humans once fashioned in-formed objects with archival powers, Flusser points out in his fable, for the sake of orientation and memory – the bent twig used to indicate a direction on a path, for instance. Once upon a time, we gathered info to disseminate it and fabricated artificial memories. Now that ever-larger quantities overwhelm our objectworld, we require special, systematic finding aids – search engines, above all. Input comes prior to information. Consider the rise of the algorithm along these lines: algorithms require archives to function, and we trade on a host of archival metaphors to talk about them, yet they are not archives. Instead, they are methods for producing systematic outputs – for cooking data, so to speak – recipes that get themselves archived and that need various archives to work. It may be that "new-style information," as Flusser puts it, is "negligible from the existential point of view," yet does this existential melancholy even matter if every ephemeral state is now collectable and available for potential use?[11]

This chapter tracks a genealogy for making literary sense of scales of input and output back to modernist literary concerns with deep time, impossible author functions, and maximal and minimal audience structures. The "oddball archive" is a futurist ersatz archive, search engines engineered for grasping what's "impossible to get a hold of," processed at inhuman scales and expanding reference beyond the Anthropocene. The murky abyss, as it were, includes speculation about deep futurity, time after human extinction, for instance, that draws on the scientific extrapolations of cosmology. It also confronts the technically assisted observation of a "reality anterior to the emergence of the human species – or even anterior to every recognized form of life on earth," as Quentin Meillassoux characterizes it. The arche-fossil Meillassoux describes – clearly rooted in modern knowledge of inhuman timescales advanced by geology and plate tectonics – is also a fossil of the future, "designat[ing] the material support on the basis of which the experiments that yield estimates of ancestral phenomena proceed – for example, an isotope whose rate of radioactive decay we know, or the luminous emission of a star that informs us as to the date of its formation."[12] Such ersatz archives are not merely eccentric; they exit the orbit of the human-scale archiving practices altogether. Seeing and hearing by technical means – devising techniques of observation, experiment, and reflection – is the crux of what Siegfried Zielinski sees as Flusser's media philosophy and also the lodestone of his own project of media variantology: "Technical media had been a pile, a treasure of possibilities (or perhaps better: potentialities), which permanently had to be explored, every day and everyday new."[13] This chapter takes such variantology as occasion for literary speculation about the scalar implications of a long inhuman turn in modernity, administering complexity of temporality as an inevitable encounter with entropy and expiration – navigating the abyss of expired databases, dated theories, and dead links.

## I.

"Take your books of mere poetry and prose; let me read a timetable, with tears of pride."[14] So says the hero of G. K. Chesterton's *The Man Who Was Thursday,* observing not only that time is information but also that it has affective texture. Let me name one of the commonplaces of the literary modern: searching for aesthetic possibilities in a newly regimented world. As modern time becomes increasingly administered on and by the clock, human timescales – seconds, minutes, years – become increasingly remote, displaced from fundamental science first by deep geological time and then by the discoveries of quantum mechanics and scientific cosmology. The new intervals of physics are so short that they are impossible to relate to, whereas the tempos of cosmos are so long that they prove similarly inhuman.

The literary modern affords special epistemological status to unforeseen circumstances beyond human control. This chapter concerns the collection of literary knowledge in inhuman quantities and the literary implications of scalar shifts in information – including temporal information – in modernity. In particular, it explores modernist interest in "collecting" absurdly long timeframes, scales of the deep future that dwarf another standard developed by remapping the psychologized, subjectivized mind with the topographies of the classical epic (i.e., on Bloom's day, June 16, 1904, or Quentin's day, June 2, 1910, or Mrs. Dalloway's day). In this regard, H. G. Wells's AD 802,701 is a critical search result for an alternative inhuman (in-Bloomian, sub-Quentinian, ex-Dallowegian) modernism that has ongoing implications. In *The Time Machine,* for instance, his thought experiments in extreme futurism reveal a decidedly literary pedigree for the engineered machines currently plying the World Wide Web. Considering the Wellsian search engines alongside other cognate versions proposed by Isaac Asimov, J. G. Ballard, and others, I argue that a conceivable end of human knowledge frameworks – the "death of the sun," using the critical shorthand proposed by Jean-François Lyotard – provides something like a new modern sublime: the cold return of the inert and the quiet, the background temperature of outer space, the unlit, unvoiced stone, the exhaustion of exhaustion. Here we might find the inhuman happiness that follows postmodern nihilism and the recent consolations of the archive: never give up on a better past.[15]

Wells (1866–1946) is the ideal literary instrument for thinking about human and inhuman time for two reasons. First, his literary name is prepossessed by the idea of generation. You see this in his own writings when Wells discusses his relation to other writers, in particular, in his *Experiment in Autobiography* composing the Wellsian brain. What Wells does again and again is place his powers of attention out of the frame of the contemporary. The fact that Wells continues to be placed paradigmatically outside the modernist cohort simply continues a procedure he rehearses in his own literary self-presentation. There's the odd way, too, that his obituarists – T. S. Eliot and F. R. Leavis, in particular – take up these cues as they dutifully place him out of phase.[16] Despite the popular reputation of Wells as a visionary, the purported originator of modern science fiction appears to suffer, however ironically, from the maxim that nothing ages faster than the future. That so many of his visions of the future "came true" – as is often remarked – seems of little moment in this regard. To the midcentury professoriate, Wells *feels* older than Henry James, the author who is a full generation younger; Wellsian style seems more *dated*. More of our times, less our contemporary. What can datedness mean, as Justin Clemens and Dominic Pettman have well observed, when we're caught in "the great aesthetic whirlpool [that] neither validates nor rejects any particular epoch"?[17]

This sense of Wellsian datedness may follow from his status as a name on the edge of this whirlpool, one of the most prominent living authors at the time when modernism happened: when John Galsworthy died in 1932, who but Wells was available as a credible choice to be president of PEN International? For Wells, the reflexive administrative moment of literary reputation never happens, because it didn't need to. The contours of his reputation were already established in his lifetime: pioneer of the high concept, social fabulist on the obsolescent side of literary history, popular historian of the steampunk future. More particular to his relevance to this concern is his work as an archtheorist of generational time – the formulaic phrase *generation after generation* appears with incredible frequency across his work. His search engines are calibrated to overleap generational scales; his alternative histories report to impossible future readerships. One might say that Wells was interested in the formula generation after generation not so much as a commonplace of sequence but as an inhuman problem: what happens to the idea of generation after generation is a zombie concept.

I'm thinking especially of *The Sleeper Awakes,* in which the protagonist goes into a trance in 1897, sleeps through the Martian wars, and wakes up centuries later to find that through compounded interest he literally owns the future. I'm thinking of the sleeper, the time traveler, the subject of the *World Set Free,* the Wellsian premise of "humanity surviving extinction, of overvaulting the end of time and historical epochs, not toward the future or the past, but toward the heart itself of time and history," to borrow some Agambenian language.[18] Before spooling to the end, some preliminary remarks about modernism and time – historicity, contemporaneity, futurity, and the concept of generation itself – may be in order. In *Graphs, Maps and Trees,* Franco Moretti notices three intervals of literary time, which he imports from the Annales school.[19] At one end of the spectrum is the very short term – the bread and butter of modernist studies – the event, the break, or the rupture. The instantaneous experience of novelty, the aesthetic effect just there that changes everything. At the other side is the very long term, the epoch, the era, or the *longue durée:* the period-spanning historical thesis that in its own way is another second mainstay of modernist scholarship. Or else, maybe more accurately, one could say that the very short is constitutive of modernist studies, whereas the very long is regulative of it. With all the emphasis on temporal particularities and generalities, we modernist scholars have ill served the middle term, the temporal span that Moretti calls the "cycle." Cycles, as he has it, "constitute temporary structures within the historical flow." These represent the "unstable" "border country" between the incremental and structure-less shock of the new designated by the event and the static and overly structured critical forensics designated by the epoch. It's no secret that what Moretti means by the cycle, his so-called temporary structure, is more commonly understood as genre. In so many words, genres are "morphological arrangements that last in time," durable but never permanent literary dispositions for, say, Imperial Gothic or teenage vampire abstinence novels.[20] In his examples derived from nineteenth-century cases, they last between twenty-five and thirty years. Whether or not the life-cycle of genres accelerate with the technomedial evolutions of the twentieth century is a key question for Moretti's methodology. Isn't the Morettian cycle in fact the Agambenian whirlpool? I want to put pressure on Moretti's insight by making an observation: thinking about genre as the life-cycle of forms – beginnings and endings, birth and death – inevitably calls forth something like generation. Genres, generations. The beginnings and endings of genres resemble the birth and death of generations by more than mere homology. A generation signals a cohort born at roughly the same time, shaped by the same generic conditions, events, shared forms of technomediality: "Each generation tallies its new talent and catalogues its new forms and epochal tendencies in art and thought."[21] It is no coincidence, I submit, that the conventional measure afforded to a generation – twenty-five to thirty years – is basically the span of time that Moretti apportions to the life of a genre.[22]

## II.

And yet the ultimate distant reader, the computational knowledge engine, Multivac, in the end, at the end of Isaac Asimov's "The Last Question," can at last report the hard-won findings to . . . no generation, the universe being finally over. Jean-François Lyotard writes that, with the inevitable exhaustion of the sun – 4.57 billion years and counting – comes the death of death.[23] And is that not a good thing? A happy end, in a manner of thinking, to thinking? *Fiat lux* and nowhere to report the search results. Here we find the nonhuman "happiness" that follows postmodern nihilism, a happy refusal of the consolations of the archive. Don't go back to the airport flyover, it tells us, like the prisoner in Chris Marker's *La jetée* (1962), blocked for the future because he can't give up on his desire for a better past.

That said, our blueprints for the administration of inhuman time include J. G. Ballard (1930–2009) and Isaac Asimov (1920–2002). Ballard, to understand the consequences of an inevitably minimal unhuman end to human knowledge frameworks. Asimov, to formulate a critical concept of the literary as a thought experiment about maximal knowledge. I file this report, however truncated and schematic, to pursue a contrarian path for criticism through a vast science fiction / speculative fiction corpus, a path avoiding the familiar Heinlein-Dick "postmodernist" axis. Instead, Asimov and Ballard get pride of place in a paleofuturist genealogy of speculative, intellectual, modernist outliers writing impossible scenarios about unhuman literary machinery, a genealogy that stretches from Ursula K. Le Guin to Olaf Stapledon to H. G. Wells and among which we could certainly count Jorge Luis Borges and Franz Kafka. The prolific Asimov has his pulp, genre-fiction bona fides and hard SF credentials, but his emigrant background (a child of Yiddish speakers, a man without papers from an impossible cultural-linguistic zone) and his standing as a committed scientific popularizer and as an actual professor of the natural sciences push his profile beyond the frothy space operas, interplanetary romances, and rocket and ray-gun escapades of many of his Cold War contemporaries.

But before we crank up the dials of Asimovian maximalism, first Ballardian minimalism. Ballard's career stretches from the mid-1950s to the present. And he may be even more difficult to classify. Less interested in the gear of hard science fiction and its attendant idiom of techno-Benthamism, Ballard liked to claim kinship with the surrealists. "My science fiction was not about outer space," he wrote, "but about psychological change, psychological space."[24] Sometimes a bright line is drawn between Ballard's early, more "conventional" SF stuff and his later, more experimental, and thus more "literary" work. Nonetheless, Ballard manages across the range of his oeuvre to remain obsessively interested in the near-term catastrophic end: the collapsing inner space of human knowledge systems. His first four novels all describe the psychological consequences of various transformations of the Earth into a hostile, alien environment; his later fiction seems to come to the conclusion that this conceit was a superfluous fantasy. The Earth was already transformed. "Earth is the only alien planet," he claimed, famously, "and the future is five minutes away." "Our concepts of past, present and future are being forced to revise themselves," he writes. "The past, in social and psychological terms, became a casualty of Hiroshima and the nuclear age. . . . [T]he future is ceasing to exist, devoured by the voracious present."[25]

He's the past master of what we could call "stalking inner space," a term he's credited with inventing in 1962: the mind scanning the tuner for weaker and weaker information signals.[26] Despite the inherent minimalism of the activity, it yields surprisingly warped and uncanny encounters, as in Andrei Tarkovsky's film *Stalker* (1979). "We have annexed the future into the present," Ballard writes. "Options multiply around us, and we live in an almost infantile world where any demand, any possibility, whether for life-styles, travel, sexual roles and identities, can be satisfied instantly."[27] Ballard's fiction is full of search engines stalking five minutes into the future. The instrument panel choked with dust and filth, social and psychological channels clogged with chatter, Ballard's fiction still probes for messages. One such story set "five minutes in the future" is "The Message from Mars" (1992). The tale has an interplanetary space crew of celebrity astronauts returning from Mars in a hermetically sealed, self-sustaining ship. Parked on the landing strip after a seemingly triumphant voyage, the passengers refuse to disembark, protected from the entreaties from without by an impenetrable space-age ceramic shell and sustained by a reactor and a well-stocked larder. "Rejecting the [outer] world with a brief wave," they choose instead to live out their lives in "a sealed [inner] world, immune to any presses from within and without" for reasons impossible to clarify by observers outside.[28] A capsule full of Bartlebys or Garbos. An allegory of the current media ecology rests on the passengers' petulant refusal to play along with a massive propaganda-and-PR apparatus set up to record and hype their mission for a global audience, a noisy Space Family Robinson reality show trading on all-too-facile plotlines and debased audience expectations.

Inner space is quieter than outer space. The allegorical capacity becomes unglued with the passage of time. Elsewhere, Ballard notes the futility of escape from the autonomous life-pod: "In the past we have always assumed that the external world around us represented reality, however confusing or uncertain, and that the inner world of our minds, its dreams, hopes, ambitions, represented the realm of fantasy and the imagination. These roles, it seems to me, have been reversed. The most prudent and effective method of dealing with the world around us is to assume that it is a complete fiction – conversely, the one small node of reality left to us is inside our own heads."[29] In the end, after NASA itself passes into history, the ship – decommissioned, forgotten, its life support still operational – ends up an inscrutable piece of hulking junk deposited on a parking lot. Another mobile home in a trailer park. A graduate student eventually rediscovers the ship and hooks up various instruments and magnetic imaging equipment – search engines of a certain kind: "An aged couple, Commander John Merritt and Dr Valentina Tsarev, now in their late eighties, sat in their small cabins, hands folded on their laps. There were no books or ornaments beside their simple beds. Despite their extreme age they were clearly alert, tidy and reasonably well nourished. Most mysteriously, across their eyes moved the continuous play of a keen and amused intelligence."[30] I find the meaning of this scene inscrutable. It has something of the quality of Ti and Bo and the Heaven's Gate Cult. Or Pong. I don't question the veracity of the data about their "keen and amused intelligence," only that the meaning of the observation remains a cipher. It could be fruitfully matched with another mysterious comment Ballard made about the task of the writer: "What is the main task facing the writer? . . . The writer knows nothing any longer. He has no moral stance. He offers the reader the contents of his own head, a set of options and imaginative alternatives. His role is that of the scientist, whether on safari or in his laboratory, faced with an unknown terrain or subject."[31] Here we can turn from the minimalist response conveyed by Ballard's minimalist time machine and make a short detour to Asimovian search engines working maximal overdrive. But first, a short detour back to Wells, who was, not surprisingly, a professed influence on both writers.

In *The Time Machine,* the Time Traveller jumps ahead to AD 802,701. The number is big but in a specific, almost too ordinary and uneventful way – a bigger version of the famous 42 in *The Hitchhiker's Guide to the Galaxy,* which I'll come back to shortly. It is as if evolutionary, epochal time, scaled for charting the origin of species, has been tacked on to the historical measure of a human lifetime, as in the joke about the museum guard at the natural history museum who tells visitors that the brontosaurus bones are 150 million and 5 years old . . . because he's been working there for 5 years. The number signals, as it were, enough lapsed time for class difference, that is, the historical driver, to take on an irreparable evolutionary form. Nearly a million years hence, with no other legacy of humanity to speak of, the over- and underclasses of economic modernity have branched into separate species, the Morlocks and the Eloi. The ironic twist is, of course, that the descendants of the upper classes have become the food source for the proles.

While the main interest of the novel may rest in this inversion, I'm more interested in an odd scene at the end of the novel. With allegory seemingly laid to one side, the search engine pushes forward to the end of the spool, 30 million years ahead. Here, on a desolate beach, the Time Traveler observes the final sunset:

> Suddenly [he reports] I noticed that the circular westward outline of the sun had changed. . . . The darkness grew apace; a cold wind began to blow in freshening gusts from the east. . . . From the edge of the sea came a ripple and whisper. Beyond these lifeless sounds the world was silent. . . . All the sounds of man, the bleating of sheep, the cries of birds, the hum of insects, the stir that makes the background of our lives – all that was over. . . . I saw the black central shadow of the eclipse sweeping towards me. In another moment the pale stars alone were visible. All else was rayless obscurity. The sky was absolutely black.[32]

This could be described as an early scene of secular, planetary snuff. Particular details to notice are the dynamic of information and noise. The time machine is, above all, an observational machine, a search engine, tasked with uncovering improbable results. The final fade-out is interesting only for its minimalism: it reports all that isn't heard, the lack of murmurs and mumbles, bleating, bird sounds, and buzzing. Curiously, even muted, non-noise counts as noise in this context. The only information is visual, minimal light inscribing the landscape as if on a photographic plate, the human observer machine, a camera basically, placed before a decidedly unhuman end, affording the time of one last, noneschatological long exposure. In any sense, save for a presence that stands in for the author function, there is nothing to be known and no audience structure to know it. This unvoiced stone under a burned-out ember says even less than Ozymandias. Without belaboring the paradoxes of observation, I will remark that Wells's point is that the meaningful human condition ended uneventfully sometime before during the span of eight hundred thousand–odd years between the present and the Morlock-Eloi scene. This final sunset is a quarrel with the humanness of endings as such.

Asimov also takes an even longer view. Most famously, his Foundation series – in fact, a cluster of interlinked stories and novels – follows through on a logic of temporal maximalism, stretching over thousands of years into the future. Fans have pegged AD 25,621 as the latest date referenced in the series, but it is a bit confusing, because new calendars are introduced at several junctures in the series. Furthermore, the entire sequence is menaced by the threat of information death, the edifice of human knowledge slouching into ruinous quagmires of ignorance, coming epochs when even the measurement of history becomes impossible. Asimov uses robots, institutions, corporations, and other durable nonhuman dispositions to overcome the narrative limitations of the human lifespan. I won't try to sum up the intricacies of a work conceived as an intergalactic retelling of Edward Gibbons's *Decline and Fall of the Roman Empire*. I only want to touch on two elements of Foundation. Each in its own way takes the form of mystified literary scholarship: the theoretical concept of psychohistory and the project of a reference work called *Encyclopedia Galactica*. In *The Time Machine*, the Traveller goes forward to discover increasing discontinuity between what he observes and human beings and their knowledge frameworks. The scene in the disused museum is paradigmatic in both Wells and the dystopian tradition. In Asimov, who is more sanguine about humanity's prospects than either Wells or Ballard, psychohistory and the *Encyclopedia Galactica* are conceived of as two durable forms extending the continuity of human knowledge frames beyond the natural lifespan. Psychohistory is essentially an extrapolative form of social science – the wisdom of crowds writ large. A computational concept engine gathers massive amounts of data about human behavior and then uses its databases to calculate future human history. The more massive the data set, the more predictive the engine gets. Eventually psychohistorians determine that humanity is doomed to enter a catastrophic phase, a ten-thousand-year span of stupidity, and they conceive of an enterprise to preserve knowledge and mitigate against the hazards of this epoch. They set out to compile a massively comprehensive *Encyclopedia Galactica* to preserve all knowledge. This task, it is said, has the power to shorten the projected dark age by a factor of 10. The efforts of the galactic encyclopedists consumes the resources of an entire planet where they are eventually exiled. In effect, the planet itself is co-opted into a giant knowledge engine, planetary sized.

Let's explore the literary dimensions of these two fictional superliterary projects and some "real-world" cognates of them. Since Asimov, the *Encyclopedia Galactica* fantasy – humanity preserved through a redemptive ark of comprehensive and curated knowledge – has become a pervasive meme. It plays no small part in inspiring the *Wikipedia* phenomenon, for instance. Douglas Adams's *Hitchhiker's Guide to the Galaxy* was a fairly self-conscious parody of it, too, a kind of *Encyclopedia Galactica for Dummies.* Allegedly filched from galactic encyclopedists, the *Guide,* Adams writes, "has many omissions and contains much that is apocryphal, or at least wildly inaccurate."[33] Of course, one doesn't need a science fiction frame to recognize that the encyclopedia from Diderot forward is in itself motivated by a principle of epistemological maximalism as an almost manic drive. In terms of *Wikipedia,* I think it is safe to say Asimov would be aghast at its open-source editing imperatives and the knee-jerk distrust of primary expert knowledge enshrined in its practices. Asimov was open source when it came to mass data collection but left the analysis, the computational psychohistory, to the positronic brain.

Asimov's related Multivac stories, a different fictional world from the Foundation series, show the fault lines of the project. In effect, Multivac draws together the two strands of inhuman humanism and puts them in a black box, to use Bruno Latour's word: first, massive information collection of the past, and second, oracle-like analysis and computational prediction of the future. As a fictional computer, the physiognomy of Multivac differs from both familiar archetypes: the humanoid robot, automaton doppelgänger with a body and the glorified space nanny, identified with the space ship itself, charged with holding steady on the instrument panel, managing human life support for interstellar express. As a knowledge engine, Multivac is a cipher for the author function itself, I submit, a disembodied search engine for information. Like Wells's Time Machine, Asimov's very long timescales and machines to probe them can be read as thought experiments about extreme configurations of author functions and impossible audience structures.

Ending ten million times further in the future than *The Time Machine,* the Multivac story called "The Last Question" (1956) surely has the record for one of the longest time frames ever conceived in fiction (and as such the least Aristotelian ever written).[34] It concerns a succession of Multivac responses to the question about the ultimate fate of the universe. Asimov gives the question both a cybernetic spin – What happens at the end of information? – and a thermodynamic one – Can entropy be reversed? In seven vignettes spaced over vast segments of cosmological time from May 21, 2061, to the event of would-be entropy death, ten trillion years later, seven varieties of this question are put to the machine and its successors. Six times the only answer returned is: "THERE IS AS YET INSUFFICIENT DATA FOR A MEANINGFUL ANSWER." The final time the question is asked, human beings and their evolutionary progeny are long gone, no data are left to be collected, and all is "completely correlated and put together in all possible relationships." The seventh computational engine (which exists only in hyperspace), an information-processing entity akin to "a computer . . . far less than was a man to Man," achieves total knowledge against the backdrop of entropy death. Asimov writes: "There was now no man to whom AC might give the answer of the last question. No matter. The answer – by demonstration – would take care of that, too."[35] Given the ingredients of (*a*) omniscience and (*b*) the universe's absolute nullity, that answer is (you probably guessed it): let there be light. A clever trick. The clue in the set-up is the idea that the answer would come by demonstration: with no information left and no matter, this is the only possible thing to say and to do. There is only one question to ask at the end of the universe: What's next?

If *The Hitchhiker's Guide to the Galaxy* anticipates *Wikipedia,* consciously or unconsciously, Asimov's futurist engineered artifacts and computational knowledge machines gesture toward the Internet. They point to one of the constitutive problems concerning the kind of epistemological maximalism that the Internet signifies, namely, interface, instrumentation, and computation. In a word, intelligence. How do you put the question and calibrate it to get back a meaningful answer from the accumulation of vast amounts of mostly undigested chatter, that is, the stuff people have seen fit to upload? You've heard the one about a million monkeys with a million typewriters eventually writing the complete works of Shakespeare. The Internet, so goes a well-known joke, proves this to be false. One can think of the Internet as a vast assemblage of information debris like the dumpster behind your apartment clotted with garbage: phone books, office materials, and the occasional appointment calendar and obsolescent Filofax. It started as a flotilla of documents lashed together by hyperlinks – various digital flotsam, jetsam, lagan that have been deposited, jettisoned, discarded, claimed, derelicted, who can say. In the early going – its incunabulum era perhaps – this assemblage of documents was countable and thus indexable. In 1993 the number of websites was in the hundreds; one year later they were in the tens of thousands; today Google estimates that the web contains one trillion links.[36]

The first search engines were simply efforts to measure the size of the information content of the web by tracing out all the links. For a while, the size was manageable, monitored by individuals who could be likened to Alexander and Bertram, the faithful attendants of the earliest Multivac. Their nonliterary cognates authored their own indexes, portals, and directories – Jerry and David's Guide to the World Wide Web, the ancestor of Yahoo!, is one such example.[37] This phase ended quickly. After the Internet became too big to be overseen by anyone began the phase of automated web-bots, which traced out the links and the search engines that allowed human users to search for key words in this mess, the same way a search feature works on their word-processing program. Even here, the results were quickly too numerous. At last, Google's algorithm came. Like its predecessors, it trawled for links, continuously scanning the cached snapshot of the Internet stored on its servers. Then, and this is the key part, it ranked the results, using algorithms designed to assign each page a ranked value based on the "quality" of its links. The most linked links ruled. In high school, the popular kids aren't the ones with the most friends but the ones with the most popular friends. Google is the same. In other words, it may not be the Multivac, precisely, but Google applies its own psychohistorical principle of massification, namely, popularity. The most likely answer is the one the most people like. Google is a hide-and-seek machine: very good at finding what's well found already and very bad at finding what's very well hidden. All this tremendous expansion signals surface area and no depth. The deep web is a myth.

Now in the contest for the title of real-life Multivac there's a new arrival, something called Wolfram|Alpha. It has already been described as an un-Google. What is it? If you type in its text-box "What are you?" Wolfram|Alpha replies, "I am a computational knowledge engine."[38] If you follow up with "What is computational knowledge?" it answers, not altogether helpfully, "That which I endeavor to compute." This circularity is instructive in its way, for computable knowledge is, in a sense, as computable knowledge does. Wolfram|Alpha aims to treat information as information, and so it's only interested in material that can be subjected to processing, calculation, or analysis rather than simply Google's hide-and-seek game of searching the static of the Internet universe for signals. Thus, it is necessary for Wolfram|Alpha to maintain an internal storehouse of refereed expert-level knowledge ready-made for computational machinery to process it. In other words, like Asimov's encyclopedists, it pursues a curatorial agenda led by experts on its own planet. Here's how the Wolfram|Alpha site explains the mission: "We aim to collect and curate all objective data; implement every known model, method, and algorithm; and make it possible to compute whatever can be computed about anything. Our goal is to build on the achievements of science and other systematizations of knowledge to provide a single source that can be relied on by everyone for definitive answers to factual queries."[39] One interesting side of the maximalist project is the decision to make its interface communicate through "free form natural language input." The theory for this seems to have as much to do with the interface between experts and nonexperts as it follows from the sense that the metalanguage between the various disciplines of knowledge can be none other than natural language. "For academic purposes, Wolfram|Alpha is a primary source"; consequently, unlike Google but like the Asimovian computers of pop culture, it is personified.[40]

III.

Wolfram|Alpha is a "citable author," so notes the FAQ, as a quasi-legal tidbit for educators and researchers.[41] If you ask this literary construct the same question asked the Multivac, "How can the net amount of entropy of the universe be massively decreased?" it answers the same way: "THERE IS AS YET INSUFFICIENT DATA FOR A MEANINGFUL ANSWER."[42] If you ask it "What is the Answer to the Ultimate Question of Life, the Universe, and Everything?" it answers, "42."[43] I take these answers to mean not that Wolfram|Alpha thinks like Multivac – or Deep Thought – but that its programmers are aware of their literary or pop cultural pedigree. The Wolfram|Alpha FAQ comments that "when computers were first imagined, it was almost taken for granted that they would eventually have the kinds of question-answering capabilities that we now begin to see in Wolfram|Alpha."[44] "Is Wolfram|Alpha an artificial intelligence?" then – a term I don't find helpful in this discussion and have so far avoided but one Wolfram|Alpha's website summons: "It's much more an engineered artifact than a humanlike artificial intelligence. Some of what it does – especially in language understanding – may be similar to what humans do. But its primary objective is to do directed computations, not to act as a general intelligence."[45] It makes sense to me to think of Wolfram|Alpha as the conditions the author function finds itself in when facing trillions of elements of data: the black-boxed front end is less artificial intelligence than it is engineered artifact for detecting semiotic red shift.

Bruno Latour's concept "black-boxing" usefully names the discursive imperative operating here through which, in Latour's words, "scientific and technical work is made invisible by its own success. When a machine runs efficiently, when a matter of fact is settled, one need focus only on its inputs and outputs and not on its internal complexity. Thus paradoxically, the more science and technology succeed, the more opaque and obscure they become."[46] In a sense, black-boxing explains the end-user's phenomenological situation in which technologies are routinized and made normative "no matter how controversial their history, how complex their inner-workings, how large the commercial or academic networks that hold them in place."[47] Open this black box and peek under the hood, as I have been suggesting, and you'll find the component dreamwork organized around a mass-mediated, postliterary fantasy. Furthermore, the engineered artifact massively mystifies the audience structures comprising it. Audience structures are not – or they are not simply – recording machines, all storage capacity and no processing power. Rather, they might be conceived of as explicit and implicit representations of mass-mediated reception, intake rendered by means of various spatial and temporal metaphorics. The Internet itself is, along these lines, a specialized audience structure. On the Internet, everyone is an author, therefore no one is an Author: the scriveners rule with squatters' rights and Bartleby-like truculence. Down with the jargon of first modernist techno-authenticity in time and space; think only of the psychohistorical predicament of readers and authors facing textual overload.

The thread that connects Asimov and Ballard here is their fascination with audience structures, maximal and minimal. Asimov's "The Last Question" identifies a point of singularity between maximum authorial capacity – the supraliterary computational Author-God who knows and has read everything – and the minimal audience structure. There are no readers left. Once the *Encyclopedia Galactica* is completed, the world necessarily ends . . . or is ended. When everything is known, we're at the end of the reel. Ballard often takes the opposite approach, dwelling on the likely possibility that we've already arrived at the end, overloaded with too much (non)information and no obvious front end on the Multivac to illuminate things. On the one hand, information is at its maximum overdrive – aggregational extremity; on the other, the only consolation is found in the minimalist path of computational quietism. Unfriending Multivac. In light of Wolfram|Alpha's trillions of elements of computable knowledge, one is tempted to say: We spooled to the end of the *Encyclopedia Galactica* pretty fast, right? And if "overhead, without any fuss, the stars were going out," as in Arthur Clarke's famous story "The Nine Billion Names of God," then don't panic.

## NOTES

1. Flusser and Bec, *Vampyroteuthis Infernalis,* 67.

2. Flusser understands the problem as one of art or artifice, but because it concerns form, inscription, and scale, I think the literary may be a more apt way to think about it. McGurl's take on scalar shift in literary theory, "competing drives toward expansion and contraction," shared by big data and deep time, overlaps the ones here to some degree ("The Posthuman Comedy," 539). McGurl critiques gestures to inhuman time-space scales in calls for "transnational" cultural history and "big" historicism. He explains that the styles of the posthuman turn are essentially a comic mode of cultural theory in which humans and their well-laid plans are variously shrunk or blown up (i.e., diminished or expanded) by inhuman forces: "The posthuman comedy . . . draw[s] together a number of modern literary works in which scientific knowledge of

the spatiotemporal vastness and numerousness of the nonhuman world becomes visible as a formal, representational, and finally existential problem" (ibid., 539).

3. Flusser, *The Shape of Things*, 86, 87.

4. Flusser and Bec, *Vampyroteuthis Infernalis*, 66–67; Flusser, *The Shape of Things*, 88.

5. Rather than nature/culture, the problem of big data concerns singular/plural. Tellingly, *data* is seldom encountered in singular form. There's so much of it. To revisit a critical commonplace, the singular *datum* means "given" in Latin in the sense of an input available for (further) processing. An Input-Output-Input model: *freely it has been given to you, freely give*. The word *date* has a similar root, as Daniel Rosenberg reminds us, and *metadata* comes semantically overburdened. See Rosenberg, "Data before the Fact," 15–40.

6. "Raw data is both an oxymoron and a bad idea. On the contrary, data should be cooked with care" (Gitelman, *"Raw Data,"* 2). The TED-like assertion by Geoffrey C. Bowker serves Gitelman's collection more as a motto than a thesis. See especially his afterword (ibid., 167–172).

7. Lévi-Strauss, *The Raw and the Cooked*, 1, 64.

8. See, for instance, Lévi-Strauss, *From Honey to Ashes*.

9. Serres, *The Parasite*, 4.

10. *The blogs will not read themselves*. See Lockwood and Coley, *Cloud Time*. Instead of reserving for raw something the illusion of uninterrupted, authentic experience, the agency of "fossil data" resembles the heap and its noises – the clamor of being.

11. Flusser, *The Shape of Things*, 86.

12. Meillassoux, *After Finitude*, 10.

13. Zielinski, "Vilém Flusser"; see also Zielinski, *Deep Time of the Media*.

14. Chesterton, *The Man Who Was Thursday*, 40.

15. If the scales of sublimity are most often imaged outside the technically unassisted reach of the human, then perhaps McGurl is correct in saying that, for all the posthumanist reach for sublimity, the mode is covertly comic in terms of a theater of experience. The search engine that results in nothing wins the Internet; the deep web represents the place where things can still be lost and therefore saved; a philosophy exists to tell us with a straight face that the web looks like realism. What should be noted is that so often posthuman comedy is deprived of a sense of satire. The History Channel program *Life after Humans* – "Welcome to Earth . . . Population: 0" – is

paradigmatic. It's a good thing, right? Keep driving. Perversely, the sublime side-effect (i.e., it dignifies human scale) now depends on fantasies of humans observing the pathos of human quiescence as pathos.

16. See respective entries in Parrinder, *H. G. Wells.*

17. Clemens and Pettman, *Avoiding the Subject,* 33.

18. Agamben, *Idea of Prose,* 88.

19. Moretti, *Graphs, Maps and Trees,* 14.

20. Ibid., 14, 17.

21. Agamben, *Idea of Prose,* 87.

22. The classic study of this concept is Mannheim, "The Problem of Generations."

23. Lyotard, *The Inhuman,* 8–9.

24. Ballard, *Millennium People,* 4.

25. Introduction to *Crash,* 4.

26. See Francis, *The Psychological Fictions,* 65–66.

27. Introduction to *Crash,* 4.

28. Ballard, "The Message from Mars," 1178.

29. Introduction to *Crash,* 5.

30. Ballard, "The Message from Mars," 1182–1183.

31. Introduction to *Crash,* 5–6.

32. Wells, *The Time Machine,* 99.

33. Adams, *Hitchhiker's Guide,* 2.

34. Asimov, "The Last Question."

35. Ibid., 300.

36. http://googleblog.blogspot.com/2008/07/we-knew-web-was-big.html.

37. http://www.guardian.co.uk/business/2008/feb/01/microsoft.technology.

38. http://www.wolframalpha.com/input/?i=what+are+you.

39. In 2009 this was the answer. As of 2012 it's this: "Fundamentally, it is the vast collection of quantities and facts that I provide, compare, and calculate for my users" (http://www.wolframalpha.com/input/?i=What+is+computational+knowledge).

40. http://www.wolframalpha.com/about.html.

41. Ibid.

42. http://www.wolframalpha.com/input/?i=How+can+the+net+amount+of+entropy+of+the+universe+be+massively+decreased%3F.

43. http://www.wolframalpha.com/input/?i=What+is+the+Answer+to+the+Ultimate+Question+of+Life%2C+the+Universe%2C+and+Everything%3F+.

44. www.wolframalpha.com/about.html.

45. Ibid.

46. Latour, *Pandora's Hope,* 304.

47. Latour, *Science in Action,* 3.

Adams, Douglas. *Hitchhiker's Guide to the Galaxy*. New York: Del Rey, 1995.

Agamben, Giorgio. *Idea of Prose*. Albany: SUNY University Press, 1995.

Asimov, Isaac. "The Last Question." In *The Complete Stories*, vol. 1. New York: Broadway, 1990.

Ballard, J. G. *Crash*. New York: Pinnacle, 1974.

——. "The Message from Mars." In *The Complete Stories of J. G. Ballard*. New York: W. W. Norton, 2009.

——. *Millennium People*. New York: W. W. Norton, 2011.

Chesterton, G. K. *The Man Who Was Thursday*. New York: Penguin, 2011.

Clarke, Arthur C. "The Nine Billion Names of God." In *The Other Side of the Sky*. New York: Harcourt Brace, 1958.

Clemens, Justin, and Dominic Pettman. *Avoiding the Subject: Media, Culture and the Object*. Amsterdam: University of Amsterdam, 2004.

Flusser, Vilém. *The Shape Of Things: A Philosophy of Design*. London: Reaktion, 1999.

Flusser, Vilém, and Louis Bec. *Vampyroteuthis Infernalis: A Treatise, with a Report by the Institut Scientifique de Recherche Paranaturaliste*. Translated by Valentine A. Pakis. Minneapolis: University of Minnesota Press, 2012.

Francis, Samuel. *The Psychological Fictions of J. G. Ballard*. London: Bloomsbury, 2011.

Gitelman, Lisa, ed. *"Raw Data" Is an Oxymoron*. Cambridge, Mass.: MIT Press, 2013.

Latour, Bruno. *Pandora's Hope*. Cambridge, Mass.: Harvard University Press, 1999.

——. *Science in Action*. Cambridge, Mass.: Harvard University Press, 1988.

Lévi-Strauss, Claude. *From Honey to Ashes*. New York: HarperCollins, 1973.

——. *The Raw and the Cooked*. Chicago: University of Chicago Press, 1983.

Lockwood, Dean, and Rob Coley. *Cloud Time*. London: Zero, 2012.

Lyotard, Jean-François. *The Inhuman: Reflections on Time*. Stanford, Calif.: Stanford University Press, 1992.

Mannheim, Karl. "The Problem of Generations." In *Essays on the Sociology of Knowledge by Karl Mannheim*, edited by P. Kecskemeti. New York: Routledge & Kegan Paul, 1952.

Marker, Chris, dir. *La jetée*. Argos, 1962.

McGurl, Mark. "The Posthuman Comedy." *Critical Inquiry* 38.3 (Spring 2012): 533–553.

Meillassoux, Quentin. *After Finitude.* London: Continuum, 2008.

Moretti, Franco. *Graphs, Maps and Trees.* London: Verso, 2005.

Parrinder, Patrick, ed. *H. G. Wells: the Critical Heritage.* London: Routledge, 1972.

Rosenberg, Daniel. "Data before the Fact." In *"Raw Data" Is an Oxymoron,* edited by Lisa Gitelman, 15–40. Cambridge, Mass.: MIT Press, 2013.

Serres, Michel. *The Parasite.* Minneapolis: University of Minnesota Press, 2007.

Wells, H. G. *Experiment in Autobiography.* Boston: Little, Brown, 1962.

——. *The Sleeper Awakes.* New York: Penguin, 2005.

——. *The Time Machine.* New York: Norton, 2008.

——. *The World Set Free: A Story of Mankind.* New York: E. P. Dutton, 1914.

Zielinski, Siegfried. *Deep Time of the Media: Toward an Archaeology of Hearing and Seeing by Technical Means.* Cambridge, Mass.: MIT Press, 2008.

——. "Vilém Flusser: A Brief Introduction to His Media Philosophy." http://www.flusser-archive.org/public/uploads/archive/projects/mecad/pdfs/introduction_II.A_brief_introduction_to_his_media_philosophy.pdf.

BELIEF

DEATH

FAITH

TROMPE L'OEIL

AVANT-GARDE

COMMON SENSE

# THE ODDBALL ARCHIVE

## BOX IV

## ARCHIVES ACTING OUT

RADIO

FRAUD

HOAX

LOVE

NECRONAUT

PHILOSOPHY

DOCUMENT

KEY WORDS

avant-garde, belief, common sense, death, document, faith, fraud, hoax, love, necronaut, philosophy, radio, reason, religion, revolution, trompe l'oeil

COLLECTION CONTENTS

## COLLECTION SUMMARY

What is it that we think we already know? If we know it, why do we gather it, ignore it, refind it as a new wonder? What kinds of forgetting do archives enable? If we put our faith in the well known, if we place confidence in common sense, to what extent do we risk credulity? Hoaxes, as Judith Roof tells us, operate through the archive of the hoax – through our unforgotten knowledge that what seems too good to be true cannot be true. Even the very commonness of such wisdom – the commonness of common sense – can, as the success of hoaxes suggests, become its own sleight of hand, concealing its own tendency to lure us in. We are suckers for common knowledge, just as we are suckers for the exceptional.

From faith to fraud, from cryptogram to trompe l'oeil, the bottomless archive of common sense (and its obverse) is the environment for all kinds of exceptional cases. The documents, signals, and founding beliefs of what we think we know are the very material for movements and systems that seek to play deliberately on our credulity, to con us with their hoaxes and frauds but also to challenge our understanding. As Grant Farred suggests, out of the greatest Rationalist of the American Revolution – Thomas Paine – comes the full force of an archive of revolutionary unreason that finds its full, reasoned rationale in works such as *Common Sense* and *The Age of Reason*. For Paine, the triumph of Reason over the irrationalisms of religion, the Crown, and the obscuring power of language arrives in the unthinkable demand of Revolution itself: the Eleventh Commandment of an all-consuming, unthinking love. What can be more unreasonable than that?

Even when sifting through the archives of twentieth-century art movements, as Seth Morton discusses, the excrescences and possibilities of the already known can still prick the conscience – and can thus still produce faith and fandom alike. We may simultaneously love and remain skeptical of the meanings we pick up, like half-formed radio signals, as we wander through the archival waste land of the all too familiar. As this archive continually reemerges, we are conned into thinking we've heard something new: this is the trompe l'oreille miracle of recycled beliefs whose reappearance produces emerging fandoms of the obsolete. We love what we hear even more – and this love, even if it is the love for our own eagerness to be duped, even if it is nothing more than autoerotic skepticism or autoerotic faith, can still shake the foundations of our reason.

Ain't it something else?

## HISTORIES OF THE CONTRIBUTORS

**Judith Roof** is William Shakespeare Chair of English at Rice University. She has authored books on feminist, narrative, and gay theory, including *A Lure of Knowledge: Lesbian Sexuality and Theory* (Columbia University Press, 1991), *Come as You Are: Narrative and Sexuality* (Columbia University Press, 1996), and *All about Thelma and Eve: Sidekicks and Third Wheels* (Illinois University Press, 2002), as well as books about concepts and trends in contemporary culture – *Reproductions of Reproduction* (Routledge, 1996) and *The Poetics of DNA* (University of Minnesota Press, 2007). She is a member of the avant-garde performance group SteinSemble.

**Grant Farred** is professor of Africana studies and English at Cornell University. He has published widely in the fields of postcolonial theory, cultural studies, the formation of intellectuals, literary theory, sport, and contemporary politics. His most recent books include *What's My Name? Black Vernacular Intellectuals* (University of Minnesota Press, 2003), *Phantom Calls: Race and the Globalization of the NBA* (Prickly Paradigm Press, 2006), and *Long Distance Love: A Passion for Football* (Temple University Press, 2008). Since 2002 he has been the general editor of the Duke University–based journal the *South Atlantic Quarterly.*

**Seth Morton** is a PhD candidate at Rice University. He's currently writing a dissertation about how modernist aesthetics inform and are informed by notions of recursivity and second-order cybernetics. He has published articles on Percival Everett's novels and on zombies as figurations of an autoimmunitary biopolitical paradigm. Though not an official member of the International Necronautical Society, he hopes that this article will help him gain access into the deepest depths of the semifictitious archive.

10

# PERSONIFYING LA CON, OR POST HOAX, ERGO PROPER HOAX

*Judith Roof*

In 1905 famous Bloomsbury hoaxer Horace de Vere Cole led a gang of costumed Cantabrigians to Cambridge under the guise of the sultan of Zanzibar and his entourage. The real sultan was scheduled to visit Buckingham Palace the same day. The group was greeted by the mayor of Cambridge at an official reception. No one questioned the authenticity of the group of four undergraduates plus interpreter, all wearing dark makeup and dressed in Middle Eastern garb. How could that be? How could the mayor not see through the makeup? What appearance did the five offer that overcame what the mayor knew he couldn't have seen?[1]

In 1910 the same Cole and his veteran compatriot, Adrian Stephen, Virginia Woolf's brother, reprised a version of the costume hoax by disguising themselves as Abyssinians for an official tour of the British warship *Dreadnought*. Again made up by costumer Willy Clarkson, four ersatz Abyssinians (including Virginia herself), with Cole as government liaison and Stephen as interpreter, boarded the ship, conversed in a made-up language, faked its interpretation, and enjoyed the crew's generous tour. When it began to rain and their makeup began to disintegrate, they pleaded the cold and retreated off the deck. They got away with it. Again.[2]

These hoaxes, like the entire cadre of frauds, deceptions, cons, and tricks, are about that which they cannot possibly be personifying as if they were just that, all the while telling us that they are doing so. Hoaxes always do this more than once; hoaxes always exist as both a series and the serious. The tone of the hoax – its aesthetic and operational necessity – is the serious, something that guarantees frankness, honesty, authenticity, "the real thing," so zealously that it is also and simultaneously its opposite. The performance equivalent of the trompe l'oeil, hoaxes are always authentically authentic and inauthentic at the same time, both/and, personifying personification. In addition to this self-reflexive, sincerely sincere personification, hoaxes premise their self-announcement as hoax on an archive of exposed cons. This archive, like most collections, in Jean Baudrillard's estimation, enables the limitless substitution and play that characterize both the hoax and the notion of the collection itself.[3] Hoaxes do not successfully mislead their targets because they introduce new and unexpected twists; they do so because they deploy well-known frauds from a culturally curated bag of pranks, frauds, and tricks. This hoaxic archive provides the necessary vocabulary by which hoaxes – in all sincerity – announce themselves as such. Prophylactic wisdom, itself a part of the hoaxic tradition, is conveyed by such homilies as "too good to be true" and signaled by the presence of too much documentation, too exclusive an offer ("we've picked you out of thousands," "it's a one-time-only deal"), too constricted a time limit, too unusual a personage (masquerading royalties, unknown heirs to millions, the possessors of time-honored secrets), payment before service, requests to transfer money to receive a much larger amount back. All of this wisdom, already a part of the hoaxic archive, announces the hoax, con, fraud *as* hoax, con, fraud. There is no such thing as a rube.

Knowledge of the hoaxic tradition exists in the various forms by which the hoax is archived, including hoax archives such as those assembled by Harry Houdini and Ricky Jay, folklore, fiction, news reportage, and, most recently, reality television shows focused on confidence crime such as *American Greed*.[4] This hoaxic archive has been part of Western cultural consciousness since Pliny the Elder reported painter Parrhasius's trompe l'oeil deception of Zeuxis or medieval Europe enjoyed tales about the fox fooling the wolf.[5] This archive is not simply a collection of great hoaxes or stories about them but also an intrinsic element of the hoaxic process, the delight in which, as Jacques Lacan suggests, occurs when we realize the hoax is a hoax. In discussing Zeuxis and Parrhasius, Lacan asks, "What is it that attracts and satisfies us in trompe-l'oeil? When is it that it captures our attention and delights us? At the moment when, by a mere shift of our gaze, we are able to realize that the representation does not move with the gaze and that it is merely a trompe-l'oeil."[6] Like the trompe l'oeil, hoaxes pretend to be one thing so expertly – and gain such trust in that one thing – that their revelation as the hoaxes they are reveals the ways their performance had always been a performance. This process raises the question of why and how hoaxes can fool people if circumstances are such that hoaxes always signal, as Parrhasius did, that what they are displaying is a painting or fraud. Why would people be duped if they are aware of the mechanisms of the trick? Maybe they aren't really fooled. They know, but all the same; they know because the hoax is always already archived, remembered, and temporarily forgotten, so that, like Parrhasius, the hoaxer can fool them again.

In 1742 renowned royal physician and experienced anatomist Sir Richard Ascot Spires discerned an apricot-colored cruciform structure in the cerebrum of a cadaver that had been laboriously harvested by grave robbers. The structure, unlike any Spires had seen previously, stood out clearly; it did not seem to have been subject to the rapid decay that usually occurs in brain matter, nor did it seem to belong to the same class of organic material. Spires could dissect it cleanly out of a brain that had pretty much already turned to mush. Spires preserved the structure in solution and sought the opinion of his anatomist brethren, who concluded, with Spires, that the structure was none other than a God organ – the bodily site of humanity's spirituality. News of the God organ spread, proving, in the minds of Enlightenment anatomists, that science was indeed in the service of the Christian deity. The preserved specimen curiously disappeared, but Spires's original drawing showing the position of the object in the frontal lobe of the cerebrum is still housed in the British Museum.[7]

As you can guess, Spires's discovery was a hoax, motivated, medical historians guess, by Spires's distaste for what he regarded as Enlightenment godlessness. The cruciform object once on display could not be examined later by more dubious fellow anatomists. Spires claimed, in the hoaxer's best tactic of loading hoax onto hoax, that the object had been miraculously transubstantiated from its storage jar. What is more likely is that it was a calcium deposit that simply dissolved in solution, if it had ever existed at all. In any case, no other anatomist ever found such a structure again. There were, nonetheless, those who still believed that physical evidence existed as signs of the subject's Calvinist election. And Spires's cerebral diagram circulated widely among the faithful as anatomical proof of God's existence.[8]

Spires's hoax lays out clearly the anatomy of a hoax. Combining older notions of the Great Chain of Being with ideas of spiritual evolution and contemporaneous insights of anatomy, Spires's "discovery" presented proof of the former based in the latter. Evidence that humans had grown more spiritually and physically sophisticated not simply was in their behavior and accomplishments but also could be located in their anatomy. That there might be such a structure as an organ devoted to spirituality also seemed to confirm the animist ideas of earlier German physician Georg Ernst Stahl, "which proposed a God-given, super-added soul (anima) as the prime mover of living beings. . . . This anima was the agent of consciousness and physicological regulation."[9] The idea that a bodily organ might host such functions accorded with folk beliefs about organs as seating particular emotions – the liver as the source of anger, for example, or the heart as the site of love.

Playing on a field of preexisting ideas was not Spires's only hoaxic tactic. He documented his findings and then documented the documentation. His drawing of the cerebrum showing the structure augmented the preserved structure itself and vice versa, both hoaxes substantiating one another. His claim that he had preserved the structure and that some colleagues had seen it also functioned as both a means of additional documentation and the basis for the hoax's continuation. In the Enlightenment era, when physical evidence was increasingly necessary to substantiate claims, Spires deftly linked such evidence to fond beliefs about the place of humans in religious schemes. When other anatomists began searching for the God organ, Spires characterized their failure to locate such a structure as the result of anatomists using cadavers whose lifetime spiritual health had been less than perfect. Spires, in other words, was able to use science against folklore and folklore against science premised on faked documentation and cultural credibility. Spires's profit in the scheme was personal renown and the apparent reestablishment of spirituality as the center of scientific endeavor.

Spires's cross-confirmational documentations also underwrote his consistent performance of seriousness and vice versa. Only a real scientist would diagram his discovery and preserve the specimen. This documentation, however, also signaled the hoaxic character of Spires's endeavor. Who would diagram a cruciform structure before it had been dissected? Why cruciform? Why dub it a "God organ"? As we work to supply a non-hoaxic motivation for Spires's discovery, we undertake the same process as Spires's victims. We want to believe. We work to sustain credibility. We offer rationales: scientific naïveté, the relativity of historical knowledge, the incipience of anatomical research, the characters of the players' religious faith. We stretch for likelihoods, when on its face, Spires's discovery had always pushed credibility.

## *FAKE!*

Even to talk about the hoax is to talk hoaxingly. Speaking seriously about the seriousness of the hoax, as Orson Welles does in his hoaxic documentary *F Is for Fake!* (1974), is also (or especially) to speak hoaxically. Welles's film explores the possible hoax of Clifford Irving's biography, *Fake! The Story of Elmyr de Hory, the Greatest Art Forger of Our Time* (1969), which explores painter Elmyr de Hory's sustained production of paintings attributed to such artists as Picasso, André Derain, Renoir, Modigliani, Kees van Dongen, and Matisse. Welles's documentary not only describes de Hory's ur-hoax but constitutes the series within which his hoax has already operated. The series, of course, is not yet ended; not only does Welles's film fashion its own hoaxic story of a fictional art forger, but the de Hory nexus burgeons with the addition of yet another hoaxic series that shifts from painting to autobiography, from Elmyr de Hory to his biographer, Irving, who authored another hoax, *The Autobiography of Howard Hughes* (1971), which hoax is itself the subject of yet another Irving book, *The Hoax* (1981). Then there is the film *The Hoax* (2007), so very loosely based on Irving's book that it, too, might as well be considered a hoax. Hoaxes hoax by loading hoaxes onto hoaxes. Each hoax moors a collection of hoaxes. All hoaxes are metahoaxes. Seriously.

Forger Elmyr de Hory's hoaxes would seem to form the origin of this series, but de Hory himself operated within a long history of art forgery. There are several well-worn versions of art hoaxes. One version involves a painter actually painting paintings like those of famous artists and passing them off as famous artists' work. Another consists of copying existing works and passing the copies off as the originals. A third mode involves reattributing existing works of art by one artist as the work of a more famous artist. All of these versions of misrepresentation play with artistic traditions, modes of documentation, and the performance of seriousness. The often under-the-table, behind-the-scenes, extraordinary circumstances in which forgers stage their performances also signal the hoaxic character of their activities. All play on the expertise of connoisseurs and deploy their victims' desire for a bargain-price acquisition or an important addition to their collection.

Re-presenting Irving's narrative of de Hory's career as a forger, Welles's documentary focuses on de Hory's charismatic personality. A charming, cultured resident of the small Mediterranean island of Ibiza, de Hory enjoyed a long career as a talented producer of paintings passed off as the works of masters. De Hory began his forging career out of the desperation typical of struggling young painters. Originally from a wealthy Hungarian family dispossessed by the war, de Hory was unaccustomed to living in penury, and he could only bear the struggle for his art for a limited period of time. He discovered he could draw and paint in the style of such respected artists as Picasso and Matisse. Armed with a modest collection of forged drawings and a credible narrative of their provenance as remainders of his family's private collection, de Hory began to survive by passing his fakes off as authentic pieces. Although he tried several times to stop forging and make his way as a painter in his own right, nothing paid him like his talent for imitation. After having met the opportunist / front man Fernand LeGros, who conned de Hory into the production end of the forgery business while he undertook the elaborate setups for sales, de Hory ultimately settled on Ibiza, where he churned out drawings, paintings, and prints, making sure to use old canvases, paper, and other materials whose authenticity could not immediately be brought into question. On his end, LeGros set up his sales by continuing false stories of provenance, even to the point of photographing de Hory's fakes and inserting the photos carefully into display catalogs. Occasionally, LeGros would con an artist or someone responsible for an artist's estate into authenticating the forgery of the artist's work. He also hung some of de Hory's forgeries in his own opulent Paris apartment and gave parties for connoisseurs, who became accustomed to seeing the paintings as part of a legitimate collection.

Given the rule of the hoax – that a hoax is always more than one – it turns out that de Hory himself was the victim of LeGros's cons. LeGros marooned de Hory on Ibiza, persistently gave de Hory false accountings of sales, and kept most of the proceeds for himself. For his part, de Hory claimed to be an imitator instead of a forger. He never, for example, reproduced or copied an existing work – and, more important, he insisted that he never signed anything. Without the signature, de Hory claimed (with perhaps the ghostly echo of Derrida in the background), he wasn't faking at all, because he was never really claiming any kind of impersonation. (His claim that he never forged signatures was also false.) De Hory's theory of forgery would seem to argue against the idea of the hoax as any kind of elaborated authentication. But that would also be the point. Lacking identification makes the authentication of the paintings all the more authenticating. The whole process becomes more painstaking, more expert, more cathected as the site of truth.

Clifford Irving also resided on Ibiza and thus knew de Hory as a neighbor. When de Hory's impersonations became public, Irving became interested in why people so easily accept personifications even if it is unlikely that the masquerades are at all plausible. Why, he asks, could Elmyr de Hory sell picture after picture to galleries with the blessing of "experts" who declared the paintings to be the works of Picasso, Modigliani, and Matisse? Fascinated perhaps by de Hory's success, Irving himself set out to produce a hoax biography of the reclusive Howard Hughes. Eschewing de Hory's simple wisdom of never overauthenticating, Irving learned to imitate Hughes's handwriting, used the exact same yellow-lined pads Hughes had used, and set out to produce a handwritten letter of commission permitting Irving access to Hughes for the express purpose of writing a biography. Inviting his friend Richard Suskind to be research collaborator, Irving sold the Hughes biography idea to McGraw-Hill on the basis of the forged correspondence. McGraw-Hill extended a contract and made Irving a substantial advance based on extensive expert authentications of the handwritten authorization. Irving and Suskind set out to delve into Hughes's life, filching materials from libraries, other biographers, and congressional records; taking trips ostensibly to secret meetings with Hughes, which left traceable evidentiary trails; and contriving communications from an irate Hughes to McGraw-Hill whenever the publishers became a bit unsure. Irving even had his wife set up a Swiss bank account with a false passport under the name H. R. "Helga" Hughes into which Irving could deposit Hughes's share of the proceeds from the project.

The entire project depended on Irving's ability to impersonate the absent Hughes, who, Irving gambled, would never appear in person, and to have that impersonation tested repeatedly. Every time the McGraw-Hill execs seemed to suspect that the project was a hoax, more hoaxic evidence appeared. At every step, the work, the notes, the information were deemed authentic by experts. Late in the project, Irving suggested to McGraw-Hill that his biography become Hughes's autobiography. Irving wrote the manuscript personifying Hughes as a first-person narrator, imitating Hughes's expression, manner of speaking, and folksy philosophical interjections. Editors at McGraw-Hill and *Time/Life,* to which the editors had sold a serial version, all read the manuscript and were convinced that it was indeed Hughes's own voice and included the voice of Hughes's last interviewer, Frank McCulloch. When finally challenged by the Hughes organization and Hughes's biographer, James Phelan, who recognized some of the book's facts as coming from his own work, Irving took a lie detector test, the results of which were inconclusive. Only when Hughes himself conducted a speakerphone interview with journalists was Irving finally exposed.[10]

The experienced professionals at McGraw-Hill and *Time/Life* fell for Irving's impersonations not only because they wanted to but also because of the power of personification itself in its layered, authenticated disavowings. Clearly a hoax from the beginning – it was a well-known fact that Hughes would never authorize a biography – Irving's documentary ploys and expert personifications played upon both a long tradition of hoaxic literary personifications and his own private series, which began with de Hory. Irving's personification of Hughes, however, took the typical literary forgery one step further. Most literary hoaxes involve one of two kinds of personification. Either fictional events are presented as nonfiction, as in the case of Edgar Allan Poe's *The Unparalleled Adventures of One Hans Pfall* (1835) and "The Great Balloon Hoax" (1840), or authors claim identities not their own in order to sell ersatz autobiographies or fiction in the guise of a specific, usually underrepresented identity category, as did Joan Lowell in her 1929 autobiography *Cradle of the Deep,* in which she claimed to have been raised on a ship.

The tradition of the literary hoax extends beyond the quarrelsome bounds of whether a literary work is fiction or nonfiction. Personifications are performed fictions only a step away from literary fiction. The difference between personification and fiction lies in whether the personifier represents the personification as a persona upon which others will determine their investment in the imaginary authenticity of the account (which authenticity authenticates the subject position of the teller). This authenticity is significant when the identity of the author, the narrator, and the narrated experience coalesce to produce, represent, and authenticate the experience and identity represented. This obvious tautology already flies in the face of what we know about narrative: that there is no narrative that is not already a fiction, no narrative that does not produce in its telling a fictional teller. That more recently than Irving's impersonations the public has been scandalized by autobiographers presenting false experiences (recall James Frey) or pseudonymous authors narrating the autobiographical experience of others (Norma Khouri's 2003 *Honor Lost* or the pretense of transgendered street youth JT LeRoy's 1994 novel *Sarah*) is a symptom of a certain cultural investment in reifying identities in obvious disavowal of the inescapably fictional character of narration.[11] All narratives are hoaxes insofar as narration is always personification.

Modernist narrative often plays on the power of personifications, no longer through the supporting ambience of realism, as in the previous century, but through the trompe l'oeil provision of interiority – of the authenticating details of a persona's inner life, which guarantee the presence of that persona whether it exists or not. Postmodern novelists play on personification's play, personifying personifications, not in an effort to reveal the hoaxic character of personification but, like the hoaxer, to enable the production of the hoaxic being that survives personification's exposures. So Percival Everett (especially in the beautiful series of personifications in *The History of the African-American People* but also in *Erasure*) and Kathy Acker (in every novel) enact personifications (and personify narrator/characters) who, by admitting their hoaxic character, become even more firmly established as personae.[12] By revealing the hoax of art, art's hoax can continue. Tempted as we are at least to take Acker's personifications as evidence that we are all already personifications, we never look for the man behind the curtain, the hoaxer who gains from it all, nor, as in Parrhasius's trompe l'oeil, do we ever even look at the curtain. But that is the aesthetic point. The constant displacements of the hoax are intrinsic to a postmodern aesthetic that, as much as a hoax, delivers the fantasy of an authentic persona somewhere in its layerings, authentic insofar as it exists as an effect of its own layered and announced fakeries.

## THE HOAX THAT IS NOT ONE

Combining Spires's detail and the *Dreadnought*'s masquerade, Irving's hoaxes depended primarily on the authenticating tactics of personification, as well as on personifying authentication. The series that sustains and enables any hoax is self-perpetuating in the sense that once a hoax begins (and it never begins *ab origine* but always on the back of another hoax, as well as on the entire hoaxic archive), the conditions that encourage serial trompe l'oeils perpetuate. The archive of hoaxes is both folkloric and oddly arcane, given the prevalence of scams, confidence games, and other frauds in the daily lives of Americans. From frauds involving impersonation (credit card fraud, identity theft) to various versions of corporate fraud, confidence games (home repair rip-offs, insurance and pyramid schemes, fake contests, stock and investment games), contemporary individuals are surrounded by examples, warnings, and stories about cons, frauds, and hoaxes. There are also hoax archivists who collect texts and other material about hoaxes, cons, and deceptions. Harry Houdini and Ricky Jay have collected and exposed the mechanisms of a large variety of hoaxes. Houdini's exposés range from the unmasking of magic and escape tricks (*Houdini on Magic; The Miracle Mongers*) to essays on deception (*On Deception, The Right Way to Do Wrong*) and carnival tricks. Ricky Jay collects and narrates incidents in his monthly magazine the *Believer* and in his own collection of books and manuscripts linked to magic, con games, and deceptions. Although frauds and stories about them circulate widely, this archive hovers as a possibility, existing as something analogous to a cultural unconscious – as that which we know and in which we delight for the same reason that the same known hoaxes will work again and again.

This hoaxic archive, which repeatedly reveals the hoaxic character of the hoax and which should by all rights prevent hoaxes, must simultaneously be both present and disavowed as a condition for the successful perpetration of a hoax. Although the philanthropic Harry Houdini published *The Right Way to Do Wrong: An Exposé of Successful Criminals* in 1906, hoping "to safeguard the public against the practices of the criminal classes by exposing their various tricks and explaining the adroit methods by which they seek to defraud," the same kinds of frauds and cons still occur today.[13] Forewarning, though it may constitute foreknowledge, more enables the perpetuation of the con than prevents its reoccurrence insofar as hoaxes depend upon a disavowal of this knowledge as the pretext for the desire they elicit. There must be desire that the hoax, which is obviously a hoax (which as a genre like all genres signals its genreness as hoax), nonetheless not be a hoax (which of course is what makes it a hoax), so that whatever the hoax appears to be offering as the upshot of the hoax – an autobiography of Hughes, a painting by van Dongen, a 21 percent return on your investment – is a foregone conclusion, aspirations to which are the inevitable effect of the disavowed inauthenticity of the hoax's authenticating moves.

Not only do hoaxes always announce themselves as hoaxes, performing a studied seriousness designed to be both credible and transparent, they also repeat familiar patterns from the hoaxic archive whose character is specifically to be disavowed. We all know that if anything is too good to be true, it is not true. We know the insincerity of unusual attentions. And yet occasionally we permit ourselves to believe that what should not logically be the case nonetheless is – that the unusual is indeed plausible and possible. We are able to maintain this disavowal partly because the hoax is a familiar story not only as part of a tradition of warnings about misrepresentation but also because it is intrinsic to the narrative of commercial success, belief in miracles, and other cultural narratives. The hoax is the underside, the other to cultural traditions of endeavor, success, divine intervention, mysticism, and technological wonder. Insofar as industrious citizens might enrich themselves, so dishonest citizens might gain weal by fooling others. Insofar as people believe there may be forces beyond what they see, hoaxes will provide the view. There is a very thin line between a hoax and cultural narratives of success whose archive is closely shadowed by its hoaxic other.

The folkloric archive by which cultural knowledge of hoaxes circulates also includes psychological theories about how hoaxes captivate their victims. As we might expect, these explanations are themselves hoaxes, sharing the same dynamic as hoaxes themselves, that is, they offer the lure of a motivation that both serves as an answer and hides another trompe l'oeil desire whose character reveals hoaxic mechanisms. Such hoaxic analyses typically offer victims' greed as motivating their participation. Accounts of victims' motivation blame a simple version of desire that is triggered and tricked by a lure – that which seduces desire by appearing to be that which it is not – which is itself a self-contained version of the same dynamic as the hoax. "Many of the best cons work because of the inherent greed of the person being tricked."[14] As de Hory describes it, "But then it came time to talk price. Then all the cultural veneer falls away, and they become what they really are – merchants in a Turkish bazaar, fighting tooth and claw to buy cheap and sell dear."[15] Desire for an offered result – the lure of wealth, profit, desirable objects, or even protection from the exposure of embarrassing secrets – hoaxically defines cons as simply offering lures. Victims of hoaxes want whatever the hoax offers – profits, valuable objects, miracles, impossibilities – so much that they are willing to ignore common sense, contribute their own resources, and hope against hope despite the utter unlikelihood of delivery. The lure is irresistible, and victims pay so much attention to this lure that their other faculties are paralyzed.

This hoaxic analysis of why hoaxes continue to work despite widespread cultural knowledge of their patterns itself reproduces hoaxic logic. By extending an account of arrangements that focus on the weakness of the victim, which is another way of focusing on the lure of the lure, the hoax becomes merely that which takes advantage of a preexisting condition. The hoax of the hoaxic account is making desire for the lure primary, when the lure is always secondary. Victims may indeed be greedy and certainly desire promised results, but this desire is secondary to the desire to be taken in. This second version of desire – the trompe d'oeil, or the disavowal of desire – is what enables hoaxes to work in the first place. Hoaxes are hoaxes not because they offer something someone wants but because they make evident from the beginning that the entire transaction is fake. In accounting for hoaxes, hoaxic accounts, like hoaxes themselves, focus attention on the wrong elements of the hoax. The hoaxic archive is thus also a metahoax, a hoax about hoaxes.

## CONNING DESIRE

Most hoaxes are hoaxically hoaxic in that they always refer simultaneously to themselves as hoaxes and to an entire tradition of hoaxes of which they are yet another incidence. The hoax and the hoaxic archive reflect, enact, belong to one another. Hoaxes simultaneously rely upon and work against the hoaxic archive as a primary means of producing a dynamic of desiring disavowal. They accomplish this through the dramatic equivalent of the sleight of hand. Sleights of hand work by attracting attention to a lure around which the performer weaves a narrative that elicits continued attention. Meanwhile, at a place to the literal or figurative side, the conjurer changes, adds, or removes an object that then turns up in an unexpected place. The lure distracts attention from other processes, while all the time something else has been going on. Shell games, for example, in which sleight of hand artists convince a watching public that they can easily discern which of three cups or "shells" hides a pea, become the pretext for a betting game during which the operator distracts the bettor's attention, effects a sleight of hand, and forces the bettor to lose. Everyone knows shell games are cons; nonetheless, just this past summer, as I was walking across Westminster Bridge in London, there were three separate shell games in progress on the sidewalk surrounded by large crowds of onlookers.

If the lure operates in this hoaxic dynamic, it operates as a desire for hoaxic authentication, which then mobilizes the form of trompe l'oeil desire that finds its satisfaction in the revelation of the hoax as hoax. This desire produced by disavowal, as Lacan's model of the operation of the trompe l'oeil suggests, is a species of peek-a-boo desire produced by an initial disavowal of a trick, then satisfied by its revelation. This trompe l'oeil desire is finally a kind of inside-out epistemological desire – a desire not to lack lack ("I want not to know that what I know is not"), which is the opposite of typical formulations of desire as the desire not to lack ("I want . . ."). This hoaxic version of disavowal desire is linked to the "I know, but all the same" disavowals of the fetish as that object that stands in for what is missing while simultaneously signaling that that same something is missing.[16] In a hoaxic economy, however, disavowal does not fix on some ultimate product lure as an ersatz fetish object but on the hoax's self-authentications, those moves that draw our attention to the authenticating processes that authenticate while not authenticating at all. Documents, Experts, Testimony, Material Evidence. All faked.

The collapse of desire and disavowal into one another is a special kind of fantasy epistemology, a desire for what can only ever really be a fantasy that operates through an obvious logic of displacement. The lure of authentication radiates desirability (and by extension desire) over all obvious evidence of displacement (which in many hoaxes is quite literal in that, say, required papers are somewhere else, or money has to be transferred, or the title is in a vault that cannot be accessed until the next day, etc.). In the hoax, that which appears to be the cause of desire not only is not there but also does not cause desire, whose cause is always somewhere else. The hoax works by repeatedly displacing desire/disavowal through its specters of authenticity produced by the hoax's layered structure of repeatedly disavowed authentications where the hoax itself becomes the bait that both draws the hoaxee in and overcomes everyday common sense in favor of the fantastic. The hoax's bait is its own cleverness. The hoax is the lure of the hoax; the hoax itself is the fantastic object of a desire that disavows that the lack of lack is not lacking.

## THE CROWN OF CROATIA

This interplay of desires becomes clearer if we consider the desires of the hoaxer. Surely con artists, Ponzi schemers, and fraudsters want pecuniary gain, but is that all? What do hoaxers want? Hoaxers generally cannot claim some triumph of originality. They must then take a certain pleasure in the performance itself–in the logistics, impersonations, stories, and general ability to fool someone else in what is perhaps simply a rehearsal of mastery. Horace de Vere Cole, hoaxer of *Dreadnought* fame, later pulled what he called the "Crown of Croatia" heist. As in his previous hoaxes, this one also required costumed impersonations. Willy Clarkson again conspired, making Horace up as a Croatian minister. In the parlor of an Eaton Place house, Cole and two impoverished Russians hired for the occasion offered the position of ruler of Croatia to a wealthy Englishman who had bragged about having gained a foreign throne. Negotiating with his mark and insinuating that there were others in competition for the position, the "Croatian" Cole managed to finagle a huge check in payment for the honor with a promise of investiture at a future date. When the man returned to claim his crown, the Eaton Place parlor was full of Horace and his friends, toasting the "king" as well as his generous check, framed and hanging on the wall.[17]

But perhaps the Parrhasian ability to put one over is not merely a desire for mastery but exactly the same trompe l'oeil desire for the revelation of the representation as such sought by the mark. It is the same impetus that drives all performance. There is no doubt that con men and fraudsters are greedy and seek fame and/or admiration, but these rewards are in addition to the successful manipulation of signifiers, desire, and cultural capital. If victims disavow their knowledge, fraudsters repeatedly triumph in it, showing in the end that the setup is far more significant than common sense, self-preservation, morality, ethics, or any other manifestations of some assumed symbolic order. Showing the ways the symbolic can trick itself, the hoax is the most symbolic of all. Operating within a complex web of desires, projections, and affirmations, all circulating within sets of cultural narratives, proscriptions, and warnings, the hoax is its archive, and its archive perpetuates a desiring economy that never tires either of repetition or of the ways it reflects more "official" culture. At the center still is the revelation that the curtain was a curtain all along.

## CURTAINS

In its impenetrable gatherings and its appearance of completion, the curtain is finally the archive – any archive. The collection of materials preserved in an attempt to define beginning and offer authority is the biggest hoax of all. What archives demonstrate is the illusion of authority in their collective avatar of a time, place, subject, oeuvre, persona. If the hoax requires a hoaxic archive, the very idea of the archive requires a hoax, a trompe l'oeil that something is there and has been there all along – an answer, the truth, a definitive history – that is not.[18] If the archive presents itself as Zeuxis's scrumptious grapes, loaded with the promise of nourishment, the archive is really Parrhasius's curtain, openly hiding that it is only a curtain that can never be opened. As such it appears to promise a plenty that never appears, because there is no behind the curtain in an archive. The archive leads only to the archive.

## NOTES

1. Martyn Downer details the sultan of Zanzibar hoax in *The Sultan of Zanzibar* (49–59).

2. See ibid., 94–121.

3. Baudrillard, "The System of Objects."

4. Ricky Jay is a well-known entrepreneur of the odd, including, as he lists them, "Conjurers, Cheats, Hustlers, Hoaxsters, Pranksters, Jokesters, Imposters, Pretenders, Sideshow Showmen, Armless Calligraphers, Mechanical Marvels, and Popular Entertainments."

See Jay, *Jay's Journal of Anomalies, Extraordinary Exhibitions,* and *Learned Pigs and Fireproof Women.* Harry Houdini wrote prophylactic pamphlets exposing the modus operandi of criminals and con men, including *The Right Way to Do Wrong, The Miracle Mongers,* and *On Deception. American Greed,* a television series aired by CNBC, documents a variety of financial cons and hoaxes.

5. In *Naturalis Historia,* Pliny the Elder recounts this contest between Zeuxis and Parrhasius to determine which was the greater painter. The tales of Renard the trickster fox and his dupe, Ysengrin the wolf, circulated throughout northern Europe in the medieval period.

6. Lacan deploys the story of Zeuxis and Parrhasius to illustrate the mechanism of the gaze in *The Four Fundamental Concepts,* 111–112. This quote is from p. 112.

7. See Sagnon, "Cerebral Etchings." This entire example derives, of course, from fictional sources.

8. For a full description of Spires's hoax, see Sagnon, "Spires' Heavenly Aspirations."

9. Porter, *The Greatest Benefit,* 247.

10. This account derives from Irving's account in *The Hoax,* which could, of course, be a hoax.

11. James Frey, author of *A Million Little Pieces* (2005), was accused of fabricating episodes in this memoir. The idea that an author could produce "fiction" as a part of nonfiction is one of the most telling misunderstandings about the nature of narrative as any kind of vector for fact. This one became a media circus to the point that "deceived readers" sued Random House and won. Never has the question of genre been so vexed by the erring conflation of author, narrator, and narrated. Norma Khouri's *Honor Lost* (2003), again purporting to be memoir, told the story of the honor killing of a friend in Jordan. This, too, was revealed as fiction. The authorial persona "JT LeRoy," reputedly a street kid, was the supposed author of *Sarah* (1999). The real author was Laura Albert, who was convicted of fraud for having signed papers as J. T. LeRoy. The "hoax" or crime, such as it is, seems to exist in the reader's misguided alignment of author, narrator, and event.

12. Everett's first-person impersonations draw attention to the function of impersonation in narrative, especially in his novel *Erasure* and in *The History of the African-American People [Proposed] by Strom Thurmond, as Told to Percival Everett and James Kincaid.* Everett's fiction openly plays with generic expectations.

In overwriting existing fiction, Kathy Acker's work personifies the personifiers as her narrators become everyone from Don Quixote to W. B. Yeats. See, for example, *The Childlike Life of the Black Tarantula by the Black Tarantula.*

13. Houdini, *The Right Way,* 2–3.

14. "Top 10 Con Games Explained."

15. Irving, *Fake!,* 49.

16. The formulation "I know, but all the same" is from Mannoni, *Clefs.*

17. Downer relates this incident in *The Sultan of Zanzibar* (213–215).

18. Jacques Derrida argues that the archive is only the breakdown of memory in *Archive Fever.*

## SELECTED BIBLIOGRAPHY


Acker, Kathy. *The Childlike Life of the Black Tarantula by the Black Tarantula.* In *Portrait of an Eye: Three Novels,* 1–90. New York: Grove, 1997.

*American Greed.* Kurtis Productions (2007–2012). Narrated by Stacy Keach.

Baudrillard, Jean. "The System of Objects." In *Selected Writings,* edited by Mark Poster, 10–28. Stanford, Calif.: Stanford University Press, 1988.

Derrida, Jacques. *Archive Fever: A Freudian Impression.* Translated by Eric Prenowitz. Chicago: University of Chicago Press, 1998.

Downer, Martyn. *The Sultan of Zanzibar: The Bizarre World and Spectacular Hoaxes of Horace de Vere Cole.* London: Black Spring Press, 2010.

Everett, Percival. *Erasure: A Novel.* New York: Hyperion, 2001.

Everett, Percival, and James Kincaid. *The History of the African-American People [Proposed] by Strom Thurmond, as Told to Percival Everett and James Kincaid.* New York: Akashic, 2004.

Frey, James. *A Million Little Pieces.* New York: Anchor, 2005.

*The Hoax.* Directed by Lasse Hallstrom. Starring Richard Gere and Alfred Molina. Miramax, 2007.

Houdini, Harry. *The Miracle Mongers: An Exposé.* Stockbridge, Mass.: Hardpress Publishing, 2010.

——. *On Deception.* London: Hesperus Press, 2009.

——. *The Right Way to Do Wrong: An Exposé of Successful Criminals.* 1906. Reprint, Whitefish, Mont.: Kessinger Publishing, 2010.

Irving, Clifford. *The Autobiography of Howard Hughes.* N.p.: Terrific Books, 1999.

———. *Fake! The Story of Elmyr de Hory, the Greatest Art Forger of Our Time.* New York: McGraw-Hill, 1969.

———. *The Hoax.* London: Franklin Watts, 1981.

Jay, Ricky. *Extraordinary Exhibitions: Broadsides from the Collection of Ricky Jay.* New York: Quantuck Lane Press, 2005.

———. *Jay's Journal of Anomalies.* New York: Farrar, Strauss and Giroux, 2001.

———. *Learned Pigs and Fireproof Women.* New York: Farrar, Strauss and Giroux, 1986.

Khouri, Norma. *Honor Lost.* New York: Atria, 2003.

Lacan, Jacques. *The Four Fundamental Concepts of Psychoanalysis: The Seminar of Jacques Lacan, Book XI.* Edited by Jacques-Alain Miller, translated by Alan Sheridan. New York: Norton, 1998.

LeRoy, J. T. (Laura Albert). *Sarah.* New York: Bloomsbury, 2000.

Lowell, Joan. *Cradle of the Deep.* New York: Simon and Schuster, 1929.

Mannoni, Octave. *Clefs pour l'imaginaire ou l'autre scène.* Paris: Éditions du Seuil, 1969.

Pliny, the Elder. *Natural History: A Selection.* Translated by John F. Healy. London: Penguin Books, 1991.

Poe, Edgar Allan. "The Balloon Hoax." In *The Works of Edgar Allan Poe,* 1:144–152. Middlesex: Echo Library, 2007.

———. *The Unparalleled Adventures of One Hans Pfall.* In *The Works of Edgar Allan Poe,* 1:18–53. Middlesex: Echo Library, 2007.

Porter, Roy. *The Greatest Benefit to Mankind: A Medical History of Humanity.* New York: Norton, 1999.

Sagnon, Eric W. "Cerebral Etchings." In *Medical Illustrations from the British Museum,* edited by Gauthier Feau, 112–120. London: Historical Reprint Press, 2009.

———. "Spires' Heavenly Aspirations." In *The Minor Myths of Science,* edited by M. N. Songe, 46–69. White Plains, N.Y.: Mad Science Press, 2010.

"Top 10 Con Games Explained." http://www.toptenz.net/top-10-con-games.php. Accessed July 19, 2012.

Welles, Orson. *F Is for Fake!* Directed and written by Orson Welles, 1973.

The just and humane principles of the Revolution which Philosophy had first diffused, had been departed from. The Idea, always dangerous to Society.

THOMAS PAINE, *THE AGE OF REASON*

The reasonable man adapts himself to the world: the unreasonable one persists in trying to adapt the world to himself. Therefore all progress depends on the unreasonable man.

GEORGE BERNARD SHAW, *MAN AND SUPERMAN: A COMEDY AND A PHILOSOPHY*

11

# THE ELEVENTH COMMANDMENT

*Grant Farred*

There is only one way to properly understand Thomas Paine. He is the expatriate Briton whose intense belief in radical republican politics made him, this son of Norfolk Quakers, the writer of the American Revolution. Paine is the thinker whose political imaginary led him, in the moment before the thirteen colonies became independent, to coin no less than the phrase the "United States of America." Paine's faith in the American Revolution led him to dedicate *Rights of Man,* a "small treatise in defence of... [the] Principles of Freedom," to President George Washington, "that the Rights of Man may become as universal as your Benevolence can wish, and that you may enjoy the Happiness of seeing the New World regenerate the Old."[1] The American Revolution would lose its radical fervor soon enough, but it would never entirely lose the proselytizing zeal that Paine understood as integral to its political mission; the United States would never relinquish its self-appointed mission to make the "Rights of Man," or democracy, "universal," beginning with the eighteenth-century "Old World," which Paine declared in dire need of "regeneration." "Every revolution," argue Michael Hardt and Antonio Negri in the wake of the political events that originated in the Arab Spring and then wended their way through Europe (Madrid foremost) and Zuccotti Park in New York, "needs a constituent power – not to bring the revolution to an end but to continue it, and keep it open to further innovations."[2] In this regard, the American Revolution would disappoint Paine. After expelling the British, the American Revolution would not "continue" on a radical trajectory; in truth, its "constituent power" was antithetical to a revolutionary impulse beyond the revolution. More poignantly, the revolution that Paine helped to author would soon have little use for him. Paine "died almost unnoticed in 1809," fully aware that the "revolutionary tide had begun to ebb."[3]

Before that "ebbing," however, Paine's work provided the political girding and the philosophical scaffolding for the American Revolution. The radicalism of Paine's thought is captured in Joseph Carrig's delineation of his career: "His most famous pamphlet, *Common Sense,* written shortly before the adoption of the Declaration of Independence, advocated the creation of an independent American republic at a time when it was quite dangerous to make such suggestions publicly. And, *Rights of Man* written in 1791 and 1792, defended the principles of the French Revolution and called for the overthrow of the British monarchy."[4] *Rights of Man* was, of course, Paine's defense of the French Revolution against his erstwhile friend Edmund Burke's attack on that self-same event in *Reflections on the Revolution in France.* In keeping with his universalist vision, Paine pronounced Burke's defense of the monarchy "an imposition on the rest of the world."[5] Burke, for his part, is full of cant – "I do not know under what description to class the present ruling authority in France. It affects to be a pure democracy" – and doublespeak – "the sacredness of an hereditary principle of succession in our government with a power of change in its application in cases of extreme emergency."[6] Looming large in Burke's consciousness is the event of 1789, so that he gives particular credence to Paine's warning, "Every place has its Bastille, and every Bastille its despot." Needless to say, this was written before Paine's almost fatal brush with Robespierre and the Reign of Terror, this coming after Paine had played "an active role in the early stages of the French Revolution."[7]

As if, that is, to prove George Bernard Shaw's point that "revolutions have never lightened the burden of tyranny. They have only shifted it to another shoulder."[8] In a strange way, Shaw's pithy and salient insight marks a rare convergence among all three of these figures. Paine, Burke, and Shaw are all concerned with what follows the revolution. However, while Burke would understand Shaw's caution as an argument against revolution (and in so doing making a case for "stable government"), the very fear that the revolution might not be true to itself is what motivates Paine's thinking – and perhaps Shaw's too. We might now understand Paine's ambition for the revolution as Trotskyist, the same impulse that informs Hardt and Negri's commitment to the revolution. For Paine, and for Hardt and Negri, the hope is that the revolution will be constitutively "open to further innovations," that it will seek to extend itself. The "open, innovative" revolution (the revolution committed to constantly remaking itself) is the only revolution that can claim itself as a revolution because it honors and then sets about exceeding itself – thereby running the risk of superannuating (such is the autoimmunity of the revolution) itself in the cause of the revolution, or, the revolution *à venir* (is that not how it always is, the revolution – even in the midst of the revolution – is always to come?); or, the impossible Revolution that will put an end to all revolutions.

America has done a very good job of unburdening itself of responsibility for the revolution to which Paine subscribed. However, what this society has not given up is reason, Paine's other obsession. *The Age of Reason* is Paine's indictment of organized religion, particularly Christianity, which he calls a "*pious fraud,*" an inveighing that owes everything to Enlightenment thinking.[9] But the United States owes reason a significant debt. Without the age of reason, there could have been no U.S. independence and no representative democracy; without the technological innovations spawned by the rationality of that era, there would have been no Industrial Revolution and, certainly, well over a century later, no Taylorism or Fordism; without technological advancements that the Enlightenment birthed, it is difficult to conceive of the United States becoming what it did and still aspires to be (however flawed and unsustainable that imagining), a postimperial empire.[10]

Paine, in his determination to play a key philosophical and ideological role in the founding of liberal democracy, gave America "reason." Now, some two hundred years after he died, more or less in anonymity in New York City, forgotten by the revolution he had helped to craft, we are confronted with how Paine is being written in being written against – his reason has become our unreason. As much as anything, a work such as Susan Jacoby's *The Age of American Unreason* (2008), a considered critique of American anti-intellectualism, reminds us that the discourse of, or, rather, the search for, the affirmation of, reason has always been central to the project of America.

What *The Age of American Unreason* might enable us to lose sight of, however, is constitutive of the "Idea" that sustains Paine's attack on religion. For Paine the "Idea" is "always dangerous to Society" because it is rooted in the revolution: what is required to combat all religion is nothing less than a "revolution in the system of religion." "It remains to reason and philosophy," Paine unhesitatingly insists, "to abolish the amphibious fraud," the "fraud" in question being what he names "Christian idolatory."[11] It is the failings of Christianity that make evident to Paine the urgent need for reason. As it stands, religion (Christianity) amounts to little more than the unthinking worship of idols – a practice forbidden, of course, by all monotheistic faiths, and yet, as Baudelaire argues in the "Pagan School," there is something profoundly pagan, at least "neopagan," about Christianity at least. Reason has to be revolutionized into science, pure science, at that, because reason is the only bulwark against not only superstition but also manipulation and exploitation by the Christian Church – be that church Catholic, Protestant, or evangelical. In Paine's understanding, the very foundation of the Christian Church militates against thinking; any subjection of Christianity to the test of reason, Paine holds, would threaten the entire structure of the Christian Church. And yet Paine, in moments a thinker as deft as he is routinely polemical, does not find religion completely inexplicable. However, even in his magnanimity Paine finds it difficult not to be dismissive of faith: "Many good men have believed this strange fable, and lived very good lives under that belief (for credulity is not a crime)."[12] How could such a way of life, one that turns on "credulity" as a system of belief, not constitute a "crime" against reason?

Paine is dissembling. He leaves us in no doubt that he considers "credulity," of the "fabulous" variety, little more than an absurdity. We must append its proper name to "credulity": it is the act of unreason (it is without thought; it has not been reasoned; it cannot withstand a logical argument), and this is a practice not to be, as Paine so easily does, summarily gainsaid or dismissed. Instead, unreason is a political force that must be approached with philosophical caution; it is, potentially, a political force to be feared, but not in the "fabulous, credulous" way that Paine imagined. The force of unreason resides in its ability to counter the force of logic; the force of unreason is not at all "strange," but it is strangely debilitating to reason. Unreason renders the "reason for reason" – as Carlos Santana sings in a 1999 song, "You're my reason for reason," melodically suggesting that the entire Enlightenment project can be succinctly captured and undermined in a single catchy line – criminally defenseless. Faith is the "fable" and the power of unreason, the living of a good life that presents itself as challenge and possibly even the revocation of the grounds of reason.

## LOVE IS "SOMETHING ELSE"

Paine condemns the Bible as a fraudulent document, a collection of writings that could certainly not have been the work of the prophets or the apostles.[13] The Bible could not possibly be, in Paine's judgment, the Word of God. In truth, what disturbs him is the power of language, a power that emanates from language's power to obscure, to render itself susceptible to hermeneutics yet remain strangely indiscernible (and still constitute the ground for belief), to retain a certain indecipherability despite several attempts to pin it down, to make it make itself finally, indisputably legible. It is this sense of being thwarted by language, but also inexorably drawn to it, that permeates Paine's critique of the Bible: "Human language, whether in speech or print, cannot be the vehicle of the Word of God. – The Word of God exists in something else."[14] Of course, Paine may be right about the limits of human language. However, in his imprecision, "something else," Paine acknowledges, through his (vague) uncategorical use of language, his paradoxical dependence on language, which is itself inadequate to the work of scientific naming. In so doing, Paine gives "something else" the greatest possible power: he makes it unnamable, a supplement that evades naming and in so doing establishes itself as a certain philosophical modality, a philosophical modality that is inexplicable only to itself. (In this way, "something else" presents us with the problem of sovereignty, a problem that might begin with language but certainly cannot be resolved without thinking language; by using language to think beyond language; to think – to – the end of language.)

In its inexplicability, "something else" presents Paine with a problem. For Paine, all that is not reason is conceivable only as "idolatory," or superstition. There is no thinking of "something else" as anything other than that which is diametrically opposed to reason. For Paine, all that is opposed to reason represents a mode of inquiry that he will not, and in truth cannot, under any philosophical circumstances, countenance. This "something else" is, more importantly, what goes against Paine's thinking. "Something else," which is nothing other than the force of unreason, is what Paine cannot think, thereby making the Bible a particular difficulty for Paine that can only be named philosophical. The "something else" that is the Word of God is that force, unreason, that cannot be found in either science or the rationality that Paine so strongly advocates. According to John 13, to Luke 10:24 ("You shall love the Lord your God with all your heart, and with all your soul, and with all your strength, and with all your mind; and your neighbor as yourself"), and to Paul's letters, especially in 1 Corinthians 13, the Word of God can be found, before all else, in love.[15]

What could be more unreasonable than that?[16] What could be more revolutionary in its absolute demand than that? To not only, as Jesus Christ commands his disciples (and also all Christians who will follow him because of his love, his self-sacrificing love for them), "love one another" ("your neighbor as yourself"), to do so in the most exemplary fashion, "just as I have loved you," to love the Other not despite but because of the asymmetrical cost of that love. As Jacques Derrida argues in *The Gift of Death,* an extended conversation with the work of Jan Patočka (*Heretical Essays*) that in key moments takes up Søren Kierkegaard's *Fear and Trembling,* "If you love only those who love you and to the extent that they love you, then you give nothing, no love." Love, then, must begin with the Other, must be shown, if it is to attain the name "love," to Other. It matters most that you love those who do not love you. Where there is mutuality (the equal exchange of affection, commitment, a measurable economy), there is no love: "You have to give without taking account and love those who don't love you."[17] Loving those "who don't love you" begins, of course, with God the Father's love for us. There is no economy, no form of exchange, only a radical – unbridgeable – asymmetry (inequity itself): God loves us; we cannot begin to approach, let alone achieve, the love God has for us. Only God can love like God does. It is God the Father's love that sanctioned the death of His Son in order that we might attain salvation. Jesus Christ's death (God's love) is the supreme and supremely radical gift, the gift of love (the promise of life everlasting). God's love commands that His Son sacrifice his life (the Crucifixion) so that all others who believe in him (and even, maybe even especially, those who do not) might be given life everlasting (the gift and the promise of the Resurrection). Because of the (irrational, asymmetrical) supremacy of this love (traceable, of course, in modern philosophy to Kierkegaard's delineation to Abraham's love for God), Jesus the Christ presents us with the unchallengeable asymmetry of love. Is it possible to emulate (this) love, a love that will sacrifice itself for the cause? What revolutionary has not had to ask such a question of herself or himself? Lodged at the core of the revolutionary's existential angst is a potentially debilitating and self-incriminating uncertainty: What is the extent of my commitment? What is the nature of my love? Do I love the revolution?

Discernible in this logic is a refiguring – the substitution of the Self for the Christ, a reverse transubstantiation, making a base element (bread and wine) of the cause – of John's Gospel: How much asymmetry can your love bear (bearing in mind, of course, that if it cannot live with asymmetry, it is not love)? Can it bear to give its life to this? Can you love as the revolution commands you? Commands what seems beyond you, in excess of what it is you have to give? Can you give your life? Are you capable of asymmetry, vulnerable as it makes you to rejection, violence, or death at the hands of the Other who does not (might not) love you? All it is you believe, for the revolution is a matter of faith, and love, as Hardt and Negri make clear in *Declaration,* you have to give? Or is your love, your commitment, Judas-like? What price your willingness to renounce your love? Jesus the Christ issues the eleventh commandment ("I give you a new commandment, that you love one another. Just as I have loved you, you should also love one another" [John 13:34]) – it is an absolute political injunction – in the immediate wake of Judas's departure ("Do quickly what you are going to do," Jesus Christ says to Judas) – Judas en route to betraying the Christ?[18] How proximate, how difficult to distinguish love from betrayal if you are not alert to it (if you, in scriptural terms, are not the Christ), how unnoticed they coexist in the same room, how vulnerable we are to the autoimmunity of love when it involves the Other who is not other. (Nietzsche, who was not enamored of Paul, dubbed his the "original betrayal" of Jesus Christ.) The greatest, most dramatic, and most memorable betrayer in history, Jesus Christ (alone) knows (prescience, knowledge before knowledge, as it were, is his Father's poisoned gift to him, the Son – Who wants this kind of foreknowledge?), was neither a stranger nor an interloper. Judas, son of Simon Iscariot, was an intimate, a disciple. Could there be a more salient example of the autoimmunity of love? A more arresting example of how love possesses, as Alain Badiou reminds us, "its own agenda of contradictions and violence?"[19] Because love is autoimmune, it will not do to ask what love meant to Judas. It is the effect of that affect that provokes the question of record: What did it mean to live in the presence of one such as Jesus Christ? A love whose violent aftermath produced nothing less than the radically unthinkable act of transubstantiation? What does it meant to be made Love, that which the commandment can instruct but surely not expect? (How asymmetrical, how unjust is that?) No wonder, then, that reason so fears unreason (love, that is, fears God or any inclining toward the notion of God). Is there anything in reason that can make so revolutionary a demand of its followers as death? The partisan is nothing before the believer. "Faith," as Kierkegaard says, "is the highest passion in a person."[20] And yet, what could be more in line with reason than to demand life, to give life its raison d'être, its very reason, in order to instigate the revolution? The revolution can only be born in – born by – love.

The revolutionary force of the eleventh commandment is that it is absolute in its demands. It is absolutely clear in its injunction: live according to this command, it is the only way to live: love: in the love of Jesus the Christ. The eleventh commandment is not the Word from the Sermon on the Mount. However, Jesus the Christ's commandment that comes after the commandment overwhelms the other ten. (Only one of which, of course, is affirming. Nine are prohibitions: "Thou shalt not . . ." The affirming commandment too invokes love, instructing us to "honor thy father and thy mother.") The eleventh commandment is the force of unreason itself: it exceeds the first writing, the tabular Mosaic writing that taught us how to write, to count, and, of course, it laid out for us the terms on which we are to live. Because it goes beyond writing, it is "something else": something other than writing that knows, intimately, the first writing that at once undoes the Word and brings it fully into itself.

"Love one another" is the only commandment that is not a commandment because it is more than that, making it the only instruction of consequence: "Love one another. Just as I have loved you" (John 13:34). Or, as it is phrased in 1 Corinthians 13: love "rejoices in the truth. It bears all things, believes all things, hopes all things, endures all things. Love never ends." It is important, critical, even, to know and uphold the Ten Commandments, but they amount to little if the One is not followed. "Love one another" is the One (commandment) that is outside the Ten, the one that comes, simultaneously, before and after; the One that makes the Ten if not inconsequential, then contingent – everything depends on love. The One inscribes itself as supreme. Without love, there can be no Commandments and no writing. Similarly, there can be no reason without the writing of the Enlightenment – the Declaration of the Rights of Man is scripted as a document to live by, for all of humanity to live by, like that first monotheistic document. In this regard, reason is born, brought to life, in and through the writing that is unthinkable without unreason.

That was Jesus Christ's revolutionary act of language in the Gospel of John: to make the one the only One. That is the power of unreason: to make itself all that matters: "Faith, hope, and love abide, these three; and the greatest of these is love." All that matters is the "new commandment": "You should also love one another." You must love one another, "just as I have loved you." This injunction begins as an invitation, but it is not an invitation. It constitutes both a rejoicing in the truth and, through the taking up of the invitation (there is no other way to come to faith – "believes all things"), the construction of love as the absolute – the first and most enduring – truth. In Badiou's terms, "To make a declaration of love," to commit to, to come to faith, "is to move from the event-encounter to embark on a construction of truth."[21] Love, whether it fails or not, whether it can sustain itself in the face of the asymmetrical, is equal to a scriptural or a Badiouean truth.

The Word of God, then, is not explicable in the ways that Paine would want it to be: it will not give itself up to reason. Nevertheless, there is a resonant logic – the asymmetrical logic of love – that governs this "something else" because this supplement that is not a supplement but a kernel of truth is something that we know, that we have always known. It is what marks us: "By this everyone will know": the faithful will be known through their love, through their achievement of this "highest passion." Love is the unreasonable word, the Word, the One Word that we already have, have always had to hand. Not only does it "bear all things," it "never ends." All truthful things are love: as temptation, the apple, as carnality, Adam and Eve, Jesus Christ and Mary Magdalene (if the Gnostic Gospels and José Saramago in *The Gospel According to Jesus Christ* are to be believed), Sarah and Lot, the most radical act of self-identification ("By this . . ."), self-determination (the decision to submit to love, the Father's love, so that God's love might make possible grace – love beyond love), and being (to believe in all things and to care for what is to hand because of this "new commandment"). Love is the unreason within us all. It is the unreason of life without which, according to Jesus Christ, there would be no life, so that even the death of the Savior, that which comes after his fear and trembling, Jesus Christ's love for his Father and his doubt, his love and his submission ("Let not my will but Thy will be done"), is the act of God's love.

Everlasting life, an unreasoned expectation in itself, life lived fully, asymmetrically, autoimmunely, in love, is the "something else" promised by and because of love. That is why "the perverse core of Christianity," as Slavoj Žižek names it in *The Puppet and the Dwarf,* matters so much.

Without the Crucifixion, Žižek argues, there can be no Resurrection, and without the Resurrection, there can be no faith. (Is that, finally, what Judas lacked? His inability to believe in all things, that love is inherently inequitable? Was Judas the archpragmatist, desiring only to be on the winning side in a political war? Did Judas doubt that the Messiah was indeed the Messiah? Was the asymmetricality of love the burden he could not bear?) The Crucifixion is the radical unreasonedness of love because it creates the conditions for agape – ἀγάπη (grace) – the love beyond love that only God can give. Paul chides Cephas for his hypocrisy in the discussion about those who are "Jews by birth and not Gentile sinners," which turns on his doctrine of grace: "We know that a person is justified not by the works of the law but through faith in Jesus Christ."[22]

Without the Crucifixion there can be no Christianity, no writing after the founding document (Ten Commandments) that contains within it the most serious critique of it – the eleventh commandment. Without the Crucifixion there could have been no Resurrection and, consequently, no possibility of achieving Paul's ultimate goal: Christianity as the universal faith, achieved through faith in Jesus Christ, available to "Jews by birth" and "Gentile sinners" alike. Jacob Taubes remarks directly on the geographical coordinates of Paul's colonialist ambitions in his commentary on the Epistle to the Galatians: "This is the only letter from Paul to a congregation that he did not found." Paul was always in the business, Taubes notes, of proselytizing: "It is a fiction or, if you prefer, a hope, that [Paul] is just passing through. Because he still wants to take his mission to the end of the world, in other words, to Spain."[23] Paul's proselytizing project extends from Rome to Jerusalem to "Spain" – the latter signals Santiago de Compostela, the "Camino de Santiago" pilgrimage (the "Way of Saint James"), which was sacred for medieval Christianity because it was believed that the remains of the apostle James were buried in the cathedral of Santiago de Compostela. Salient, of course, is that for Taubes's Paul, "Spain" signaled the "end of the world." How circumscribed was the geographical imaginary of the early Christian world – a religious world in which the Second Temple still stood.

Taubes's engagement with Paul (first published in German in 1993) came about a decade before Žižek, Alain Badiou (*Saint Paul: The Foundation of Universalism*), and Giorgio Agamben (*The Time That Remains: A Commentary on the Letter to the Romans*) all took up Paul as a thinker for the contemporary moment. Paul is a figure of fascination (a preacher whose teachings are always aimed at increasing the flock: "I have often intended to come to you . . . in order that I may reap some harvest among you as I have among the rest of the Gentiles") for contemporary philosophy because he is the only apostle who was not present to witness the Crucifixion or the Resurrection.[24] Paul is unpresent at the event. ("He didn't know Jesus, as he himself says. He must be a new kind of apostle.")[25] However, as we know, his unpresentness does not diminish his hermeneutic claims upon the Christ or his right to convert (which Paul understood as a sacred duty). In fact, Paul's constitutive lack – and his political commitment to working from that lack, making of that lack a fundamental virtue – is precisely what makes his legendary conversion so troubling. In Taubes's estimation, "Paul is a fanatic! Paul is a zealot, a Jewish zealot. He is totally illiberal."[26] Donald Harman Akenson considers him homophobic and "brilliant, god-drunk."[27]

"Illiberal," "fanatic," "zealot," Paul is indeed all of these things. However, from time to time he is studied (often with a singular intensity) because he is such a compelling figure of the political. His entire standing among philosophers, and surely among the many converts he made, derives from his ability as convert to deploy his lack – his absence at the event – into his greatest asset. It is what makes him like us because, like him, we were not there – Peter and the other disciples were, so they have, as it were, reason to believe. Paul's lack is the very basis of his faith and his proselytizing; what other option is available to the "new apostle"? What other path to the faith does he have? The other apostles have, on the face of it, everything. As the "loyal" disciples, the eleven were present at the event, bore direct witness to the Crucifixion, and welcomed Jesus Christ back after the shock of Judas's betrayal and absolute miracle of the Resurrection. Paul uses his lack to bring Gentiles and Jews, all those many who did not witness the event, to Jesus Christ by offering redemption through his life, death, and radical rebirth. For Paul, all things begin and end with commitment to Jesus Christ, "for from him and through him and to him are all things."[28]

Paul, to whom the love of the Father comes only secondhand (if Paine is impatient with revelation, he is infinitely less tolerant with mediation, so he has no use for Paul – it is, of course, "mediation" that makes Paul's love, unlike Peter's, so constitutively radical), takes it upon himself to keep the tradition of Christian alterity alive; Paul's writing of the Word is a writing against the writings of Rome and Jerusalem. "At the time of their writings, [Paul's] writings were just letters, nothing more," but they are documents of a faith steeped in unreason.[29] Paul stands, in truth he has no choice, since he was not there (the absence that he translates into his foundational virtue), constitutively against the "revelation" of Peter (against Peter's founding presence – "first" among the disciples, present, if only to betray thrice, at the Garden of Gethsemane; Peter the apostle to whom the Church is entrusted). The revelation, the event, experienced by Peter and the remaining disciples is epitomized by Peter so that Peter's Church stands as a testament to (their) presence at the event, so that Peter's Church is the testament to Presence. Peter founds the Church of Presence (Roman Catholicism), the Church that stands in the name of the Presence that is, as Taubes puts it, the Church founded upon faith and the "kinship of the promise."[30] "Kinship," in Taubes's sense, begins with the "promise" of the event: the Christ's Church's "promises" are only possible because the Crucifixion reveals itself as the act of death that is also the definitive act in birthing love. It is the very asymmetricality of love. The Resurrection reveals what is already present in the Crucifixion – the "promise" that through faith, through love of the Christ, all will be joined in the "kinship" of eternal life; the Crucifixion is the beginning of life everlasting. Love can, according to the Scriptures, bear everything, including (the death that is not) death. And love, as Kierkegaard knows and Paul incarnates, is restless, even relentless: "The person who has come to faith (whether he is extraordinarily gifted or plain and simple does not matter) does not come to a standstill. . . . I have my whole life in it. . . . 'One must go further, one must go further.'"[31] As an apostle, Paul is "extraordinarily gifted," he has his "whole life in it." Paul has given his whole life to love, his love of Jesus Christ. He is possessed of the "highest passion."

Paine barely mentions the Crucifixion, although he grasps its significance. He names it the "sacrifice of the Creator," but he is, in the main, derogatory about the event: "The Christian mythologists tell us that Christ died for the sins of the world, and that he came on *purpose to die*. Would it not have been the same if he had died of a fever or of small pox, of old age, of anything else."[32] Paine is, characteristically, at once trenchant in his skepticism ("he came on purpose to die") and quotidian in his dismissiveness (equating the Crucifixion with death by "fever," "small pox," or "old age," as if this would have amounted to the same thing; it never could, of course). Even Badiou, who is skeptical of the place of love in Christianity (and all religions), understands the importance of Jesus Christ's sacrifice: "to achieve the acceptance of suffering in the name of the supreme interest of the community and not just on behalf of individual survival."[33] There is a real political consequence to Paine's almost jocular rejection of the Crucifixion. It causes him to overlook the eventness of the event (Crucifixion): the nature of Christ's death is as important as the death. Christ's was a revolutionary death (a political category for which smallpox is decidedly unsuited), so that it cannot be said, as Paine does, that the "sentence was death, not the *manner of dying*."[34] On the contrary, the "manner of dying" was everything.

The political work of the Crucifixion is a singular undoing. The Crucifixion overturned everything, beginning – but by no means ending – with death – and love. It is the felicitous unreasoned act – Abraham is faithful to God, not to humanity, not to his family, his community, not to his son, no matter how painful such a fidelity to God must have been – that finds its apogee in the Crucifixion. Condemned to die in public, Jesus Christ rose again after three days, revealing God's power: the power to restore life, and, in so doing, to give the prospect, the hope, of new life – life everlasting, life through the Christ, life that can triumph over death – to all other lives, lives that are, lives that have been, lives that are to come. Love never ends, love that goes "further," and "further." Indeed, the "sentence was death," but it was the "manner of dying," a political death, the most politically ordained death of all, that was crucial to the event. The event is born out of putting to death a threat – God's only begotten Son – to the Roman Empire. The event could not have been made through a man expiring in his bed from natural causes or meeting with a fatal accident on the road to Galilee.

It is because of the manner of his death, to phrase the matter as George Bernard Shaw might, that Jesus the Christ is followed. Jesus the Christ has no intention of adapting to the world. His only goal, one Paul seizes on with the zealot's vigor, is to make the world adjust to him. That is why the event, the progress of faith (Paul's mission, to go far, and then farther still), if you will, depends upon him being crucified, because only the unreasonable man can give himself to the Father's promise, can believe the Father's promise, the Kierkegaardian fear and trembling notwithstanding, that he will rise from the dead. (How could Jesus Christ not tremble in the face of the Crucifixion? What radical love there is in that is known only to Abraham and Jesus Christ. But of this we are sure: the Son of God trembles before man, in the presence of man, before his violent death. The Crucifixion is the event that has its immediate origins in the gathering of a group of scared men divided into two highly unequal groups – eleven for Jesus Christ, one against him, one who knew that the Christ's death was imminent but did not, could not, know of the Resurrection, late one Thursday night a long time ago on the Mount of Olives.) For the reasonable man, death is the end; for the unreasoning one who glimpses, just barely, the asymmetry of love, death is merely a transient moment. Death lasts but three days; the life made by God's love secures eternity.

The poignant, politically charged scene where the frightened men are gathered takes place in the Garden of Gethsemane: "Let not my will but Thy will be done."[35] Where is the reason in giving the Self up to death? (The revolution demands sacrifice.) What is this decision but the very incarnation of radical unreason? (Kierkegaard promises that after the decision everything will be different.) Or it may be unreason itself. What does it mean to abdicate any sense of self, absolutely, in the face of certain death? It is only possible to preach about love as an absolute, the eleventh commandment, if the Son loves the Father absolutely, if the Son both believes in and submits to the promise of the kinship to come, if the Son is willing to go infinitely farther because he knows his love cannot "come to a standstill." The kinship, moreover, that only His death (and Resurrection) can make possible. (One is simultaneously sure that Paul understands the kinship of faith in this way and that it is entirely beyond his colonialist grasp – that kinship with Jesus Christ matters absolutely to him and that the only matter of consequence is submission through faith, submission in the way preached by the "new apostle.")

That is why, in this context, the Old Testament, so disparaged by Paine, matters. Because Isaac did not know that he would be sacrificed, his salvation resides not in his father's love but in their mutual unknowingness (though it is simultaneously a doubt and love-filled unknowingness, to be sure; neither Abraham nor Isaac knows that they will be spared the violence that only Abraham is aware of and yet Isaac is not entirely blind to). Isaac had no foreknowledge of the event, much as he sensed that something consequential, involving him and his father, was afoot; Isaac could not have known that in one moment he would be potential victim (of his father's love for and absolute fealty to God) and in the next the living embodiment of God's love (spared only by God because his father, Abraham, loved God more than him). In the New Testament, the Son is the Son who knows, and, knowing, the Son accedes, albeit with trepidation and reluctance and in the face of a double betrayal – or triple, if you follow Paine, because he would add the Father's "betrayal" to that of Judas (sealed with a kiss – "Judas, is it with a kiss that you are betraying the Son of Man?") and Peter ("Before the cock crows today, you will betray me three times").[36]

Through love, and only through love, the Son knows the promise of the injunction of love. To have faith is to know, above all else in the face of the event, the political force of "Thy will" – the very sovereignty of sovereignty. It is the event that enables, nay, empowers, the Son to issue to humanity the One commandment, the one that must be kept above all others. The eleventh commandment must be kept, in the face of death, because it is so unreasoned: love one another as the Son loved the Father, who commanded the Son crucified, who let the Son hang next to "common thieves," the Father, who spared Isaac by summoning up a sheep for Abraham to slaughter instead of his son. The Son loved the Father (yet the Son could not love as only the Father can – asymmetry itself), and in so doing the Son gave his life to love. Judas was not open to – might we say capable of? – this love, either to receiving it or to inclining toward the asymmetry of love. Judas was nothing but a catalyst; without him there could have been no event. So the act of betrayal was cataclysmic, it made Life itself possible, because betrayal alone is what made the event possible. Peter could only come to this love after his historic denial.

## PAULINE LOVE, PAINE'S ARCHIVE

To think "something else" is to submit, at some fundamental level, to the vagaries of the unreason. (Paine submits too but does so without any form of genuflection; the force of reason is that it demands that you not bend the knee be/for God.) It is to know, as Paine does, that the only proper name for the "Idea" is the revolution – the revolution against the imperial state (*Common Sense*), the claim of the right to revolt against the monarchy (*Rights of Man*), and the determination to replace religion through the triumph of reason. To think "something else" is also to acknowledge that it is only because of unreason that there can be a revolution (politically speaking, faith is that passion that refuses what is; faith in the revolution is asymmetrical – it exceeds – the revolution), that the act of love can produce the revolution. Without love, love that is both asymmetrical (catalyst of possibility) and autoimmune (the threat that the revolution will fail, or, worse, fail itself), there can be no thinking of unreason; love, like the revolution, is never unthinkable in itself. It is in the act of revolution, Derrida's love "*without reserve,*" that both the unthinkable – that which has been imagined, even if does not yet possess its own conceptual name – and the unreason – that "something else" that can only be encountered in the act of thinking for what is not known, that which has not been imagined as knowable – are possible, can, in the very same moment, occur.

Love is, oddly, the Pauline truth (and, in different ways, of course, also the Kierkegaardian or the Badiouean one) that constitutes Paine's archive. There is no way to know this except through the unease – skepticism – that Paine's fidelity to reason provokes. What is unwelcome in Paine's thinking, in his dedication to the revolution, is unreason – love. In its turn, love, love that can be thought in relation to that mode of being, faith, to the scriptures, and Paul's writing in particular, reveals itself to be – despite Paine's best political efforts to negate it, to condemn it for precisely its unreason – immovable and recalcitrant. But the love that Paine so vehemently resists is exactly what grounds his archive and comprises the philosophical treasure trove that makes up the collection of thinking that resides there.

Paine's Pauline archive invites nothing so much (irony of ironies and yet not ironic at all, of course, because of how love structures the revolution, inheres in it from – before, even – the beginning of the revolution) as a thinking of and for the deeply religious (specifically Christian) and political nature of love.

The revolution is feared, according to Paine, by all religions – not only the monotheisms, Christianity, Judaism, and Islam, but all their adherents – because the revolution is the only event in which the thought and the unthought, reason and unreason, find each other. That is because there can be no revolution that does not know, or move toward knowing, love. That is what the revolution threatens: the death of reason, of life as it is known and the promise of an unimaginable kinship. Paine, for these very reasons, was hounded because he proposed exactly such a death in *The Age of Reason.* Paine was castigated, outcast because he was an atheist (even though he says he is a "theist": "I believe in one God, and no more; and I hope for happiness beyond this life"), because he wanted to ensure the death of religion, the prevailing reason for which he could find no reason.

This is what made Paine a revolutionary. He was agitating for the death of life as it was known (how those who opposed Paine forgot their own debt to the event of death): What could be more terrible, more unreasoned, than that? That is why unreason must be feared. It is the repository of love, asymmetrical, autoimmune, gifted to humanity as the – in the name of a – supreme sacrifice. Love that is at once utterly inexplicable (What kind of love is it that could even make the father contemplate killing his son?) and profoundly reassuring (because of the Father's love, everything will be different, beginning with how we understand life itself). The asymmetrical singularity of love: without love, no unreason. Without unreason, as Paine surely knew from his proximity to both the American and the French Revolutions, there could be no revolution. What could be more unreasoned (because there is, we have to admit, nothing unreasonable about it) than love for, love of, the revolution?

We might, therefore, in light of the event, take issue with both Paine and our earlier reading of the pivotal phrase. In looking again at "something else," it would be reasonable to conclude that *The Age of Reason*'s singular utterance is neither directed as a critique of an ineffectual religion (or all three of them, to be entirely accurate, though he reserves for Christianity and Judaism a special venom) nor a random possibility ("some thing," as if it were any/thing, any random object or encounter, as if it did not matter where or when such an encounter took place, if it had a name or not). "Something else": it is the very thing, the very substance of Paul's lifelong commitment to Jesus Christ and the inexplicable core of coming to truth about the eleventh commandment itself: the unreason of love. Love is only fully itself when it offers itself asymmetrically, without any expectation, when it bans reciprocation, when reciprocation is condemned to beyond its horizon of possibility. Love gives everything, as Paine did – to the revolution. Paine knows love. Paine knows love, oddly enough, as Paul did. They shared a passion for going farther. And not farther from each other but farther in the direction of the other. How difficult such a recognition would have been for Paine. And yet how entirely appropriate that two figures of revolution should illuminate each other. To phrase this mischievously: it is only by making Paine and Paul love one another that it becomes possible to discern how Paul's love is archived by Paine. Or, the eleventh commandment allows Paine's archive of unreason, one that he might struggle to identify, to give entirely new philosophical life to Paul's love.

1. Paine, *Rights of Man,* 3.

2. Hardt and Negri, *Declaration,* 46.

3. Taffel, introduction, viii.

4. Carrig, introduction, xii.

5. Paine, *Rights of Man,* 5.

6. Burke, *Reflections,* 21.

7. Paine, *Rights of Man,* 18, 8.

8. Shaw, *The Revolutionist's Handbook,* 6.

9. Paine, *The Age of Reason,* 65.

10. In 1989 the "management theorist" Charles Handy, inventor of "shamrock organization" (core workers, freelancers, and part-time/temporary workers each form one "leaf" of the shamrock), argued for the innovativeness of "discontinuous change" in his work *The Age of Unreason.* Handy was born in Ireland and became an economist based in London, and his work has attracted a great deal of attention in the United States. Almost twenty years later, 2008, Susan Jacoby wrote a scathing critique of American anti-intellectualism, *The Age of American Unreason.* Jacoby, impatient with how thought is being undermined in every sphere of American life (she wrote *The Age of American Unreason* during a moment when the sitting president seemed unable to construct a grammatically correct simple sentence; he certainly could not pronounce the word "nuclear" properly), writes against what she considers "a virulent mixture of anti-intellectualism, anti-rationalism and low expectations." It is appropriate that Handy and Jacoby, the British-based Irishman and the American, through their national heritage (which does not exactly match Paine's but evokes it through Handy's close links to British capital), should return us to the eighteenth-century revolutionary.

11. Paine, *The Age of Reason,* 5, 9.

12. Ibid., 17.

13. In this regard, Donald Harman Akenson's work is useful. In *Saint Saul: A Skeleton Key to the Historical Jesus,* Akenson argues that the Gospels, especially, were produced not by the Apostles but those he names "author-editors," suggesting that the Scriptures were subjected to substantial revision – to say the very least.

14. Paine, *The Age of Reason,* 24.

15. The entire thirteenth chapter of 1 Corinthians is a dissertation on love. It centralizes love insofar as everything depends on it – if I "do not have love, I gain nothing," Paul declares. The chapter is also relentlessly descriptive – love is "patient," "kind," not "envious," and so on. Love, most important, ranks as the

supreme virtue: "And now faith, hope and love abide; and the greatest of these is love." It is on this note, the supremacy of love, that Paul concludes the chapter.

16. In *What Is Called Thinking?* Martin Heidegger argues that reason is "supra-sensual," that is, beyond the sensual (58). It is humanity's ability to exceed the sensual that is the first condition – the unerring sign – of humanity's reason.

17. Derrida, *The Gift of Death,* 106.

18. John 13:27.

19. Badiou, *In Praise of Love,* 61.

20. Kierkegaard, *Fear and Trembling and Repetition,* 122.

21. Badiou, *In Praise of Love,* 42.

22. 2 Galatians:15–16.

23. Taubes, *The Political Theology of Paul,* 15, 16.

24. Romans 1:13.

25. Taubes, *The Political Theology of Paul,* 14. Akenson contends that it was the intention of neither Jesus-the-Christ ("Yeshua" is his proper name for Akenson; "Jesus-the-Christ" marks the Hellenization – itself a struggle against "Yeshua's" Semitism) nor Saul (Paul) to found a new religion. Instead, "Yeshua's" was one of many "Judahisms" that existed before the destruction of the Second Temple (70 CE). After the fall of the Temple the world of Rabbinic Judaism and Christianity came into being – much of the latter due, in the estimation of many (not least among them Akenson and Nietzsche), to Paul's zeal as a proselytizer. In Akenson's estimation, "the religion that eventually rules much of the Gentile world is unmistakably a repackaging of late Second Temple Judahism" (*Saint Saul,* 53).

26. Taubes, *The Political Theology of Paul,* 24.

27. Akenson, *Saint Saul,* 8.

28. Romans 11:36.

29. Akenson, *Saint Saul,* 9. Paul's life is also recounted favorably in Acts, which is written by Luke, an admirer of Paul.

30. Taubes, *The Political Theology of Paul,* 28.

31. Kierkegaard, *Fear and Trembling and Repetition,* 122.

32. Paine, *The Age of Reason,* 18, 27.

33. Badiou, *In Praise of Love,* 65.

34. Paine, *The Age of Reason,* 28.

35. In *The New Oxford Annotated Bible* this line reads: "Father, if you are willing, remove this cup from me; yet, not my will but yours be done" (Luke 22:42).

36. Luke 22:48, 61.

# SELECTED BIBLIOGRAPHY


Agamben, Giorgio. *The Time That Remains: A Commentary on the Letter to the Romans*. Stanford, Calif.: Stanford University Press, 2005.

Akenson, Donald Harman. *Saint Saul: A Skeleton Key to the Historical Jesus*. Oxford: Oxford University Press, 2000.

Badiou, Alain. *Saint Paul: the Foundation of Universalism*. Stanford, Calif.: Stanford University Press, 2003.

Badiou, Alain, with Nicolas Truong. *In Praise of Love*. Translated by Peter Bush. New York: New Press, 2012.

Baudelaire, Charles. "The Pagan School." In *Baudelaire as Literary Critic*. Edited and translated by Lois Boe Hyslop and Francis E. Hyslop, Jr. University Park: Pennsylvania State University Press, 1964.

Burke, Edmund. *Reflections on the Revolution in France*. Oxford: Oxford University Press, 1999.

Carrig, Joseph. Introduction to *The Age of Reason*. New York: Barnes & Noble Books, 2006.

Derrida, Jacques. *The Gift of Death*. Translated by David Wills. Chicago: University of Chicago Press, 1995.

Handy, Charles B. *The Age of Unreason*. Boston: Harvard Business School Press, 1990.

Hardt, Michael, and Antonio Negri. *Declaration*. New York: Argo Navis Author Services, 2012.

Heidegger, Martin. *What Is Called Thinking?* Translated by J. Glenn Gray. New York: Perennial, 2004.

Jacoby, Susan. *The Age of American Unreason*. New York: Pantheon Books, 2008.

Kierkegaard, Søren. *Fear and Trembling and Repetition*. Edited by Howard V. Hong and Edna H. Hong. Princeton, N.J.: Princeton University Press, 1983.

Paine, Thomas. *The Age of Reason*. New York: Barnes & Noble Books, 2006.

———. *Rights of Man*. New York: Barnes & Noble Books, 2004.

Shaw, Bernard. Foreword to *The Revolutionist's Handbook and Pocket Companion*. N.p.: Floating Press, 2012.

———. "Maxims for Revolutionists." In *Man and Superman: A Comedy and a Philosophy*. Baltimore, Md.: Penguin Books, 1952.

Taffel, David. Introduction to *Rights of Man*, by Thomas Paine. New York: Barnes & Noble Books, 2004.

Taubes, Jacob. *The Political Theology of Paul.* Translated by Dana Hollander. Stanford, Calif.: Stanford University Press, 2004.

Žižek, Slavoj. *The Puppet and the Dwarf: The Perverse Core of Christianity.* Cambridge, Mass.: MIT Press, 2003.

**12.1.** Inside the INS broadcast crypt.

12

# THE ARCHIVE THAT KNEW TOO LITTLE

## THE INTERNATIONAL NECRONAUTICAL SOCIETY AND THE AVANT-GARDE

*Seth Morton*

Over one hundred years after the first Futurist manifesto, the historical avant-garde looks like an oddity that died long ago. Perhaps nothing has served the avant-garde better than its own death. In death, the avant-garde is memorialized and archived. Its antiart position has been absorbed by the art world, and its logics inform mass culture and high art alike. Although the historical avant-garde failed to make good on revolutionary ideals, avant-garde logics continue to evolve and diversify across our entire cultural media landscape, from Dada to Monty Python and *Saturday Night Live*. This is the odd thing about the avant-garde: its style thrives in a cultural era overwrought with aesthetic and cultural cynicism. If a productive tension between its own cynicism and its revolutionary ideals energized the early twentieth century's avant-garde, then the relocation of the avant-garde in the museum and in popular culture turns that tension into a perverse parody of "the avant-garde that was." From today's vantage point, the avant-garde seems to have cultivated a very real death wish. Its death was not stylistic or aesthetic but rather a failure *to be*. In the wake of its death, the object lesson of the avant-garde appears to concern the necessary failure of any project that sets radical forms of being as its goal.

But what if today's avant-garde – if there even is such a thing – knows that already? And what if in knowing that it also knows that in order to maintain the collective spirit that has nourished all avant-gardes despite their very difference, today's avant-garde had to turn itself into an archive, to turn the institutional and bureaucratic structure of death into the baseline for aesthetic invention? Promoting this practice is the International Necronautical Society (INS), a twenty-first-century avant-garde that appears to have only ever been an archive. Its archive offers a contemporary object lesson for a recent historical phenomenon that challenges notions of historical or ontological priority and pushes against a tacit belief that the archive holds some kind of transcendental truth that can make a claim on the past and present.

This lesson begins by separating the archive and the achievable. In the INS, the archive is the only thing that exists. The events, practices, pieces, and other historical errata come into being through the moment of archiving. For the INS, the avant-garde is more than a warehouse of techniques, it is a study in the relation between the practice and the institutionalization of art. The INS's project returns to the avant-garde's original critique of a transcendental humanism, now focused on a cryptotranscendental secular world. The INS offers an idiosyncratic critique of humanism's indulgences, especially with regard to any form of a metaphysics of presence. The archive is the INS's primary mode of parody because the archive exists within the humanist imaginary as a sort of material fundament for thinking and being. The archive provides more than an apt trope for challenging long-held beliefs about the status of knowledge and truth; its recursive structure challenges notions of temporality and ontology that inform the most basic claims on knowledge production. In aestheticizing this recursivity, the INS charts out its own version of a double finitude – which is, in the first place, the knowledge that our knowledge is incomplete and, second, that our tools for knowing are themselves always limited and flawed. In doing so, it offers a way of overcoming the nihilistic threat that this finitude portends, through the very practice of the archive itself. The INS develops a set of terms that engage with this struggle against finitude, against the lingering feeling that there is no substrate beneath the archive that can shore up the shortfalls that our incomplete knowledge leaves us with. The INS uses the avant-garde as an institution of oddities that allows the INS to archly explore the archive as a crypt, cypher, transmission scrambler, and, ultimately, failure. These attempts, flawed and failure they might be, provide an alternative system for how one goes about thinking the archive. The INS's use of the archive reveals a countervailing desire within the archive toward quiescence. The INS shows that the energies housed within the archive are a mesh of destructive and constructive forces, neither of which can answer the question of meaning. Rather than giving up on the archive, the INS has used this impasse to appropriate the idea of the archive as a joke that makes fun of our own need to find a true and authentic meaning in our experience of art.

These are grand claims to make about an institution that to most only appears as a strange website documenting the events and publications of a society described by the popular press as a "semi-fictitious" avant-garde network. They are even grander, considering that the INS website archives an avant-garde group intent on its own self-effacement and destruction, modeled after some early twentieth-century avant-garde movements like the Futurists, the Vorticists, and the diaspora of Dada. The site itself parodies a kind of bureaucratic Cold War fantasy of underground operations bunkers managing a system of global intelligence in the shadow of total nuclear collapse.

The style of the site encourages an aesthetic of paranoia and meta-analysis. The INS is quick to remind visitors to its archive that it has agents everywhere and that all readers are always, already a part of the INS. Many discover the INS inadvertently through the bibliographies of either philosopher Simon Critchley (INS chief philosopher) or author Tom McCarthy (INS general secretary). The INS is an important touchstone that fuses the artistic and critical aspirations shared by both thinkers. In this light, we can read Critchley's and McCarthy's work as necronautical transcripts that chart out the ways and means of an INS worldview. Framing the INS in relation to either of these two thinkers raises a problem of priority. Is the INS merely a pet project of two British friends who share a common affection for the avant-garde and contemporary critical theory? Or is the INS the metadiscourse for unlocking the undercarriage in both thinkers' work? These questions ask us to make a claim about the logical priority of the archive and its relation to objects that exist outside the frame of the archive. The INS resists this question by turning the archive into the aesthetic act itself. By turning the archive into a piece of art, it makes the institutional structure of truth and knowledge a site of experimentation and play.

The INS not only makes art out of archives but also makes a game of epistemic veracity. Every dead end might yield some new discovery, every well-known truth might bottom out as mere gag. In light of this, it's better to think of the organization's literary executors (Critchley and McCarthy) as heretofore unexplored areas in the INS archives rather than as the epistemic fundament for INS knowledge. The desire to turn McCarthy and/or Critchley into *fathers* of the archive is really a desire to nail down the law of the archive, master it through administration, and therefore transcend it, the very desire that the INS seeks to evade. The INS claim of infinite dominion does not represent a universal and transcendent declaration but rather flattens and opens all things up to the effects of its archontic principle. To take the INS at its word, then, to pore over the myriad strata of communications *as if* the INS not only is "real" but presents an imminent threat to the archive and the avant-garde as such, may be the only means of approaching the question that frustrates every avant-garde: But what does the avant-garde actually *mean,* really? The INS cannot answer this question, but its archive develops a way of thinking that allows us to ask different questions, questions that are less interested in the truth or meaning of a thing and more interested in how to account for its variability and the impossible gap between our experience of the thing and our ability to represent that experience.

The INS made its first public declaration in 1999 with its first manifesto, published in the *Times* of London:

> We, the First Committee of the International Necronautical Society, declare the following:
>
> 1. That death is a type of space, which we intend to map, enter, colonise and, eventually, inhabit.
>
> 2. That there is no beauty without death, its immanence. We shall sing death's beauty – that is, beauty.
>
> 3. That we shall take it upon us, as our task, to bring death out into the world. We will chart all its forms and media: in literature and art, where it is most apparent; also in science and culture, where it lurks submerged but no less potent for the obfuscation. We shall attempt to tap into its frequencies – by radio, the internet and all sites where its processes and avatars are active. In the quotidian, to no smaller a degree, death moves: in traffic

accidents both realised and narrowly avoided; in hearses and undertakers' shops, in florists' wreaths, in butchers' fridges and in dustbins of decaying produce. Death moves in our apartments, through our television screens, the wires and plumbing in our walls, our dreams. Our very bodies are no more than vehicles carrying us ineluctably towards death. We are all necronauts, always, already.

4. Our ultimate aim shall be the construction of a craft* that will convey us into death in such a way that we may, if not live, then at least persist. With famine, war, disease and asteroid impact threatening to greatly speed up the universal passage towards oblivion, mankind's sole chance of survival lies in its ability, as yet unsynthesised, to die in new, imaginative ways. Let us deliver ourselves over utterly to death, not in desperation but rigorously, creatively, eyes and mouths wide open so that they may be filled from the deep wells of the Unknown.

* This term must be understood in the most versatile way possible. It could designate a set of practices, such as the usurpation of identities and personas of dead people, the development of specially adapted genetic or semantic codes based on the meticulous gathering of data pertaining to certain and specific deaths, the rehabilitation of sacrifice as an accepted social ritual, the perfection, patenting and eventual widespread distribution of Thanadrine™, or, indeed, the building of an actual craft – all of the above being projects currently before the First Committee.

This blending of artistic, scientific, philosophical, and political tropes continues a long line of avant-garde manifestos. The INS makes death its object of understanding and the purpose of its project. It delivers its Herculean task archly, but this archness is equally serious and comical. Death is a ridiculous, unintelligible concept on the same order of "Truth" or "Reality," but it is also a very serious attempt to grapple with finitude. In the ensuing years, the INS has released a few dozen–odd declarations, statements, and reports regarding its activities and ideas about art, reality, and culture. It has held public and private events, broadcast its absurdist-inspired rhetoric on pirated bandwidths, held exhibits about its own work, and endorsed the work of others. The horizon of death remains withdrawn, yet it continues to steer the INS's output. While death remains a condition of being, the INS manifesto suggests a second order for death that questions our very inability to conceptualize death's withdrawnness.

If not for the INS's insistence on encryption, the opened-up space of the INS archive might seem like a pointless postmodern exercise in multiplicity. The motto of the International Necronautical Society reads: "Tomorrow we shall (re)traverse the enormous space/sea."[1] The enormity of this space is the function of INS encryption, which attempts to render all things within the frame of its ever-expanding archive. Where does one begin to describe and how can one account for a system of aesthetic production that aspires to produce production itself? Vilém Flusser's diagnosis of postindustrial production offers a useful insight. Flusser describes the advent of the non-thing in twentieth-century production.[2] In the world of non-things, information is more accurately understood as *un*formation, an exchange of the material world for the virtual as it appears through gadgetry and electronics. The non-thing describes late modernity's transition from objects to processes, from hardware to software. Following Flusser's insights, the INS might be best understood as an aesthetic that un-in-forms its public. The INS wagers that the systematic process of taking away any sense of truth or certainty produces, ironically enough, better art and better thinking. Better because it incorporates a second-order level of thought. The first order engages with the problem at hand; the second order engages with the ramifications of that problem. Thus Death for the INS means both dealing with the ever-present reality of finitude and dealing with the knowledge that we cannot understand finitude at the same time.

This parallax view of the world prevents the first-order object from reifying into a transcendent form.

Once you enter the INS crypt, is there ever any longer an outside structure, or are you trapped between the two horizons of death? The codings and decodings of culture that are processed through the INS crypt explode in all directions, always portending collapse into a code with an as-yet-undiscovered key. Or as broadcast in a London pirate radio address:

> Calling all agents. Listen, I repeat Message to follow.
> Calling all agents. I repeat Message Following:
> FLIGHT PATH Jealousy and discontentment will come to he or she who dreams of living beneath a flight path. A dream of planning flight paths drawing lines between cities, countries or continents of the world is a sign of restlessness.
> When I land when the weather is bad, I pop up on the other side of the cloud. When you are in the cloud, you can see nothing.[3]

The tropic resonances in this broadcast flirt seductively with meaning. Blindness and insight, truth, knowledge, and elevation – these broadcasts generate their own sort of archive for thinking about the kinds of desires that come bundled with new forms of telecommunication. The INS revels in the production of chatter, a kind of noise that promises meaning just over the horizon. The desire lines and axes that crisscross between art and philosophy or meaning and nonsense can be broadly contained within two poles: the archive and the avant-garde. How the INS handles these institutional substrates exemplifies its return to the question of the aesthetic and mobilizes its critique of the dominant tendencies in humanities research today, which first turns to the archive as a locus of meaning and then temporalizes that locus around a historical narrative. The hope of the avant-garde – whether aesthetic, political, or playful – is always held on a promise of some other possibility. The oddity of the INS is that it produces a critical practice that productively perverts these institutions into a general economy that maps the practice of critique onto an aesthetic object. The archive is the only possible product for the INS because the archive relies on a double vision, one that sees its object and its trace in a way that is formally coincident and yet impossible.

## ARCHIVING WAS ALWAYS A DIFFICULT ART

The sum total of INS exploits, manifestos, collected reports, schematizations, novels, philosophical tomes, photographic records, and broadcasts goes hand in hand with briefs, public statements, and notes to explain and clarify exactly what happened. It is this autoexplicating exchange between the thing and the commentary on the thing that motivates one critical axis of the INS's project, which attempts to short-circuit any gesture that essentializes the aesthetic as a source of truth. The INS's commitment to blur the lines between art, art object, and criticism is part of its general goal to challenge epistemic connections that promise to ground meaning in something else (an author's journal or the historical context of the piece). The INS shorthands this imperative within a rubric of the "failure of transcendence." That failure is better described as the failure to make good on the humanist project of enlightenment. Samuel Beckett surmises the humanist impulse nicely in his famous line from "Worstward Ho" (1983): "All of old. Nothing else ever. Ever tried. Ever failed. No matter. Try again. Fail again. Fail better."[4] The INS wants to brightline the way that many are unable to cope with this failure in a substantial way by undermining Beckett's last word in favor of the line's more general sentiment: to continue despite the absolute promise of failure. In the general secretary's first report, *Navigation Was Always a Difficult Art,* the INS discovered that part of the reason for this failure is a problem of ends. Transcendence fails because it is based on a logic of arrival or completion. The INS questions how one can ever know when one has arrived and also questions the knowledge given from one's "arrival." Instead, it reads the topos of destinations and the discovery of new modes of knowing and being as bad-faith fantasies. In response, it proposes a system of navigation and its attendant emphasis on reading, interpretation, journeying, and a ceaseless drive into that which will never be known.

The INS is thus a systematic working through of contemporary culture vis-à-vis the topology of the failure of transcendence through the metaphorics of death. The archive is essential to this project because it's where the trace of dead things is thought to live. To most, the INS appears *merely* as an archive – *nothing but* a collection of documentation on the web unified under a single voice and crest. The INS archive takes on a strange shape; rather than being an object-document relation where the former precedes the latter, the INS archive looks like an institution filled with documents that gesture toward the possibility of an archivable moment. The effect is to produce an archive that revises the move toward the archive as a validating substrate by pulling apart the archive's own performance of a self-sustaining order. The ouroboros has finally had its fill. This order emerges from the illusion of a play between the law of the archive (the principle that grants membership to objects) and the materials housed within it (those things that represent the archive's law), rather than through the logic of a general economy that would reveal the archive as it is: a system where order emerges as an afterthought, retroactively through the administration and organization of things.

The INS reveals this retroactive emergence of meaning by disentangling the articulated relation between the object and the recording of the object. On the side of the archive, all published documents on the INS website end with: "Issued by INS Department of Propaganda. Official INS propaganda may be freely distributed, distorted, appropriated or adapted as the reader sees fit." This statement nods to the logic underpinning Derrida's *Archive Fever,* where the very institution of the archive is constituted by a coupled desire to expand and destroy the archive in the same move. In light of this, the INS archly welcomes the knowledge that with the first archivist comes a series of misinterpretations that open the archive itself to an unending horizon of permeability and expansion. This invitation to distort qualifies all the archived material as potentially distorted. The necessary presence of distortion, impurity, misinterpretation, or any other kind of signal noise is the only qualifying way for something new to enter the archive. Every text is a code to be decoded through every other text.

On the other side of this relation is the object to be archived, which in the logic of the INS doesn't exist. Consider the "nonevent" on 25 September 2007. According to the documentation (published and authorized under "The INS Statement of Inauthenticity"), the general secretary and chief philosopher presented "The Joint Statement on Inauthenticity," a live performance of "The INS Statement of Inauthenticity." All transcripts and recordings are available but were disavowed. Along with the documentation was a set of photographs that showed McCarthy and Critchley look-alikes reading the statement with other photos showing the real McCarthy and Critchley in another location entirely. Adding to this confusion was the similarity – an imperceptible difference – between the voices of the "actors" and the voices of McCarthy and Critchley. The INS went out of its way

**12.2.** Not the general secretary and not the chief philosopher.

to make the archivable into an impossible object while at the same time declaring its work in terms of a positive and expansive production. Quoting David Lynch's *Lost Highway,* the general secretary declared: "We're in your house."[5] The concept of the archive – reified and utilized primarily as an institution and on behalf of institutions – therefore performs what the INS calls the "failure of transcendence." In one register, this failure addresses the impossibility of pure, unequivocal communication. After this failure – as the conditional experience of modernity – the aesthetic split between form and matter becomes asymmetrically aligned with matter on one side and nothing on the other.

The INS explores the awareness of this experience through the topos of death, which is why, according to its first manifesto, "death is a type of space, which we intend to map, enter, colonise and, eventually, inhabit." It would appear that this first declaration, with its attention to the language of mapping as recording, is merely an attempt, at best, to invert or, at worst, to reconstitute the archive through the asymmetrical dynamic of matter over form. Because of the tendency to revise through inversion, the INS can only maintain its integrity by undermining the logic of the archive while at the same time feverishly archiving itself. The wager is not dialectical but residual: "from the individual to the dividual, thence to the residual . . . and further to the residual, a laughable doubling."[6] This doubling is a doubling-over, structurally made possible by making fun of the severity of the archive as an institution of truth. "The remainder that remains" is the unaccounted-for element that persists after the leveling of both the archive and the archivable. This residual thing contains both the mark of the archive and the mark of that which cannot be archived – the conditions for its possibility are also the conditions for its impossibility. The INS shorthand for this thing is the sponge – a formless form that absorbs and oozes without any directive. This "form" calls back to Flusser's notion of the non-thing. For Flusser, the age of the archivable thing is over. Sounding its death knell is the accumulation of junk that piles up around people as they process the non-thing: in-formation (read: un-formation). The transformation is one that moves from accumulation (archiving) to processing (thinking). In this way, the archive of the INS is an attempt to map a particular experience of matter onto the topos of a process. The archive makes matter *matter* differently and as such returns the prospective necronaut to the scene of death: the radical finality of matter. Our inability to understand either matter's finitude or our experience of this finitude forms the two planes of death between which the INS's impossible project comes into focus. The INS makes an important slippage by combining a discourse of death and finitude with a notion of failure. The emergence of failure as a trope that may or may not collide with death brings its project in line with the same trials and tribulations as those of the historical avant-garde.

## FAILING THE AVANT-GARDE

Radicalizing the archive in its own impossible demand, the INS firmly grounds its project within the tradition of the avant-garde that seeks to establish a set of aesthetic practices that operate within a logic antithetical to the major contours of aesthetic sensibility in the main. The INS makes the archive the site of the avant-garde and in doing so questions the popular narrative of the avant-garde as a missed opportunity or failed revolution. The INS shows how failure is not only intrinsic to the logic of the avant-garde but also the very engine that legitimates and opens up the possibility for something like an avant-garde to have meaning.

Enframed in the avant-garde aesthetic is the concept of two orders of failure. The first order of failure takes place with the embrace or admission that the INS's project is fated to fail. Hans Richter describes this fate when writing about the early days of Dada: "Its only program was to have no program. . . . [I]t was just this that gave the movement its explosive power to unfold in all directions, free of aesthetic or social constraints. . . . [T]he frailty of human nature guaranteed that such a paradisal situation could not last."[7] Richter's celebratory tone praises Dada while admitting a frailty that doomed the project from the beginning. Thinking of failure in this way already reconfigures how the avant-garde has been received at the beginning of the twenty-first century. The failure that Richter admitted to then is used as a metaphor today for the failure of the European intelligentsia to make good on its ideals in the face of a rapidly declining political world.

The work of the INS is to turn failure into success and thereby establish a second order of failure. In a certain sense, the process of failure that Richter describes is bound up with a conception of the future or of a failure on the horizon of experience; it can't but fail. Richter deploys a logic of futurity that situates the avant-garde as a being unto death. Part of this narrative places the avant-garde uncomfortably within a narrative that engages on some level with the idea of a telos. The avant-garde names the tip of the spear – the forward movement into the future. This underlying logic of progress until death is precisely the failure that the INS wants to reframe by turning death into a mode of production instead of a marker of completion. The INS's failure is not the failure of an avant-garde but rather a failure *to be* an avant-garde, if what it means to be an avant-garde is wrapped up with the logic of progress.

The INS takes as an object lesson the first manifesto of futurism, specifically how the event of futurity is bound up with its own writing and how that writing is itself the narrative of a car crash. For the INS, this catastrophic moment can only be understood as a rejection of "the *idea* of the future, which is always the ultimate trump card of dominant socioeconomic narratives of progress. . . . We resist this ideology in the name of the sheer potentiality of the past and of the way the past can shape the creative impulses and imaginative landscape of the present. The future of thinking is its past."[8] The avant-garde aesthetic that the INS cultivates is archival in that its attempt is paleofuturistic – mining the past in order to not give up on a better version of it.

In the INS's own words, taken from the "Proclamation on Democracy and Art," "art is the annihilation of all positions." Turning the failure of the avant-garde into the failure to be an avant-garde as an aesthetic practice allows the INS to capture the ephemerality of the avant-garde without giving up the responsibility to attend to the present as a site of aesthetic practice. The care of the now as a practice becomes the residual remainder of the INS's engagement with the avant-garde aesthetic, and in doing so it recovers for the INS archive the secret code that validates its position within an idiosyncratic tradition of the avant-garde. Death is not synonymous with failure; rather, it is the INS's answer to the avant-garde's legacy. Death means embracing finitude in all its guises. The avant-garde's claim to truth is one that is always ready to fail and change and fail again.

## EXHAUSTIVE AND EXHAUSTING ENDINGS

The torsion between death and failure is felt strongest at the end of McCarthy's novels. Considered as INS documents, these novels suggest the possibility of an un-ending, an ending that is always staging itself as an ending, as the final front for engaging with the desire for truth. In a strong sense, the end as a concept is diametrically opposed to the vivifying structure of what the novelist and philosopher are *supposed* to do. The end doesn't continue to inspire thinking or questioning; the end provides relief from the ever-failing attempt to know. The end, when understood as a kind of satisfying closure, fails because the text continues to generate despite being reshelved. Celebrating this failure to end is why the INS triumphs the comic Wile E. Coyote over the tragic Oedipus; only the comic sensibility of the former, who dies and dies again, can embody the necessary humor and wit needed to face the catastrophe of the material order, namely, that things merely are and go on without beginnings or endings. It's not enough to claim the end of all things and the radicality of this finitude. A permanent diagnosis constantly needs to reproduce the conditions of that finitude. Taking a cue from Nietzsche, we (new and old members of the INS) must guard against the shadow form of the divine that lives on in countless caves around the world.

To this end the INS directs its apparatus of thinking toward the world in a radical way. Reappropriating the past into its archive of unreason, the INS claims that you are always already a necronaut, you just don't know it. As it relates to the topos of failure, this claim offers another way into how the INS troubles the very idea of failure and death. It comes as little surprise, then, that General Secretary Tom McCarthy's novels have fantastically bad endings. The collection of unresolved narratives has become a signature gesture in the general secretary's work. *Remainder* (2007), *Men in Space* (2008), and *C* (2011) all portray characters who are driven in the wake of a catastrophic experience of materiality to quiesce into a state where form and content are radically coincidental.

Most emblematic of these characters is the unnamed narrator from *Remainder,* whose efforts to stage that coincidence of meaning take the form of increasingly elaborate reenactments in which he can occupy the space of his imaginary within the material confines of the world. The narrator allegorizes the INS concept of art, seeking to understand the nature of failed transcendence through the attempt to restructure form and matter in a way that affirms the radical unavoidability of the material. In *Remainder,* the staging for these reenactments always takes the form of repeating structures, infinity loops that try to exceed the conditions of their materiality by creating a perfectly closed system. "Matter," the narrator remarks: "my undoing."[9]

McCarthy's narrators exemplify a meta-ending that is really no ending at all. The ending of endings should not be confused for a beginning but rather requires a different kind of knowledge system. As with the archive and the avant-garde, simply inverting the underlying dynamic (turning the ending of endings into a beginning) or naming the negative a positive for its own sake only reproduces the very thing that it decries. For the INS, the end might be read as the catastrophic experience that names modernity, but the inversion of that experience as a resistance to a tradition of closure would only affirm and reproduce the values it seeks to contort.

Sliding from death, to failure, to endings and all their attendant concepts leaves behind another remainder: exhaustion. The INS raises the stakes on its project by developing an exhausting aesthetic of the un-ending or of the quiescent ending. Quiescence is the death of death; it is the experience of stillness that follows a decline of energy: entropy. More than a hyperbolic redundancy, quiescence thought of as the death of death underscores the radicality of a radical finitude, a complete and totalized exhaustion that continues to exhaust. The death of death names a space where death, as a substrate of meaning, no longer organizes the principles or values for being. Being-unto-death withers and along with it the promise of a horizontal futurity that promises *something more.* Quiescence as a desire finds its form in Freud's *Beyond the Pleasure Principle:* "It is clear that the function [of the pleasure principle] thus described would be concerned with the most universal endeavor of all living substance – namely to return to the quiescence of the inorganic world."[10] *Remainder* compounds this universal endeavor because in being brought back to life the narrator experiences two distinct modes of quiescent desire. The first attempts to pull him back into history; the second draws him toward infinity, the silence of a perfectly closed system. In both instances, figurations of remainders, extras outside and in addition to the system, make quiescence an impossible act. These lines lead toward quiescence, but as quiescence becomes a category of near-infinite delay, the process itself, the static hum of the machine, functions itself in quiescent form as an exhaustion that haunts all of the codings and decodings in the INS archive. These novels end with ambivalent gestures toward a structure of silence found in the pause one feels when falling from a building, in the figure eights of a hijacked plane while the police wait below, or in the churning lines of a ship's wake seen by no one played against the hum of a static transmission heard by no one.

The aesthetic of the quiescent end is an alternative to the reproduction/annihilation dynamic that opens up the possibility of an inhuman technology unto death. In this the INS archives its most successful failure. By ending a narrative in a cryptic silence, it engenders a desire to rewrite and reconfigure the structure. The permission to distort becomes the operating principle for the possibility of meaning. Distortion evokes Lyotard's idea of modernity as rewriting. In Lyotard's idiom, the failure of the postmodern is nothing but a series of attempts to exceed the limit of modernity while failing to recognize that modernity itself, as a result of its fluctuating relation to the "now," always attempts to exceed itself. Lyotard instead wants to think of modernity as a series of attempts to rewrite itself. These reenactments appear like Lyotard's second sense of the "re-," namely, "*Durcharbeitung,* ie. A working attached to a thought of what is constitutively hidden from us in the event and the meaning of the event."[11] *Durcharbeitung* (working through) is a search whose parameters are defined by the subject's cathexis. The point for Lyotard is that modernity is engaged in a never-ending cycle of rewritings. At its simplest the quiescent un-ending seeks to cathexitize experience into that which allows for thoughts disparate and outside the transmissions of what the INS calls the "mediasphere." Un-endings as un-formation shoot for Lyotard's first concept of "re-," the fresh start, passing through the death of modernism, modernity, late modernity only to turn back in order to discover the quiescent as the deviant logic that structures the archive.

## TRANSMISSIONS FROM THE CRYPT

By now the INS archive seems full of stuff yet also eerily empty. There are things to be saved, but those things aren't supposed to mean anything, and that's supposed to mean something. Does this non-thing archive the whence and whither of the avant-garde? It could only do so by having a belief in nothing, in a type of nihilism that is rendered as a productive technology in these moments of ending and un-formation. The work of the INS archive is about a demand to stage this question again and again. As a result, Critchley and McCarthy must repeat and rehearse the terms of their commitments, always appearing different, yet always the same. Repetition is not about a more true representation but about staging the question of the nothing that is and the nothing that isn't.

The persistence of the end in the work of Simon Critchley and Tom McCarthy and throughout the INS archive at large demands a collaborative working through; this work is about a rift that opens up between their writing around the problem of the end that cannot be answered solely in the framework of either thinker. The rubric of the end orients all things toward finitude. The beginning is the end. In *Remainder,* technology falls from the sky and kills the unnamed narrator. *C* opens with a caul that portends the end of a humanist genealogy that can only "give and gives itself again" and the beginning of a distributed network of codes and signs that are constitutively indecipherable in the final analysis.[12] *Men in Space* ends again and again; the seams of the novel pull apart until the series of endings reads as the only thing that was holding the novel together. The final voice, channeling Beckett, finishes unraveling the narrative spool: "Soon I will stop. Soon . . ." The end of one cycle constitutes the beginning of another, ad infinitum.

Thinking about the vagaries of nothing begins, fittingly, with where most of Critchley's books begin: disappointment. Philosophy for Critchley, we are reminded time and time again, begins after the onset of political and religious disappointment: that there is no justice and there is no god. This reality precipitates into two flavors of nihilism, passive and active, that in Critchley's work must be resisted to the very last. This version of nihilism affirms the nothing and allows itself to be consoled by meaninglessness itself. Critchley said so much to McCarthy in a 2001 interview on the INS archive: "It's the question of nihilism that I want to put at the center of my agenda. . . . It's a question that's been deemed to be almost indecent because in a sense we can ironize our way out of it."[13] Indecent why? Critchley correctly puts pressure on a cultural tendency to avoid nihilism either by manning the so-called barricades of meaning or by embracing and reveling in an ironic embrace of claiming a *belief* in nothing.[14] These two slopes of nihilism establish a frame in which a third iteration of nihilism – one that is better understood as a posthuman technology of finitude – can be thought through as an answer to the demand of finitude, which expresses itself in necronautical declaration: we want to make matter *matter* differently.

The end, anecdotally read as the end of the novel, more "seriously" as finitude or as a personal experience of death that one does not experience, can only find a sufficient response in a nonrepresentational discourse that is not based on an epistemological metric of "more or less true." To do otherwise would be to write under the sign of romanticism, to supplement the fallout of the divine with a new, "more true" aesthetic reality. The final call, the call at the end of the novel, the end of the philosophical argument, is not toward an itinerary of actions but rather looks like the final image in Walter Benjamin's "On Language as Such and the Language of Man," "comparable to a secret password that each sentry passes to the next in his own language, but *the meaning of the password is the sentry's language itself.* All higher language is a translation of lower ones, until in ultimate clarity of the word of God unfolds, which is the unity of this movement made up of language."[15] The collaborative work in Critchley and McCarthy is to think through how meaning becomes formalized as the discursive substrate itself. Rather than writing a supplement to a divine order or announcing the futility of the project, the topoi of encryption, archives, and remainders describe a set of alternatives to the predictable set of problems brought on by the knowledge of the end. These alternatives bracket out the problem of the end by pointing out and laughing at the absurdity of it all. The arched eyebrow of the suspicious necronaut is also the arched grin of the comic, who is able to frame the meaninglessness of the everyday as the source of humor. The INS does its best job in framing a set of alternatives when it tackles the problem of the nothing, or nihilism, itself.

Nihilism, the *belief* in nothing, is understood as a cipher for the available modes of finitude as they relate to a certain experience of nothing. Written in the key of C, the communicability of this nothing arrives in Serge's fever dream, a burst of static that erupts from Sophie: "Sophie's going to say the word that will complete the ceremony, bring about its climax, sealing his and her anointment. . . . [T]he word is welling, not so much in Sophie's lungs and thorax as in space itself." It arrives in the first wave as a pure signal, "a static that contains all messages ever sent, and all words ever spoken; it combines all times and places too, scrunching these together as it swallows them into its crackling, booming mass. . . . [E]verything is spilling . . . the dead being catapulted back out of the earth."[16] The first promise of the cipher, nominalized through Sophie as wisdom itself, is pure potentiality, a fantasy of decoding – that all things can be translated, archived, known, and put to rest. Immediately the image collapses through excess. There is simply too much signal for the available container; a cut is made, and the rest is spilled. The overflow of signal flips into a second burst of noise,

> a second burst, heading the other way, like an enormous echo or the backrush from the first explosion. . . . [H]e feels himself rushing backwards, through a black and endless void. He's merging with the void. . . . [A]ll these scenes and objects have been reproduced inwardly, as though injected through some kind of time-syringe into his stomach, in whose blackness they're suspended like small, lit-up screens, contained by the walls of a new syringe that frames them and injects them further inwards, again and again, the scenes and objects miniaturizing more and more as they regress.[17]

The urgency of both transmissions are rendered as the twinned faces of wisdom: Is the world to be decoded according to a divinity of potentiality, an infinitely complicated explosion of meaning that any being, in its finitude, cannot hope to contain? Or is it to be given up into a system of diminished returns, where the void disintegrates all things into an un-ending decay of meaninglessness? The answer is not quite neither; both models are incorrect answers to the demand that is given; however, their incorrectness has nothing to do with the content of the transmission. What determines the semantic content of the signal in either case is a certain kind of positionality, a relation to static that allows the signal to be known as signal. Both responses are rendered in relation to a finitude that is understood as the constitutive structure of life. Carrefax's last utterances, ssss, c-c-c-c, are perhaps a call for Simon Critchley to make sense of the last transmission, as he does in the "Last Words" of *The Book of Dead Philosophers:* "Human existence is limited. It is shaped by evolutionary forces beyond our control and by the movement of a desire that threatens to suffocate us in the clutches of its family romance. . . . [I]f we can begin to accept our limitedness, then we might be able to give up certain fantasies of infantile omnipotence. . . . [I]n speaking of death and even laughing at our frailty and mortality, one accepts the creaturely limitation that is the very condition for human freedom."[18] C gives shape to the forces that are beyond our control. As a response to finitude, these last two transmissions are important because they radically disposed of Carrefax, and they are both iterations of an inhuman technology that allows the problem of finitude to be iterable; that which carries the force of the human, then, is paradoxically rendered visible through that which is ultimately and importantly inhuman. The nihilistic texture of technology is death itself, that which is uniquely and completely ours but which we can only experience, following Critchley's reading of *Being and Time,* through the death of another.[19] This dynamic is motoric and enframing; it cuts equally between the first and second transmission and is echoed in Serge's last words: "Dummy chamber, everywhere, what's not, it came through, through me, the call: I'm being called."[20] Every code is a craft, a vehicle for understanding and delivering one over to an experience of finitude. Every craft is therefore a crypt, a house for dead things: an archive.

Document Ends

Issued by the INS Department of Propaganda. Official INS propaganda may be freely distributed, distorted, appropriated, or adapted as the reader sees fit.

## NOTES

1. INS First Committee, "Briefing Notes."

2. Flusser, "Non-Thing 1."

3. INS Broadcasting Unit, "Calling All Agents," 87.7 FM, April 8, 2004. Full transcript of radio broadcast is made available by the INS Broadcasting Unit at http://necronauts.org/caa_script .htm.

4. Beckett, "Worstward Ho," 7.

5. INS First Committee, "Joint Statement."

6. Ibid.

7. Richter, *Dada,* 34.

8. INS First Committee, "Declaration."

9. McCarthy, *Remainder,* 17.

10. Freud, *Beyond the Pleasure Principle,* 76.

11. Lyotard, "Rewriting Modernity," 25, 26.

12. Derrida, "Geschlecht II."

13. INS First Committee, "Interview."

14. Here belief is understood in its religious, rather than pragmatic, variation.

15. Benjamin, "On Language as Such," 74.

16. McCarthy, *C,* 307.

17. Ibid., 308.

18. Critchley, *The Book of Dead Philosophers,* 248.

19. Critchley, "'Death' on *Being and Time,* Part 6."

20. McCarthy, *C,* 309.

## SELECTED BIBLIOGRAPHY


Beckett, Samuel. "Worstward Ho." New York: Grove Press, 1983.

Benjamin, Walter. "On Language as Such and the Language of Man." In *Early Writings 1910–1917,* translated by Howard Eiland. Cambridge, Mass.: Harvard University Press, 2011.

Critchley, Simon. *The Book of Dead Philosophers.* New York: Vintage, 2009.

——. "'Death' on *Being and Time,* Part 6." *Guardian,* 13 July 2009, http://www.guardian.co.uk/commentisfree/belief/2009/jul/13/heidegger-being-time.

Derrida, Jacques. *Archive Fever: A Freudian Impression.* Translated by Eric Prenowitz. Religion and Postmodernism. Chicago: University of Chicago Press, 1998.

———. "Geschlecht II: Heidegger's Hand." In *Psyche: Inventions of the Other,* vol. 2, edited by Peggy Kamuf. Meridian: Crossing Aesthetics; Stanford, Calif.: Stanford University Press, 2008.

Flusser, Vilém. "Non-Thing 1." In *The Shape of Things: A Philosophy of Design.* Translated by Anthony Matthews. London: Reaktion Books, 1999.

Freud, Sigmund. *Beyond the Pleasure Principle.* Translated by James Strachey. New York: Liveright Publishing Corporation, 1961.

INS First Committee. "Briefing Notes." http://necronauts.net/pdf/ins_key_events.pdf.

———. "Declaration on the Notion of 'The Future.'" *Believer,* November/December 2010, http://www.believermag.com/issues/201011/?read=article_necronautical.

———. "Founding Manifesto." *Times* (London), 14 December 1999, advertisement, http://necronauts.net/manifestos/1999_times_manifesto.html.

———. "Interview with Simon Critchley by Tom McCarthy." March 2001. http://www.necronauts.org/interviews_simon.htm.

———. "Joint Statement on Inauthenticity." Public Statement, Drawing Center, New York City, 25 September 2007. http://necronauts.net/declarations/ins_inauthenticity_new_york/inauthenticity_precis.html.

———. *Navigation Was Always a Difficult Art.* London: Vargas Organisation, 2010.

———. "Proclamation on Democracy and Art." 2008. http://necronauts.net/proclamations/art_democracy.html.

Lyotard, Jean-François. "Rewriting Modernity." In *The Inhuman: Reflections on Time.* Translated by Rachel Bowbly. Ann Arbor: University of Michigan Press, 1992.

McCarthy, Tom. *C.* New York: Vintage, 2011.

———. *Men in Space.* Updated edition. New York: Vintage, 2012.

———. *Remainder.* New York: Vintage, 2007.

Richter, Hans. *Dada: Art and Anti-art.* London: Thames & Hudson, 1965.

AFTERWORD

# "TO PROPHESY *POST HOC*"

## THE CURIOUS AFTERLIVES OF ODDBALL ARCHIVES

*David L. Martin*

It is a curious, if not downright odd, first thing to say about *The Oddball Archive* that, above all else, it has spoken to me at the level of politics. After all, particularly as it is practiced in the contemporary academy, politics or political science is a discipline famed for its "seriousness"; its social-science predictive ways; its focus on institutions, structures of power, and governance; and its avoidance of the messy stuff of culture, agency, and desire. Could anything be less oddball, less hospitable to the playfulness of hoaxers and hoarders, or the incongruity of dissected fish and Dixie cups? What of the explorations at the limits of rationality, the flush of excitement at reveling in the irrational, and the constant, quite odd, slip between them both that *The Oddball Archive* performs so well?

But politics it is! I say this because at the heart of *The Oddball Archive* I see a series of questions – no, a call to arms, if you will – centered precisely on the *politics* of knowledge production: its practices, its objects, and our place as practitioners of and within it. What the uncanny, the heterogeneous, the curious, and the downright odd do for us is show us the manifold ways in which knowledge formation is a deeply political act – all those streams of thought shut down as quaint, deluded, or categorically dangerous blind alleyways of inquiry by the relentless monotheism of modern science historiography; all those states of being – ecstatic, fractious, excessive, divine – curtailed, shunned, and ultimately disciplined for being out of step with a dominant mode of knowledge production whose contemporary form can only countenance Being shackled to a notion of productivity; and all those ways in which things, objects, treasures, and plain and simple "stuff" are stripped of their ability to demand attention, circulate, resonate, and coalesce within worlds and spheres of knowledge, reduced as they are to mere possessions of more "Enlightened" beings. These are things that we have not just inherited as the way the world happens to be; these are things that are a reflection of the world we have produced – the acts of repression, the conquests, and the disciplinings; the hard-fought negotiations and compromises; the bigotries, fears, and violences; as well as the more modest whims and fancies, forgetfulnesses and out-and-out dumb luck associated with how it is that something comes to stand as "known."

However, in getting lost in the curious collections of objects, places, words, and temporalities of *The Oddball Archive,* what we find is the way in which this collection – like all good collections – points not only to its own death but also to the effervescence of its many possible afterlives. This archive of archives, odd and curious, furtively calls upon us to acknowledge and resist the ways in which our disciplinary trainings are just that: disciplining as much as they are enabling. It beckons to us as practitioners of knowledge production to *perform* and *enact* the archive rather than merely explicate its worth. And finally, it calls to us to recognize the ways in which the things, peoples, and places collected within the archive have an ability of their own to throw us, to move us, and, dare I say, to act upon us as if agents of their own desires. Thought of in this manner, I cannot think of a more apt term than "politics" to describe how we might take a collection like *The Oddball Archive* forward: it captures both the urgency and the ethics of working with those things that for any number of reasons have found themselves as being "Other" to contemporary concerns.

## FROM REPRESSION USEFUL THINGS RETURN

There is a somewhat neglected early essay by Georges Bataille, a rudimentary theory of Fascism, that I have found particularly enlightening – less for its subject matter per se than for its role in enabling us to understand a general condition of knowledge that lies at the very heart of modernity. In "The Psychological Structure of Fascism," Bataille opposes a "productive," bourgeois element of society whose most significant trait was its "tendential homogeneity," with a nonproductive element of society he described as "heterogeneous." Although essentially a division concerned with the ownership of the means of production, interestingly enough for our purposes, Bataille extends this description to include the very structures and formations of post-Enlightenment thought and knowledge formation as well. Thus we find that by its very nature scientific knowledge is allied with the homogeneous elements of society: "Compelled to note the existence of irreducible facts . . . the object of science is to establish the homogeneity of phenomena."[1] Using the psychoanalytic metaphor of the exclusion of the unconscious from the conscious ego, Bataille characterized homogeneous scientific knowledge as necessitating the exclusion not only of the "restricted heterogeneous" elements of taboo and mana but also of anything deemed heterogeneous resulting from "unproductive expenditure": violence, excess, madness – the elements of heterogeneity that surface in persons or mobs when the laws of homogeneous society have broken down.

For Bataille, this exclusion of the heterogeneous from the homogeneous elements of society was governed by an active "intentionality" on the part of the bourgeoisie in an effort to maintain control over the means of production (hence he often called it "censorship"). But if we were to put this notion of exclusion alongside Martin Heidegger's wider epistemological deployment of Edmund Husserl's phenomenology of perception and the suggestion that every act of knowledge is necessarily accompanied by a simultaneous and unavoidable act of concealment and unknowing, then what we begin to approach is, to my mind, an understanding of this process of exclusion *as the general condition of post-Enlightenment knowledge production itself.* Taken in this way, we can suggest that a homogenizing tendency is inscribed into the very structures of scientific knowledge production at the level of discourse, which operates above all by the inclusion of certain elements deemed fit and worthy of rationality along with a simultaneous exclusion of those elements to be deemed "Other" to it. Put another way, we can claim that the structures of post-Enlightenment rationality are as much about the suppression of heterogeneous elements as they are about the generation of knowledge claims.

Elsewhere, I have pushed on with Bataille's psychoanalytic metaphor by characterizing the operations of this general condition of post-Enlightenment, scientific knowledge as being akin to an act of repression.[2] In doing so, I suggested that as much as the Enlightenment may be seen as an active campaign for the eradication of other ways of knowing and being that were heterogeneous – primarily those that were enchanted, magical, and sacred – this eradication, or rather repression, was necessarily an incomplete one, and that elements of these other ways of knowing and being not only coexist with scientific rationality to this day but, more to the point, are constitutive of them *in their repression.* Thus, *Curious Visions of Moder-*

*nity,* as that book was called, essentially become an effort at unearthing the repressed heterogeneous underbelly of a scientific modernity triumphantly pronouncing its own Enlightenment through the homogenizing violences it would unleash across the globe.

Imagine my delight, then, when first rummaging through *The Oddball Archives* to discover Beth McCoy's stunning recuperation of the FEMA emergency signs in post-Katrina New Orleans as ancient sorceries of the law, talismanic signs giving up black bodies and possessions both as a sacrifice to ward off the knowledge that many more will be subsumed by the rising tides of capitalism and white liberalism's living death for black people and as conjuring forth from memory the wish of sacrifice as internal reprisal for the humiliation of 9/11. These glyphs FEMA inscribed on half-submerged properties in New Orleans represent nothing less than "vengeful incursions of the sacred," to paraphrase Bataille, upon the supposedly rational surfaces of modernity's knowledge claims. This is indeed a magic of the State.

Likewise, Timothy Sweet's description of Shawnee, Iroquois, and Delaware narratives of the "eradication" of the Great Buffalo from the lands of the Ohio Valley as these narratives surfaced in European narratives of "extinction" of the woolly mammoth is instructional first and foremost of the ways in which such negotiations always happen within the "contact zone" of colonialism: the dismissal of the knowledge acts of one system as fanciful "myth," yet a reliance on them as evidence (albeit perverted), followed by an act of translation into the language of rationality, thereby licensing the eradication of the original narrative. But more than this, what Sweet's own excavations unearth is the way in which the Enlightenment may have shifted agency from God to "Man" as *the* knowing being, but almost as if, in mourning the license that narratives of God-as-agent gave, we moderns constantly felt its pull, deploying it in our analyses of breaks in the fossil record, even as we denounced as "myth" similar indigenous calls to supernatural agency. Far from being something confinable to the early, half-formed fumblings of eighteenth-century science, this pull of agency in knowledge production and this recourse to nonhuman agents are still very much with us today.

This is, in effect, part of the important work that *The Oddball Archives* undertakes for us: to demonstrate "that great trove of unreason that nourishes reason's archive," as its editors put it in the "History of the Collection." And we can see these unreasonable reasons, occluded visions, and less useful efficacies at work right through the collection – the hoarders, the hoaxers, the necronauts, the political and philosophical thinkers at the edge of what it is to think, and don't forget the fish-dissecting filmmakers. We can see the way in which reason operates and how their thoughts, actions, and outputs may even be directly in conversation with more reasonable logics and rationales. Yet there is often that some-thing-else, that little bit extra, that excess that tips them over into the not entirely reasonable. At the same time there are those who were never part of the canon of reason and rationality but were always already constituted at its margin as "Other."

But whereas I am in staunch solidarity with the editors' notion that "we approach oddity and even unreason as irremediable elements of all thought" (How could I not be with my own narratives of repressed heterogeneity lurking in the shadows of scientific knowledge structures?), I think we need to do more than just revel in, document, and archive these oddball practitioners, these curious collections of things and objects, and these asynchronous synchronicities. One of the provocations of *The Oddball Archive* is the editors' hypothesis that "archives of idiosyncratic thinking reveal as much about the shape of intellectual history . . . as any taxonomy of the work of great minds." True enough! However, it would be wrong to say that they reveal so much because their inclusion into discourse through our unearthing of them makes a picture more complete – this would in fact be a dangerous proposition. Rather, in defining that which cannot be, these archives mark out the limits and limitations of our knowledges; but more to the point, they elucidate the mechanisms through which such knowledge is produced, which is itself a marker of interests, struggles, negotiations, betrayals, hijackings, and even genocides in the worlds that sustain and nurture them. So while I agree that we should not dismiss the richness of these alternative thinkers, their thoughts, and the worlds they produced merely as offshoots of the regressive or self-destructive tendencies within Enlightenment reason, I also think that if we are to honor their visions rather than merely domesticate them, then we need to address how it is that the label "oddball" may have come to be associated with people who might themselves have thought they were anything but; places and things that were once central to the march of rationality and reason but suddenly found themselves on the outer edge; and those whose heterogeneity was marked as dangerous, foreign, or inhuman from the very beginning.

Acts of repression are often productive, but very rarely innocently so. What I want to do for the purposes of this afterword is to dwell in this lack of innocence as a way of showing how a collection like *The Oddball Archives* should call upon us to be responsive not just to the pleasures of dabbling in the forgotten side paths of modernity but also to the analysis of how such archives have been sidelined in the first place *and may yet be again* by our own interactions with them. What I want to do, then, is to push into the realm of politics to explore the exclusions and heterogenizing tendencies of a rationality that still takes sustenance in its homogenizing exclusions.

To do this I will need to indulge in some odd, perhaps even irrational, and certainly excessive ways . . .

## REMEMBER, THE GUILLOTINE IS AN INSTRUMENT OF ENLIGHTENMENT!

In a scathing rebuke of the subdiscipline of political science known as international relations, Sankaran Krishna characterizes the field as being more than just race blind; he characterizes it as actively amnesic of the part it plays in the continued maintenance of a racialized status quo. Toward this end, and in faint echo of Foucault, Krishna zeros in on the political side effects of the academic commonplace of abstraction, acknowledging it to be an inescapable analytic device that makes knowledge practices possible in the first place but also as something never innocent of power. In the case of international relations, this lack of innocence has a sharp political edge: "IR discourse's valorisation, indeed fetishization of abstraction is premised on a desire to escape history, to efface the violence, genocide and theft that marked the encounter between the rest and the West."[3] In this regard, Krishna sees the discipline as being predicated on a number of "disciplining" abstractions: the taboo against overly descriptive or historical analysis in favor of theory building, the reduction of social beings to utility maximizers, the evisceration of violence and its effects through its reduction to mere statistics in graphs and tables, the persistence with an archaic system of states that discredits imagining noninstitutional ways of being, the preservation of hypermasculine insecurities on matters of gender, and the elision of themes such as land theft, racism, slavery, and colonialism.[4] In Krishna's eyes, these otherwise commonplace academic abstractions come to constitute the way in which the discipline preserves its own ideology as the legitimate author(ity) of academic pronouncements about the international. Krishna is unequivocal in his naming of this maintenance of disciplinary self in the face of historic violence and complicity: "Founded as it is on discourses that justified, abstracted, and rationalised the genocide of populations of the so-called New World, the enslavement of Africans, the colonisation of Asians, the discipline of International Relations is one giant strategy of containment."[5]

There are a number of things I find compelling about Krishna's overtly politicized account, things that will eventually help me reveal the political effects of the oddball. The first is the way in which these very specific "heterogenizing" tendencies are the direct and inevitable outcome of a key cornerstone of rational discourse itself: abstraction, that logic that makes contemporary academic knowledge possible in the first place through its ability to draw equivalence and make mobile information for comparative purposes. The second, although somewhat incidental, is the way in which Krishna grounds this accusation in the replication of the discipline via its everyday pedagogic practices. In this case, the way students are encouraged to display their virtuosity in techniques of abstraction and are berated as being "too historical," "too descriptive," "not analytic enough," or "lacking in intellectual rigor" if they do not. To this we could add any number of additional "trainings" that international relations propagates: the antagonistic and combative argumentation; the masculinist valorization of "power politics" as the only "real" politics and the belief that institutions are the only site of such politics; the denigration of personal, local, or even internal state politics as somehow "feminine"; the derision of racial politics as something "to get over"; and so on and so forth. Finally, what I find captivating about Krishna's account is the way in which the particular carries with it an air of the general: this is not something confined to a "problem discipline" called international relations (in fact, in many ways IR is known as an exemplary social science), this is a general condition of the Western academy. Yes, the details may differ from institution to institution, discipline to discipline, but whether it is politics, economics, history, law, art history, or philosophy, there are elements of what Krishna has been describing in all of them.

In essence, what Sankaran Krishna's account of the disciplining effects of international relations does is call attention to the political ramifications of how our academic disciplines replicate themselves, our part as academic agents of that replication, and, more to the point, how this replication is not innocent of the maintenance of certain conditions in the world or of a status quo. Like any system of knowledge, academic disciplines cannot help but do this at a purely structural level – Enlightenment or otherwise, any system of knowledge will consist of a series of mechanisms for its own coherence and replication. By bringing Bataille into conversation with Krishna, the suggestion I want to make is that the epistemological status of the oddness at the center of *The Oddball Archive* should be seen not merely as the incidental by-product of Enlightenment rationality, although there is no doubt an element of happenstance to its immediate content. Rather, this oddness is the consequence of an active expurgation from an Order of Things by a system of knowledge production that has, at its core, a need to do more than just maintain internal coherence but actively to repudiate and repress those other ways of knowing and being that are not its own. This we can see in the excesses of Enlightenment rationality. The Enlightenment was an effervescent flowering of knowledge: it was the birth of a technique of knowledge production that would enable wondrous invention and advance; it would herald the coming of "Man" as *the* knowing subject;

it would bring a globe within that subject's purview through its standardized times and flows, new forms of communication and exchange; it would liberate subjects from older forms of subjugation; and it would allow for the birth of political communities capable of bringing tens of thousands of subjects under the sway of a single flag. And yet we must not forget the excesses of violence, dispossession, and destruction that came with it.

## TOWARD AN ODD REFLEXIVITY

If anything of the above account has chimed with the reader, then hopefully it is in sounding a word of warning regarding our encounter with the heterogeneity of the oddball and the place we academics might yet play in its further domestication and marginalization. Precisely because we all too often view the oddball as a thing otherwise just existing as curious and off-centered in the world, we tend to overlook the ways in which it has been produced as such. And if what Krishna insinuates has even a kernel of truth to it, then this domestication can be as much a function of the structures and logics of our disciplinary formations as it is of any active negligence on our behalf. We may be the most sympathetic of collectors, most nuanced of archivists, and most skilled of historians yet still be complicit in the erasure of that thing in which we delight and wish to revel.

Precisely because it is not perfect in this regard, I propose we read *The Oddball Archive* as a call to arms, a call to the kind of reflexivity that would bring recognition of our own positionality and the techniques of exclusion and domestication we are inadvertently agents of to the fore of our research and writing on the oddball. This is not a romantic and unproblematic call to occupy the space of knowledge of "the Other"; that is, it is not the suggestion that we may be external to the systems and functions of power that bring us as researchers, writers, interested amateurs, and aficionados into discourse, even as we search at the margins of that discourse for the traces of oddity that enchant us so. Rather, what I am intimating is that we might take the work of a book like *The Oddball Archive* forward by focusing on the ethical and political position of working on epistemologically vulnerable material from within a system predicated on producing that vulnerability.

In this manner I am reminded of the early call made by subaltern studies scholar Dipesh Chakrabarty to a project of history writing he would later describe as "provincializing Europe." Starting from the realization that, particularly as it is practiced in the institutional site of the university, the act of History writing was one that necessarily brought "Indian History" into a position of subalternity to a master narrative otherwise known as the "History of Europe," Chakrabarty sought to redress the deep collusion between history and the modernizing narratives of citizenship and nation (which could only ever read Indian histories in terms of lack) with an effort to invert this structural positioning of Europe as the referent of all histories by casting *it* to the provinces of history writing itself.[6] This was neither a call to reject the rationality of modernity per se nor a call to a shallow cultural relativism or atavistic nativist history. Rather, it was an appeal to a history that would make visible within the structures of its narrative forms its own repressive strategies and practices.[7] But in making this appeal Chakrabarty made known the doomed nature of his own enterprise: "This is a history that will attempt the impossible: to look toward its own death by tracing that which resists and escapes the best human effort at translation across cultural and other semiotic systems, so that the world may once again be imagined as radically heterogeneous."[8]

Doomed because of the impossibility of conducting this project within the institutional site of the university, whose knowledge protocols will always take one back to the terrain where all contours follow that of Europe, Chakrabarty nonetheless perseveres. He perseveres because of the political and ethical imperative to do so.

## IN PURSUIT OF LEFT-HANDEDNESS

> The assembly of shadows, the organisation of optical phenomena which resist the light, the look of things that suggest a face, the depth of bodies that cannot be concealed – all these things fall under dark writing's jurisdiction. Like the ground, the meaning of dark writing cannot be excavated; it lies in the footstep, the leap and the instance between two strides.
>
> Paul Carter, *Dark Writing: Geography, Performance, Design*

If *The Oddball Archive* calls to us at the level of being responsible to the ways of knowing and being produced by the disciplinary exclusions and homogenizing tendencies of our academic abstractions, then in what way does it also point toward further work, techniques of investigation, and modes of inquiry that might take this political call forward in responsive and responsible ways?

In the same "elsewhere" that I referred to earlier in *Curious Visions of Modernity,* I attempted to write to a series of premodern curiosities in as left-handed a way as possible, that is, in a way that confounded and frustrated the desire of the right hand to domesticate, to draw equivalence, to square the circle, to lock sign and signifier into a one-to-one relationship; to write to genre, discipline, or type. In that instance, the divide between modern and premodern, although increasingly blurred the further I journeyed, did act as a kind of guide in this venture. So it was to semblance, sympathy, and similitude that I wrote, my own kind of dark writing.[9]

But on this occasion two fragments have surfaced from the pages of *The Oddball Archive* that I briefly want to sketch, as I see potential in them for the development of other left-handed techniques: the need to perform, not merely explicate, the archive, and the archive as agent.

### *The Need to Perform*

In many ways the archives written about in this collection already point us in the direction of new modes and techniques of academic inquiry themselves: in their fragmentary and opaque structures, in their elusive and unreasonable claims, their oddness unfurls before us like a blueprint to be studied, replicated, and, above all, *performed*. Jonathan Eburne's archive of David Lynch's "kits" neatly shows us this. In the absurdity of Lynch's Fish Kit – of assembling a living fish from the kit of its dissected parts – what comes to the fore is Lynch's own characterization of ideas as being tangible things, and in this case the thing that is the "substance" or "materiality" of the idea is also a vital and animating spirit, both blueprint for action and something in excess of it. It is thus not difficult to see Lynch embracing his own eclectic "fish kit" of transcendence edited from his cut-up wanderings through world religions, as, in essence, this is precisely what he is chasing: the animation, the "click, click, click" of film through camera, the vital spirit that sees dead and inanimate things rise again.

Following on from the Eburne/Lynch Kit, we could suggest that metaphor, excess, the uncanny, and the heterogeneous are as much techniques to be deployed as they are anything else. One of the all-too-common dangers of dealing with epistemologically fragile archives is that the archive disappears from our work amidst the reams of explication we make of its worth, rather than the archive being allowed to surface itself in all its oddness and disruptive and illusive qualities. Not all of the chapters in *The Oddball Archives* were able to avoid this, but some did with noteworthy skill.

In the complex interplay of hoax, hoaxer, and hoaxed, Judith Roof deftly reveals a two-way (at least) operation: for the perpetrator of the hoax, because it is always already a repetition, the triumph of originality is rarely there to be had (pleasure is to be derived from the performance of hoaxing itself); whereas for the recipient of the hoax, the hoax is already known through its repetition and transparency (not that this means people are not willing to be hoaxed). In this way, the play of a hoax is nothing less than that of the public secret – that thing that is known but not admitted to in everyday discourse. In fact, it is only through its "knownness" that the hoax can even be. But in the twists and turns of Roof's hoaxers and hoaxed, one almost starts to feel a prickle of recognition, the recognition that comes with the slow dawning that one is being played, and that "played" here was not a dishonesty or a failing of argument; rather, it was an uncanny repetition or performance of the argument itself, the fulfillment of "desire for the revelation of the representation as such sought by the mark," according to Roof.

When metaphor is pushed to its limit and breaks, something happens; there is that hemorrhaging of a kind of "presence" often associated with the negative labor of defacement. It is an animating force that, if performed, can produce curious disruptions and odd disjunctures indeed.

When the category of "man" heretically ascended to the position of *the* knowing subject in the early modern period and thereby assumed the Adam/Christ figure's power to name, something was lost: that demiurgic trace written into all things, which activated them as the agents, and not the patients, of knowledge. But in confounding the taxonomic categories of a rationality that structures knowledge as an evolving series of named inert things (even if they are actually living things), the oddball, like Lynch's Fish Kit, often starts to come close to something "vital" in and of itself. How else do we explain its pull on us, that immediate flash of recognition when we stumble across it in our research travels? It is not so much that we notice it; it is more like it notices us, beckoning often as something jarring and out of place, but equally as something to be treasured.

As someone familiar with the academic writings of a few of the authors assembled in this collection, I found it interesting to ponder the manner in which many of the chapters had been written. For some whose writing I already knew, this project would have been but more of the same of a writerly way honed elsewhere. But for others I got the sense of the license that the material itself gave, if not demanded. More than just the notion that this is trivial or amusing material that can afford a lighter touch, what I sensed with some chapters was a coming to terms with a new set of imperatives for writing about the thing that somehow seeks to evade or elude our standard academic explications with their well-worn structures, so familiar that they announce "expertise" and "scholarliness" well before one even reads a single word. In other words, what I sensed was the way in which the archives themselves were speaking back, demanding of their authors that they do justice to these avoidances and oddities.

What calls us to an archive, and this is particularly true of the allure of the oddball archive, is the power of its ability to throw us, to unsettle, to unnerve, to worry, as well as to delight. This power is the archive's vital spirit, generated often precisely because it is at odds with the rationality of its day. But it is also this very spirit that is targeted when we innocently enough go about working with our archives; working in ways that serve us and our research agendas; working on them so that they can be compared, contrasted, qualified, quantified, systematized, and temporalized – in a word: homogenized.

Being self-reflexive of the positionality from which one writes carries with it the possibility of admitting that other ways of knowing and being are entirely possible. Occupying those "other" positionalities may well be beyond our reach, but in striving to be responsible to the objects of our research, we may come close to knowing what it is to acknowledge their needs and desires rather than always following our own. It is this above all else that *The Oddball Archives* teaches us.

## NOTES

1. Bataille, "The Psychological Structure," 141.
2. Martin, *Curious Visions of Modernity.*
3. Krishna, "Race, Amnesia," 401.
4. Ibid., 407.
5. Ibid.
6. Chakrabarty, "Postcoloniality." And later: Chakrabarty, *Provincializing Europe.*
7. Chakrabarty, "Postcoloniality," 23.
8. Ibid.
9. Carter, *Dark Writing,* 1.

Bataille, Georges. "The Psychological Structure of Fascism." In *Visions of Excess, Selected Writings, 1927–1939.* Minneapolis: University of Minnesota Press, 1985.

Carter, Paul. *Dark Writing: Geography, Performance, Design.* Honolulu: University of Hawai'i Press, 2009.

Chakrabarty, Dipesh. "Postcoloniality and the Artifice of History: Who Speaks for Indian Pasts?" *Representations* 37 (Winter 1992): 1–26.

———. *Provincializing Europe: Postcolonial Thought and Historical Difference.* 1998. Reprint, Princeton, N.J.: Princeton University Press, 2008.

Krishna, Sankaran. "Race, Amnesia, and the Education of International Relations." *Alternatives* 26 (2001): 401–424.

Martin, David L. *Curious Visions of Modernity: Enchantment, Magic and the Sacred.* Cambridge, Mass.: MIT Press, 2011.

# INDEX

This book was designed by Jamison Cockerham and set in type by Tony Brewer at Indiana University Press, and printed by Thomson-Shore, Inc.

The fonts are Arno, designed by Robert Slimbach in 2007, and Univers, designed by Adrian Frutiger in 1954. Both were published by Adobe Systems Incorporated.